Our Punitive Society

Second Edition

Our Punitive Society

Race, Class, Gender, and Punishment in America

Second Edition

Randall G. Shelden
University of Nevada, Las Vegas

Morghan Vélez Young
California State University, Fresno

WAVELAND
PRESS, INC.
Long Grove, Illinois

For information about this book, contact:
    Waveland Press, Inc.
    4180 IL Route 83, Suite 101
    Long Grove, IL 60047-9580
    (847) 634-0081
    info@waveland.com
    www.waveland.com

Contents

Preface to the Second Edition

Published in 2010, the first edition of this book had a steady following, primarily in academic settings. Morghan Vélez Young, whom Randall Shelden mentored years prior to this second edition, was a particularly enthusiastic supporter, assigning *Our Punitive Society* in her courses on gender and racial bias in the juvenile and criminal justice systems, as well as in training sessions for community-based programs. She offered to be a coauthor for the second edition, and the book you have in your hands is the outcome of a partnership cultivated around her enthusiasm.

In the original preface, Shelden wrote:

> This book represents a good deal of my thinking about crime and punishment in the United States. I have been involved in the study of this subject matter for the better part of four decades, beginning in the early 1970s. In all these years of research and thinking about the subject I have arrived at some general conclusions, all of which are discussed in this book. In general, I have reached the conclusion that you cannot possibly discuss in any honest way the subject of crime and punishment in America without reference to class, race, and gender inequality. Indeed, given the fact that this country has the highest degree of inequality among all industrialized democracies—a fact extensively documented in this book—what other conclusion can one make?

The first edition emphasized that you cannot have equal justice in an unequal society. The French philosopher Anatole France cleverly made reference to the relationship of laws to equal justice when he said: "The law, in its majestic equality, forbids the rich as well as the poor to sleep under bridges, to beg in the streets and to steal bread."

Deterrence is one of the basic principles of the classical school of criminology, which dates back to the publication of *On Crimes and Punishment* by Cesare Beccaria in 1764. The *deterrence* argument states that society can prevent crime by making the punishment so severe, swift, and certain that people (with the assumption that all people are on equal footing) will think twice before committing a crime. According to this line of thinking, *fear* is the main instrument of the control of human behavior, especially fear of *pain*. Punishment, as a principle method of creating fear, is seen as necessary to influence human will and thus to control behavior. More than two hundred and fifty years later we see the horrific results of this failed philosophy as the foundation of the criminal justice system. The focus of this book is the documentation and analysis of this failure.

We do not make any claims of originality. We are, as the saying goes, "standing on the shoulders of giants." Many scholars over the past century have advanced some of the same ideas we are elevating for discussion in this second edition. These scholars are cited repeatedly throughout this book.

The book covers several dimensions of the punitiveness of our society. One of the most important questions to be asked is: *Why is the United States so punitive?* This issue is raised in the introduction, and the chapters that follow explore potential answers for both academic and popular audiences.

Chapter 1 reviews recent trends in the use of incarceration. The United States imprisons more people as a percentage of its overall population than any country in the world—it has 5% of the world's population and 25% of the world's prisoners. Although the number of people incarcerated has declined somewhat in recent years, about 2.1 million people are jailed or imprisoned. Another 4.4 million are on probation or parole, bringing the total in the criminal justice system to almost 6.5 million.

The prison-building boom from 1980 to 2000 resulted in what some call a "Gulag" effect. Prisons were constructed in rural areas (sometimes multiple prisons were clustered in a small area, resembling "penal colonies"). US immigration and military prisons add to confinement facilities—mostly hidden from public view and discussed in the media only briefly after a sensational incident. Years back, Shelden and Vélez Young toured one of the first American prisons in Philadelphia whose founding purpose was based on repentance and the opportunity for redemption. The almost immediate change of purpose to punishment was the foundation for today's mass imprisonment.

Locking people up is a booming business. Chapter 2 discusses the prison industrial complex. We provide a detailed discussion of the many dimensions of the profitability of this system, ranging from the building of prisons and jails to their daily operation. Literally hundreds of companies, both large and small, are reaping profits. Many professional organizations such as the American Correctional Association and various unions such as the California Correctional Peace Officers Association support and benefit from the existence of numerous prisons. All have a vested interest in the existence of crime and their prominent role in controlling it. As one writer commented, crime may not pay, but punishment certainly does. Chapter 2 highlights the concept that the system of punishment cannot afford a significant reduction in crime because too much money is at stake.

Chapter 3 covers a key component of the penal system, the jail. The subtitle—temporary housing for the poor—states the basic theme of the chapter. Jails are the modern equivalent of eighteenth- and nineteenth-century poorhouses in that the bulk of the prisoners detained in jails are poor. Jails have served as temporary holding facilities to control or manage the *dangerous classes*. The definition of who comprises the dangerous classes has changed very little in the last several hundred years. Jailed prisoners are primarily persons of color, economically disadvantaged, and often with disabilities. More advantaged people committing the same types of crimes are rarely jailed.

We consider chapter 4 the most important chapter of all because it deals with the fundamental subject of race and racism in the United States. As the title suggests, our penal system is little more than a new form of slavery. In fact, as we also document in chapter 3, penal institutions and slavery have paralleled each other throughout US history. Many scholars note the similarity between the treatment of slaves and prisoners and the interchangeable use of the terms. One of the original forms of punishment was transportation of prisoners to foreign lands as galley slaves. In early Roman society, slaves and prisoners performed the same labor; they built the Colosseum, Pantheon, Roman Forum, and many other famous structures. In southern states, slaves became convicts via race-based laws passed after the Civil War—in fact the oldest prisons in the South were called "plantation prisons" (some are still standing, such as the infamous Parchman and Cummins Prisons). The chapter reviews trends that highlight the rate of incarceration for Black Americans, which is 5.5 times higher than that of whites. The justice gap is even greater when considering the racial disproportionality of the drug war. The chapter concludes with discussions of hyperghettos and disenfranchisement.

Chapter 5 reviews the ultimate form of punishment: the death penalty. This form of legalized homicide is aimed almost exclusively at the poor. It is no accident that legal forms of execution increased as illegal forms, such as lynching, declined. Racism continues to affect when and how persons are executed. Historical facts show that capital punishment has no deterrent value—yet innocent people have been subjected to this punishment that eliminates exoneration. A complete historical review is provided with up-to-date statistics on the death penalty, including a review of key court decisions.

Chapter 6 addresses a subject noticeably missing in most books on punishment, namely the experiences of women in the criminal justice system. A truly forgotten minority when it comes to imprisonment, women are the fastest rising segment of the prison population with an incarceration rate zooming upward by a phenomenal 650% from the mid-1970s to the present day. The major cause of the increase was the war on drugs.

Chapter 7 is new to the second edition and deals with another forgotten minority, the LGBTQ community. The authors added this chapter to highlight the experiences of LGBTQ persons in the criminal justice system. Although the proportion of this community processed through the system has always been high, those affected were not recognized or widely "seen" until recent years. LGBTQ persons historically have been charged with committing minor crimes, and the LGBTQ lifestyle itself has been criminalized to pull this population into the criminal justice system.

Chapter 8 examines still another key dimension of our punitive society, namely the punishment of young offenders. A significant segment of this chapter focuses on the excessively large proportion of minority youth confined in institutions. Indeed, looking at rates of confinement in both detention and correctional facilities, we see that Black youths are five to seven times more likely to be locked up than their white counterparts, even for the same offenses. Vélez Young draws on her years of working inside juvenile facilities to discuss the many failures and dangers of juvenile incarceration. One segment of this chapter is devoted to the crisis in detention centers filled to capacity with kids who do not really need to be there. The main culprit has been criminalization of status offenses. One recent controversy involves the mental health status of many juveniles—thousands are locked up in detention centers awaiting placement in mental health facilities or out-of-custody services. Juvenile facilities are plagued with inadequate and developmentally inappropriate services. We also address the widespread phenomena of physical and sexual abuse in these spaces.

Chapter 9 highlights the problems associated with reentry and the many barriers that returning inmates face as they are released from prisons, which can lead to recycling people through the system. Much has been written about collateral consequences, including the second-class citizenship experiences of persons reentering society, such as denial of voting rights, housing, and jobs. We summarize the effects ex-offenders experience from these collateral punishments. Approximately 875,000 people are on parole—a system that far too often ensures that prisoners fail and recycles them through the system. National recidivism rates consistently hover around the 65%–70% mark.

Finally, chapter 10 provides some of our own—and others'—recommendations for alternatives to the current criminal justice responses to crime and delinquency. Here we recommend, among other things, an end to the war on drugs, starting with the legalization of marijuana (treating it like alcohol), which a number of states have already implemented. From there we move to a discussion of diversion programs that avoid the problem of net widening. After a discussion about curbing prosecutorial power, we look at gender-responsive programming and then cover some broad-based national programs to address social inequalities. We conclude with the necessity for a new paradigm that rejects retributional punishment in favor of restorative practices.

In closing we quote Richard Quinney, one of Shelden's mentors and arguably one of the most influential criminologists of the twentieth century.

> A society that separates people through the institution of the prison creates populations of incomplete and wounded lives, whether we are *inside* the prison or *outside* the prison. This is the dance of slave and slaveholder, inmate and captor, prisoner and non-prisoner. No one escapes the damage caused by the fact that the prison exists. The damage is pervasive—on levels economic, social and psychological, and ultimately spiritual. (Quinney, 2006, p. 270)

One interpretation of Quinney's analysis is that our punitiveness damages all of us—one of the themes of this book.

Acknowledgements

Some final words of thanks are in order. Writers rarely if ever come up with original ideas. Most writing is a process of borrowing words and ideas from others and reshaping them in some other form to encourage a new audience to engage in societal transformation. Shelden and Vélez Young consider themselves "assemblers" who ingest ideas from many brilliant minds and add interpretations that leverage the message. Therefore, they extend their thanks to all the people cited in this second edition. Obviously, they are too numerous to list here. The following people are personal acquaintances; without them and their unique insights, this book would be little more than blank pages. They are, in no particular order of importance: Bud Brown, Richard Quinney, Noam Chomsky, Howard Zinn, Meda Chesney-Lind, Michael Hallett, John Irwin, Dan Macallair, and Victor Rios.

Shelden would also like to extend his thanks to his colleagues in the Criminal Justice Department at the University of Nevada–Las Vegas for their generous support over the years (especially Terry Miethe and Joel Lieberman) and to the university itself for the continuing support throughout his 40+ years there. Vélez Young would like to extend her gratitude to the Anthropology and Sociology Departments at California State University, Fresno for their support and collegiality over the years, allowing this second edition and other social change projects to materialize.

A very special thank you goes to Carol and Neil Rowe of Waveland Press for their overwhelming encouragement and time for this and previous books. It is a pure joy to work with both of them.

Finally, Shelden wishes to express his deepest thanks and love to his wife, Virginia, and stepdaughter, Marcie, for their unconditional love and support during this and previous book projects. Likewise, Vélez Young offers the deepest appreciation to her son, Sebastián, and her family for the many ways that their lives inspired this book.

Introduction
Why Are We So Punitive?

This book is about punishment in the United States. The US system of punishment is filled with ironies. Direct expenditures on the three major components of the criminal justice system (police, courts and the correctional system, which includes both probation and parole) in 2016 were almost $295.6 billion (Hyland, 2019). An additional $67 billion is spent on private security systems (security guards, gated communities, thousands of security devices, etc.) (Freedonia Group, 2019). Yet the crime rate, especially violence, remains the highest in the world.

Simultaneously, our system of punishment is a source of rewards for those working within it and for those who build and maintain the system. Terms such as *crime control industry, criminal justice industrial complex,* and *prison industrial complex* describe the symbiotic relationship between criminal justice, politics, and economics. The shorthand description is that punishment pays and pays very well. Efforts to prevent crime, however, do not receive nearly the funding that punishment does, nor are the profits for private industry as high.

Politicians infrequently support prevention efforts, avoiding the risk of being labeled soft on crime. Calls for more cops on the streets and more prisons resonate with public fears about crime and criminals. Those fears highlight an irony. In what is touted to be the most liberated and richest country in the history of the world, we are not just the most punitive—we are the most fearful. Indeed, despite all the measures taken and money spent for security, the fear of crime remains high (Glassner, 2018).

Embedded within the Constitution, the Bill of Rights, and the Declaration of Independence is the assumption of inalienable rights. The distinction between inalienable rights and legal rights is that the first is a natural

1

right bestowed on all humans at birth while the other is coded in law (Legal Dictionary, 2015). Inalienable rights supersede governmental laws and cultural norms. These natural rights include freedom of movement and freedom in decision making. The Constitution provides for exceptions to inalienable rights, which can be suspended after an arrest and criminal charges. The suspension lasts through investigation and trial, with the accused protected by due process. Conviction means the right to freedom can be taken away.

Punishment itself is not new, nor is the use of prison to produce pain for its inhabitants (Johnson et al., 2017). What is new in modern societies is the length of prison sentences *as an expression of the deprivation of liberty*. Today the United States incarcerates more people than any other country in the world. The US incarceration rate of 555 inmates per 100,000 residents leads the industrialized world (Gramlich, 2020). For forty years, the United States has expanded its criminal justice system and made every element more punitive. Incarceration is the default response to crime—70% of convictions result in jail or prison terms. How do we explain this?

Indices of Change

David Garland (2001) provides an insightful analysis of what he describes as the "accelerating movement away from the assumptions that shaped crime control and criminal justice for most of the twentieth century" (p. 3).

> As the character of everyday life changes, its changing habits and routines often have consequences for the structure of informal controls that can, in turn, cause problems for the functioning and effectiveness of the institutions of formal control. We have to bear in mind, therefore, that the field of crime control involves the social ordering activities of the authorities *and also* the activities of private actors and agencies as they go about their daily lives and ordinary routines. . . . A reconfigured field of crime control involves more than just a change in society's response to crime. It also entails new practices of controlling behavior and doing justice, revised conceptions of social order and social control, and altered ways of maintaining social cohesion and managing group relations. . . . Behind these new responses to crime, there lies a new pattern of mentalities, interests, and sensibilities that has altered how we think and feel about the underlying problem. (p. 6)

He attributes the transformation away from the less punitive approach that had previously dominated thinking about crime to twelve indices of change.

First, there has been a rapid decline in the rehabilitative ideal (Garland, 2001). The loss of faith in rehabilitation began in the early 1970s, based in part on a misunderstanding of a controversial work by Robert

Martinson (1974). In a summary of a study that reviewed evaluations of rehabilitation programs, Martinson said that while some programs showed promise of reducing recidivism, most of the evaluations lacked evidence of effectiveness and had been seriously flawed. He never said "nothing works," but many commentators interpreted his findings to mean exactly that (see, for example, Wilson, 1975).

The second index of change is the rebirth of very punitive sanctions and "expressive justice" (Garland, 2001, p. 8). Use of the death penalty increased; chain gangs were reinstated; and prisoners once again were assigned striped uniforms. Public shaming and humiliation had been regarded as demeaning, but attitudes shifted toward embracing punishment for precisely that value. The open expression of vengeance and condemnation was accepted as a justifiable outlet for the angers and fears of the public.

The third index parallels the second and marks a change in the tone of discourse about crime and punishment. In the past, people vocalized commitments to treat offenders decently and humanely, but the tone shifted in the opposite direction beginning in the 1980s. Disgust and anger toward offenders became prevalent versus the concern in previous years about the various social and psychological causes of crime and delinquency. By the 1990s the rhetoric included terms like *superpredators* and incorrigible *career criminals*. Rather than seek to address the many causes of crime, the primary tone changed to "a collective anger and righteous demand for retribution" (Garland, 2001, pp. 10–11).

The fourth index is the "return of the victim" (Garland, 2001, p. 11). The response to crime shifted rather dramatically from a focus on the criminal (and his or her shortcomings and prospects for reformation) to the victim. *Victim's rights* became a dominant theme, with many politicians attracting votes by expressing concerns over crime victims, even though nothing much was done to make them safer (see Elias, 1993). Laws were passed named for specific victims (e.g., Megan's Law, Jenna's Law, Brady Bill). Many crime bills were passed after a sensational crime ("three-strikes" legislation in California was enacted after the kidnapping and murder of Polly Klaas in 1993). Garland (2001) emphasizes that one outcome of basing legislation on cases receiving national publicity is that the victim is seen as someone whose experience is "common and collective, rather than individual and atypical" (p. 11). Many new laws with extremely harsh sentences are guided by exception-based policies and could be termed "legislation by anecdote."

The fifth index is the elevation of security as an urgent need exceeding all others, highlighted by such procedures as community notification laws (especially for sex offenders). Civil rights are de-emphasized and become secondary to the search for security. People accept surveillance cameras on city streets and encroachments on procedural safeguards such as the exclusionary rule. "The call for protection *from* the state has been increasingly displaced by the demand for protection *by* the state" (Garland, 2001, p. 12).

Sixth, "the policy-making process has become profoundly *politicized and populist*" (Garland, 2001, p. 13). Policy is decided for political advantage under the glare of publicity. Sound bites have taken the place of more careful analysis, with catch phrases like "three-strikes and you're out," "zero tolerance," "do adult crime, do adult time," etc. The opinions of experts and professionals are rejected in favor of public opinion and the views of victims. Instead of relying on expert opinion and research, the emphasis shifted to "common sense" or "what everyone knows" (Garland, 2001, p. 13).

The seventh index of change is the *reinvention of the prison* (Garland, 2001, p. 14). Incarceration is no longer viewed as a method of reforming criminals but rather as a means for incapacitation and punishment. The emphasis on the harshness of punishments satisfies a growing public demand to punish those who threaten public safety and to remove offenders from society.

Eighth, there has been a shift in emphasis within the field of criminology—a return to the classical school and its theme of "let the punishment fit the crime." Rather than stressing the importance of why people commit crime (underlying causes), there is a strong emphasis on *control theory*. Crime is not viewed as being caused by various forms of deprivation; rather, it is perceived as the result of inadequate controls. Crime is seen as "normal" and "routine," a "common occurrence" in modern societies (Garland, 2001, p. 15). Like the weather, there is nothing much in the way of prevention except to "batten down the hatches" or, like in the days of the "wild west," guard the forts and hope that reinforcements come before the next attack. The assumption of these new theories (e.g., routine activity, rational choice) is that crime will occur naturally as long as there are inadequate controls.

Ninth, Garland (2001) identifies an aspect of crime control that differs from punitive segregation and expressive justice. There has been a tremendous growth in the local infrastructure of crime control and community safety. "Today's most visible crime control strategies may work by expulsion and exclusion, but they are accompanied by patient, ongoing, low-key efforts to build up the internal controls of neighborhoods and to encourage communities to police themselves" (p. 17). Prevention, security, harm reduction, loss reduction, and fear reduction are the priorities in these preventative partnerships.

The tenth index is *civil society and the commercialization of crime control* (Garland, 2001). The assumption previously was that crime control and corrections were the responsibility of the state and government employees. The commercialization of crime control straddles the line between public and private enlisting the help of citizens, communities, and businesses to control crime. Public sector agencies have been remodeled to reflect the values of private industry. This development also includes a growing number of businesses and households investing in various forms of security devices and private security companies. One of the fastest growing industries is the private security industry. In 2018 there were 1,154,300 security guards employed in the United States, compared to around 808,700 police officers and detectives (Bureau of Labor Statistics, 2019).

The eleventh index of change is the development of new styles of management and working practices by those involved in crime control efforts. Rather than an emphasis on social work practices and rehabilitation, agencies like prisons and departments of probation and parole focus on monitoring offenders. Discretion in sentencing was displaced by the mechanical application of guidelines and mandatory sentencing. Professional discretion throughout the system has been reduced in favor of tightly regulated working practices. There is an emphasis on cost-effective management of risks, funneling resources in policing, for example, to hot spots. Garland (2001) notes the contradictory nature of some of the practices—cutting programs that have proven effective such as drug treatment programs and prison education in favor of ineffective practices supported by the public such as mandatory sentences, the war on drugs, and mass incarceration.

Finally, Garland (2001) notes that there is a perpetual sense of crisis pervading the crime control establishment. Unrelenting upheaval in practices since the 1970s and rapid change have exposed employees to sustained periods of uncertainty and disruption.

> Expertise of the professional groups that staff the system has tended to become discredited, both by others and by members of the groups themselves. . . . The public has increasingly lost confidence in criminal justice, and politicians have become more and more unwilling to entrust decision-making powers to criminological experts or criminal justice personnel. . . . [The system is often seen as a] danger zone—a constant generator of risks and scandals and escalating costs—whose officials can no longer be entrusted with autonomous powers and grants of discretion. (p. 20)

With Garland's analysis as background, we now return to the question posed in the title of this introduction.

Public Discourse on Punishment

Ta-Nehisi Coates (2015) examined the special character of American punitiveness and prison population growth.

> The Gray Wastes—our carceral state, a sprawling netherworld of prisons and jails—are a relatively recent invention. Through the middle of the twentieth century, America's imprisonment rate hovered at about 110 people per 100,000. Presently, America's incarceration rate (which

accounts for people in prisons and jails) is roughly 12 times the rate in Sweden, eight times the rate in Italy, seven times the rate in Canada, five times the rate in Australia, and four times the rate in Poland. America's closest to-scale competitor is Russia—and with an autocratic Vladimir Putin locking up about 450 people per 100,000, compared with our 700 or so, it isn't much of a competition. China has about four times America's population, but American jails and prisons hold half a million more people. "In short," an authoritative report issued last year by the National Research Council concluded, "the current rate of incarceration is unprecedented by both historical and comparative standards."

The Conservative Philosophy

The huge increases in imprisonment rates in this country beg for an explanation. Have the number of crimes increased exponentially? Have we passed more laws defining specific activities as crimes? The war on drugs is one significant source of the rapidly expanding number of people sentenced to jail or prison. Two of the questions to ask are: Why was a "war" declared in the first place?; and—again—Why have we become so punitive?

We need to look deep into US culture to understand the tendency toward punitiveness. There is a strong cultural belief in rugged individualism, accompanied by the belief that people succeed largely through their own efforts. Another strong image is that of the traditional nuclear family, often with overtones of patriarchy where the father is in control and sometimes is the major breadwinner. This pattern is usually marked by behaviors such as obeying the rules—in order to become a good and moral person, a child must learn to respect authority. Proper behavior is taught through threats of punishment. Within such a system, "the exercise of authority is itself moral; that is, it is moral to reward obedience and to punish disobedience" (Lakoff, 2016, p. 67).

Punishment, according to this philosophy, is the only way to become a self-disciplined and moral person. The system of rewards and punishments builds character and teaches children how to survive in a dangerous world. To be successful requires becoming self-disciplined. More importantly, rewarding someone who has not worked to earn the reward is immoral. Adherents to this philosophy reject various forms of welfare, affirmative action, lenient punishments and the like, for they see this as rewarding deviance, laziness, etc. (Lakoff, 2016). There is an erroneous assumption that those who are rich and famous arrived there through their own efforts, with little or no help from others. Luck and the privileges of birth are often ignored within this philosophy.

Related to this worldview is a belief in a morality of strength. The world is divided into good and evil. In order to stand up to evil, one must be morally strong; one becomes morally strong through a system of rewards and punishments that teaches self-discipline. A person who is morally weak cannot fight evil. If one is too self-indulgent, he or she is immoral. Crime and deviance are immoral and should be punished. There-fore, it logically follows that crime and deviance are the result of moral weakness. Teenage sex, drug use, and other behavior labeled deviant stem from lack of self-control. "If moral people always have the discipline to just say no to drugs or sex and to support themselves in this land of opportunity, then failure to do so is moral weakness, and hence immorality" (Lakoff, 2016, p. 75).

It should be pointed out that the entire criminal justice system (and to a somewhat lesser extent, the juvenile justice system) is based on a similar punitive philosophy, generally known as *deterrence*. Such a view argues that the best way to deter—that is, prevent—crime from occurring is the threat of punishment or the fear that one will be caught and punished. There are two kinds of deterrence. *General* deterrence is aimed toward the population as a whole. Thus, you punish one person in the hopes that others will "get the message" and refrain from committing crime. *Specific* deterrence is the punishment of a one individual in the hopes that he or she will learn from the punishment and never violate the rules again. It is based in part on the idea that all humans are rational with free will and will seek to minimize pain and maximize pleasure. Thus, the pleasure of committing a crime should be offset by the pain of punishment.

It can certainly be debated whether or not humans actually behave in this manner. What cannot be debated is that increasing the punishments for crimes has not worked very well. Yet we seem to keep sounding the same horn, louder and louder—saying to those who might be tempted to commit crime "we're sending you a message that you will be caught and punished to the full extent of the law if you keep doing this."

The philosophy described above has become a more dominant force in US culture since the 1980s (Mauer, 2001). Underscoring this development has been the concomitant growth in the number of conservative think tanks (Herman, 1997). Part of this philosophy comes from religious teach-ings. More specifically, it derives in part from the Protestant ethic, which refers to a belief system that one must make sacrifices, be thrifty, and engage in hard work; success in this world was seen as an indicator of eternal salvation (Weber, 1958).

The Role of Religion

The earliest form of law in this country was shaped by puritan reli-gious beliefs. In the Massachusetts Bay Colony, Governor John Winthrop expressed a desire to build "a City upon a Hill, the founding of a society that would be an example of godliness to the world. Religious interests were to play a predominant role in the creation of a social and legal order in early Massachusetts" (Quinney, 1970, p. 61). The Puritans believed that government exists to regulate imperfect man and that political leaders must be obeyed because they had been ordained by God. Many laws were taken almost literally from the Bible, including those prohibiting idolatry, blasphemy, bestiality, sodomy, and adultery, all of which were punishable by death. Even after the American Revolution, which stressed a separation of church and state, many religiously based laws remained on the books.

Helen Ellerbe (1995) argues persuasively that orthodox religions are inherently punitive. Orthodox Christianity "is embedded in the belief in a singular, solely masculine, authoritarian God who demands unquestioning obedience and who mercilessly punishes dissent" (p. 1). Fear is the tool used to sustain belief in a hierarchical order in which God reigns at the pinnacle. Christians were taught to fear earthly rulers just as they feared God; in many cases rulers were believed to be agents of God. "This confined power and authority to a small few and established a specific chain of command" (p. 9). In the fourth century, St. John Chrysostom issued a statement that could easily provide the theoretical underpinnings of the classical school of criminology: without magistrates "and the fear that comes from them," entire nations would fall because there would be no one "to repress, or repel, or persuade them to be peaceful through the fear of punishment" (p. 5). In short, people will coexist only through the threat of punishment.

Religion played a key role in the establishment of the first prisons. Quakers and other religious groups in the late eighteenth and early nineteenth centuries confined prisoners in quarters where they could contemplate their crimes and seek penance—*penitentiaries* were named to reflect this goal. Prisoners were locked up in solitary confinement almost 24 hours per day, with nothing to read but the Bible; the only outsiders allowed to visit were members of the clergy. Going to prison was supposed to be a "monastic experience" (Welch, 1999). The Pennsylvania model has been reconstituted in supermax prisons today where inmates are confined in single cells with no human contact.

Vengeance and retribution are concepts common to many religions; they have also dominated discussions of crime control policies. Rational arguments against the death penalty, for instance, are often ignored because the crimes committed produce such strong feelings of vengeance. If members of the public focus on retribution—"an eye for an eye" in the Bible or "lex talionis" in Roman law (Shicor, 2006, p. 26)—the desire to punish will override the facts that the death penalty is not a deterrent, that it is more costly than life in prison, and that it discriminates against racial minorities.

There are a number of facilities for teenagers operated under the auspices of religious organizations. Some parents confronted with teenage behavior such as drinking, smoking, and truancy turn to faith-affiliated programs that claim to build character through strict obedience to rules. Because the facilities are affiliated with churches, parents assume their children will be safe. The facilities often dismiss governmental regulations as religious persecution (Joyce, 2011).

A number of fundamentalist Christian facilities for troubled teens trace their roots to a Texas radio evangelist, Lester Roloff. He founded the Rebekah Home for Girls in Corpus Christi in 1967, which employed disciplinary tactics such as isolation and corporal punishment (Joyce, 2011). Reports of abuse surfaced, and the state of Texas investigated (Escobedo, 2004). It took 12 years for Texas to close the Rebekah Home for Girls. Roloff referred to his efforts to fight the regulators as the Christian Alamo.

Two of the people who worked with Roloff moved to Florida and opened the first New Beginnings. When Florida officials began investigating the facility, another couple took over and moved the home to rural Missouri. Openings and closings and moving from one state to another to avoid prosecution became a common pattern for such facilities (Joyce, 2011). One mother heard a presentation at her Maryland church by the headmaster and some of the girls at New Beginnings touting the Missouri home as a place where girls could restore broken relationships and get on track academically. Her 17-year-old daughter had been assaulted while jogging, and the trauma affected her behavior. Her mother sent her daughter to New Beginnings as a place to heal. Instead, she was monitored day and night and was subjected to rigid discipline. Girls were micromanaged down to the number of squares of toilet paper allowed. They were not allowed to converse except from 6 to 9 p.m. each Friday. Making eye contact with another girl was an infraction, as was not finishing a meal. Girls were not allowed contact with their families during their first month, or with anyone else for six months. They were told that their families abandoned them and that the world outside was a sinful, dangerous place where girls who left were murdered or raped. After three months, the mother removed her daughter; the trauma experienced resulted in an eating disorder and severe depression.

Another Rebekah spin-off, New Bethany Home for Boys and Girls, opened in Louisiana. Complaints by youths formerly housed there prompted investigations. Studies consisted of memorizing Scripture (mistakes were punishable by paddling). Discipline ranged from belt whippings to being forced to scrub pots with undiluted bleach. Youths were beaten, locked in isolation, refused bathroom privileges, and denied contact with their loved ones (Joyce &Mechanic, 2011). New Bethany finally closed after numerous investigations; related facilities continue to exist (Catalanello, 2014).

As shocking as these cases are, they are really nothing new, for such abuse extends far back in the history of juvenile justice. The victims are labeled "troubled teens" (thereby justifying their incarceration). Perhaps a more accurate description would be that the parents are the ones who are troubled, not knowing how to cope with unwelcome behaviors. Seeking a simplistic solution to perceived rebellious behavior, they opt for "tough love" approaches.

Religion continues to be a foundation for some politicians. In a speech at Notre Dame University in 2019, the attorney general of the United States discussed the absence of faith as a threat to society and to our system of government (Chapman, 2019). He took issue with an Illinois law that requires history classes in public schools to review the contributions of lesbian, gay, bisexual, and transgender people. He alleged secularists had "marshaled all the force of mass communications, popular culture, the entertainment industry, and academia in an unremitting assault on religion and traditional values"—forcing religious people to "subscribe to practices and policies that are antithetical to their faith" (p. 16).

In the speech, the attorney general suggested that every measure of social pathology—including suicide and illegitimate births—is gaining ground because of moral relativism, adding that people remain free only if they are moral and religious. However, countries ranked the most free are New Zealand, Switzerland, Australia, and Canada where citizens are much less religious than in the United States, which is ranked seventeenth in freedom (Chapman, 2019). Rich countries are generally less religious than poor countries. People in the United States are the exception, as 68% say religion is very important, compared to 39% in Canada, 27% in Australia, 12% in Germany and France, and 11% in Great Britain (Marshall, 2018).

Crime is more common in the United States than in secular countries such as Japan and Sweden. The two states with the highest rate of births to unmarried mothers are Mississippi and Louisiana, which are also among the highest in church attendance. New Hampshire has the lowest murder rate—and the second lowest church attendance. Religion is no guarantee against social ills; secularism does not cause them (Chapman, 2019). Adults under the age of 40 in the United States are less likely to pray, to attend church services, and to identify with any religion (Fahmy, 2018); 23% of Americans claim no religion.

Social and Political Factors

In *Thinking about Crime*, Michael Tonry reviews a number of possible explanations for the increase in punitiveness. He sets the stage for his analysis by noting:

> The ways people think about contentious issues change slowly but predictably. Social scientists use the word "sensibilities" to refer to prevailing social values, attitudes, and beliefs, and show how sensibilities change slowly over time and shape and reshape what people think and believe. Current American crime control policies are to a large part an outgrowth of American sensibilities of the last third of the twentieth century. (Tonry, 2006, p. 5)

Attitudes toward crime in the United States are cyclical. Prevailing sensibilities affect what laws are passed and the policies pursued, as does the ongoing cycle of tolerance and intolerance.

Tonry notes that some people, including David Garland, point to economic and social disruptions as causing a postmodern angst—extreme concerns about the future accompanied by vast insecurity. Governments cannot insulate citizens from the disruptive effects of economic recession, globalization, and multiculturalism. Crime, however, differs. The state can take swift, punitive action. The goal is not crime reduction but the credibility of the state. Policy makers must be perceived as doing something; vigorous enforcement is expressive rather than functional. Why are harsh, expressive policies accepted?

> Because the groups most affected lack political power and are widely regarded as dangerous and undeserving; because the groups least affected could be reassured that something is being done and lawlessness is not tolerated; and because few politicians are willing to oppose a policy when there is so little political advantage to be gained by doing so. (Garland, 2001, p. 132)

Tonry (2006) also discusses Theodore Caplow and Jonathan Simon's attribution of harsh punishment to the breakdown of broad-based political parties, the rise of single-issue interest groups (e.g., environment, civil rights, abortion, taxes, etc.), and an overall lack of public confidence in government programs. Politicians needed to find an issue to attract support without offending specific interest groups. Crime offered a point of consensus and a means of winning votes. Criminals were convenient scapegoats, along with welfare recipients and immigrants. "Criminals are among the most vulnerable and viscerally plausible scapegoats, and politicians have tried to placate voters' discomforts and win votes by being tough on criminals" (p. 24).

Tonry (2006) strongly suggests that race plays a major role in increased punitiveness. The vast differences in the rates of incarceration for Blacks and for whites provide ample evidence of this factor. Linked to the factor of race is the drug war. Tonry argues that both drug and crime policies have been the result of

> recurring patterns of tolerance and intolerance of deviance to produce widespread public susceptibility to calls for adoption of unprecedentedly repressive policies. The emotional force of ubiquitous mass media coverage of such events as the crimes of Willie Horton [suspension of weekend furloughs], the murders of Megan Kanka [sex offender registration and community notification laws] and Polly Klaas [California's "three-strikes" laws], and the crack overdose death of Len Bias [federal 100-to-1 crack cocaine sentencing law] produced moral panics that provided occasion for such calls. (p. 60)

During moral panics, people exaggerate the dangers of things they fear (e.g., fearing crime when crime is actually declining or when the odds of being a victim are extremely low), and they become more rigid and moralistic. Examples include the furor over crack babies and teen mothers. Clear majorities believed the hype surrounding these two issues and supported punishing the individuals involved severely (Reinarman & Levine, 1997). As Tonry (2006) observed:

> For two decades, Americans thought they wanted single-minded toughness and they got it. The question is why they thought they

wanted it. "Moral panics" are part of the answer. They typically occur when horrifying or notorious events galvanize public emotion, and produce concern, sympathy, emotion, and overreaction. . . . Moral panics relating to crime lead to poorly considered and overly harsh reactions. In recent decades, moral panics have magnified the effects of longer term changes in values and attitudes. (p. 5)

As will be discussed throughout this text, minorities suffer disproportionately from the punitive nature of society—from arrest to detention to imprisonment. It is much easier to impose severe punishments on people "with whom we have little in common or do not know in any personal sense . . . the more stratified a society, the easier it becomes for the well-off to advocate greater pain for those less fortunate" (Mauer, 2001, p. 15). Well over half of all of those imprisoned today are racial minorities, yet there is limited public debate about the disparity in treatment. Imagine if the police suddenly began arresting middle and upper-class whites and placing them in prison in numbers approaching the arrest and conviction rates for Blacks.

We're the Tough Guys

Todd Clear and Natasha Frost (2015) refer to the punitive spirit that was the rationale for mass incarceration as the punishment imperative and describe the prison boom as a policy of expanded social control.

The punitiveness of the 1970s was nothing compared with the years to come. For the next forty years, virtually every aspect of the punishment system, from the way people were processed before trial to the way people were confined after conviction, grew harder. Like a drunk whose life descends increasingly into the abyss, penal policies grew steadily and inexorably toward an ever harder edge. Thresholds of punitiveness people never thought our democracy would ever have to confront became a part of official policy: life without parole and death penalties for young people; lengthy detention before trial; humiliation and long periods of extreme isolation during confinement; decades behind bars for minor thefts and possession of drugs. Such developments would have been unthinkable in the 1960s, but they would become the leading edge of penal reform in the years that followed. (p. 2)

We live in what might be termed a macho culture marked by a belief that might makes right. The history of the United States contains many examples of invasions of foreign countries (Chomsky, 2000, Johnson, 2001, Kinzer, 2006). Militarism extends to our treatment of criminals (with the notable exceptions of corporate offenders and crimes of the state).

Europeans have moved away from the *degradation and humiliation* of offenders (Whitman, 2003). They treat ordinary offenders of low social status with the dignity and honor formerly reserved for high status offenders. The United States practices status degradation ceremonies whereby the very personhood of offenders is ignored (Garfinkel, 1956). Europe distanced itself from the harshness and meanness of the ultra-authoritarian punishments associated with Fascism and Nazi Germany. In contrast, the United States moved in the opposite direction.

> Cultural differences in the perception of the "harshness" of particular acts of punishment are only the beginning. Deeper difficulties grow out of the fact that criminal justice systems are *systems*. Criminal justice is a complex machinery that begins with investigation and arrest; continues with trial, conviction, and sentencing; and ends only with the reintegration, or as the case may be, with the death of, the offender. (Whitman, 2003, p. 33)

James Whitman (2003) looks at harshness/mildness by the range and types of conduct treated as criminal offenses. The first measure is the degree to which various behaviors are *criminalized*. In the United States, relatively minor offenses (especially those categorized as morals offenses) are prohibited by law. His second measure is the extent to which numerous *classes* of persons are subject to potential criminal liability, ranging from treating minors as adults via certification to violations of drug laws to various forms of zero tolerance. A third dimension of harshness is *grading*—determining whether an offense is a felony or a misdemeanor. For example, in the United States many drug offenses are felonies, whereas in Europe they are misdemeanors. The fourth dimension is inflexible doctrines of criminal liability—one indication is whether a criminal justice system treats ignorance of the law as an excuse. The system typically does not. The fifth dimension is *enforcement* of the law. Criminal justice systems where the police often ignore violations of the law are considered mild.

Whitman also looks at the harshness/mildness of punishment. The first measure is the length of sentences. The second dimension of punishment is the *application* of punishment. Does the system maintain harsh conditions within prisons or administer rough treatment at the station house or on the streets? The third dimension is the *inflexibility of punishment*. A system that is very harsh tends to apply the same punishment regardless of individual circumstances. Whitman delineates two measures of mildness: respectful treatment and the use pardons, amnesties, and commutations. Respectful treatment includes addressing prisoners in a dignified manner and avoiding undignified customs. A number of practices in prisons that are unquestioned (perhaps not even noticed) in the United States have been eliminated in Europe: keeping inmates in cells through which they are observed and all activities exposed; uniforms; prison regulations about personal grooming such as hair length and facial hair; restrictions on visitation, regimentation in when, where, and what to eat; deprivation of the right to vote; cell and strip searches; and letters censored. Europe tends to be more respectful of its prisoners as well as exercising the discretion of pardons more frequently.

The movement toward determinate sentencing reflects the harshness practiced in the United States. People expressed anger that different offenders received different sentences for committing the same crime. The crime now determines the punishment, regardless of individual differences or circumstances. Determinate sentencing fits the goal of the classical school of criminology to make the system predictable and efficient.

A Concluding Thought

In the previous section, we mentioned that the belief that might makes right leads to wars. Part of the same mentality asserts that you can change behavior through force or the threat of force. These attitudes have created jails and prisons that confine more than 2 million people and police departments primed to arrest those who get out of line. The challenge that faces us today has existed for centuries: create true alternatives in dealing with our problems—alternatives to the "might makes right" ideology.

Bryan Stevenson (2017) notes that color emerged as the defining feature that would shape the cultural, social, political, and economic development of the United States. White settlers viewed indigenous people as inferior and unworthy of the resources and opportunities of the land in which they lived, resulting in decades of exploitation and violence. The population of 10 million indigenous people was reduced to less than 500,000. Disease accounted for most of the deaths, but forced migration and war also played a role. Over the next two centuries, slavery added to the mythology about the racial inferiority of people of color.

There is a presumption of guilt and dangerousness that burdens people of color in the United States. Racial disparities cannot be attributed only to biased police officers or judges.

> There is a narrative of racial difference that contaminates the thinking of most Americans. We are burdened by our history of racial injustice in ways that shape the way we think, act, and enforce the law. Without understanding this narrative, confronting it truthfully and repairing the damage created by our history, we will never truly experience the equality and fairness we value so highly in our legal system. . . . We need to own up to the way racial bias and legalized racial subordination have compromised our ability to implement criminal justice. (Stevenson, 2017, p. 5)

If we ask the right questions, we could change our policies about a number of issues. Stevenson uses capital punishment as an example. The question is not whether people deserve to die for the crimes they commit. Instead, we should ask whether we deserve to kill. If we don't question how to confront implicit bias, we will repeat our history of racial injustice. If we don't ask why we imprison people for drug use, we will continue to spend billions of dollars on a drug war that has been ineffective for decades.

1

Incarceration in the United States

The processing of offenders through the criminal justice system is a huge undertaking. In 2019, the police made almost 10.1 million arrests (FBI, 2020a). Although few arrestees are sentenced to prison, the number of incarcerations increased exponentially for decades until 2010. At the end of 2019, the US prison population (state and federal) was 1,430,800 (Carson, 2020b).

People under Criminal Justice Control

Since 2010, there has been a gradual decrease in the number of people incarcerated (see figure 1-1). The decline can be attributed in part to "tightened state budgets, plummeting crime rates, changes in sentencing laws and shifts in public opinion" (Goode, 2013, p. 11). Changes to sentencing laws included reducing punishments for lower-level offenses to reduce prison population size. In California, for example, voters in November 2014 passed Proposition 47, which changed certain low-level crimes from felonies to misdemeanors. Two years later, voters approved Proposition 57, which increased parole and good behavior opportunities for offenders incarcerated for nonviolent crimes. Further, many states expanded diversion programs, slowing the growth of prison populations. Some states changed parole policies regarding parole violations.

Many conservative states realized the importance of lowering the cost burden of prisons and supporting less punitive solutions for nonviolent offenders, as evidenced by reductions in states like Texas and Arkansas. Right on Crime (2019) is a conservative website based in Texas. It advo-

15

U.S. State and Federal Prison Population, 1925–2017

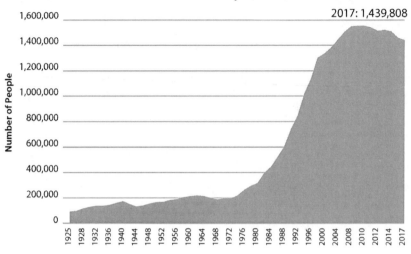

Figure 1-1   Trends in U.S. Corrections, 1925–2017

Source: Bureau of Justice Statistics *Prisoners Series*

cates increasing the use of custodial supervision alternatives such as probation and parole for nonviolent offenders and linking these programs to mandatory drug addiction treatment and mental health counseling to prevent recidivism. The website compares average daily prison costs of almost $79.00 to less than $3.50 daily average cost for probation. It also suggests considering geriatric release programs. The cost of incarceration increases substantially for the approximately 200,000 prisoners over age 50 because of health care needs.

In addition to state and federal prisoners in 2018, another 738,400 persons were incarcerated in local jails (Zeng, 2020), bringing the total number of incarcerated people to more than 2.2 million. The most significant increases occurred after 1975, roughly coinciding with the onset of the war on drugs (Shelden & Vasiliev, 2018).

The United States versus the World

The United States has the highest prison incarceration rate in the world—655 per 100,000 (Walmsley, 2018). The rate is much higher than the rates for other industrialized democracies (see figure 1-2). Canada, for example, has a rate of 107, while the United Kingdom (England and Wales) has a rate of 141. The Scandinavian countries rank the lowest: Iceland, 37; Finland, 51; Sweden, 59; Netherlands, 61; Norway and Denmark, 63. Most European countries have a rate under 100.

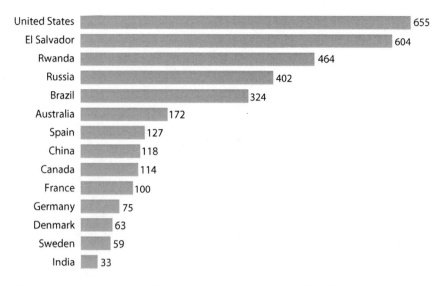

Figure 1-2 International Rates of Incarcerations per 100,000

Source: Walmsley, 2018

The European Union has 512 million people and incarcerates 1,404,398 prisoners, an incarceration rate of 116 per 100,000 (Council of Europe, 2019). The incarceration rates for many of these countries, unlike the incarceration rates in the United States, include people housed in various community-based facilities. While the exact number of persons housed in community-based facilities in the United States is not known, about 1 in 58 adults nationwide was under some form of correctional supervision in 2018 (Kaeble & Alper, 2020). For Black Americans, the proportion under supervision was drastically different, reflecting 1 in 23 adults. Another aspect of supervision rates is that they differ by state. For example, 1 in 35 across the adult population are supervised in Ohio versus 1 in 18 in Georgia.

Expansion of the Correctional System

Between 1980 and 2010, the four segments of the correctional system grew by 286%. Jails and prisons led the way, increasing by 389 and 356% respectively. The number on probation went up by 262%, while the number on parole increased by 269%. The overall adult population increased by just 18% during this period, and arrests increased 41%—compared to an overall *decrease* in reported index crimes. What this clearly shows is that there was a significant increase in the number of less serious offenders being arrested, with a corresponding increase in the number being convicted and sent to prison or jail.

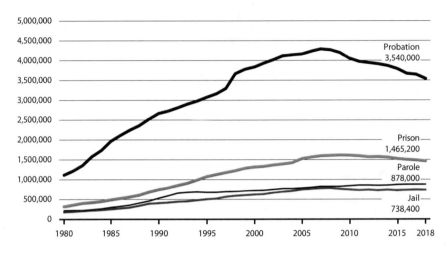

Figure 1-3 Number of Adults Under Community Supervision More Than Tripled Over 38 Years

Source: Bradner et al., 2020

Many different kinds of facilities house people sentenced by the courts: diagnostic/reception centers, work release centers, transfer facilities, boot camps, prison medical centers and hospitals, etc. Other people are detained under the jurisdiction of US Immigration and Customs Enforcement (ICE)—39,322 in 2018 (Cullen, 2018). In 2018, there were 37,529 youths in juvenile residential placement (OJJDP Statistical Briefing Book, 2020). The number of juveniles in residential placement peaked at 108,802 in 2000. From 1975 to 2000, youth in placement more than doubled. In contrast, juvenile placement rates in 2018 were almost one-third less than in 2000—a 65.5% decrease. More than half of the youth in 2018 were held in local facilities.

Incarceration Rates

Incarceration rates vary considerably from one state to another. As shown in table 1-1, Louisiana ranks first with a rate of 887 per 100,000 state residents age 18 or older, followed by Oklahoma with a rate of 840. Notice that states with particularly high rates are in the South, a region that has led the United States in rates of incarceration and also rates of violence (Stebbins, 2019). Southern states rank the lowest in several indicators of well-being, including child mortality, child poverty, unemployment, health insurance, wages, income inequality, etc. (Hitchcock & Miringhoff, 2008). We explore the link between Southern rates of incarceration and slavery in chapter 4.

Table 1-1	State Rankings of Incarceration Rates, Age 18 or Older, 2019				
Louisiana	887	Arizona	719	Georgia	663
Oklahoma	840	Texas	709	Idaho	632
Mississippi	830	Kentucky	665	South Dakota	566
Arkansas	762				

Source: Carson, 2020b

Crime Rates and Mass Incarceration

In recent years, there has been a considerable amount of commentary concerning the connection between the rise in imprisonment rates and the drop in crime. A superficial reading could suggest that there was a correlation between incarceration and decreasing crime. Between 1990 and 1999, the incarceration rate increased 56% while the overall crime rate decreased 26% (Shelden et al., 2016). Violent crimes went down by 28%; the murder rate dropped 39%; and property crime declined 26%. These figures could be interpreted to mean that more people in prison equals less crime.

The Impact of Imprisonment on Crime

It may seem intuitive that increasing incarceration reduces crime through incapacitation and, perhaps, deterrence through fear of being punished. However, increased incarceration rates have minimal impact on reducing crime—at significant costs (Stemen, 2017). Any crime reduction benefits of incarceration are limited to property crime. Research consistently shows that higher incarceration rates are not associated with lower violent crime rates. Since 2000, increased incarceration rates were responsible for almost zero percent of the reduction in crime. Other factors—including an aging population, increased wages, increased employment, increased graduation rates, and changes in policing strategies—accounted for 75 to 100% of lower crime rates. Nineteen states from 2000 to 2015 reduced both imprisonment and crime rates through crime prevention and alternatives to incarceration. New Jersey reduced incarceration by 37%, with a 30% decrease in crime rates. West Virginia's incarceration rate increased 83%, and its crime rate increased 4%. During that time period, only four states experienced increased crime rates—all four also had increased incarceration rates.

Researcher David Roodman (2017) reviewed empirical research on the impact of incarceration on crime. He cautions that any discussion of impact should specify the alternative to incarceration. The studies he reviewed compared incarceration to supervised or unsupervised release.

Other options exist such as drug treatment and restorative justice pro-grams, but those alternatives have not been researched extensively.

> Since plausible theories point in each direction, the question of the net impact of incarceration on crime must be brought to the data. Having reviewed and revisited published analyses in unprecedented depth, my best estimate is that the best estimate of the impact of additional incar-ceration on crime in the United States today is zero. And, while that estimate is not certain, there is as much reason overall to believe that incarceration increases crime as decreases it. (p. 7)

Most studies suggest that the harmful aftereffects (e.g., felony record affecting employment and housing; alienation from society) of incarcera-tion are strong enough to offset any crime benefits of incapacitation. Roodman notes that we must remember the complexity behind examining the impact of incarceration given different people, different crimes, differ-ent places, different ways to adjust sentencing guidelines and laws, etc. He cautions that his conclusion of zero benefits from incarceration regarding the crime rate does not tell us how much decarceration is possible without crime increasing.

"Get Tough" Policies

The unprecedented growth of the penal system and the dismantling of welfare programs developed simultaneously, fueled by the challenges of responding to inequality and the disorder that crested in the 1970s (Kohler-Hausmann, 2019). Politicians reacted to the slowing economy and protests by abandoning individual rehabilitation that had been the founda-tion for both penal and social programs for decades. Strategies of punish-ment, surveillance, and containment replaced rehabilitation. The repeated enactment of punitive policies convinced many Americans that social investment was a failure—coercion and force were required to manage the underclass. Ironically, the US "get tough" policies, which included the "end of welfare," resulted in another form of welfare. Instead of taxpayer money going to provide some subsistence for the marginalized in communities, the money is routed for housing marginalized populations in prisons. The financial cost is far greater than typical welfare expenditures—from about $20,000 to $40,000 per individual annually depending on the prison.

Harm to Families

In addition to the financial waste, there is a tremendous cost to fami-lies. More than five million children—1 in 14 or 7% of all children—have had a parent who lived with them go to jail or prison (Murphey & Cooper, 2015). The number is "almost certainly an underestimate, since it does not include children with a nonresidential parent who was incarcerated" (p. 1).

The incarceration of a parent is most common among children who face other barriers to opportunity. The percentages of children whose parents are incarcerated are higher for Black children and children who are poor (Murphey & Cooper, 2015). About twice as many Black children (1 in 9 or 11.5%) have experienced parental incarceration than have white children (1 in 17 or 6%). For Black children ages 12 to 17, the percentage is 13.6%. Children living in poverty are more than three times as likely to have experienced the incarceration of a parent than are children living in families with incomes at least twice the poverty level—12.5% versus 3.9%.

The harm associated with parental incarceration compounds the already difficult circumstances of vulnerable children. One of the variables most strongly related to juvenile chronic delinquency is having one or more parents in prison (Shelden & Troshynski, 2020). Parental incarceration is also linked with childhood health problems, behavior problems, problems in school, and poor mental and physical health in adulthood (Murphey & Cooper, 2015). Reducing reliance on imprisonment as a sanction for some criminal behavior would mitigate the harm caused to children.

Expenditures and Crime Control

Part of the reason for the growth of the criminal justice system is that many have decided that a technocratic solution to crime control is the best course of action. The President's Crime Commission in 1967 clearly linked two knowledge bases with efforts to combat crime.

> More than 200,000 scientists and engineers have applied themselves to solving military problems and hundreds of thousands more to innovation in other areas of modern life, but only a handful are working to control the crimes that injure or frighten millions of Americans each year. Yet the two communities have much to offer each other: Science and technology is a valuable source of knowledge and techniques for combating crime; the criminal justice system represents a vast area of challenging problems. (President's Commission, 1967a, p. 1)

Those holding political power took up the challenge; the criminal justice system today extends into other social institutions. Many observers suggest that the criminal justice system replaces some of the *military industrial complex,* using military equipment to squelch protests and to target internal enemies (Balko, 2013). The new enemy is crime—specifically crimes committed by marginalized populations. In the last 30 years, expenditures on crime control increased twice as fast as military spending (Shelden et al., 2016).

One can clearly see the expansion in the size of the criminal justice system by looking at expenditure increases during the past four decades. In 1982 total expenditures came to around $36 billion; in 2016 the total was $295.6 billion—a 721% increase (Hyland, 2019). Annual expenditures for the war on drugs at the federal and state levels total more than

Table 1-2	Criminal Justice Expenditures, 1982, 2002, and 2016 (in billions)		
	1982	**2002**	**2016**
Total	$36	$190	$295.6
Police	$19	$84	$142.5
Judicial	$8	$43	$64.7
Corrections	$9	$63	$88.5

$47 billion (Drug Policy Alliance, 2019). Since 1971, the economic impact of the war on drugs has been $1 trillion in criminal justice expenditures (Pearl, 2018).

A Boom in Prison Construction

From 1970 to 2000, prison construction was a booming business. The number of prisons increased from 511 in 1970 to 1,663 in 2010 at a cost of more than $23 billion; the average population at each facility was 758 prisoners with 231 staff members (Eason, 2017b). The prisons constructed in those years covered 580 square miles—about half the size of Rhode Island. The apex of the prison building boom was in the 1990s, when almost one-quarter of all prisons were constructed. Between 1970 and 2006, there were 1,152 new prisons—more than in all the years before 1970. Of the new prisons constructed, 70% were in rural communities. Building slowed after 2000 to an average of 17 new prisons annually in the first decade of the twenty-first century. Renovations, however, increased; 250 prisons were renovated.

Southern states built the most prisons, although every state built at least 1 new prison from 1970 to 2010 (Eason, 2017b). Texas built 133 facilities (11% of the total constructed). Georgia built 69, followed by Florida with 58, Oklahoma with 55, New York with 52, Illinois with 46, California with 43, North Carolina with 38, Virginia with 35, and Michigan with 32. Those 10 states accounted for 49% of all prisons constructed. Prisons were not evenly dispersed. Of the 133 facilities in Texas, 7 were in Huntsville and 6 were in Gatesville. Cañon County has 7 of the 34 facilities in Colorado. In Florida, 45% of the state's counties had a prison in 1979 compared to 78% in 2000; in New York 31% of counties had a prison in 1979 versus 52% in 2000 (Lawrence & Travis, 2004).

On a driving trip through the northern peninsula of Michigan, Shelden and his wife were admiring the rolling hills and farms and the serene quality of the landscape, a throwback to an earlier era when farming was the dominant occupation in the United States. When they reached the town of Newberry, they were surprised to find several chain motels, chain restaurants, gas stations, and mini-marts. It all seemed totally out of place. Outside the town, they noticed an old brick building surrounded by barbed wire, sitting on several acres of land; male prisoners were in the yard, and most of them appeared to be Black. They subsequently learned that the institution had been a mental facility until deinstitutionalization in the 1970s; it was converted to a prison in 1996. They counted an additional five prisons before leaving the state. More than 90% of the prisoners (primarily Black) housed in the 6 correctional facilities in the Northern Peninsula of Michigan came from Detroit.

In 2020 there were 1,833 state prisons, 110 federal prisons, 3,134 local jails, 80 Indian Country jails, and 1,772 juvenile correctional facilities in the United States (Sawyer & Wagner, 2020). There were almost 7,000 correctional facilities nationwide plus military prisons, immigration detention facilities, civil commitment centers, and state psychiatric hospitals.

Gulags American Style

The gulag was a system of labor camps first established in 1919, but Josef Stalin's dictatorship (1924–1953) vastly extended the system. *Gulag* is an acronym for the bureaucratic institution (Glavnoe Upravlenie ispravitel'no-trudovykh LAGerei) that administered the corrective labor camps. The camps were located primarily in the remote regions of Siberia and northernmost areas. The forced labor contributed to the economy, and the camps also served as prisons and detention camps for political prisoners (Conquest, 1995). After the publication of Aleksandr Solzhenitsyn's (1970) *The Gulag Archipelago*, the term was used to describe the Soviet penal system. The number of camps grew from around 350,000 in 1929 to more than 1.5 million by 1931.

One might conclude from the above that the Gulag phenomenon is typically seen as either an aberration or something restricted to totalitarian societies. However, a close look at the modern US prison system might suggest otherwise. Norwegian criminologist Nils Christie (2000) suggested that the "crime control industry" was beginning to look like the equivalent of the Russian *Gulag*. Journalist Mark Dow (2004) referred to US immigration prisons as an *American Gulag*. Before immigration prisons, Japanese Americans were removed from their homes and businesses and sent to "relocation centers" during World War II. Ruth Wilson Gilmore (2007) described the California prison building boom as the *Golden Gulag*.

Today the US prison system has many of the same characteristics of Gulags. There are many human rights abuses in prisons (and also jails and juvenile correctional facilities), including cruel and unusual punishment (e.g., long periods in solitary confinement) and extreme brutality and violence. Moreover, there is forced labor, much of which produces profits for corporations.

Texas has been one of the most punitive states. Since 1976, Texas has executed 574 people. Its peak year of incarceration was 2010 when it incarcerated more than 173,600 people. There has been a 4.5% reduction in the prison population since then, and Texas closed 8 prisons (Hart, 2018). In 2019, Texas had 108 incarceration facilities. In 1993, Texas created a state jail felony program to divert some inmates, such as drug offenders, from state prison, but the program never funded rehabilitative programs to reduce the likelihood of recidivism. There are 17 state jails in Texas and 61 prisons (10 run by private corporations). Texas has the largest inmate population in the United States.

Earlier we mentioned the 6 prison facilities in Gatesville, Texas. The town of about 12,400 people is the home of 5 of the 9 Texas state prisons/jails for women. With the men's prison, Gatesville houses a total of 7,505 prisoners. There are four prisons housing more than 6,000 men in Rosharon, Texas. The population of the city is 1,152. In chapter 2, we discuss how prison populations skew census figures to the advantage of towns in which prisons are located and to the disadvantage of the home communities of inmates.

The Geography of Prisons

John Eason (2017a) argues that the prison boom is best understood from the perspective of the rural southern towns that wanted prisons. As the number of prisoners increased and the country embarked on prison building, rural towns sought opportunities to halt their decline. "Some rural leaders see attracting a prison as a way to achieve order in a world that seems to be rapidly changing in ways that are increasingly beyond their control (p. xii). When economic opportunities like factories or mills were available for rural towns, prisons were frequently viewed as aesthetically unattractive and as NIMBY (not in my backyard) because of the populations housed. Unraveling why rural leaders pursued prisons reveals the social, political, and economic shifts that drove the prison boom—which Eason refers to as the largest public works projects in modern history. He sees nonmetropolitan municipalities where federal, state, or private prisons were constructed as a strategic site for investigating the intersection of race, spatial disadvantage, and the expansion of the criminal justice system.

Eason (2017a) notes that the expansion in the number of prisoners alone does not explain why some states build more prisons than others, pointing out that Illinois and Georgia each had approximately 50,000 state prison inmates but Illinois had 55 prisons compared to 82 in Georgia. Prison towns are diverse in size, region, socioeconomic status, and racial composition. The average rural southern town was twelve times more likely to receive a prison than a Midwestern or northeastern town. Prisons were usually placed in towns of concentrated rural disadvantage with high poverty and residential segregation. At the height of the prison boom, most prisons were built in southern towns with higher percentages of Blacks and Latinos. Roughly a third of all corrections officers nationally are Black or Latino.

The War on Drugs

Let's begin this section by considering some statistics.

- Every 25 seconds, someone in the United States is arrested for drug possession (Pearl, 2018).
- In 2018, there were 1,654,282 arrests for drug offenses; 663,367 arrests were for marijuana; 86% of arrests were for possession compared to 67% of arrests in 1989 (Stellin, 2019).
- Blacks and Latinos comprise 31.5% of the US population but 46.9% of people arrested for drug law violations (Drug Policy Alliance, 2019).
- Almost half a million people are incarcerated for a drug offense (Sentencing Project, 2020b).
- Blacks are almost 6 times more likely to be incarcerated for a drug offense than whites. Almost 80% of people serving time for a federal drug offense are Black or Latino; people of color comprise 60% of state prisoners serving time for a drug offense (Pearl, 2018).
- Twenty-five percent of women in prison have been convicted of a drug offense, compared to 14% of men; the proportion of imprisoned women convicted of a drug offense has increased from 12% in 1986 to 25% in 2017 (Sentencing Project, 2019a).
- 200,000 students have lost federal financial aid eligibility because of a drug conviction (Drug Policy Alliance, 2019).

These figures are just a sampling of the human wreckage resulting from more than four decades of punitive policies.

The war on drugs has targeted mostly the poor and racial minorities. People of color are disproportionately represented among those imprisoned for drug offenses. This is not because of greater involvement in the use or sale of drugs. Minority offenders possess and sell drugs that are the most frequent target of arrest (Kennedy et al., 2018). There are more arrests for crack cocaine than for methamphetamine and heroin.

The media emphasize highly organized drug dealers making vast sums of money. The war on drugs, however, is waged primarily against people possessing or selling very small amounts of drugs (Kennedy et al., 2018). Forty percent of drug arrests are for possessing or selling a quarter of a gram or less. Another 20% of arrested offenders possessed between one-quarter and one gram. For cocaine, heroin, and methamphetamine, 40% of arrests were for trace amounts (a quarter of a gram or less). A quarter-gram of crack costs between $10 and $20; the effect will last less than an hour. The felony liability, however, is the same as possessing a quarter-gram of heroin, which costs 2 to 3 times as much with effects lasting a day or more.

The war on drugs repeats the failed policies of prohibition (Coyne & Hall, 2017). The Eighteenth Amendment to the Constitution in 1920, banned the manufacture, sale, and transport of alcohol. Proponents claimed eliminating alcohol consumption would cure multiple social ills. It would reduce crime and corruption; it would reduce the money spent on prisons and jails, and it would improve health and prevent the disintegration of families. Instead, illegal alcohol varied in quality and potency, leading to deaths related to alcohol poisoning and overdoses. Prohibited from purchasing legal alcohol, many former users turned to other drugs such as opium and cocaine. Criminal syndicates manufactured and distributed illegal liquors. Crime increased, as did corruption. The Eighteenth Amendment was repealed in 1933. The drug war, similarly, is marked by disastrous policies—repeatedly leading to waste, fraud, corruption, violence, and death.

Reporter Dan Baum (2016) advises that people's desire to alter their states of consciousness creates a market. By attempting to suppress that market, drug prohibition has created violence, overdoses, and criminality. Interdiction has cost billions of dollars, deaths in Mexico and other countries in the supply line, deaths on US streets, and millions of lives destroyed by punishment that continues after imprisonment. One of every eight Black men has been disenfranchised because of a felony conviction, which also limits access to housing, employment, and education.

There has been a change in public attitudes. In 1990, 73% of Americans surveyed favored a death sentence for drug traffickers; about 57% believed police should be allowed to search the residences of known drug dealers without a court order (Coyne & Hall, 2017). Several decades later only 26% of respondents believe prosecution should be the focus versus 67% who think the government should implement policies focused on treatment.

There is wide public support for changing US drug policies. In about two decades, public opinion on marijuana reversed—from 63% of people surveyed in 2000 saying marijuana should be illegal to 62% in fall 2018 saying marijuana should be legalized (Geiger, 2019). Numerous states have enacted laws reducing criminal penalties for some marijuana-related convictions; 34 states have approved a medical marijuana program; and 15 states have legalized the use of marijuana. The federal government, however, continues to classify marijuana as a schedule I drug. Schedule I drugs are the most restricted; they are considered to have a high potential for abuse and no legitimate medical use.

When asked what substance is more harmful to a person's health, 69% of respondents said alcohol was more harmful than marijuana; 63% said that would be the case even if marijuana were as widely available (Coyne & Hall, 2017). The number of crimes committed in which alcohol plays a role number in the hundreds of thousands. It has long been recognized that alcohol plays a huge role in criminal behavior. It has been linked with assaults, aggression, sex-related crimes, serious youth crime, family violence, and homicides (Dilulio, 1996). One survey found that about 40% of offenders under some sort of supervision within the criminal justice system (probation, parole, jail, prison) were using alcohol at the time of the offense for which they were convicted (Greenfeld, 1998).

In 2018, an estimated 139.8 million people used alcohol in the past month compared to 27.7 million users of marijuana, 1.9 million users of cocaine, and 1 million users of methamphetamine (SAMHSA, 2019). Half of the people surveyed used alcohol compared to 1 in 9 people who used an illicit drug. In 2016, drug users in the United States spent about $150 billion on cocaine, heroin, marijuana, and methamphetamine (Midgette et al., 2019). While numbers of chronic users can be estimated more accurately than spending, the annual totals of money spent on drugs fluctuated between $120 billion and $150 billion from 2006 through 2016. The markets for these drugs now approximate the value of the US alcohol industry. Heroin consumption increased 10% annually between 2010 and 2016. Heroin users spent $31 billion in 2006 and $43 billion in 2016; there are about 2.3 million chronic heroin users in the United States.

These figures raise an important question: why do we continue this drug war in the face of such obvious failure? Our answer to this is not the standard answer; we believe the drug war was never really intended to reduce drug abuse. The purpose was to do two things: control the growing population known variously as the underclass or the surplus population and to add to an already bloated criminal justice system—thus adding to the profits of both private industry and agencies of the criminal justice system.

As history shows, anti-drug legislation has consistently targeted drugs used almost exclusively by the poor and/or racial minorities. (We return to this topic in chapter 4.) A prominent official in the Nixon administration stated that the agenda was to criminalize drug use to disrupt communities that posed a threat (Pearl & Perez, 2018).

> The disproportionate impact on communities of color is no coincidence. President Nixon waged the war on drugs in response to public demonstrations led by civil rights activists and Vietnam War opponents, pushing a narrative that linked Black communities and protesters with drug use. . . . Nixon's policy agenda took hold across all levels of government, leading to exponential growth in incarceration without any discernible health or safety benefits. (pp. 1–2)

Nixon's invention of the war on drugs as a political tool was cynical, but many politicians have found it useful (Baum, 2016).

In the 1980s, law enforcement officials requested a tool with which to punish drug traffickers. An amendment to the Comprehensive Drug Abuse Prevention and Control Act created the Asset Forfeiture Fund. Police, prosecutors, and other law enforcement agencies can seize assets (cash, cars, homes, etc.) believed to be used in the commission of a drug crime. Asset forfeiture laws allow seizures based on *suspicion* of wrongdoing; there is no requirement of a criminal conviction or even a criminal charge (Shelden & Vasiliev, 2018). Police departments fund salaries and equipment through forfeiture activities. Civil forfeiture creates perverse incentives, making corruption more likely if an agency's budget is tied to forfeited assets (Coyne & Hall, 2017).

After his father's death, Tyson Timbs used proceeds from his father's life insurance policy to purchase a Land Rover for approximately $42,000. When Timbs was arrested for selling a small amount of heroin worth several hundred dollars to an undercover agent, police seized the vehicle. He accepted a plea bargain, was sentenced to home detention, probation, and a court-supervised treatment program for addiction (Barnes, 2019). Timbs sued for the return of his vehicle. The trial court ruled the forfeiture was an excessive fine under the Eighth Amendment because the maximum statutory fine for his felony offense was $10,000. The ruling was affirmed by an appeals court, but the Indiana Supreme Court reversed, concluding that the US Supreme Court had never clearly incorporated the Eighth Amendment against the states under the Fourteenth Amendment. In February 2019, the Supreme Court ruled unanimously that the Constitution's prohibition on excessive fines applies to state and local governments. *Timbs v. Indiana* did not take a position on whether Indiana's seizure of the Land Rover was excessive. It held only that the Indiana Supreme Court was wrong to say that the Eighth Amendment did not apply. Critics of civil asset forfeiture viewed the ruling as supporting their efforts to terminate civil asset forfeiture, which they term "policing for profit" (Barnes, 2019). Briefs in support of Timbs noted the nationwide trend for municipal and county agencies to rely on forfeiture for their budgets. The Institute for Justice represented Timbs; Scott Bullock, the general counsel, described the trend as not only ominous but dangerous.

Historically, law enforcement provided domestic security while the military dealt with external threats (Coyne & Hall, 2017). In 1981, the Military Cooperation with Law Enforcement Act allowed the Department of Defense (DOD) to participate in local counter-drug operations and to share information with local police departments. It also allowed the transfer of military equipment to domestic law enforcement to combat illegal drugs (the property transfer was later expanded through sections 1208, 1122, and 1033). Property worth more than $5.1 billion has been transferred to law enforcement agencies (Kappeler & Potter, 2018). The drug war has militarized the police. Intensified street-level drug enforcement by Police Paramilitary Units (PPUs) or Special Weapons and Tactics (SWAT) teams has changed the fundamental nature of law enforcement and the relationship between the police and the public. PPUs and SWAT teams, trained by active duty armed forces members, primarily execute no-knock search warrants. An estimated 80,000 annual deployments take place (Coyne & Hall, 2017). There have been hundreds of incidents where police raided the wrong residence, sometimes killing or injuring innocent civilians or nonviolent offenders.

Current drug policies hamper health and public safety. For example, it is illegal to use federal funds for syringe service programs (SSPs) that provide free sterile syringes to drug users to prevent the transmission of HIV/AIDS and hepatitis (Coyne & Hall, 2017). SSPs effectively reduce disease and also make neighborhoods safer for police, sanitation workers, and the general public by providing for the safe disposal of potentially infectious needles. By providing users with information and access to treatment programs, they can also help drug users quit. SSPs can save taxpayers millions of dollars. Heavy drug users are more likely to rely on public assistance. The Foundation for AIDS Research estimates that every $1 spent on SSPs saves an estimated $3 in health care costs.

As noted above, the public and some states have moved to decriminalize or legalize marijuana. Some argue that current drug war policies are necessary to reduce crime, improve health, and to support US foreign policy regarding the war on terror (Coyne & Hall, 2017). Others argue that numerous entrenched interests (e.g., police and prison guard unions and public and private interests connected with US drug policies) pursue the continuation of the war on drugs. Communities across the nation have seen an unprecedented rise in substance abuse fatalities (Pearl & Perez, 2018). White Americans have been hardest hit by the opioid epidemic, which has been linked with increased public support for harm reduction strategies. In 2017, there were 70, 237 drug overdose deaths—47,600 from opioids. The crisis has seen some communities redouble efforts in the war on drugs—despite overwhelming evidence that arrests and incarceration do not lower drug use. Other cities treat substance abuse as a disease rather than a crime. They focus on saving lives and reducing the harmful effects of drug use.

Current drug policy, as shown above, has been an abject failure. It is time to focus on treatment rather than punishment and to consider broader decriminalization or legalization. Change would have positive effects on the disproportionality regarding people of color, who currently are more likely to be incarcerated and to experience negative interactions with the police. Liberalizing drug policies would eliminate many raids and traffic stops, perhaps easing the trend toward increased militarization.

For more than a century, the primary reaction to illicit substances in the United States has been prohibition. Changing that orientation might seem unthinkable regarding cocaine and heroin (Coyne & Hall, 2017). However, Portugal provides an example of what is possible. In 2001, Portugal changed its focus from prohibition to treatment and harm reduction. It decriminalized possession of all illicit drugs but retained criminal sanctions for trafficking. Drug usage did not increase; the rate of use in Portugal is well below the rate in the United States and is below the European average. The use of drugs by adolescents has dropped. The number of people seeking treatment increased 60%, even as usage rates remained the same or declined. Drug-induced deaths also fell.

We have highlighted some of the disastrous consequences of the war on drugs. The real drug problem is addiction, which is relatively small—fewer than 4 million people (Baum, 2016). Addiction is as difficult for friends and family as it is debilitating for the addict. Addressing addiction would require far less than the billions of dollars currently spent on enforcement and incarceration. We need to "replace the war on drugs with a fairer, more effective model that treats substance misuse as a public health issue—not a criminal justice issue" (Pearl, 2018, p. 1).

2

The Punishment Business

Fighting crime is big business. What many have called the *crime control industry* is part of a much larger network of social control, as we discuss throughout this book. An extensive network of thousands of public and private corporations profit directly or indirectly from punishment—companies that operate private prisons; companies that supply goods and services to prisons, jails, and detention centers; companies in the bail industry; subcontractors that provide telecommunications, transportation, medical services, and food; and companies that use or profit from prison labor. Importantly, this larger network of social control players includes the American people as employees of these companies; family members of incarcerated persons who are required to interact with the companies; the general public who engages the prison labor downstream for their livelihoods and/or circular cultural commitment to our punitive society; and the majority of members of the US political establishment who pass legislation in support of the network of social control. This deep involvement in the punishment business invites all of us into its study.

Connections to Crime

More than 100 years ago, Karl Marx listed some of the myriad links to crime generally overlooked in most conceptions of the topic.

> The criminal produces not only crime but also the criminal law; he produces the professor who delivers lectures on this criminal law; and even the inevitable text-book in which the professor presents his lectures as a commodity for sale in the market. . . . Further, the criminal produces the whole apparatus of the police and criminal justice, detectives, judges, executioners, juries, etc. . . . Crime takes off the labour

31

market a portion of the excess population, diminishes competition among workers, and to a certain extent stops wages from falling below the minimum, while the war against crime absorbs another part of the same population. The criminal therefore appears as one of those natural "equilibrating forces" which establish a just balance and open up a whole perspective of "useful" occupations. (Marx, 1977, pp. 52–53)

Marx is bringing our attention to the many pieces of the puzzle that co-construct and normalize the business of punishment. Marx's outline of the myriad links in the network of social control is outside of the twenty-first century US context where the invention of the prison industrial context contributed to a new apartheid for minorities (see chapter 4), but his outline remains relevant for understanding the punishment business.

The Media

Crime has always been front-page news. It dominates the local nightly newscasts, complete with film footage of victims and perpetrators. Crime provides story lines for prime-time television and movies. Reality television portrays police in action catching criminals. Color of Change, a racial justice organization, conducted a study assessing 26 television series in collaboration with the Norman Lear Center at the University of Southern California (Metz, 2020). The series examined the following: *NCIS* and *FBI* on CBS; *Law & Order: SVU* and *Chicago P.D.* on NBC; *Bosch* on Amazon; and *Narcos* on Netflix. *NCIS* was broadcast television's most watched drama with an average of 15.3 million viewers, followed by *FBI* with 12.3 million viewers.

The report found that crime shows imply that rules are broken so that justice is accomplished with special emphasis on racial bias and systemic racism as nonexistent and that current police methods keep people safe and are necessary for solving crime (Metz, 2020). Rashad Robinson, president of Color of Change, commented:

Series focused on crime and law represent an outsized share of television entertainment across platforms: broadcast, cable and streaming. The viewer attention they command cannot be underestimated. Series focused on crime and law dominate television, whether scripted, reality, documentary or feature/investigative news programming. . . . More crime shows were on the list of the top 100 most watched shows than shows from any other genre—reality, comedy, sports, news or non-crime drama. Crime shows like *NCIS, Blue Bloods, Chicago P.D.* and *Law and Order: Special Victims Unit* had higher total viewership than any other category of show. In the fall 2019 lineup, 21 of the 34 prime-time dramas that aired on the 4 main broadcast networks were series focused on crime and law—more than 60%. (Color of Change, 2020, p. 9)

Media misrepresentations are significant because what the public views on television can have profound effects on attitudes and perceptions for both the inventing of cultural imagery that misinforms viewers and normalizes the imagery as well as the hypnotic function that television watching plays psychologically.

Media, primarily television and online television-like sources such as YouTube, lend themselves to strategic political misuse of the situation. Crime is a hot item during every election year, with opposing candidates paying for media spots, advertising their tough-on-crime approach. Crime is also the subject of thousands of books, both fiction and nonfiction; over 90,000 books appear when searching "crime" within online book seller websites. Even academic discourse is flooded with the subject of crime; for example, as this book goes to press, Google Scholar has more than two million search results for "crime."

The myriad links that Marx points our attention to—police, courts, prisons, etc.—have become huge, self-serving, and self-perpetuating bureaucracies with vested interests in keeping crime rates at certain levels. Political and media leadership, to name a few, need victims and criminals, even if they have to invent them (as they have throughout the war on drugs and war on gangs).

Elected officials and many others talk about the need to turn the corner on the crime problem and to make the streets safe, as if street crime is the only or largest source of injury to the public. However, the society that Americans have built cannot afford to reduce crime. In fact, the traditional reasons for putting people in prison—incapacitation, retribution, rehabilitation—may be giving way to another reason: increasing business profits and providing economic uplift in rural communities. In short, crime is linked to billions of dollars in profits and the employment of hundreds of thousands of people (including the authors of this book). Fighting crime, in effect, stimulates the US economy.

Fear of Crime

Despite decades of falling crime rates, the public's fear of crime has not diminished (Glassner, 2018). During recent history as the crime rate decreased, polls showed a rising fear among the public. For instance, a Time/CNN poll in 1995 found that an overwhelming majority (89%) believed that crime was rising, and just over half (55%) were concerned about being a crime victim (Blakely & Snyder, 1997). More recent surveys show continued fear. Public perceptions about crime in the United States frequently differ from actual statistics. Since 1993, at least 60% of respondents in 18 of 22 Gallup opinion surveys said there was more crime in the United States compared with the previous year—despite falling violent and property crime rates during most of that time (Gramlich, 2019). Pew research found a similar pattern. More than half (57%) of registered voters in its 2016 survey said crime had increased since 2008, although the crime rate showed a decline by double-digit percentages over those years.

The Crime Control Industry

The crime control industry can be defined as an assortment of public agencies and private companies that profit, to some extent, from the existence of crime. In some cases it is their raison d'être (e.g., criminal justice agencies, private security firms, and so on). In other cases, benefits come more indirectly. Examples of the latter include the system of higher education, with thousands of criminal justice programs within colleges and universities and distance learning programs. Educating people for occupations in criminal justice is a big business, given the large number of those majoring in criminal justice or criminology and planning on a career in related fields.

There are numerous examples of various businesses that profit indirectly from crime, e.g., insurance companies that issue policies covering crime and hospitals that treat patients injured during crimes. Similarly, there are profits from the sale of books (e.g., college textbooks, trade books), magazines, journals, and newspapers as well as profits from television crime shows (and their advertisers) and movies about crime. The profits made help pay the salaries of insurance agents, doctors, nurses, paramedics, writers, reporters, actors, and actresses.

Punishing Poverty

Further examples of the businesses receiving profits from crime include the money collected by courts through various fines (traffic tickets, jaywalking, driving without insurance) and fees (e.g., fees for electronic monitoring, fees for drug testing, fees for courses mandated as a condition of a sentence, including traffic schools, anger management, counseling, cognitive restructuring therapy, parenting classes, alcohol or drug rehabilitation). The bail system (including bail bondsmen and insurance companies) collects $1.4 billion in nonrefundable fees from defendants and their families. The industry lobbies to block reforms that would threaten profits (Wagner & Rabuy, 2017). Those who cannot afford bail may face pay-to-stay jail fees.

In 43 states, defendants must pay fees related to being represented by a public defender, a constitutional right (Krimsky & Foster, 2019). In most states, fines and fees can be levied against juveniles for minor infractions such as skipping school. In 17 states voting rights are restricted until all debts are paid; in 43 states, nonpayment of fines and fees can result in the suspension of one's driver's license. If caught driving on a suspended license, there may be additional criminal charges, monetary penalties, or incarceration. Fines and fees are regressive and disproportionately affect low-income people of color—perpetuating cycles of debt and incarceration. Interest charges and collection fees are typically imposed for unpaid fines and fees; several jurisdictions charge a fee to set up a payment plan. People must return to court repeatedly to make payments or to explain why they have not been able to pay their debt.

Low-income offenders in many towns and cities are faced with paying fines and fees they simply cannot afford, often leading to even more fees and late charges. Nonpayment can lead to driver's license suspensions and even to incarceration. In some cases, people convicted of violating a minor infraction, for which only a fine and no jail time is a penalty, end up going to jail anyway because they cannot afford to pay the fine or are chronically late in making payments. It is difficult to hold a job in the United States without a driver's license; it is impossible while in jail. (Smith et al., 2017, p. 1)

We put people in jail for failure to pay debts. The main difference today is that the debt is to the criminal justice system, especially failure to pay fines. We send people to jail for, in effect, being poor (Maxwell, 2018). As discussed in chapter 1, *Timbs v. Indiana* may provide the precedent to halt excessive fines. The ACLU filed a brief in support that noted 10 million people owed more than $50 billion in criminal fines, fees, and forfeitures (Barnes, 2019). A $100 ticket for failure to stop at a red light in California carried an additional $390 in fees. A fine of $100 for marijuana possession in New Jersey could cost a poor person represented by a public defender $1,000. A *Washington Post* investigation found that aggressive policing tactics resulted in hundreds of millions of dollars taken from motorists not charged with crimes.

Sociologist Alexes Harris (2016) points out that while contemporary social control may not be as physically brutal as that of the past, court systems impose fines and fees that create a two-tiered system of punishment—one for those who are financially secure and one for those who are poor. Legal financial obligations (LFOs) are imposed in addition to jail or prison and disproportionately punish the poor.

The imposition of monetary sanctions is consistent with prior forms of American "justice." Like the colonization of the indigenous peoples, the enslavement of people from Africa, the Black Codes and Jim Crow laws that managed and isolated nonwhites, and convict leasing and forced labor camps for prisoners, the contemporary use of monetary sanctions is disproportionately imposed on the impoverished and socially isolated. These sanctions keep poor and racially marginalized people under constant surveillance and living in poverty and perpetual punishment. Thus, the contemporary criminal justice system remains essentially unchanged from earlier incarnations, which were understood to be necessary to control populations deemed in need of management and punishment. As a system that uniquely disadvantages people in poverty, the American criminal justice system generates and sustains inequality and closes off successful societal integration for many people it touches. (pp. xxii–xxiii)

Law professor Alexandra Natapoff notes that misdemeanors make up 80% of the criminal cases in the United States; these cases are the primary way most people experience the justice system (Watkins, 2019).

> The enormous misdemeanor system remains an influential layer in the historical drama over class and race in America. . . . The petty-offense process repeatedly uses its criminal authority to accomplish noncriminal policy ends. Southern states deployed misdemeanors to reinstate slave labor practices that were otherwise illegal—strategically treating common conduct as "criminal" in pursuit of racial and commercial goals. That era stands as a dramatic reminder that the petty-offense process is available as a cover for disreputable social and economic agendas that might not pass muster on their own terms. (Natapoff, 2018, p. 185)

The sprawling, poorly understood archipelago of local institutions and laws that comprise the misdemeanor process is an engine of social and racial inequality (Watkins, 2019). Today, the misdemeanor system relies on fines and fees that target the poor and communities of color.

> Although much of the social control literature focuses on mass incarceration and violent crime, the petty-offense process has long provided one of the clearest examples of how the criminal system functions as a mode of social control in general and as a means of controlling the disadvantaged in particular. (Natapoff, 2018, p. 197)

A recent trend is that those on probation or parole are assessed various supervision fees—supervision is a requirement of release, and offenders are charged for this mandatory part of their sentences. Georgia passed a law in 2012 that allowed private companies to manage probation. Private probation companies advertise their services as offender rather than taxpayer funded. They collect the fines assessed by the courts and then charge additional fees for their own revenue. If people receive a traffic ticket in Georgia and cannot afford to pay the fine, they are placed on misdemeanor probation typically managed by a for-profit company. There were 29 private probation companies in Georgia; in the first 3 quarters of 2011, they collected almost $18 million in fees (Schwartzapfel, 2017).

Sentinel Offender Services and Judicial Correction Services (JCS) were two companies participating in this type of business. Sentinel settled a lawsuit filed by 12 people in Georgia for more than $2 million for illegally putting them in jail for failure to pay their fees (Cook, 2017). The Southern Poverty Law Center (2017) filed suits against private companies, judges, and municipalities in Alabama for illegally jailing the poor for nonpayment. One suit charged JCS with racketeering under the RICO Act. The judge in the case observed that an apt description of the Harpersville Municipal Court would be a judicially sanctioned extortion racket. It was determined that defendants were essentially trapped into paying sizeable multiples of their original fees.

A series of lawsuits in Georgia argued that the state's practice criminalized poverty by placing people on probation and sometimes jailing them solely because of their inability to pay fines. Companies were also sued for requiring drug tests and making probationers pay for the testing. In 2015,

Georgia passed a law limiting companies to three months of fees for people on probation because they could not pay a fine (Schwartzapfel, 2017). As a result, Sentinel pulled out of its contract with the Atlanta Municipal court (JCS submitted the winning bid to replace Sentinel) and sold its remaining contracts (more than 50) to another private probation company.

In a federal class action suit, the ACLU and local counsel represented a group of people incarcerated for unpaid fines and fees stemming from traffic violations and misdemeanors in Biloxi, Mississippi. One member of the group, Qumotria Kennedy, was a 36-year-old single mother with teenage children. She was a passenger in a friend's car when the police pulled them over for running a stop sign (Pilkington, 2015). The police database showed a warrant for her arrest for failure to pay $400 in court fines for traffic violations dating back to 2013. Kennedy had told her probation officers—employees of the private probation company JCS—that she was so poor she could not pay the fines. Kennedy was jailed for five nights following her arrest on the warrant. She was not informed of her right to request counsel, was not appointed counsel, and was not provided a court hearing on her ability to pay. She was fired from her part-time cleaning job because she missed work while jailed.

A private court settlement agreement in 2016 resulted in Biloxi implementing sweeping reforms. The court retained jurisdiction for three years, and the settlement required termination of contracts with for-profit probation companies; adoption of new court procedures, including ability to pay hearings and recall of failure to pay warrants more than two years old; establishment of a public defender office to represent indigent people at hearings for nonpayment; consideration of alternatives to payment of fines and fees; no minimum requirement for monthly payment plans; no fees imposed for community service; and training for city officials.

In the state of Massachusetts, 3 of 4 people under state correctional control are on probation; service fees cost probationers more than $20 million annually (Sawyer, 2016). Lower income communities pay more of these fees than higher income communities. The majority of probationers live in the poorest communities, which means the state raises revenues by charging those least able to afford it—a regressive tax that punishes poverty. If the probation fee is not paid, the court issues a warrant, which carries a $50 fee; if arrested on the warrant; there is an additional $75 fee—both of which are added to the existing debt. These actions create more work and expense for the court. If someone is jailed for failure to pay fees, the state must pay for housing the offender in jail—the downward spiral has significant costs for both the offender and the state.

One critic pointed to the serious ramifications of nonpayment of probation fees.

> Supervising agents in some jurisdictions may be strongly encouraged
> to focus on collecting these fees. Thus, supervising agents focus more
> on bill collecting than on ensuring compliance with sentencing condi-

tions or helping to promote offender change to avoid recidivism. Failure to pay such fees may be viewed as a probation or parole violation,
which could result in a sanction such as jail time, or worse, revocation.
While there are constitutional limitations on incarceration of the poor
for failure to pay monetary sanctions, these limitations often do not
protect those low-income individuals who are deemed to have some
ability to pay, even by borrowing money. (Ruhland, 2016)

Sometimes the system turns probation officers into bill collectors. In one
Texas county, "half of the office payroll comes from probation fees. If those
on probation don't pay, paychecks can't get cashed" (Lieber, 2016).

Human Rights Watch (2014) reported on profiting from probation.

Every year, US courts sentence several hundred thousand people to
probation and place them under the supervision of for-profit companies for months or years at a time. They then require probationers to
pay these companies for their services. Many of these offenders are
only guilty of minor traffic violations like speeding or driving without
proof of insurance. Others have shoplifted, been cited for public
drunkenness, or committed other misdemeanor crimes. Many of these
offenses carry no real threat of jail time in and of themselves, yet each
month, courts issue thousands of arrest warrants for offenders who fail
to make adequate payments towards fines and probation company
fees. (p. 1)

The Human Rights Watch report noted that poor people (who constitute
the bulk of those arrested) remain the longest on probation simply
because they have such a hard time paying fees charged by the private
company hired by local governments to collect fees.

Employment

Fighting crime is a big business with literally hundreds of companies,
large and small, itching for a slice of a growing pie of profits. Employment
in this industry offers careers for thousands of young men and women,
many with college degrees in criminal justice programs from more than
3,000 colleges and universities nationwide.[1] The criminal justice system
alone provides a steady supply of career possibilities as police officers,
prison guards, probation officers, and many more secure their livelihoods
through the punishment sector. Most of these jobs offer not only good
starting pay but also excellent benefits and a promise of future wage
increases and job security. Many criminal justice employees have formed
unions, some of which are robust in size with significant political clout.

Further, a multitude of businesses have found it profitable to participate in the punishment sector as adjuncts to criminal justice institutions,
ranging from small mom-and-pop security businesses to huge corporations
listed on the New York Stock Exchange with the formal purpose of fighting
crime. The employment opportunities among both institutions and businesses orient high school and college graduates to enforce the retributive

paradigm, touching the lives of countless Americans without questioning the relevance and consequences of these jobs. These employment outlets are framed as opportunities for careers as in any other field. In addition to framing criminal justice employment opportunities, in particular, as normative, the distribution of these jobs saturates some locations more than others. This location-specific saturation furthers the norming element of employment in this sector.

Overall, in the United States, the number of people working for the justice system is larger than the number of people working to grow food. While the growth in the justice system slowed in the second decade of the twenty-first century, its enormous size has a substantial effect on the economy (Widra, 2017). The nation's investment in mass incarceration and overcriminalization reflects a transformation in priorities. The next section discusses the prison industrial complex in terms of profits.

Cashing in on Crime

The prison industrial complex (PIC) represents an interconnection among the criminal justice system, the political system and the economic system—just as the military represents an interconnection of the political and economic systems. PIC refers to a combination of government and private-sector interests that profit from spending on prisons. "PIC is criticized as a convergence of self-serving special interest groups that openly encourage new prison construction, while discouraging the advancement of reforms intended to reduce the inmate population" (Longley, 2019). The special interest groups include politicians who play on fear when running for election, lobbyists who represent companies that profit from cheap prison labor, depressed rural areas that depend on prisons for economic survival, and private companies that view the billions spent on corrections as a lucrative market.

Politics and economics go hand in hand: How are politicians elected, and whose interests do they serve? Think also of the large number of lobbyists in the nation's capital and working at the local and state level—try to see your senator, congressman, city councilman, or other representative and chances are you will have to wait in line until after they have seen corporate lobbyists. Think for a moment about the building of prisons, jails, courthouses, and police departments and furnishing them with everything they need to keep going (construction costs, electrical, plumbing, furniture—down to toilet paper) and you will have an idea of the intersection of politics, economics, and the criminal justice system.

Prisons as a Market for Capitalism

Within a capitalist society there tends to be an insatiable desire to continue "converting money into commodities and commodities into money"

(Heilbroner, 1985, p. 60). Everything, it seems, is turned into a commodity—from the simplest products (e.g., paper and pencil) to human beings (e.g., women's bodies, slaves). Indeed, within a capitalist society "daily life is scanned for possibilities that can be brought within the circuit of accumulation" (p. 60). Any aspect of society that can produce a profit will be exploited; life itself has been commodified.

Part of this drive for profits stems from the ideology of the free market, which is a system of beliefs that undergirds the entire capitalist economic system. According to this ideology every individual pursues his or her own personal interests, and the result is a collective good for the entire society. It is Adam Smith's invisible hand at work. Corporations are free to do whatever they want.

This free market includes the prison system (Gottschalk, 2015). The amount of money that flows into the coffers of the prison industrial complex from tax dollars alone is quite substantial (Johnson et al., 2017). A good illustration of how companies are cashing in on the boom in corrections is found in the amount of advertising done in magazines related to this industry. Two of the major trade magazines are *Corrections Today* and *American Jails*.

There are at least two websites that list company ads aimed at the prison market. One is corrections.com. Under the tab "Correct Source," one can search vendors by category (23), state, or business.[2] Examples include: apparel and linens; building, grounds and maintenance (cleaning and sanitation, laundry equipment, landscaping, hardware, etc.); business and finance (credit card services, office supplies and equipment, patches and badges, etc.); doors, locks, windows (windows glazing covering, power doors, etc.); food and kitchen; and gifts (books, jewelry, greeting cards, magazines, online courses, videos). One of their leading advertisers is the Keefe Group. Through its various affiliates, the company "is the nation's leading supplier of food products, personal care products, electronics, clothing, technology, telecommunications and software solutions to the correctional market" (Keefe Group, 2020).

The American Correctional Association (ACA) is one of the largest national organizations in the country. Their annual meetings draw hundreds of vendors (e.g., Western Union, Aramark, CoreCivic, and the College of Criminal Justice at Sam Houston State University), usually taking up an entire floor of a hotel or convention center. The main meeting is held each August, and another is held in January.

As discussed previously, almost 1.3 million people are incarcerated in state prisons, about 740,000 in local jails, and approximately 180,000 in federal prisons. The numbers do not reflect the churn in and out of correctional facilities or the much larger universe of people (families, friends, and communities) affected by the criminal justice system (Sawyer & Wagner, 2020). In 2019, almost 540,000 people entered prison (Carson, 2020b). The churn in jails was even higher with 10.7 million jail entries

(Zeng, 2020). Some of those arrested and jailed will post bail within hours or days of entry. Many cannot afford to pay bail and will remain jailed until a trial or case disposition; 26% of jail inmates are charged with a misdemeanor offense.

The United States detains more individuals in pre-trial detention than most other countries have in their prisons and jails combined. In 2018, 490,000 people were confined in jails who had not yet been convicted or sentenced. As these individuals await disposition of their cases, the "prison industrial complex" generates revenue from them and their families.

> Time in jail is psychologically and physically traumatizing. It is also economically destabilizing for individuals and families. Even a single night in jail can lead to the loss of a job and a cascading series of consequences. For families, an incarcerated loved one means lost wages and lost support, from childcare to elder care. Additionally, families have a new range of costs to pay in order to support and stay connected to their incarcerated loved one, including the cost of phone calls, transportation for visits, and commissary. (Schaffer et al., 2019, p. 5)

Phone calls and commissaries are two forms of financial exploitation in jails and prisons. Elevated prices for phone calls interfere with access to legal counsel and contact with loved ones. Local governments transfer the costs of basic necessities (i.e., hygiene products) onto incarcerated people and their families through jail commissaries—at unreasonably higher prices than found in brick and mortar and online stores. The food service provider is sometimes also the commissary vendor. Cost cuts in the kitchen (i.e., low-quality meals) push the captive audience to compensate for inadequate food by paying exorbitant prices in the commissary for substitutes such as instant coffee, popcorn, and food bars. "For-profit corporations reap millions of dollars through jail service contracts and repay their government partners with kickbacks" (Schaffer et al., 2019, p. 6).

In March 2020, governors across the United States issued stay-at-home orders to flatten the curve of the COVID-19 virus pandemic. Institutions such as schools and businesses were expected to send the public home to wait out further study of the virus. For months, nonessential businesses were closed and workers remained home. People in closed settings such as nursing homes, jails, and prisons where social distancing could not be practiced were at highest risk of contracting COVID-19; as indicated by the U.S. Department of Public Health, social distancing is needed to avoid spreading the virus through respiratory droplets and touch. Health experts described such institutions as petri dishes for the virus.

> As factories and other businesses remain shuttered across America, people in prisons in at least 40 states continue going to work. Sometimes they earn pennies an hour, or nothing at all, making masks and hand sanitizer to help guard others from the coronavirus. Those same

men and women have been cut off from family visits for weeks, but they get charged up to $25 for a 15-minute phone call—plus a surcharge every time they add credit. They also pay marked-up prices at the commissary for soap so they can wash their hands more frequently. That service can carry a 100% processing fee. As the coronavirus cripples the economy, leaving millions unemployed and many companies on life support, big businesses synonymous with the world's largest prison system are still making money. (McDowel & Mason, 2020, p. 24)

To avoid further public health crises within jails and prisons, some states released persons who committed low-level offenses and medically vulnerable individuals and/or reduced bail amounts to $0 (Prison Policy Initiative, 2020b). All but two states (Hawaii and Nevada) suspended medical co-pays for inmates during the height of COVID-19 for symptoms related to the contraction of the virus. However, social distancing cannot be adequately addressed in the current design of jails and prisons where bringing as many people as possible into small spaces is part of the financial plan for the prison business. In California, for example, 3,200 inmates contracted COVID-19 by May 2020 and 16 inmate deaths from the virus were confirmed (Levin, 2020).

Reach Out and Touch Someone

The cost of telephone calls for the average citizen is negligible today—but not for the incarcerated. There has been progress over the last decade (Wagner & Jones, 2019). The Federal Communications Commission (FCC) capped the cost of out-of-state phone calls from both prisons and jails at about 21 cents a minute and also capped other abusive fees of providers. Most state prison systems lowered the cost of in-state calls as well. Predatory contracts continue to exist in jails run by counties and cities; in-state phone calls can cost $1 per minute, or more, and hidden fees are common. As noted above, two-thirds of the people held in jails have not been convicted; they are at risk of losing their jobs, housing, and custody of their children. Charging high prices for phone calls punishes people who are legally innocent—making it expensive for them to contact family members and inhibiting contact with attorneys and others who might help build their defense.

A phone call for someone incarcerated in an Illinois prison costs less than a penny a minute, the cost of the call in an Illinois jail is 52 times higher (Wagner & Jones, 2019). In Michigan, a typical 15-minute call from a jail is about $12 (and as high as $22) compared to $2.40 for the call from a Michigan state prison.

While the rates for a call from a jail are high, the fees charged are even more lucrative for the provider. There are fees to open an account, to fund an account, to maintain an account, to close an account, to receive a paper bill, to receive a refund, and to listen to voice mail. Fees can increase bills by 40%. The fees allow some providers to meet rate caps yet continue to generate additional profit—and they don't pay commissions to facilities on

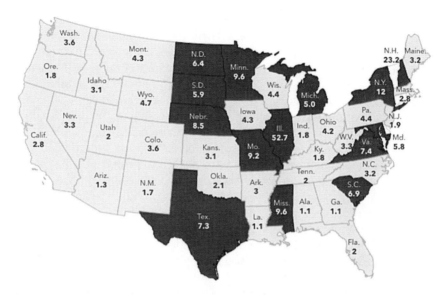

Figure 2-1   Disparity between Prison and Jail Phone Calls: Multiples by State

Source: Wagner & Jones, 2019

fees. In 2015, the FCC capped the fee charged for a credit card purchase at $3 (still a significant charge). The people most likely to be incarcerated do not have bank accounts or charge cards. They often pay their bills by money transfer via Western Union or Moneygram, whose standard fees are $6 to send a payment to a company. However, Securus and Amtel have "revenue sharing" or "referral fees," raising the cost of money transfer to $10–$12.

Two companies—GTL and Securus—control most of the correctional phone market (Wagner & Jones, 2019). Both companies also offer packages of services to facilities. Bundled contracts include video-calling technology, electronic tablets, and money transfer for commissary accounts. Providers can shift profits from one service to another to hide the real costs of each service. Bundling makes it more difficult for facilities to change vendors because phone, commissary, and banking systems are combined.

The prison industrial complex has benefitted from incarcerating individuals and charging astronomical rates for telephone calls, and new technology is adding more profit while restricting communication with loved ones. The American Correctional Association, the American Bar Association, and the National Institute of Justice do not recommend replacing in-person visits with video calls. Problems include high costs for families, poor quality of the technology, and the loss of human contact (Watson, 2019).

Some institutions have implemented the use of video visitation provided by Global Tel Link (GTL). According to a GTL website, video visitation "can help facilities of any size improve security while allowing time to be reallocated to more critical tasks" (GTL, 2018). Family members no longer meet their loved ones in a designated area. Instead, the communication is through a phone and monitor. The institution does not have to be concerned with the possible introduction of contraband; the visitation requires less staff. Such visits significantly limit the quality of interactions that take place between inmates and visitors. Rather than face-to-face interaction, visits are limited to a two-dimensional screen. Anyway you spin it, the prison industrial complex makes it harder to "reach out and touch someone."

Critics have achieved some success in abolishing the use of video and high fees for telephone calls. Illinois passed a bill to protect prison visits in 2016 that prohibited prisons from replacing in-person visits with video calls (Prison Policy Initiative, 2020a). The bill also prohibited charging high rates for video calls. In June 2017, California required jails to provide in-person visits rather than video calls (jails that had replaced in-person visits with video calls before 2017 were permitted to ban in-person visits but were required to provide the first hour of remote video at no cost). In April 2018, Massachusetts required its jails to provide at least two in-person visits per week, and the state prohibited the replacement of in-person visits with video calls. In early 2019, the newly elected sheriff of Mecklenburg County, North Carolina, reintroduced in-person visits after more than two years. It also provided one free video call per week, and reduced call rates by approximately 60%. In July 2018, New York City became the first to make phone calls from city jails free. San Francisco followed suit in June 2019.

The growth in the building of prisons had several unintended consequences, both political and economic. A close look at where most prisons were built is revealing.

Uplifting Rural Economies?

In this country there are more prisoners than there are farmers. It would not be too much of an exaggeration to say that rural America has been pretty much destroyed by factory closings, corporate downsizing, and the shift to service occupations. Many rural towns became "dependent on an industry that itself is dependent on the continuation of crime-producing conditions" (Huling, 2002, p. 198).

For most Americans, prisons are distant and out of sight. Brett Story's documentary, *The Prison in Twelve Landscapes,* examines the impact of mass incarceration from outside the prison walls. One of the landscapes is a Kentucky mining town that now depends on the local penitentiary for jobs. The Elkhorn Coal Company founded Wheelwright in 1916 (Independent Lens, 2017). Economically, the town depended completely on the coal industry. When that failed, the local economy turned to the 600-bed Otter Creek Correctional Center owned by the Corrections Corporation of America (CCA, now CoreCivic) that opened in 1981. The population of

Wheelwright was 556; the prison created almost 200 jobs for one of the poorest communities in the South. CCA paid Wheelwright about $30,000 a month for utilities and paid 50 cents per prisoner per day. In 2005, Indiana notified CCA that it was removing 620 male inmates from the private prison (Meadows, 2019). Kentucky began housing 400 female inmates at Otter Creek that year; Hawaii also sent female inmates there. Reports surfaced about female prisoners who were sexually abused by prison staff. Six Otter Creek employees were charged. Hawaii pulled its female inmates from Otter Creek in 2009, and Kentucky did the same in 2010.

In 2010, Kentucky paid CCA $21 million for prisoners housed at Otter Creek and 2 other private facilities (Meadows, 2019). The state transferred male inmates to the facility, paying $53.77 per day versus $31.34 at Kentucky jails. Otter Creek closed in February 2012. In 2019, the state of Kentucky signed a 10-year lease with CoreCivic for the 650-bed facility. It will reopen as Southeast State Correctional Complex in early 2020, providing 193 positions at a starting salary of $30,000 plus benefits. Officials claimed the reopening was a regional investment that would impact several counties and emphasized that it was a huge investment for Wheelwright.

In three Oklahoma cities (Hinton, Sayre, and Watonga) the population increased by more than 40% after prisons were built (Kilborn, 2001). One example was the North Fork Correctional Facility in Sayre (population 4,375).[3] North Fork Correctional Center was completed in 1998 and originally operated as a private prison run by CCA, housing 1,440 inmates (expanded in 2007 by 960 beds). When the facility opened, CCA was the largest taxpayer ($411,000 in property taxes) and spent $2.5 million for goods and services in Oklahoma (mostly around Sayre); the company paid about $7 million in wages. Many of the prisoners were from Wisconsin until the state objected to high long-distance telephone rates. Subsequently, many prisoners were from California. Those prisoners rioted in October 2011; 46 were injured (Horn, 2019). The company closed the facility in 2015. The following year, the Oklahoma Department of Corrections established it as a state prison through a 5-year lease agreement that paid $37.5 million to CoreCivic. In 2018, the town of Sayre sued the private company, saying it owed impact fees. Until 2004, the town received all revenue from the inmate phone system; that year, it agreed to let the company collect the fees in exchange for impact fees based on the number of prisoners. CoreCivic stopped paying the fees in 2016. The town received a $975,000 settlement in 2019.

The small southern Illinois town of Vienna (population 1,500) is home to the Vienna Correctional Center (a minimum-security male facility; capacity 1,155) and Shawnee Correctional Center (a medium-security male facility; capacity 1,863). Vienna also operates the Dixon Springs Impact Incarceration Program, a coed boot camp (capacity 300). There is no other industry in the town aside from the prisons. Between 1990 and 2001, Illinois "built or planned 21 prisons, work camps and juvenile detention centers at an estimated cost of $818.7 million" (Landis, 2002). In one instance, a maximum-security prison in Grayville "offered typical economic incentives to prospective communities: $140 million in state construction spending, 350 construction jobs, 750 corrections jobs and an annual prison budget estimated at $55 million." Politicians viewed prisons as a significant form of regional economic development, but budget crises halted decades of growth.

There are many states that have several prisons built within a few miles of one another, sometimes described as "penal colonies." The town of Ionia, Michigan (population less than 11,000), houses 4 of the state's 29 prisons, which cover 4,000 acres (about one-third of the city). Ionia previously housed two other institutions. When the state closes a prison, the community—which does not own the facility—is vulnerable; Michigan has closed 24 facilities since 2005 (Clark, 2019). Prior to the closing of Ojibway Correctional Facility in Michigan's Upper Peninsula in 2018, Marenisco Township sued the state over the economic harm to Gogebic County if the facility closed. The case was dismissed.

Ionia hoped the state would approve the 2019 sale of the Deerfield Correctional facility (closed in 2009) to a for-profit detention company that planned to house detained immigrants (Dickson & LeBlanc, 2019). After a year of negotiations with Immigration Centers of America, the newly elected governor vetoed the sale. Communities lose revenue for water and sewer, income tax revenue, and state sharing revenue (Clark, 2019). There is also an impact on schools and local businesses when people leave town because jobs (corrections officers, health care workers, counselors, maintenance staff, etc.) are lost. Closed prisons that sit empty for years are a blight on communities. Developers are often reluctant to find new uses for huge facilities in isolated locations. The facilities are generally not well maintained and require environmental remediation for hazards such as asbestos, lead paint, and fuel storage tanks. Riverside in Ionia has been sitting vacant since 2007. Michigan State Police used part of the facility until May 2019 when they left because of degraded conditions. Riverside's 46 buildings—half a million square feet of bricks, mortar, and cement—are scheduled for demolition when tear-down financing becomes available.

Cañon City, Colorado, is the county seat of Fremont County, known as "prison valley." The website for Fremont County (2020) has a section entitled "Correctional Capital of Colorado," which begins: "Correctional facilities have long been an integral part of Fremont County. From the 1871 opening of Territorial Prison ("Old Max") in Cañon City to the present, prisons have provided a stable element to the area's economy and added an interesting character to its communities." There are 4 federal facilities in Florence (population 3,800), including ADX Florence, the "Alcatraz of the Rockies"; the federal facilities house 2,900 inmates. Cañon City (population 16,000) is home to 9 state correctional facilities, incarcerating about 5,000 prisoners.

Inmates comprise 38% of the population of Cañon City and Florence (Glionna, 2015). Residents have a saying about life in prison valley: "Even those on the outside live on the inside." Territorial prison officers once brought inmates to town for house repairs, and low-security female prisoners walked the streets in their prison uniforms. Today, some locals express tension about living among stressed-out prison guards, some of whom suffer from corrections fatigue and extend suspicious, cynical, hardline attitudes from the prison into the community. Prisons can stimulate the economy and create jobs, but they also have a significant impact on people in the community (Independent Lens, 2017).

The prison industry accounts for more than half of all the jobs in the county (*Economist*, 2017). When the Colorado Territorial Correctional Facility opened in 1871, legislators lobbied for the penitentiary to provide employment for new settlers. Other prisons followed, built on ranchland owned by the territorial correctional department. As in other rural towns, the economics of prisons is not stable. Colorado built the $200 million Centennial South facility in 2010 to house prisoners in solitary confinement; it closed two years later when the prison population dropped and the state changed its policy about long-term isolation for inmates. In March 2020, Colorado reopened the facility after the GEO group closed its private prison in Colorado Springs three months early. The state needed to find a new facility to house the 600 prisoners from Cheyenne Mountain (Herrick, 2020a).

In previous years, the three biggest employers in Pueblo, Colorado, were the steel mill, the chemical plant, and the state mental hospital (Norton, 2018). The workforces at all three have declined during the past few decades. A woman's prison is now on the campus of the former state mental hospital. People from Pueblo work in the prison, and others commute to the prisons in Cañon City or Florence. As employment in steel and coal dwindled, prison employment increased both in scale and in relative importance within the county. Colorado's state-level reforms have increased pressure on local jails. Voters in Pueblo have rejected proposals to expand the jail twice, despite rising opioid use across the region resulting in more jail incarceration in the county. Facing similar problems, Alamosa doubled the size of its jail. One Pueblo resident commented that the town needs a treatment center not a jail. Another commented "People are tired of putting money into this same system instead of investing in the actual development of the community." He said he judges the priorities in a town by looking for the newest and nicest buildings. In his area, those buildings are the justice center, the police station, and the jail.

Downsides to Depending on Prisons

Officials sometimes turned to private prisons, which were appearing in a number of small towns across the nation, to save their cities. Impoverished rural America—desperate for jobs—became the setting for the expansion of private facilities. During the 1990s, a prison opened its doors at some location in the rural United States every fifteen days (Eisen, 2017b). When the boom slowed, private corporations funded much of the twenty-first century's prison construction. Almost all new prisons that opened their doors from 2000 to 2005 were private. Sixty-five percent of all immigration detention beds—most prominently in rural areas of Texas, Arizona, and California—are operated by for-profit prison corporations. John Eason (see his discussion of the geography of prisons in chapter 1) notes that the economies of communities where prisons were constructed in the earlier stages of the prison boom received a short-term boost, but the effects did not last. A study that examined 25 years of economic data for seven rural counties in New York that hosted a prison and seven rural counties that found no significant difference (King et al., 2003).

The town of Appleton, Minnesota, opened the 500-bed Prairie Correctional Facility in September 1992 at a cost of $28 million (Eisen, 2017b). In its first four years of operation, the facility struggled to fill its beds with prisoners. In the fall of 1996, Corrections Corporation of America (CCA) offered to refinance and manage the facility. It also spent $25 million to expand it, and signed contracts with Colorado, Idaho, Minnesota, and North Dakota to house prisoners. Even at full capacity, Prairie Correctional struggled financially. CCA announced it was closing the facility in 2010. The $1.1 million the facility provided to Appleton annually for property taxes and utilities made up almost 60% of the city's budget. When Prairie Correctional closed, Appleton's pizza parlors and restaurants were boarded up, unemployment soared, and younger families moved away. These types of histories have not deterred rural communities with soaring unemployment rates and few economic opportunities from hosting a private prison.

About one in four people live below the poverty line in Letcher County, Kentucky. The median household income is less than $32,000, with employment at twice the national rate. For five years, residents were told about plans to build a high-security, 1,200-bed federal facility in the coal country town that would create up to 300 jobs plus the jobs associated with constructing the facility. Hal Rogers, a 20-term congressman who served on the Appropriations Committee for 33 years, told reporters in 2006 that the prison business is essentially recession proof. Rogers clearly thought so—he had already brought three other prisons to Eastern Kentucky. Those three counties remained among the poorest in the country after the federal prisons were built. The Bureau of Prisons (BOP), in its 2016 budget report to Congress, extolled the significant positive impact on rural communities. "By bringing in new federal jobs, stimulation of local businesses and housing, contracting with hospitals and other local vendors, and coordinating with local law enforcement, the BOP improves the economy of the town and the entire region where these rural facilities are located."

Promises often don't match reality. Research suggests that prisons rarely bring significant economic improvements to rural communities One study compared how counties with prisons perform versus those without; the research examined the change in employment for every county in the lower 48 states from 1976 to 2004 (Hooks et al., 2010). The researchers found that after 1990, there was no link between prisons and growth in employment. For counties with lower rates of educational attainment, prisons negatively impacted employment growth. Towns with new prisons experienced lower retail sales, household wages, and home values (Meagher & Thompson, 2016). Jobs at new prisons primarily go to people who already work in the system. In California, an average of 20% of jobs at new prisons went to county residents; in Missouri less than one-third of the jobs were filled by locals. Corrections officers employed at the new prison often don't move into the community; there are few gains in home ownership, tax base, or other civic investment. Building a prison doesn't necessarily attract other businesses that bring more jobs. Prisoners are a source of cheap labor for custodial, laundry and food service jobs within a facility; local residents find themselves competing with prisoners for jobs. In Louisiana, local factories, gas stations and churches have hired prisoners. Locals often don't have the skills or union connections necessary for the work constructing the prison.

Rogers spent more than 10 years securing the $510 million for the construction of USP Letcher, which would have been the most expensive federal prison in history—despite a steady decline in federal prisoners (Tsolkas, 2019). The BOP repeatedly said it did not need a facility in Letcher County, but it required a federal lawsuit by prisoners and activists to derail the project. In March 2015, the Human Rights Defense Center coordinated the first national opposition, with over 20 organizations commenting on the environmental impact. The litigation focused on concerns about the proposed facility being located on a former mountaintop removal coal mine and near an active mine and coal sludge pond. The following year, Letcher County residents launched a social media campaign opposing the prison. One resident told an NBC reporter: "I refuse to have our community's future built on the backs of other people." On June 17, 2019, federal officials cancelled the prison.

New York's prison population declined 37% since 1999 (Arnold, 2020). The state closed 17 prisons from 2011–2019, saving taxpayers $193 million annually. The number of workers in the prison system decreased by about 3,000 in the last decade. Governor Cuomo has said prisons are not a jobs program and should not be economic drivers. In 2020, the governor sought authorization to close an additional unspecified number of prisons in the state. The state's Corrections Officers and Police Benevolent Association condemned the proposed closures, saying shuttering additional facilities in the state would disrupt workers and endanger the lives of correction officers.

As noted above in the discussion about Pueblo, Colorado, state-level reforms have reversed dependence on prisons but have increased pressure on local jails. In the country's largest cities, there has been a reduction in jail populations. National headlines such as closing Rikers Island have obscured a quiet jail boom in hundreds of small cities and towns building new and larger jails (Mai et al., 2019). Research has examined where and why prisons are built, how prison construction has impacted host communities, local perceptions of the impact of new prisons, and the relationship between increases in the number of prison beds and increases in incarceration levels. The Vera Institute of Justice points out that the parallel growth in local jail beds has not yet received consistent scrutiny. However, new scholarship reveals the use of the language of economic development to promote jail expansion—just as it was used to promote prison expansion in the past. The Institute's report explores the persistence of jail expansion, the arguments made by county officials to build new jails, and the potential negative consequences of jail construction.

> The growth of mass incarceration in communities across America was accompanied by a boom in jail construction, vastly increasing the capacity of local governments to incarcerate hundreds of thousands more people. Nationwide, this growth continues, with thousands of new jail beds added each year, a hugely expensive investment for local governments—especially in an era of falling crime rates. As jails grew more overcrowded, concerns about safety and conditions, especially in old or out-of-date facilities, have driven many counties to build larger jails. The organizations and individuals that stand to benefit from jail expansion build support for these projects using the justifications that most resonate with the community—whether it be economic development, safety, better jail conditions, or substance use and mental health treatment. In many counties, decision makers and the consultants they hire take for granted that a larger jail is needed. They frame the debate as a question of how to use the larger jail, rather than considering whether a new jail is needed or how they can reduce the jail's size. . . .
>
> A growing number of counties view the assumption of perpetual growth with suspicion. These places are renovating older facilities instead of building larger jails, maintaining smaller jail populations, and voting down proposals to build bigger. They are also looking for ways to invest in community-based treatment services, rather than locating such services within a jail expansion project. By pushing back against the cycle of construction, these counties can save money, hold fewer of their community members behind bars, and dedicate more resources to evidence-based practices that more effectively ensure community safety. These are places that are breaking new ground. It's a model all of America's counties should consider. (pp. 42–43)

Exploiting Prisoners to Enhance Rural Populations

State officials use census data numbers when they redraw legislative districts. The Census Bureau, unless state law directs otherwise, counts prisoners as residents of the town in which prisons are located. Until the era of mass incarceration, this practice had minimal effect (Prison Policy

Initiative, 2019b). As the numbers of prisoners increased and prisons were constructed in rural areas, so did the consequences of counting prisoners where they are housed. Prison gerrymandering is most dramatic in rural, low-population communities, giving disproportionate political power to areas housing a prison.

Counting incarcerated people at the location of the facility reduces the accuracy of Census data about communities of color. African Americans and Hispanics are disproportionately incarcerated. Counting incarcerated people in the wrong location distorts the demographics of African American and Hispanic communities (Prison Policy Initiative, 2018). The prison facility is a permanent structure, but the people within the prison are in flux, depending on the length of their sentences. For example, most of the people incarcerated in Rhode Island spend less than 100 days in the state's correctional facilities. If those people spent 100 days at a summer residence, the Census Bureau would count them at their primary address. The same principle is not followed for prisoners.

The Census Bureau does not consider the realities of incarceration—inmates are not members of the community hosting the prison; they are not free to interact with other residents. The Census Bureau invited public comment on their practices before the 2020 census. Despite almost unanimous opposition to counting prisoners where they are incarcerated, the Bureau announced it would retain the practice for the 2020 census. Only two states (Maine and Vermont) allow prisoners to vote. Counting prisoners who cannot participate in the electoral process inflates the power of those in the district who can vote. The Prison Policy Initiative (2019b) has argued that allowing mostly white rural districts to claim urban Black prisoners as residents for purposes of representation resembles the clause of the Constitution that allowed the South extra representation for its slaves.

The NAACP filed a lawsuit against Connecticut in October 2019 after the state used 2010 census numbers that counted prisoners where they were imprisoned to redraw voting maps (Wang & Devarajan, 2019). The civil rights organization argued that the redistricting plan inflated the voting strength of districts of predominantly white voters and violated the 14th Amendment's "one person, one vote" principle (which is violated when prisoners cannot vote). Since the 2010 census, California, Delaware, Maryland, Nevada, New York, and Washington passed laws requiring that counts of prisoners be reallocated from where they are incarcerated to their last known home addresses for redistricting.

Exploiting Prison Labor

Prison labor, often called prison industries, has a long history; it can be traced back as far as the early 19th century with the emergence of the congregate labor system (Shelden & Vasiliev, 2018). Convict labor is alive and well throughout the country. Prisoners make office furniture, work in call centers, take hotel reservations, work in slaughterhouses, and manufacture textiles, shoes and clothing (McCormack, 2012). Wages range from 93 cents to almost 5 dollars a day.

The Cañon City prison complex has numerous industries (Wood, 2017). It has the country's largest water-buffalo dairy, which produces buffalo mozzarella. Supermarket chains sell tilapia raised on the prison's grounds. The goods/services produced (which range from honey to zebrawood fishing rods to partridges sold to hunting clubs to breaking wild mustangs to training dogs) aren't marked as the product of prison labor. Colorado Correctional Industries collects about $63 million annually. Top prison laborers earn about $125 per month, approximately $1.50 per hour.

Indiana University professor Alex Lichtenstein notes that the prison system has always been tied to labor (Wood, 2017). Eastern State Penitentiary was among the first to compel inmates to work; prisoners created handicrafts alone in their cells as part of their penitence. Prisons later turned to a model that more closely resembled a factory. Prisoners were expected to work to pay off the financial costs of their crimes. Lichtenstein describes large state prison-work programs (Texas being one example) as enormous corporations operating with slave-like labor. The state is the primary beneficiary. Typically, inmates earn 50 cents or less per hour. In California, enterprise revenue from inmate labor totaled almost $265 million, with a profit of almost $60 million (CALPIA, 2019). The California Prison Industry Authority manages more than 100 manufacturing, service, and consumable enterprises in 35 correctional institutions, with more than 8,000 offender assignments in manufacturing, agriculture, consumable goods, and service/support functions. The goods and services provided by CALPIA's enterprises are sold predominately (about 63% of all sales) to departments of the State of California and other government entities (i.e., the Department of Motor Vehicles, the Department of Healthcare Services, the Department of Forestry and Fire Protection, the California Military Department, the California Department of Parks and Recreation).

Prison industries that sell goods directly to consumers are a small fraction of all prison production (Wood, 2017). If the goods cross state lines, they are subject to the Prison Industry Enhancement Certification Program (PIECP, or PIE). Since 1979, PIE regulations apply to inmates in about 35 state prison systems. The program stipulates that prison workers must receive wages no lower than the federal minimum wage—$7.25 per hour. However, taxes, fees, restitution, or other court-ordered payments generally reduce payments to about $3 per hour. States can avoid PIE regulations by selling to in-state businesses that then re-package the products and sell them elsewhere. Generally, both PIE and state prison industries must make sure that they do not compete with private enterprise. As a result, most of the products are for niche markets and sufficiently invisible that outside businesses, organized labor, and consumers don't notice and object.

While the wages are extremely minimal, most prisoners want to do something productive and to relieve the monotony of prison life. Even critics who find the prison labor system morally problematic believe it would be an overreaction to shut down prison labor entirely. Lichtenstein asks: "What's the alternative? Have them sitting idle and lifting weights?" Yet he also cautions that prison workers are subject to exploitation.

Companies across the United States take advantage of the cheap labor inside prisons. Examples include: Whole Foods (sells food from Haystack Mountain Goat Dairy and Quixotic Farming, private vendors that use prisoners to raise fish and milk and herd goats), Wendy's and McDonald's (inmates help process beef for burgers), Walmart (inmates clean products of the bar codes so that products can be resold), Starbucks (inmates help package holiday coffee), Sprint and Verizon (work in call centers), Victoria's Secret (South Carolina female inmates used to sew products) (Schwartzapfel, 2009).

The Bureau of Prisons operates Federal Prison Industries that pays inmates roughly 90 cents an hour to produce mattresses, eyeglasses, road signs, body armor and other products for government agencies, earning $500 million in sales in 2016 (Paton & Zarate, 2019).

> The federal prison industry produces 100 percent of all military helmets, ammunition belts, bullet-proof vests, ID tags, shirts, pants, tents, bags, and canteens. Along with war supplies, prison workers supply 98 percent of the entire market for equipment assembly services; 93 percent of paints and paintbrushes; 92 percent of stove assembly; 46 percent of body armor; 36 percent of home appliances; 30 percent of headphones/microphones/speakers; and 21 percent of office furniture. Airplane parts, medical supplies, and much more: prisoners are even raising seeing-eye dogs for blind people. (Buczynski, 2014)

In the 1990s with a record number of people imprisoned, there was a boom in private companies employing prisoners for telemarketing, manufacturing circuit boards, and producing clothing for private brands (Paton & Zarate, 2019). Pulitzer-prize winning journalist Chris Hedges (2015) comments: "There are nearly 40 states that allow private corporations to exploit prison labor. And prison administrators throughout the country are lobbying corporations that have sweatshops overseas, trying to lure them into the prisons with guarantees of even cheaper labor and a total absence of organizing or coordinated protest." His list of corporations engaging in this practice includes: Abbott Laboratories, AT&T, AutoZone, Bank of America, Bayer, Berkshire Hathaway, Cargill, Caterpillar, Chevron, Costco, John Deere, Eddie Bauer, Eli Lilly, ExxonMobil, Fruit of the Loom, GEICO, GlaxoSmithKline, Glaxo, Hoffmann-La Roche, International Paper, JanSport, Johnson & Johnson, Koch Industries, Mary Kay, Merck, Microsoft, Motorola, Nintendo, Pfizer, Procter & Gamble, Quaker Oats, Sarah Lee, Sears, Shell, Sprint, State Farm Insurance, United Airlines, and UPS.

A prison product subcategory that has grown internationally is small, niche brands selling clothing made by inmates. Carcel is a Danish fashion brand founded in 2016 to provide incarcerated women worldwide with jobs and training (Paton & Zarate, 2019). When the company introduced a new line of silk garments produced from women's jails in Thailand, social media exchanges raised the issue of opportunity versus exploitation. One person wrote that the company was advertising the use of slave labor as a reason to buy the product. Another decried a sustainable business model that depends on women being imprisoned. [Carcel halted sales in the United States in 2019 when it became aware of a federal law that bans the import of goods made by convicts.] Prison Blues is an example of this type of brand in the United States. the products are made by inmates at the Eastern Oregon Correctional Institute in Pendleton, Oregon. The facility states it created a work program that provides inmates the opportunity to help taxpayers, pay restitution, build a work ethic, and gain a skill. Prison Blues Retail Center advertises: "made on the INSIDE to be worn on the OUTSIDE."

In 2012, Arizona decided to issue pre-paid debit cards from Bank of America (BOA) to prisoners when released. "Prisoners are given no choice other than the fee-laden cards to obtain their own money from inmate accounts. Charges include some that ordinary consumers would not have to pay, such as $15 to withdraw money at a bank teller window" (Aubin, 2016). A class-action suit was filed in federal district court. JPMorgan Chase & Co paid $446,822 to settle a similar action stemming from its BOP contract to issue debit cards to ex-inmates. In 2017, BOA agreed to halt the collection of debit card fees and to return the $168,000 in fees that it had already collected from about 70,000 Arizona prisoners (Gilna, 2018). Sue Ellen Allen, founder of Reinventing Reentry, commented about the settlement: "This is a message to departments of corrections and to banks that charging exorbitant fees to people who are getting out and desperately want to be members of the community again is really not the message we want" (p. 15).

Fire protection in California relies on the Conservation Camp Program, run jointly by the California Department of Corrections and Rehabilitation (CDCR) and the California Department of Forestry and Fire Protection (Cal Fire).[4] The Conservation (Fire) Camps were organized to support government agencies (local, state, and federal) responding to emergencies such as fires and other natural or man-made disasters. During World War II, the state created 41 interim camps (CDCR, 2019). In 1946, the state established the first permanent facility, Rainbow Conservation Camp. In 1983, Rainbow was converted to a female camp. Today, CDRC, Cal-Fire, and the Los Angeles County Fire Department jointly operate 43 fire camps in 27 counties. The camps house approximately 3,100 inmates in minimum-security facilities staffed by correctional employees.

The inmates receive pennies on the dollar to risk their lives and fight wildfires—they are paid $1 an hour to brave some of the deadliest conditions in the workplace; Cal Fire employees are paid ten times that wage (Gomez, 2017). CDCR inmates make up as much as 7% of California's firefighting force, saving the state over $100 million a year. Not surprisingly, these facts have drawn alarm from legislators, celebrities, and the general public.

Inmates in 17 states went on strike in August 2018, refusing to eat or work in order to draw attention to troubling aspects of mass incarceration including their exploitation as a work force. Law professor and Co-Director of the UNLV Workplace Law Program, Ruben Garcia (2018) noted that inmates have been exploited for labor with very low or no wages performing duties such as answering customer service phone calls, fighting wildfires, and packaging Starbucks coffee. The exploitation is a clear violation of the Thirteenth Amendment barring slavery and indentured servitude, the Fair Labor Standards Act of 1938, which requires that prisoners with jobs receive at least minimum wage, and the codes of conduct of private sector companies. The US government has admonished other countries such as Burma and China for using forced labor, yet the practice is just as prevalent in the United States. The Department of the Navy and Minnesota are among the governmental entities sued for minimum wage violations in prisons. The United States belongs to the International Labor Organization, which established a convention on forced labor in 1930 that prohibits the use of forced labor by private individuals, companies, or associations. The United States is one of only nine countries that have not ratified the convention. The prison industrial complex is being used to generate wealth for the rich and to suppress the poor, specifically those who are incarcerated.

We have discussed profits being made from building and supplying prisons with various products, as well as from cheap prisoner labor. Another key component of the prison industrial complex is the trend of states turning to private companies that specialize in the entire operation of prisons, from the design to the daily operation. The next section explores this topic in more detail.

The Privatization of Prisons

Privatization involves a private corporation managing the operations of an existing jail or prison or building and operating its own facility and contracting with governments to house inmates. Several years ago researchers warned about the tremendous growth in privatization. One source called this phenomenon *creeping capitalism*—the transfer of services and responsibilities that were once monopolized by the state to profit-making agencies and organizations (Spitzer & Scull, 1977). It should be noted that privatization is a trend that includes more than the criminal justice system. This *contracting out*, as it is often termed, involves a number of services formerly provided by state and local governments, such as public education, health care, waste collection, and many more (Shelden & Vasiliev, 2018).

Economist Edward Herman (1997), a critic of the market system, described privatization as "one of the mantras of the New World Order. Economic, political and media elites assume that privatization provides undeniable benefits and moves us toward a good society." The core beliefs of this ideology are that private markets are more efficient and public enterprise is inefficient. The Government Accountability Office has repeatedly concluded that there is no evidence that private prisons are more cost-effective than public prisons (Eisen, 2018). Through privatization, states can get around voter resistance to prison construction bonds by having private corporations build the prison. Private corporations then bill the state and thus taxpayers, which socializes the costs while privatizing the benefits (Shelden & Vasiliev, 2018).

The Market and Players

In the 1980s, the War on Drugs and harsh sentencing policies fueled a rapid rise in the prison population; state and federal prisons were overcrowded. Corrections Corporation of America (now CoreCivic) was established in 1983. Its founders saw an opportunity to meet the demand for more prison beds and established the world's first modern for-profit prison company (Kim, 2019b). In 1985, Texas became the first state to outsource incarceration of its prisoners (Gorman, 2019). Other companies that made money from government contracts soon followed. Public prisons eventually outsourced numerous services—healthcare, food, transportation, communication—to private companies. Private industries are also involved in reentry, electronic monitoring, and drug treatment programs (Armstrong, 2019). There are approximately 4,000 private sector companies involved in the criminal justice system. More than half of the $80 billion spent annually on incarceration by government agencies is paid to thousands of vendors that serve the criminal legal system.

Today, CoreCivic (based in Tennessee), GEO Group (based in Florida), and Management & Training Corporation (MTC, based in Utah) dominate the private-prison business. GEO Group and CoreCivic are publicly traded, with revenues of $2.3 billion and $1.8 billion in 2018. The chief executive of GEO Group received $6.66 million in total compensation, while CoreCivic's chief executive received $4.09 million. MTC is privately held; details are not public. The companies have entrenched their positions through a variety of strategies, including hiring former corrections officials for high-level positions. CoreCivic hired two of the past four directors of the Federal Bureau of Prisons. The companies also make campaign contributions and spend between $3 and $4 million annually on lobbying (Williams & Oppel, 2018). As states seek alternatives to prison, the companies have expanded into rehabilitation programs.

From 2000 to 2005, private correctional facilities accounted for nearly all of the increase in the number of adult correctional facilities—and most of that growth was in facilities under contract to the Federal Bureau of

Prisons (Stephan, 2008). In 2000, 9,400 federal prisoners were held in private facilities (Kaeble & Cowhig, 2018). In 2018, the number was 24,900 (Maruschak & Minton, 2020). Jurisdictions vary in their reliance on private prisons. Six states (AZ, IN, OH, FL, GA, and TN) more than doubled their private prison populations from 2000 to 2016 (Sentencing Project, 2018). In contrast, 8 states (AR, KY, ME, MI, NV, ND, UT, and WI) eliminated their use of private prisons at some point in those years.

In 2019, 116,000 prisoners were held in private facilities (Carson, 2020b). The number of state prisoners held in private facilities (7%) decreased 2% from 2018 to 2019; 15.7% of the federal population was confined in private facilities. Five states housed at least 20% of their prison population in privately operated facilities: Montana (47%), New Mexico (36%), Tennessee (29%), Oklahoma (25%), and Hawaii (24%). In addition to incarcerating about 7% of the country's prisoners, private prisons hold 70% of detained immigrants; those detentions increased 442% between 2000 and 2016 (Armstrong, 2019).

Twenty-two states do not house incarcerated people in for-profit prisons. Illinois, which banned for-profit correctional centers in the 1990s, expanded the law to include privately-run immigration detention centers. In October 2019, California passed legislation to ban for-profit prisons. The author of the bill said: "By ending the use of for-profit, private prisons and detention facilities, we are sending a powerful message that we vehemently oppose the practice of profiteering off the backs of Californians in custody, that we will stand up for the health, safety and welfare of our people, and that we are committed to humane treatment for all" (Kim, 2019b). Supporters pointed to private prisons being driven to maximize shareholder profits, lacking proper oversight and incentives to rehabilitate inmates, and contributing to a culture of mass incarceration. The bill will close three private prisons in four years when the contracts expire. Four private detention facilities that hold about 4,000 federal detainees were scheduled to close in 2020 when the federal contracts expire. There are, however, loopholes in the bill; facilities that provide educational, vocational, medical, or other ancillary services are exempted. Rather than Nevada's outright prohibition of private prisons, California's law may allow the private prison industry to continue.

Controversies over Private Prisons

Private prisons in more than two dozen states are often located in relatively remote regions where jobs are scarce. The crime in metropolitan areas is seen by some as the engine of economic development for a rural area (Haberman, 2018). Eloy, Arizona, depends on the four private prisons located there for $2 million of the town's $12.5 million annual operating budget (Williams & Oppel, 2018).

Colorado's prisons are 99.7% full, and the state uses private prisons to house 18.8% of its 19,586 inmates (Herrick, 2020a). CoreCivic has a 20-

year partnership with Colorado. The company operates 37 facilities (primarily re-entry and treatment facilities). Two of the facilities are private prisons: the Bent County Correctional Facility in Las Animas and the Crowley County Correctional Facility in Olney Springs.

Colorado in 2020 was an excellent example of divergent approaches to private prisons. For twenty years the state employed the services of private companies, but the state had been changing its policies and practices regarding prisoners in the latter years of that partnership. Its prisons were full, but the Colorado legislature considered a bill in 2020 to close the state's for-profit facilities by 2025. When Bent and Crowley county officials learned about the bill, they hired lobbyists and organized residents to testify against the bill. Closing the prisons would cost Crowley 54% of its property taxes and Bent County 25% (Goodland, 2020). Commissioners for both counties said the closures would bankrupt their communities.

While the bill was being considered, another interest surfaced. The state of Idaho, which had not altered its approach to criminal justice, did not have the capacity to house its prisoners (Editorial, 2020). The Idaho Department of Corrections was negotiating with CoreCivic to send more than 1,000 close-custody inmates to the Kit Carson Correctional Center in Burlington, Colorado. The facility closed in 2016, but CoreCivic planned to reopen it to house Idaho prisoners for a daily fee of $75.50 per prisoner versus the $57.94 paid by Colorado at CoreCivic's other two facilities. The Colorado Department of Corrections would have to approve housing out-of-state inmates (Herrick, 2020b). Complicating the issue was that Colorado law prohibits housing close-custody inmates in a private prison unless the governor declares a correctional emergency. A state representative living near Burlington said re-opening the facility would bring 300 jobs to a town of 3,500 (Goodland, 2020). When Kit Carson closed in 2016, the city lost $1 million in property taxes for the local schools.

Private facilities do not have to report how many inmates they hold in isolation. The ACLU interviewed hundreds of immigrants detained in private prisons (Thompson, 2014). People were placed in solitary confinement at intake and held there for days or weeks because beds were unavailable in the general population. The interviews also revealed that detainees were sent to solitary for reasons ranging from filing a complaint to asking for new shoes. The lack of adequate BOP oversight and the lack of transparency created by private companies being exempt from public records laws such as the Freedom of Information Act shields for-profit private prison companies from public scrutiny of operations. Since 2005, various versions of a private prison information act have been introduced in Congress that would require correctional and detention facilities holding federal prisoners or detainees to make available to the public the same information that federal facilities must provide. Private prison firms have successfully lobbied against all the bills. The November 2019 version was referred to the judiciary committee.

Activists have long decried investment in companies whose profits depend on imprisoning people (Eisen, 2017a). In June 2017 New York City was the first large public pension system to fully divest from CoreCivic, the GEO Group, and other such companies because of concerns about health and safety violations and human rights abuses. Columbia became the first private college in the nation in 2015 to divest from private prisons. Shortly thereafter, the University of California became the first public education system to divest, selling its $25 million stake in GEO Group, G4S, and CoreCivic. There was a domino effect with Harvard, Swarthmore, Yale, Northwestern, Princeton, and City University of New York all divesting.

In March 2019, JPMorgan Chase announced it would no longer finance private prisons and detention centers; CoreCivic and Geo Group had received at least $254 million in loans from the bank (Kim, 2019a). The companies also lost funding from Wells Fargo after pressure from activists. Bank of America (BOA) announced in June 2019 that it would no longer fund private prisons or the detention industry. The decision was reached after bank officials toured the Homestead Center, a private shelter near Miami. Previously Bank of America had loaned $380 million to the company running the shelter, plus a $75 million revolving credit line. Government-run facilities must release a child after 20 days, but private facilities do not have to follow the same standards. Homestead detained migrant children for long periods in poor conditions. Its abuses attracted public attention; the facility shut down in November 2019. Louisiana State University political science professor Anna Gunderson said the publicity surrounding the abuses caught people's attention; the problems with private prisons resonated more deeply because those incarcerated were children (Kim, 2019b). Gunderson commented it raised questions of "if the federal government is privatizing immigration, what is my state doing?"

Lauren-Brooke Eisen (2017a) is the director of the Brennan Center's Justice program and leads that organization's work to end mass incarceration. She notes that divestment will have only minimal effects. Activists should petition policy makers to reform contracts to improve practices, which would affect incentives, transparency, and accountability. One method would be to implement performance-based contracts. For example, the companies would earn more money if recidivism were reduced. Australia and New Zealand are experimenting with this model. Two relatively new private prisons (one operated by GEO) have contracts that provide bonuses if their released inmates have less recidivism than inmates released from government prisons. The contracts charge prison companies for what the government deems unacceptable events, such as riots, escapes, and unnatural deaths.

Repeated Failures

Despite large-scale failures, states continue to issue contracts to private companies. After a riot broke out at a facility run by MTC in 2015, Arizona revoked the company's contract and hired the GEO group—

despite a ruling by a federal judge three years earlier that GEO inmates in an East Mississippi facility had not been protected from gang violence (Williams & Oppel, 2018). After that ruling, GEO Group had surrendered its contract; Mississippi replaced GEO with MTC. The warden at East Mississippi had been the warden during the Arizona riot. Before the riot, three prisoners had escaped from the facility and murdered a vacationing couple. Arizona's investigation said the riot was sparked by MTC's "culture of disorganization, disengagement, and disregard" for fundamental inmate management and security principles (Williams, 2018). Arizona attempted to reduce the number of inmates held in that prison, but MTC claimed the state was violating its contract that guaranteed a certain number of beds would be filled. State attempts to extricate themselves from private prisons have been hampered by contracts, lack of state facilities to house inmates, and by economic interests (as discussed above).

Controversies surrounding privatization include riots, deaths, and allegations of improper financial influence from for-profit prison companies (Sentencing Project, 2018a). After a Department of Justice report in 2016 revealed that private prisons had higher rates of contraband, violence, and use of force than public prisons, the White House issued a directive ordering the Justice Department to reduce the use of private prisons for federal prisoners. The attorney general of the next administration rescinded the directive in 2017.

Mississippi has the third highest rate of incarceration (636 per 100,000) in the United States (Carson, 2020b). In 2019, 16.2% of the 18,915 prisoners in the state were held in private facilities. Its corrections system has been marked by violence, maltreatment, and corruption. Christopher Epps, commissioner of the Mississippi Department of Corrections from 2002 to 2014, was sentenced to prison for almost 20 years for receiving $1.4 million in bribes and kickbacks from the $800 million in state prison contracts he signed (Pauly, 2019).

In January 2019, the Mississippi state attorney general announced that his office had recovered $26.6 million in settlements with companies in connection with the Epps racketeering conviction. In addition to MTC ($5.2 million) and GEO Group ($4.6 million), other companies included in the settlements were Global Tel*Link ($2.5 million), Wexford Health Sources ($4 million), Keefe Commissary Network ($3.1 million), and Sentinel Offender Services ($1.3 million)—major national providers of prison phone services, medical care, commissary management, and electronic monitoring, respectively. The Mississippi Department of Corrections continues to do business with several of those corporations. MTC runs three prisons holding 3,121 state prisoners; Global Tel*Link (GTL) provides phone service to inmates, and Sentinel Offender Services monitors Mississippi prisoners released on probation or parole.

In Mississippi, private prisons must operate at a 10% lower cost than state-run facilities (Williams, 2018). State officials once boasted that Mississippi spends significantly less on prisoners than most other states. The state pays MTC $26 a day—about $9,500 a year—for each minimum-security inmate. Alabama spends $15,000, and New York spends $73,000. The warden at the MTC facility receives incentives for staying within budget and is not penalized if inmates die under questionable circumstances or fires damage the prison.

A federal civil rights lawsuit filed by the American Civil Liberties Union and the Southern Poverty Law Center sought wholesale changes at the East Mississippi Correctional Facility. Testimony described dangerous conditions, lack of oversight, and problems attracting and retaining qualified staff (Williams, 2018). Security staff earn less than the $12-an-hour starting wage of public service counterparts. Private prison guards receive only three weeks of training, which is less than half the training time required of state prison guards. At the Wilkinson County Correctional Facility, a 950-bed maximum security prison managed by MTC, more than a third of the low-paying jobs of guarding prisoners are not filled; turnover annually is almost 90% (Neff & Santo, 2019). Violence is widespread; inmates refer to the prison as the "killing field." Without sufficient staff, gangs are in control. The Southern Poverty Law Center filed two class action lawsuits against MTC over conditions in Mississippi prisons. The lead lawyer commented: "It's like a hospital saying we can't perform the surgery, but we'll have another patient do it, and we're getting paid anyway."

Reporter Shane Bauer (2018) became a guard in a CCA-run private prison in Louisiana to investigate how prisoners are treated in a profit-making institution. To lower costs, guards were paid $9 an hour. In a prison of more than 1,500 inmates, there were often only 24 guards on duty. In training sessions, guards were taught not to intervene if inmates were stabbing one another. Prison violence was rampant. About 200 weapons were found during a 4-month period—23 times more than in the state's maximum security prison. One of the prisoners lost his legs to gangrene after months of unfulfilled requests for medical care. CoreCivic resisted sending prisoners to the hospital because the company had to pay for outside medical visits. Another inmate, who weighed 71 pounds, committed suicide after repeated hunger strikes to demand mental health services. The prison had one part-time psychologist. To save money, educational programs were discontinued.

In May 2017, Bauer bought one share in CoreCivic in order to attend the annual shareholder meeting. He watched corporate executives discuss the company's objective of serving the public good. He wondered how many times people sat in company headquarters or in legislative offices far removed from their prisons and convinced themselves that they were in the business of punishment because it makes the world better—not because it makes them rich. Worth Rises (2019) is a nonprofit advocacy organization that works to expose the commercialization of the criminal legal system. Its website describes the problem of building industries based on caging people and controlling them—capitalizing on crime and preventing justice.

Closing private prisons will end the abuses that stem from cost-cutting procedures to enhance profits, but eliminating private prisons will have a minimal effect on the criminal justice system as a whole (Kim, 2019b). The private prison problem was created by mass incarceration; the industry sprang up because of the numbers of people being punished by incarceration in the United States. True reform involves changing tough-on-crime legislation (and attitudes) and removing profit incentives from the justice system. Questions and criticisms have surrounded private prisons since their inception. The government acts as society's representative when someone violates the law. Can the responsibility for punishment be contracted to a profit-seeking entity? As early as 1985, the sheriff of Fairfax County, Virginia, asked, "What next will we be privatizing? Will we have private police forces? Will we have private fire departments? Will we have private armies?" (Haberman, 2018). Whether or not privatization of prisons continues, prisons and jails will continue to operate, guaranteeing steady employment for a large workforce and profits for businesses that supply the many goods and services needed to run the institutions.

Private Security: Crime Is Good for Business

The private security business is perhaps one of the fastest growing industries globally. More than 40 countries (including Australia, Canada, China, the United States, and the United Kingdom) have more private security workers than police officers (Provost, 2017). Security officers are hired to protect specific people, places, and things. Private security companies became a symbol of the global wealth divide (McCarthy, 2017). The global physical security industry is expected to reach $291 billion by 2025.

The security services industry consists of companies that provide private security guards as well as cyber security, background screening, investigation, risk analysis, loss prevention, alarm systems, remote video monitoring, and security consultancy services. In 2018, revenues for the industry were $40 billion (Mazareanu, 2019). Freedonia Group (2019), a market research company, said revenues for private security services in the United States are projected to grow to $80 billion through 2023. One of the key factors cited for growth was the perceived risk of crime. Freedonia noted that crime rates continue to fall, but highly publicized events cause consumers to feel an elevated sense of risk. There are 8,000 companies in the United States providing outsourced security (White Paper, 2019). In 2018, there were 1.1 million security guards in the United States with median pay of $28,490 (Bureau of Labor Statistics, 2019).

Private security products for the home is another example of cashing in on fear of crime. Consumer spending for smart home surveillance cameras alone was $7 billion in 2018 (McCue, 2019). Home security systems combine software with hardware devices (security cameras, sensors, motion detectors, smart locks) to detect intrusion or environmental dangers (such as fire, flood, etc.). In addition to traditional security companies (e.g., ADT and Honeywell), there are technology companies such as Ring. Its mission statement declares stronger communities are the key to safer neighborhoods; the company is driven to create products to protect what matters most at home and to empower connection with neighbors from any location to make neighborhoods safer. Media companies (e.g., AT&T and Comcast) are also involved in home security in the transference of video surveillance data. The revenue per active household (20 million in 2019) was $300; the number of active households is expected to be more than double by 2024 (Statista, 2020).

Companies have capitalized on the fears of being a victim of gun violence (Chan, 2019). In 2017, schools spent $2.7 billion on security systems. The chances of a school shooting are small. In 2018, there were 94 gun-violence incidents in the 130,000 K–12 schools in the United States—a probability of 0.07% (MacBride, 2018). Individuals spent $768 million on items such as bulletproof backpacks, despite the fact that there is no known case of such items saving students from being wounded (Chan, 2019). Critics note that the only beneficiaries of such alleged security measures are the people profiting from their sale. While the items might protect against handguns, they would not withstand the assault weapons used at Parkland and Sandy Hook.

Athena security sells a smart-camera system that detects 900 types of guns and alerts law enforcement with a video feed if it senses a threat (Chan, 2019). More than 50 schools, malls, and businesses use Athena software, which charges $100 per month for each camera monitored. Malls typically have 100 cameras, which means Athena earns $100,00 per year monitoring one mall.

The top four security companies in the United States are Allied Universal (140,000 employees; $5.3 billion annual revenue) Securitas (110,500 employees; $4.5 billion), G4S USA (57,000 employees;, $2.4 billion), and US Security Associates (51,000 employees; $1.4 billion) (Finkel, 2018).

The latest in security technologies are robots (Finkel, 2018). In 2018, less than 500 robots had been deployed for physical security, but industry insiders believe the next generation of security personnel will need to be trained to work with robots as well as drones. Robots will reduce human workloads and are unaffected by tedious repetition. Humans may be less effective if performing monotonous tasks.

Paralleling the growth in the private security industry is the emergence of gated communities. This is perhaps most apparent in Southern California where, beginning in the late 1960s, literally millions of affluent whites fled to outlying regions of Los Angeles such as Simi Valley to the northwest (i.e., site of the first Rodney King trial) and Orange County to the southeast. As social critic Mike Davis (2003) shows, these flows outward have created "fortress cities" that are divided between the "fortified cells" of the affluent suburbs and "places of terror" in the inner cities "where the police battle the criminalized poor" (p. 203). A study of the national growth of these communities found that the number of gated communities went from less than 5,000 in the early 1970s to more than 20,000 in the 1990s (Blakely & Snyder, 1997). Between 2001 and 2009, there was a 53% increase in homes in gated communities—about 10% of Americans lived in such communities (Benjamin, 2012). "Gated communities churn a vicious cycle by attracting like-minded residents who seek shelter from outsiders and whose physical seclusion then worsens paranoid groupthink against outsiders" (p. 27). The bunker mentality of these communities is codified by laws that permit the use of deadly force for self-defense in one's home (castle doctrine or "stand your ground" laws).

Over two decades of research, Setha Low (2003, 2017) found that some individuals experience a loss of place as increased social diversity changes neighborhoods. They feel unsafe and insecure and respond to loss by moving to a defensive space—a walled and guarded community. Fears of violence and crime prompt the move; residential segregation and class-based exclusion strategies are rationalized and legitimated. Low's work illustrates the fort mentality that sees crime as something inevitable. From this perspective, fortifying your community is required.

Low (2003) argues that many individuals move into gated communities as a way of recapturing their childhood or at least the emotional security they had in their old neighborhoods. In other words, they miss their childhood home. She quotes one woman who moved into a gated community with a guard house and away from one without this feature, saying that the guard house makes her feel secure. However, all of this fortification comes at a price, both social and psychological. Low asks whether children growing up in such communities become much more fearful than other children. Are such children more vulnerable to drugs, suicide, and other problems? She notes the growing child-protection industry that has capitalized on these fears "as a way to remake the home as citadel and to sell private protective technologies" (p. 109). These fortifications shift the responsibility for protection from the state to private firms—reminiscent of feudal societies where elites lived behind high walls with a moat separating them from the peasants on the estate.

NOTES

[1] These programs typically rank among the top five as far as the number of majors is concerned. The senior author is at UNLV where the undergraduate program has over 1,000 majors—the second highest in the university.

[2] For more see this website: http://www.corrections.com/vendor/by_category

[3] To view this prison, visit http://doc.ok.gov/north-fork-correctional-center

[4] One of the 12 landscapes in the documentary is about inmate firefighters in Marin County, California.

3

Jails
Temporary Housing for the Poor

During the course of a year, more than 10 million people are arrested and taken to jail. The US culture has a strong belief in using "edifices," such as jails, to enforce the law through coercion. The vast majority of those who end up in a local jail do not receive a "get out of jail free card" as in game of Monopoly. Most have little or no capital with which to secure their release, reflecting the saying "those without capital get punishment."

Virtually every large city and small town has at least one jail. Many old jails—dating back to colonial times—have become tourist attractions. The modern jail is a purely local institution (mostly city or county operated). Usually you will find four types of prisoners in jails: (1) those serving short sentences for misdemeanor convictions (normally "public order" crimes like disturbing the peace, drunkenness, vagrancy, loitering, petty theft, or "contempt of court"—often failure to pay traffic fines), (2) those who have been convicted of a felony and are awaiting transfer to a prison, (3) those who are being held temporarily for other jurisdictions (including federal offenders), and (4) those awaiting their final court disposition. The last category accounts for the largest number of jail prisoners. They have not yet been convicted of a crime (although most will eventually plead guilty). They are usually in jail because they cannot afford bail, which is normally a relatively small amount ($500 or so). Jails are the modern-day equivalent of eighteenth and nineteenth century poorhouses, or as one writer has suggested, "the ultimate ghetto of the criminal justice system" (Goldfarb, 1965, 1975).

The Historical Context

The modern jail originated in England with the Norman Conquest in the eleventh century. Under Henry II, the jail (the English term is *gaol*) began to take on the characteristics and functions recognizable today. By the thirteenth century, all but five counties had a jail. The county sheriff was a royal appointment, "a functionary who upheld his master's interests against local powers" (McConville, 1995, p. 299). The illusion was that localities exerted control, but the power remained with the king. Masking the source of the power was a sophisticated method of social control.

One of the most famous gaols was Newgate in London. Built in 1188 at the corner of Newgate and Old Bailey, it was referred to as the "old city gate and prison." According to law, it was to be managed by the local sheriff; he then contracted the duties to private "gaolers," or "keepers," in return for fees. (Today we would describe this as a form of "privatization.") The keepers charged fees to the inmates housed there—a very profitable business. Some very famous people were imprisoned in Newgate, including: Daniel Dafoe (author of *Robinson Crusoe*), Captain Kidd (infamous pirate hunter), and William Penn (founder of the state of Pennsylvania). Some of the novels of Charles Dickens (e.g., *Oliver Twist*, *A Tale of Two Cities*) made the prison famous. On many occasions, Newgate housed prisoners awaiting execution at the gallows at Tyburn (Grovier, 2008; Halladay, 2007; Hay et al., 1975).

In the American colonies, several "gaols" were built, including one in Williamsburg, Virginia (designated as the capital of the colonies). Opened in 1704, it was known as the "Public Gaol." Among those who were confined in this institution were debtors, runaway slaves, and sometimes the mentally ill. During the American Revolution, the gaol held Tories, spies, military prisoners, deserters, and traitors.

Eventually, gaols became temporary holding facilities for those awaiting court appearances or serving short sentences. People who could afford to do so secured their release pending their day in court through the system of bail. The use of bail dates back to early English society (at least as early as AD 1000) and was originally established to insure that an accused appeared for trial. It was an outgrowth of mutual responsibilities of the collective where groups of ten families (under the control of the "tythingman") worked together to insure obedience to the law (Shelden & Vasiliev, 2018). The families, in effect, pledged to ensure that the defendant would appear in court. Crime prevention was a collective responsibility, which was very practical in small, agrarian communities. Such a concept no longer applies in modern societies, characterized by mobility and anonymity. Bail is now a monetary or property pledge, often provided by the defendant's family, relatives, or friends.

Since the earliest history of jails, most of the people confined in them came from the poorest sectors of society.

No other public institution so well embodies the contradictions among which we live. Certainly symbols and instruments of order and law—to hold a prisoner implies deliberation and process rather than summary disposal—jails have equally been identified with grand and petty tyranny, sadism, corruption, extortion, debauchery, contamination, ruin, and despair. Refuges of last resort, the door from which the mad, sick, destitute, and unwanted could not be turned away, jails have also been, and are, places of terror, degradation, and suffering. (McConville, 1995, p. 297)

Debtors' Prisons

From the time jails were established, they were used almost exclusively to house the poor. In fact, *debtors' prison* is a term often used interchangeably with jail. Ironically, the financing of local jails depended on user fees paid to jailers, yet the majority of prisoners were from the poorest classes—the fees adding to their misery (McConville, 1995). Although the Magna Carta (1215) declared that a man's body could not be taken for the failure to pay a debt, several laws were subsequently passed that made it easy to jail a man who was in debt. By the middle of the seventeenth century, an estimated 10,000 were in prison because of debts.

Debtors in England could be locked up indefinitely. Horror stories of the treatment of people in these prisons began to leak to the outside world. Charles Dickens drew attention to the problem in his novels. The setting for *Little Dorritt* is Marshalsea Prison. Dickens was 12 in 1824 when his own father was sent to that prison for a debt of £40 and 10 shillings to a baker. Dickens was sent to work 10 hours a day putting labels on jars of boot polish while his mother and younger siblings lived in the prison with his father.

Marshalsea Prison opened around 1329, closing more than 500 years later in 1842. It was a privately run prison that housed mostly debtors but also smugglers, men charged with sedition, and those under court martial. It was essentially operated as an extortion racket—men who could afford the fees charged for housing them paid for the privilege of being able to leave during the day to work. Those who could not pay were crammed together into nine small cells, and their debts grew from nonpayment of fees (Ginger, 1998).

The Cry of the Oppressed, written in 1691, revealed "shocking miseries prevailing in debtors' prisons." The exposé prompted further investigations, including one by James Edward Oglethorpe, who headed up a special parliamentary committee that exposed conditions in prisons. The investigation revealed "the sale of offices, breaches of trust, enormous extortions, and the highest crimes and misdemeanors"—all prevalent in debtors' prisons such as the Fleet, Marshalsea, and Westminster. Oglethorpe's investigation resulted in a series of trials of four wardens (Lewis, 2009).

The Bankruptcy Act of 1869 abolished debtors' prisons. Although technically the jailing of people for debts was no longer legal, people still went to jail on the charge of "contempt of court," which essentially served the same purpose. Then and today the contempt usually means failure to pay a fine (Goldfarb, 1975). Corruption was rampant with little effort to correct the problem. Then, as now, profit was available because of the existence of crime. The jails of London functioned as "brothels, taps, criminal clubs, and asylums for thieves, robbers, and fraudsmen, and when their raw material—prisoners—threatened to run out, minions would bring false charges to replenish the supply" (McConville, 1995, p. 301) The well-being of the prisoners was virtually ignored. As a result of their poverty, many either starved to death or died from disease.

About two-thirds of the Europeans who came to the American colonies were debtors.

> Some colonies were, basically, debtors' asylums. By the seventeen-sixties, sympathy for debtors had attached itself to the patriot cause. The American Revolution, some historians have argued, was itself a form of debt relief. In 1787, just before the Constitution was drafted, New Yorkers formed the Society for the Relief of Distressed Debtors. They launched an investigation and found that of 1,162 debtors committed to debtors' prison in New York City in 1787 and 1788, 716 of them owed under twenty shillings. (Lepore, 2009)

The Elizabethan Poor Laws and the Emergence of Poorhouses

Jails have served still another function. As far back as the mid-fourteenth century, jails were almost synonymous with *poorhouses*. The Statute of Cambridge in 1388 restricted the movements of all laborers and beggars. This is often regarded as the first English poor law, but it had a very limited impact because of lack of enforcement. The *Vagabonds and Beggars Act in 1494* decreed that: "Vagabonds, idle and suspected persons shall be set in the stocks for three days and three nights and have none other sustenance but bread and water and then shall be put out of Town." Then in 1547 the *Statute of Legal Settlement* provided that a "sturdy beggar could be branded or made a slave for two years (or for life if he absconded)." The Act of 1564 empowered parish officers to find places for the "habitations and abiding" of beggars. This was one of the first references to what would eventually become the "workhouse."[1] In 1597, an *Act for the Relief of the Poor* "required every parish to appoint Overseers of the Poor whose responsibility it was to find work for the unemployed and to set up parish-houses for those incapable of supporting themselves." Finally, in 1601 the *Elizabethan Poor Law* consolidated earlier decrees, declaring the parish as the administrative unit responsible for poor relief. Any able-bodied pauper who refused to work was liable to be placed in a "House of Correction" or prison. It also provided for the apprenticeship of children.

The next noteworthy development was the passage of the Settlement Act in 1662, which included the first specific reference to a workhouse. *Sir Edward Knatchbull's Act* of 1722–3 amended the Settlement Act, enabling local parishes to establish. One study estimates that there may have been as many as 700 workhouses in England by 1732 (Slack, 1995). By 1777, the estimate grew to 2,000 parish workhouses in both England and Wales.

The 1834 *Poor Law Amendment Act* established "Poor Law Unions" among the approximately 15,000 parishes in England and Wales, each one with its own workhouse. Ireland and Scotland eventually set up a similar scheme. The first workhouse to be opened under the new scheme was at Abingdon in 1835. "Hard labor" (which evolved into the "chain gang" and similar punishments) became a standard form of punishment for the poor, who had never been convicted of a crime. It became difficult to distinguish between the *pauper* (the common term for a person living in poverty) and the *vagabond* (those who wandered about the country without working). Eventually, in the United States, these two terms were replaced by *welfare dependent, petty persistent offender, vagrant,* and the mentally ill (McConville, 1998).

The Elizabethan Poor Laws and its predecessors turned thousands of propertyless and powerless peasants into a mass of wage-laborers (or proletarians) forced to emigrate to cities and towns in search of work. However, there were more people than there were occupations and jobs available (a standard condition throughout the history of capitalism). This created a problem for controlling the newly created *surplus population* (the chronically unemployed—in later years due to mechanization that rendered them useless for producing profits).[2] This segment keeps wages down and is absorbed back into the general working population when labor is scarce. This group is also "a condition of existence of the capitalist mode of production" (Giddens, 1971, p. 57). Paupers, vagabonds, beggars and vagrants were criminalized by the state and sentenced to a term of confinement at hard labor in the houses of correction.

The poor laws and the subsequent institution of the workhouse were methods of controlling the poor, the surplus population. In many cases workhouses were not permanent homes for the poor, as some were known as the "ins and outs." People entered and left quite frequently, depending upon the availability of work. Throughout the twentieth century and to the present day, jails have functioned in a similar manner, with some (especially the homeless) going from the streets, to shelters, to jail and then repeating the cycle.

Workhouses and Houses of Correction

The first house of correction/workhouse opened in 1596 in Amsterdam (Sellin, 1944). The *Rasphuis* housed young male offenders; it represented a significant shift in the thinking about crime. On the entrance gate were the words "Wilde beesten moet men temmen"—"Wild beasts must be tamed by men." (The gate remains standing today near a shopping center.) Offenders were sentenced for a short term; they shaved wood from a Brazilian tree and then "rasped" it into powder (hence the name of the institution). The product was then made into a dye. For a time, the Rasphuis had a monopoly on this process (Lewis, 2009, p. 11). Within a few years this institution "began to be exploited as a source of cheap labour and the rehabilitation goals envisaged by the founders were lost." Increasingly, adults were incarcerated there; it closed in 1815.

In this and similar institutions that sprang up throughout Europe and later in America we find the beginnings of the shift toward punishment of the *mind* in the form of the inculcation of "habits of industry." One purpose of the Rasphuis was to impose the kind of discipline and regimen similar to a factory. Furthermore, the organization of these workhouses anticipated "the compulsive regimens of isolation and hard labor to be pursued far more thoroughly in the penitentiary" (Ignatieff, 1978, p. 14). These workhouses were more fully developed in the late eighteenth and early nineteenth centuries for industrial workers (Marx, 1977). Indeed, the prison system was at least partly modeled after the factory.

Eighteenth century philosopher Jeremy Bentham's invention of the *Panopticon* design for a penitentiary was used almost simultaneously as a design for the early factory system.[3] In fact, he developed this model not just for prisons but for "houses of industry," "poor houses," hospitals, factories, mental institutions, and even schools (Hallett, 2006, p. 41). Both the early prisons and factories emphasized regularity and punctuality. By "instilling order in its inmates, the prison was, in effect, helping to guarantee discipline and regularity in those who arrived each morning at the factory gate" (Rothman, 1971, p. 111). Bentham derived the idea from the plan of a factory designed for easy supervision—conceived by his brother Samuel as a solution to the complexities involved in the handling of large numbers of men. Prisons and other hierarchical structures (army, school, hospital, and factory) have evolved through history to resemble Bentham's Panopticon design.

Some prison reformers, including John Howard, were influenced by hospital reformers of the period. The hospital reformers wanted to habituate the poor to cleanliness, since the sicknesses of this class of people "were interpreted as the outward sign of their inward want of discipline, morality, and honor" (Ignatieff, 1978, p. 60). Physical diseases were correlated with moral problems; the poor needed to be taught to be clean and to be self-disciplined. "Once the bodies of the poor were subjected to regulation, their minds would acquire a taste for order" (p. 61).

It is hardly a coincidence that similar behavior was required of factory workers. Among the men who actively supported Howard's reforms were leading scientists, academics and manufacturers. Some prison reformers, including Howard, were influenced by hospital reformers of the period. The hospital reformers wanted to habituate the poor to cleanliness, since the sicknesses of this class of people "were interpreted as the outward sign of their inward want of discipline, morality, and honor" (Ignatieff, 1978, p.

60). Physical diseases were correlated with moral problems. People believed that "once the bodies of the poor were subjected to regulation, their minds would acquire a taste for order" (p. 61).

Howard and other reformers believed that crime was a product of unregulated, undisciplined, and immoral lives. The required corrective was a strict regime of routinization and regulation, including the "repentance" of one's sins (hence the name "penitentiary"). Foucault (1979) described the new form of punishment as:

> Exercises, not signs: sign-tables, compulsory movements, regular activities, solitary meditation, work in common, silence, application, respect, good habits. And, ultimately, what one is trying to restore in this technique of correction is . . . the obedient subject, the individual subjected to habits, rules, orders, an authority that is exercised continually around him and upon him, and which he must allow to function automatically in him. (pp. 128–129)

Prisons, workhouses, jails, and poorhouses were controlling institutions "designed to shape an emerging industrial proletariat" (Weiss, 1987, p. 338). Control of crime and humanitarianism were not the major factors in the development of these institutions; rather, "discipline and surveillance were the objectives of the new institutional web" (p. 339).

Abingdon (mentioned earlier as the first official workhouse under the new scheme of the 1834 *Poor Law Amendment Act*) was one of hundreds of workhouses built and opened throughout England.

> Life inside the workhouse was intended to be as off-putting as possible. Men, women, children, the infirm, and the able-bodied were housed separately and given very basic and monotonous food such as watery porridge called gruel, or bread and cheese. All inmates had to wear the rough workhouse uniform and sleep in communal dormitories. Supervised baths were given once a week. The able-bodied were given hard work such as stone-breaking or picking apart old ropes called oakum. The elderly and infirm sat around in the day-rooms or sick-wards with little opportunity for visitors. Parents were only allowed limited contact with their children—perhaps for an hour or so a week on Sunday afternoon. (Workhouses.org, 2018)

Upon entering a workhouse, paupers forfeited the responsibility for their children, who often were forced into an apprenticeship. The paupers wore uniforms like other inmates (Fowler, 2007). "Proponents of workhouses saw them as educational institutions where the poor, and especially the children of the poor, would learn habits of work" (Morgan, 1975, p. 322).

Colonial America developed its own version of workhouses following the English model. The New York City Workhouse, for instance, was filled with "disorderly persons, parents of Bastard children, Beggars, Servants running away . . . Trespassers, Rogues, Vagabonds, poor persons refusing to work" (Wagner, 2005, p. 40). Some of these institutions were called "almshouses." Most were organized as total institutions (Goffman, 1961) with many rules and regulations and an internal order not unlike prisons.

The Portland Almshouse opened in 1763. At this institution, there were a detailed set of rules including when to get up each morning, when to eat, when to go to bed (with bells ringing throughout the day reminding everyone of these times) and rules about cleanliness (e.g., all "entries and stairways, cells and cellars, must be swept clean every morning") (Wagner, 2005, p. 41). Meals were highly regimented, with one bell 10 minutes before each meal and another to signal entry to the dining room after washing up for the meal.

In addition to workhouses and almshouses, there were "poor farms" throughout America during the late eighteenth and nineteenth centuries. Rockingham County, New Hampshire, opened a poor farm in 1868; it remained in operation until the late 1970s. Worcester, Massachusetts, opened a workhouse in 1772, which was converted to an almshouse and poor farm in 1818. The poor farm in Haverhill, Massachusetts, opened in 1820, existed until the late 1940s, and then became a nursing home (pp. 16–17, 46).

There was feminization of poverty throughout New England cities and seaport towns prior to the American Revolution. "Women and children were often forced to enter workhouses because many towns, including Boston, were reticent to apply large amounts of relief to an increasing population of poor people within the city" (Turner, 2003, p. 199).

One of the first poorhouses in Boston opened on Beacon Street in 1686. As the poor population continued to grow, another poorhouse opened in 1738, designed as a workhouse. "Town officials intended the poorhouse to receive the aged, sick and impotent poor, while the new workhouse would house the able-bodied poor who could be put to work to defray the cost of their upkeep" (Turner, 2003, p. 199). In Boston's early records, the term *poorhouse* indicated an institution for paupers who could not work, while the term *workhouse* designated an institution for paupers who were able to work; over time, the distinctions blurred and the terms were used interchangeably.

Jails in Early America

In America during the eighteenth and well into the nineteenth century there was a huge growth of detached persons variously referred to as the "dangerous classes," "rabble," or similar terms. Many of these were children who had been separated from their parents because of wars, illnesses, deaths in the family, and other problems. In rapidly growing cities in the northeast (such as Philadelphia, New York, and Boston), authorities confronted the problem of social control over detached persons. Similar problems emerged in the Midwest and the western frontier as the nineteenth century grew to a close. In the latter areas, local citizens faced "drunken miners, trappers, cowboys and outlaws"—they began to build small wooden jails to house them (Irwin, 1985, pp. 7–8).

The law of vagrancy was commonly employed and often resulted in a short jail sentence (Shelden & Vasiliev, 2018).[4] The first vagrancy statute was enacted in 1349 in England. The original law stipulated that it was a crime to give alms to any person of sound mind and body who was unemployed. In actual fact, the law was passed in order to provide a steady supply of cheap labor to landowners and to regulate the labor force. The prime force behind this law was the Black Death of 1348–1349, the pestilence that reduced the population in England by about one-half. The disease reduced the size of the labor force—and the profits of the lords of the manors and other employers.

This period witnessed a significant change in social class relations and in the composition of the work force. More people were making a living by working for a wage, versus working the land as serfs. Workers were becoming more mobile, searching for the best jobs at the highest wages. In short, it was the beginning of a capitalist economic system, which became a constant battleground between owners and workers (still going on today). The conflict is at the heart of the capitalist social order: it is the inherent contradiction within a capitalist system whereby the process of producing commodities is essentially a public process involving many different people, while the results of such production (in this case the profits) are privately owned.

In response to this significant change, the landowning class passed a series of laws known as the Statutes of Laborers in 1349. The new law stipulated that every man "when offered service at these wages must accept it . . . if any laborers, men or women, bond or free, should refuse to accept such an offer of work, they were to be imprisoned" (Cheyney, 1913, p. 107). It was a period when "bread riots were common and landless farmers poured into English cities," and vagrants were perceived as being a challenge to "social order" (Adler, 1989, p. 213).

The vagrancy laws were consciously designed to control the mobility of the laboring classes and to protect the interests of the landowners. The laws were designed "to curtail the mobility of laborers in such a way that labor would not become a commodity for which the landowners would have to compete" (Chambliss, 1975, p. 11). The application of such laws was widespread, focusing not only on "vagrants" but "rogues" and thieves, along with "gypsies, Irishmen, fortune tellers, university scholars found begging without permission, and peddlers" (Adler, 1989, p. 213).

The law was altered to adapt to changing social and economic conditions. In 1530 the law was reactivated (after being dormant for several years) as the focal concern shifted from the idle and those refusing to work to people who developed criminal careers because of their marginal positions in society and the shortage of employment opportunities. Merchants and other capitalist entrepreneurs needed protection from those whose life conditions forced them to steal in order to survive.

From colonial times into the twentieth century, vagrancy laws were enforced against those on the margins of society. After the Civil War the legal system worked to keep African Americans in their "place," with vaguely worded vagrancy laws (reactivated after being dormant), Black Codes, and Jim Crow laws that enforced segregation in the South (Shelden, 1979). Enforcing these and similar laws helped contribute to the convict lease system, which existed throughout the South until World War II.[5] Throughout the southern states following the Civil War until World War II, jails were constantly filled with young, able-bodied Black men charged with minor crimes (or in some cases no crimes at all) who were subsequently convicted and fined. Because they could not pay their fines, they were "sponsored" by owners of local mines and factories who agreed to pay off the fines. In return, these Black men were forced to work for their sponsors in what amounted to slave plantations. They often languished in these mines and factories for several years, many ended up dying there (Blackmon, 2008).

The first known jail in the colonies was in Virginia in 1792. Other states, including Massachusetts, New Jersey, Maryland, and South Carolina established jails in rapid succession. Most of the inhabitants of jails were debtors, children, and the mentally ill accused of petty crimes (Shelden & Vasiliev, 2018). A survey of inmates in the Boston House of Correction (a local jail) in 1837 found that 44% were convicted of being "common drunkards," while 31% were charged with larceny; the third most common offense was "lunatic" (6% of the cases) (Moynhan & Stewart, 1990, p. 51).

In colonial times jails were often filled with those who violated laws related to religion. As discussed in the introduction, the legal system in New England was shaped by puritan religious beliefs. One study of a justice of the peace court found that three offenses constituted almost one-third of the cases—profane swearing, profane cursing (it is not clear what the difference was), and profaning the Sabbath. The crime known as "breach of peace" constituted almost half of all cases (Osgood, 1984).

Religion was woven into codes throughout the colonies but was most evident in the Massachusetts Bay Colony. There were several laws punishable by death and each of these "came equipped with citations from the Bible" (Friedman, 1970, p. 34). The Massachusetts Code of 1648 made the following offenses punishable by death: "Idolatry, witchcraft, blasphemy, bestiality, sodomy, adultery, rape, man stealing, treason, false witness with intent to take a life, cursing or smiting of a parent, stubbornness or rebelliousness on the part of a son against his parents" (Haskins, 1969, p. 37). Most of the codes were based on text from the Old Testament; the reliance on scripture illustrated the strong religious influence that infused Puritan thinking about the administration of justice.

In the spring of 1692, hysteria erupted in Salem, Massachusetts; 200 people were charged in the infamous witchcraft trials. In addition to witchcraft, offenses included heresy (which was often the foundation for the offense of witchcraft), blasphemy, Quakerism, and violation of the Sabbath.[6] By May, the Salem jail was packed with 200 people accused of witchcraft—primarily women. The trials took place from June to September. Twenty-nine people were convicted, and nineteen were sentenced to death. The lives of those who confessed were spared.

Most jails in colonial America were ordinary dwellings, resembling households in structure and routine. The keeper and his family resided in one of the rooms; inmates occupied other rooms. Classification was nonexistent; men, women, and juveniles were mixed together. These jails held not only those who were awaiting trial but also debtors, the homeless, and the unemployed (Rothman, 1971). No one regulated the daily routine; few inmates worked; security was nonexistent. Some colonists feared the jails were too comfortable and that there would not be sufficient fear of punishment to prevent inmates from returning. The distinctive architecture of fortified, massive structures emerged in the nineteenth century.

Typical of many jails was the one located at the corner of Third and Market streets in Philadelphia that housed men and women, the old and young, Black and white in crowded conditions. The jailer supplied spirits at inflated prices to the prisoners. There were also fees for food, heat, clothing, locking and unlocking cells, and for attaching and removing irons before a court appearance (Johnston, 2009). In 1773 a new jail was built on Walnut Street, directly behind the State House. The new facility continued the practice of selling spirits to inmates; some women would arrange to be arrested to gain access to the male prisoners. (The Walnut Street Jail eventually became a prison to house long-term prisoners.)

Financial arrangements were common among jailers and county sheriffs—often the same person held both jobs. As happens with other people in powerful criminal justice positions, the jailer was often corrupt, known for embezzling public funds, soliciting bribes from prisoners and their families, selling whiskey to the prisoners, and abusing the inmates.

Revival of Debtors' Prisons

In the section on punishing poverty (chapter 2), we discussed the burden of fines and fees on lower income offenders. The new debtors' prison is incarceration for failure to pay obligations to the criminal justice system—fines and fees and legal financial obligations (LFOs). As noted in chapter 2, misdemeanors—which are punishable by jail—make up 80% of the criminal cases in the United States.

In *Bearden v. Georgia* (1983), the Supreme Court ruled: if a state determines a fine or restitution to be an adequate penalty for a crime, it may not imprison someone solely because of lack of resources to pay the fine; imprisoning someone because of the inability to pay a fine or restitution is contrary to the fundamental fairness required by the Fourteenth

Amendment. Despite the ruling, the practice of jailing people too poor to pay fines still exists (Atkinson, 2016; Kuttner, 2015).

> Thousands of people throughout the St. Louis metropolitan area are routinely sent to jail because they cannot pay local court fines and fees. These people are poor, and they tend to be Black. While there are many terms to describe this—including, importantly, unconstitutional—there is one with historical resonance reserved for such a practice: debtors' prison. . . . City governments, incentivized by their own budget goals and shortfalls, encourage local police to increase the number of citations in order to drive up revenue. Municipal courts are the mechanism for collection. (Benns & Strode, 2016, paragraphs 5 and 11)

In Mississippi, there are four restitution centers where judges confine people until they have earned enough money to pay court-ordered debts (Wolfe & Liu, 2020). The sentence is unusual because it is for a dollar amount rather than a period of time. Beginning in the 1970s, a few other states experimented with restitution programs but abandoned them as expensive and ineffective. A study of 200 people in the restitution centers found that most received suspended sentences for nonviolent felony convictions; half of the people confined in the restitution centers owed less than $3,515. Most did not owe restitution (20% were convicted of drug possession) but owed fines and court fees. The average time spent at the centers was four months. Inmates worked for private employers (who benefit from access to cheap and reliable labor) to earn the money owed to the court. Their debts grew because they were charged for room and board, transportation to jobs, and medical care. The average pay was $6.76 per hour.

The director of the MacArthur Justice Center at the University of Mississippi, Cliff Johnson, said it is a futile system that penalizes the poorest residents of the poorest state in the country. He described debtors' prisons as an effective way of collecting money but said there are constitutional, public policy, and moral barriers to the practice (Wolfe & Liu, 2020). Jailing the poor has an inordinate impact on people of color, and many states are reconsidering the practice. There has been a requirement in Mississippi since 2018 that judges must determine that a person willfully failed to make court-ordered payments before sending them to jail or prison. Yet the restitution-center program continues, primarily affecting people on probation for low-level offenses related to drug addiction or poverty. One-quarter of the money earned by inmates was for restitution; the remainder went to the corrections department and the courts.

Historian Alex Lichtenstein said the restitution-center program—as a form of penal labor—has unfortunate parallels with Mississippi's past. After the abolition of slavery, Mississippi leased prisoners to private industry (Wolfe & Liu, 2020). After public outcry over deaths and mistreatment, the state ended convict leasing in 1890 and founded Parchman Farm, which was modeled after a slave plantation. It houses more than 3,000 of the state's 21,000 prisoners today.

More than 20% of the incarcerated population has lost its freedom for financial reasons such as failure to pay a fine (Maselli, 2019). The poor are the most adversely affected but those who have fallen behind on student debt are also at risk. The budgets of counties depend on fines and fees. Repeated jailings for failure to pay court costs and probation fees—and then fees for being jailed—result in an endless cycle of people jailed for debt.

Who Is in Jail?

At mid-year 2018, county and city jails held 738,400 prisoners, with an incarceration rate of 226 per 100,000 population (Zeng, 2020). That jails are "temporary housing" is illustrated by the fact that the weekly turnover rate is 55%; there were 10.7 million admissions in 2018 with an average stay of 25 days. From 2005 to 2018, the percentage of the jail population that was white increased from 44% to 50%, while the percentage that was Black decreased from 39% to 33%. In both years, Hispanics accounted for 15% of all jail inmates. The incarceration rate for Blacks was 592 in 2018 (803 in 2005), compared to 182 for Hispanics (263 in 2005) and 187 for whites (167 in 2005). The incarceration rate for males (387 per 100,000) was almost 6 times the rate for females (69 per 100,000). The percentage of female jail inmates exceeded 15% in 2018. Most jail inmates (68%) were charged with a felony, and most (66%) had not been convicted.

Understanding mass incarceration requires a detailed view of systems of confinement. Often overlooked are local jails, which play a critical role as incarceration's front door (Sawyer & Wagner, 2020). There are 3,134 jails in the country plus 80 Indian County jails. Jail churn is high; most people have not been convicted. Those who can make bail leave within hours or days; those who are too poor to post bail remain locked up with people (about 160,000) serving misdemeanor sentences of less than a year. About 25% of people in jail—usually those dealing with poverty, mental illness, and substance abuse disorders—will be arrested again in the same year. Incarceration aggravates those problems. Contributing to the churn are people on probation or parole jailed for violating their supervision; when parole and probation officers file a detainer, that person is ineligible for release on bail. For people struggling to rebuild their lives after incarceration, returning to jail for a minor infraction is deeply destabilizing. Data suggest that more than one-third of some jail populations are detained for probation or parole violations.

As discussed previously, the misdemeanor system is another driver of overcriminalization and mass incarceration. An estimated 13 million misdemeanor charges—for behaviors as benign as jaywalking or sitting on a sideway—sweep people into jails (Sawyer & Wagner, 2020). The punitive response to very minor offenses accounts for more than 25% of the daily jail population nationally—and higher percentages in some states and counties. The charges are for petty offenses, but the punishment carries significant financial and personal costs. People charged with misdemeanors often are not appointed counsel; they are pressured to plead guilty and to accept probation to avoid jail—but not the collateral consequences of a criminal record and the risk of future incarceration for a probation violation.

Above, we referred to jail as incarceration's front door. A small minority of people constitute almost one-half of all admissions to jail—the same people cycle through the system repeatedly (Subramanian et al., 2015). Many are charged with nonviolent misdemeanors and are held in jail "for minor violations such as driving with a suspended license, public intoxication, or shoplifting because they can't afford bail as low as $500" (p. 2). The collateral consequences of being in jail—even for a very short period of time—include lost wages, potential loss of housing, impaired access to public benefits, weakened physical and mental health, and possible loss of custody of children.

These consequences are usually ignored when discussing criminal justice processing. Almost 40 years ago Malcolm Feeley (1979) entitled his book The Process Is the Punishment. Entry into the criminal justice system has multiple punitive aspects beyond the final sentence or even if the case is dismissed. The experience of going through the process of arrest (often being handcuffed in front of family and/or friends), sitting in jail (often more than one night) and trying to make bail, getting a lawyer (or being assigned one), appearing in court in a jail uniform (often bright orange or yellow), etc. is a form of punishment. Following this, if one is sentenced to probation there will be fees of various kinds (as noted in chapter 2) or special classes to take (e.g., DUI school), which means having to take time off work (if you still have a job). This is all in addition to the other consequences mentioned above. For minorities and the poor, the process exacerbates an already precarious existence.

Conditions in Jail

Many commissions have documented appalling jail conditions over the years, and the media have published journalistic exposés dating back as far as the 1930s (President's Commission, 1967b; US National Commission on Law Observance and Enforcement, 1931; Wildeman et al., 2018). Studies of the effects of jail overcrowding document adverse effects and horrible living conditions in many jails. Physiological effects include increased blood pressure and coronary problems; assaults by inmates and other behavioral problems are numerous. More general problems include lack of recreational and educational opportunities, poor food service, and lack of treatment programs (especially for drugs and alcohol). Problems with the jail staff include disciplinary practices and abuse from officers.

Jails function as a social institution of last resort—a place where people struggling with problems are sent when all else fails (Ford, 2019). Chicago's Cook County Jail, one of the nation's largest pre-trial detention centers, is also effectively the largest mental health hospital in the United States. Funneling at-risk individuals into a hostile environment can have fatal consequences. Between 2000 and 2016, suicides accounted for 31% of jail inmate deaths (Carson, 2020a). In 2016 the suicide rate in local jails was 46 per 100,000 inmates (compared to 13 per 100,000 in the US population). Of the 5,207 jail inmates who committed suicide from 2000 to 2016, the median time served was 9 days.

The Los Angeles County Sheriff's Department (LASD) is the largest in the country with 10,000 sworn deputies serving a population of almost 10 million. It operates the largest jail system, with an average daily population of almost 22,000. The Los Angeles County jail system has a history of violence. There have been a "litany of reports and recommendations to address the problem of violence in the County jails issued by multiple bodies over more than two decades" (Citizens Commission on Jail Violence, 2012, p. 1). A federal investigation into excessive force by guards and conspiracy to obstruct an FBI investigation prompted criminal charges against more than 20 deputies and high-ranking officials including Sheriff Lee Baca, who was sentenced to 3 years in federal prison (Ortiz, 2020). LASD agreed in 2015 to a federal monitor to ensure that its jail system curbs rampant prisoner abuse and improves conditions for mentally ill detainees.

The ACLU conducted an exhaustive investigation and issued a report detailing pervasive abuse of inmates by deputies and an ongoing climate of violence that existed for years under Sheriff Lee Baca, who covered up claims of savagery. The ACLU reviewed more than 4,500 complaints from inmates and interviewed experts, jail chaplains, a volunteer tutor to jail inmates, and others.

> Inmates suffered a shocking litany of severe injuries at the hands of deputies, including a fractured jaw, a broken collarbone, eye wounds so severe that they required surgery, broken blood vessels, and long-lasting dizzy spells. One former inmate, who is now a drug treatment counselor, witnessed multiple deputies beat another inmate so severely that he "let out the most awful scream I have ever heard in my life," the memory of which still causes the counselor to "shiver." (Liebowitz et al., 2011, p. 2)

Thomas Parker, formerly of the FBI's Los Angeles Field Office, conducted a number of the ACLU interviews. He described the violence as systemic and unchecked for decades. "In my opinion, this has provided the 'seedbed' for continued lax supervision, violence, and corruption within LASD and the county jails it administers" (p. 1).

The notorious Stanford Prison Experiment demonstrated how conditions inside even a simulated prison can produce a culture of violence and abuse. Otherwise normal undergraduates who volunteered began to engage in all sorts of verbal and physical abuse, whether they were prisoners or guards. Some student "guards' became sadistic overlords who abused the "prisoners," many of whom began to see themselves as real prisoners. The interactions became so disturbing that Zimbardo stopped the experiment after just six days (CBS, 2018).

There are multiple examples of intolerable conditions at jails. The DeKalb County Sheriff's Office manages DeKalb County Jail in Decatur, Georgia (just west of Atlanta), which is the largest pre-trial detention facility in the state detaining an average of 33,000 men and women each year. The facility implemented video conferences. Inmates wrote messages on lunch trays, including: "DeKalb Jail is mistreating us"; "We sleep and breathe mold"; and "Please help, we are dying" (Dilawar, 2019). A relative posted the screen shots on Instagram to publicize the conditions at the jail. While the posts stirred public outrage, they also resulted in guards at the jail retaliating by beating the men in the pictures and placing them in solitary confinement (which facility administrators denied). Mold has been an ongoing problem at the facility and in the food, but the Sheriff's Office claims the mold poses no health risks. Instagram posts prompted messages from former inmates or their families alleging jail administrators denied inmates medication, neglected people with serious medical conditions, and violently retaliated against anyone who spoke up.

Between 2003 and 2018, there were 68 in-custody deaths at Hampton Roads Regional Jail in Portsmouth, Virginia—and millions of dollars paid in legal settlements (Morrison & Ben-Menachem, 2019). The Department of Justice (DOJ) released a report in 2018 about the unconstitutional conditions of confinement at the jail, which houses approximately 1,100 people per day. The facility's oversight board proposed adding 113 officers and a full-time psychiatrist (at a cost of $7 million) to satisfy the DOJ's demands to improve its conditions of confinement. Critics alleged surveillance was not the most effective means of improving conditions of confinement. At the Cherokee County Detention Center, a North Carolina jail, two guards ordered incarcerated men to act as "enforcers" by beating other men held in the jail (Equal Justice Initiative, 2018). Detention staff coerced fights between those incarcerated and refused to protect the vulnerable.

Problems at the Cuyahoga County Corrections Center include civil rights violations and unsafe conditions. There have been civil lawsuits, an FBI investigation, and criminal charges against corrections officers (Zaveri & Garcia, 2019). A video showed two corrections officers repeatedly punching an inmate who was strapped to a chair. (The officers eventually pleaded guilty; one was sentenced to 9 months in prison, the other to 10 days in jail.) In October 2018, a Cleveland municipal court judge cited safety concerns as his reason for releasing people charged with low-level crimes rather than sending them to jail for pretrial detention. He said six deaths at the facility indicated it was not safe; people should not die before they appear in court. A November 2018 report by the United States Marshals Service found that inmates were not getting enough food and were held in cells far exceeding capacity—a cell designed for two people held 12. In February 2019, the Ohio Department of Rehabilitation and Correction inspected the jail and found that it failed to comply with 84 state standards. Inmates were denied hygiene products, clean linens, and visitation hours. Four months later, the jail still failed to meet 66 state standards.

Kevin Ring (2019) served 20 months in federal prison on corruption charges connected with his work for a lobbyist; he is president of a nonprofit criminal justice reform advocacy organization, Families Against Mandatory Minimums. He sees two primary reasons for barbaric conditions in jails and prisons. The first is that many people believe individuals who commit crimes deserve whatever happens to them. The second reason is ignorance about abusive conditions. There is very little oversight of corrections institutions and employees. Complaints are often unheeded, and abuses remain hidden. Legislation has made it nearly impossible for prisoners to seek relief from the courts when their rights are violated. In 1996, the Prison Litigation Reform Act (PLRA) restricted the ability of prisoners to sue over the conditions of their confinement. The strict exhaustion requirement prohibits any legal action by a prisoner confined in a correctional facility until all available administrative remedies have been exhausted.

The COVID-19 pandemic of 2020 highlighted conditions at jails—and the serious implications for society. Jails are ideal environments for the spread of an infectious disease (Lopez, 2020b). Visitors and correctional staff interact in close proximity with inmates. Law professor John Pfaff comments that jails pull people from many neighborhoods into the same cramped quarters under unsanitary conditions and then quickly release them back to their communities. He describes jails as a powerful, centralizing, and diffusing vector of disease.

The American Civil Liberties Union and the public defender's service in Washington, DC filed a lawsuit on behalf of four inmates in Washington, DC's city jail. The court filing starkly portrayed the lack of sanitary supplies in some jails and the difficulty of stopping the virus from spreading (Polantz, 2020). One defense attorney commented that even the most humane and medically up to date jail is a giant petri dish with people living in close quarters where social distancing is impossible. The lawsuit called the situation inside the jail cruel and unusual punishment. At entry, inmates receive one bar of soap. The lawsuit asked the court to rule that inmates should be provided with hand soap, paper towels, toilet paper, running water, tissues, no-touch trash cans, hand sanitizer, clean laundry, and access to daily showers.

Criminalization of the Mentally Ill

Jails are increasingly filled with people with serious mental disorders. This trend began back in the 1970s with the movement to deinstitutionalize mental patients. Proponents of deinstitutionalization wanted to end what they viewed as the warehousing of mental patients in facilities they believed were essentially dungeons and snake pits. Two other reasons were the desire to save money and the hope that new antipsychotic medications would offer a cure (Yohanna, 2013). The end result of this movement was the closing of many institutions and the release of mental patients into communities. While many were helped by this move, others suffered. The dollars that had formerly supported the institutions were to have been diverted to outpatient services, but that happened all too rarely and there was a lack of planning for alternative facilities and services (Talbott, 2004).

> 2.2 million of the severely mentally ill do not receive any psychiatric treatment at all. About 200,000 of those who suffer from schizophrenia or bipolar disorder are homeless. That's one-third of the total homeless population. Ten percent are veterans who suffer from posttraumatic stress disorder or other war-related injuries. More than 300,000 are in jails and prisons. Sixteen percent of all inmates are severely mentally ill. There were about 100,000 psychiatric beds in both public and private hospitals. There are more than three times as many seriously mentally ill people in jails and prisons than in hospitals. (Amadeo, 2019)

A study in Pennsylvania looked at the "transinstitutionalization" of the mentally ill—the process of moving mental health clients from one institution (e.g., hospital) to another type of institution (e.g., shelter or jail). As psychiatric hospital beds decreased, incarceration rates increased (Primeau et al., 2013). When not in a treatment facility, the mentally ill are usually found on the streets trying to survive as best they can; some of the petty crimes committed can be seen as survivalist behaviors (e.g., loitering, stealing, or trespassing) (Peternelj-Taylor, 2008).

Local jails and state prisons now bear the responsibility of managing the problem of the mentally ill, even though they do not have the facilities, training, or resources to do so. People in a mental health crisis are more likely to encounter the police than to get medical help—resulting in 2 million people with mental illness booked into jails each year (NAMI, 2020).

> Today, the country's largest providers of psychiatric care are not hospitals at all, but rather the jails in Chicago, Los Angeles, and New York City. Across the country, correctional facilities are struggling with the reality that they have become the nation's de facto mental health care providers, although they are hopelessly ill-equipped for the job. They are now contending with tens of thousands of people with mental ill-

ness who, by some counts, make up as much as half of their populations. (Roth, 2018, p. 1)

Almost 15% of men and 30% of women booked into jails have a serious mental health condition. "In 44 out of 50 states, prisons and jails hold more individuals with serious mental illness than the largest state hospital. In local jails, 64% of people experience symptoms of a mental health condition, which represents over 7 million people (Docherty, 2017, p. 1). Mentally ill prisoners are locked up longer, cost more to house, are more frequently placed in solitary confinement, and are more likely to commit suicide (Lyon, 2019).

In effect, deinstitutionalization has been replaced by the *criminalization of mental illness*, and those who are jailed receive little or no treatment.[7] The O'Brien Fellowship in Public Service Journalism at Marquette University conducted a study into people with mental illnesses dying in jails. In an interview, the sheriff of Nashville commented: "We are arresting people who have no idea what the laws are or the rules are because they're off their medications. You'd never arrest someone for a heart attack, but you're comfortable arresting someone who is diagnosed mentally ill. No other country in the world is doing it this way" (Harki, 2018).

Jails spend two to three times more money on people with mental illnesses that require intervention than on those without those needs—but there is little improvement to the health of the individuals nor to public safety. Counties that attempted to address the problem frequently encountered significant obstacles, such as minimal resources and lack of coordination between criminal justice, mental health, substance abuse treatment, and other agencies. In 2015, the Council of State Governments Justice Center, the National Association of Counties, and the American Psychiatric Association Foundation launched Stepping Up, a national initiative in response to the disproportionate number of people with mental illnesses in jail (Herman, 2018). Since 2015, more than 500 counties in 43 states have signed on to participate. California, Ohio, and Pennsylvania have statewide initiatives. A major component of the initiative is evidence-based screening tools to identify inmates with a serious mental illness. Congress passed the Mentally Ill Offender Treatment and Crime Reduction Act in 2004; in 2020, funding was $35 million. Grants can be used to fund mental health courts, training for responding appropriately to individuals with mental illnesses, programs supporting cooperative efforts by criminal, juvenile justice and mental health agencies, and programs that support state and local cooperation regarding the mentally ill offender.

After implementing its Criminal Mental Health Project, Miami-Dade County reduced its daily jail population of 7,000 in 2008 to 4,000 in 2018 (Morrison & Ben-Menachem, 2019). People who undergo voluntary treatment are diverted from the criminal legal process and sent to a mental health care provider. If individuals follow the treatment plan developed, criminal charges are reduced or dropped. The program also provided training for crisis interventions to 5,600 Miami-Dade law enforcement officers. Crisis intervention teams responded to more than 11,000 calls in 2017 and made only 19 arrests. The program prevented the accumulation of more than 15,000 jail days and contributed to closing a Miami jail—saving taxpayers approximately $17 million annually. Bexar County, Texas, with almost two million residents is one of the most populous counties in the United States. It implemented a jail diversion program for people with mental illness. For every person diverted, taxpayers saved $2,800. Leo Beletsky, Northeastern University law and health sciences professor, said we need to deflect people from the traumatic and counterproductive encounters with the criminal justice system.

Functions of Jails: Managing the "Rabble" Class

The typical jail population has been described variously as "social refuse," "social junk," "riffraff," "social trash," "dregs," and many other degrading descriptions. After a detailed study of the San Francisco City Jail, John Irwin (1985) concluded that most jail prisoners have two essential characteristics: "detachment" and "disrepute." He uses "detachment" in the sense that the prisoners are not very well integrated into mainstream society, with few ties to conventional social networks. Irwin uses the term "disrepute" to mean that prisoners are offensive, irksome, often threatening, and perhaps dirty, smelly, and lacking social graces. Irwin uses the term *"rabble"* to designate the disorganized, disorderly, "lowest class of people" (pp. 1–2).

Irwin concludes that the characteristics of detachment and disrepute are larger factors in decisions by the police to arrest than are the crimes committed. The jail functions as a means of managing this rabble class. In this sense, the jail is a subsidiary of a much larger welfare system that regulates the poor (Piven & Cloward, 1972). The most serious offenders of this class—those who commit serious violent and property crimes—are eventually sent to prison. Although not all of the people in jail are *only* detached and disreputable, the jail still serves the overall purpose of managing people characterized by such traits.

Irwin's study parallels a study by Miller (1996) in Jacksonville, Florida. In both locations, the majority of the offenses committed by jail prisoners were rather petty in nature. Irwin conducted extensive interviews with many of the prisoners and classified them according to the degree of seriousness of the charges against them and the degree of offensiveness they displayed. In general, using a seriousness scale devised by several prominent criminologists (Wolfgang et al., 1981), Irwin (1985) determined that only a very small percentage of crimes could be categorized as serious (around 4%), while the vast majority were classified as petty (scoring from 0 to 5 on a seriousness scale that goes as high as 35.7). Three was the average seriousness score from Irwin's sample.

Irwin then classified the prisoners according to one of several types, the most common of which were what he termed "petty hustlers" (29% of his sample). This type was followed in frequency by "derelicts" and "corner boys" (each at 14%, for a total of 28%); followed by "aliens" (9%), "junkies," "gays," and "square johns" (each constituting 6%); and "outlaws" (really serious types, 4%), "lowriders" (4%), and "crazies" (4%). Most of these individuals (57%) represented a mild degree of offensiveness and committed mostly petty crimes.[8]

Clearly, most jail prisoners do not fit the popular image of the dangerous felon so often portrayed in both the media and by politicians. The authors have observed local campaigns to expand jail capacities and even build more jails based on such misconceptions, advanced by those with vested interests in building new jails. Moreover, data reveal that most people jailed will be released within two to three days—indicating a minimal level of dangerousness.

A study testing Irwin's hypothesis of the functions of jails used interview data from 47,592 inmates in local jails in 30 US cities (Fitzpatrick & Myrstol, 2011). The study was part of the "Arrestee Drug Abuse Monitoring program." Bivariate analysis of the data supported Irwin's rabble management thesis. Homeless people were overrepresented in the study; the homeless were jailed because of their "offensiveness," not their dangerousness.

Another study of the Marion County Jail in Salem, Oregon, further reinforces Irwin's thesis (Shelden et al., 2016, pp. 246–255). The inmates at this jail displayed characteristics typical of those in other jails, including the one Irwin studied. Most had not graduated from high school and had very sporadic work histories (most were unemployed at the time of their most recent arrest). The majority had used a number of drugs, and most had been diagnosed with a variety of mental health issues. The majority had been arrested for property and drug offenses. These factors fit the general description of the "rabble."

Jails confine people with whom society doesn't want to deal out of sight where most citizens can forget about them—enabling horrendous conditions (Matthews, 2020), Pandemics are times of scarcity, and scarce goods are distributed according to existing social inequalities. COVID-19 highlighted those inequalities. It disproportionately affected Black Americans, people without access to medical care, people living in impoverished conditions in close proximity to one another in inner cities, people in nursing homes, and people in prisons and jails. Power differential creates social estrangement, which enables differential treatment. Political theorist Judith Shklar points to Machiavelli's claim that people can only rule inferior subjects—not equals—with cruelty. COVID-19 was a brutal reminder of the consequences of inequality—but it also presented an opportunity for change. The United States can reduce the number of people warehoused in jails; it can create social supports and economic opportunities for the impoverished.

NOTES

[1] For a look at a workhouse in the United States, visit http://www.correctionhistory.org/html/chronicl/nycdoc/html/penitentiary2.html

[2] The term "surplus population" was popularized by Karl Marx (1977).

[3] See the following web site for an illustration of *Bentham's Panopticon Prison Design.* http://en.wikipedia.org/wiki/Panopticon.

[4] For a more detailed discussion of the law of vagrancy, see chapter 1 in Shelden and Vasiliev; for one of the best studies on the subject see Chambliss, W. S., "The Law of Vagrancy." In W. S. Chambliss (ed.), *Criminal Law in Action.* New York: John Wiley, 1975.

[5] One of the best treatments of convict leasing is found in Blackmon, D. (2008). *Slavery by Another Name: The Re-Enslavement of Black Americans from the Civil War to World War II.* New York: Doubleday.

[6] For more information see Shelden and Vasiliev, 2018, pp. 110–112.

[7] For a summary, see Shelden et al., 2016, pp. 242–244.

[8] Austin and Irwin (2012), in their study of the prison system, discovered a similar distribution of offenders to what Irwin found in his jail study.

4

Slavery in the
Third Millennium

Privately-owned plantation prisons emerged in the southern states shortly after the end of the Civil War. Not surprisingly they were modeled after the slave plantation in terms of the use of space, the monetizing of crop-based work, and the emphasis on Black incarceration and labor. Practically all of the prisoners were Black, both male and female. "After the civil war, newly emancipated African Americans would be incarcerated on the flimsiest pretexts and then put to hard labor in the fields of these prisons, often in chain gangs" (Johnson et al., 2017, p. 42).

Over the years, the atrocities in these prisons became well known, with the Cummins Prison Farm the most notorious. In the 1960s a reform-minded warden, Tom Murton, discovered numerous bodies of prisoners buried in the fields. The scandal, while one of many in the twentieth century, received significant attention (Bauer, 2018). The movie, *Brubaker*, starring Robert Redford, was based in part on the scandal. Prisons like Parchman in Mississippi and Cummins in Arkansas were little more than slave plantations that, along with convict leasing, extended the slave system long after emancipation (Mancini, 1996; Oshinsky, 1996). This chapter explores historical, legal, and demographic evidence of the extension of slavery into the twenty-first century.

Social Control, Prisoners, and Slavery

Throughout history, people in power have sought to control groups they perceived to be a threat and/or groups they wished to dominate for political or economic gain. The methods of control have varied from economic marginalization to thought control via propaganda to subjugation to the control of the legal system to total or partial segregation—and, in extreme cases, total extermination (e.g., genocide) (Chomsky, 1989, 1993). In the United States, social control has targeted Native Americans, African slaves, labor agitators, and many others (Shelden & Vasiliev, 2018).

Seeking Cheap Labor

The use of inmates as a form of cheap labor has been part of the capitalist system since its origin. Owners attempt to maximize profits however they can, including using the law to legitimize the targeting of specific populations for cheap labor. Whether those groups are slaves, immigrants, or inmates, they have been strategically targeted by market forces through the use of legal measures (Alexander, 2020).

In the Roman Empire the term *slave* included prisoners of war, sailors captured and sold by pirates, or slaves bought outside Roman territory (Bradley, 1987). Taking advantage of those imprisoned—in various forms, including slavery—has been common among many nations for centuries (Sellin, 2016). In contrast, "low-density" slavery in some African empires created less exploitive enslavement practices (Stillwell, 2014). In these contexts, slaves became members of families rather than a lower class of outsiders; in some cases, children of slaves were not automatically slaves, and slaves could manage businesses of their own.

The various forms of channeling people into slavery included the use of transportation, which was common until replaced with imprisonment in the early nineteenth century (Shelden & Vasiliev, 2018). In the seventeenth century, private merchant shippers transported prisoners to North American plantations for a period of indentured servitude. It was one among many methods of amassing large fortunes during this time. Most of the transported prisoners were white. The end of transportation coincided almost exactly with the increased use of slavery in the colonies.

Capitalists soon learned that there were even more benefits from the African slave trade than from white indentured servants. One writer noted that among the many advantages of slaves was the fact that they "were held to perpetual instead of temporary servitude, they were cheaper to feed and clothe, they replaced themselves to some extent by natural breeding, and they endured the hot climate of the plantation much better than white men" (Smith, 2012, p. 29).

> Beginning in the seventeenth century, millions of African people were kidnapped, enslaved, and shipped across the Atlantic under horrific conditions: starvation and death were the rule. For the next two centuries the enslavement of Black people created wealth, prosperity, and growth for free people of European descent while an elaborate and enduring mythology about the racial inferiority of Black people took hold to legitimate, perpetuate, and defend slavery. The ideology of

> white supremacy survived the Civil War and endures in ways that are
> evident even today. (Stevenson, 2017, p. 6)

Slaves were important to the colonial economy, providing much needed
cheap labor for a relatively small group of landowners. The slaves were
classified as chattel or property. From its inception, the United States—
despite its stated foundation on principles of equality—allowed slavery.
The Declaration of Independence declared the self-evident truth that "all
men are created equal"; unstated was the actual situation that *white* men
were created equal. Women were treated almost as if they were slaves
socially and even legally through coverture laws, which indicated women's
legal identities were literally "covered" by the legal presence of the male
authority (i.e., husband or father) (Moore, 2016; Stretton et al., 2014).
The white, male ruling class created an economic and political system
complete with a set of laws that guaranteed slavery would remain intact
(Elkins, 1976; Fogel, 1995; Kolchin & Foner, 1995).

Maintaining Control

History books inform us that the Civil War "freed" the slaves. Well, not
exactly. After the war, the South faced serious economic, political, and
social problems. One crucial problem was what "to do with" the newly
"freed" slaves. From the standpoint of the white power structure, this was
a problem of social control. The response to what eventually became
known as the "Negro problem" was the systematic oppression of Blacks
and the maintenance of a system of *caste* rule that would replace a system
of slavery (Oliver, 2015; Shelden, 1979). The legal abolition of slavery did
not eliminate the racist ideology created to defend it. "In place of slavery,
belief in a racial hierarchy took virulent expression in newly defined social
norms, including lynching and other forms of racial terrorism; segregation
and Jim Crow; and unprecedented mass incarceration" (Stevenson, 2017,
p. 8).

The South created a system of racial hierarchy and subordination of
African Americans. One of the defining features of slavery—and one of its
most potent legacies—was the exclusion of Blacks as legitimate members
of the community (Patterson, 2020).

> After the Civil War, the radical Reconstruction movement recognized
> the need to incorporate Blacks into the body politic and initially suc-
> ceeded in doing so, but once federal forces withdrew and power was
> restored to the local Southern elite, there was a vicious program of
> suppression of both Black freedoms and their access to land. (p. C-2)

Prison systems were integral in the extension of the dehumanization and
exclusion of Blacks.

"Negro crime" was a powerful narrative at the time, linking rape and
other violent crimes with Black Americans (Freedman, 2013).

Fears of interracial sex and marriage have deep roots in the United States. The confluence of race and sex was a powerful force in dismantling Reconstruction after the Civil War, sustaining Jim Crow laws for a century and fueling divisive racial politics throughout the twentieth century. (Stevenson, 2014, p. 27)

Sharecropping was another "legal" method of replacing slavery and controlling the bodies and labor of African Americans. Sharecropping was the practice of enacting rigid surveillance of farm laborers (almost all of whom were Black), tracking their labor, production hours, living arrangements, movement off the farm, and so forth. Black laborers were allowed to live on the owners' land for the cost of working that land. Ultimately, a system of agricultural (and eventually industrial) "peonage" emerged, which was supported by informal (vigilantism and intimidation) and formal (Jim Crow laws) methods (Weiss, 1987).

Bryan Stevenson[1] makes the point that the great evil of American slavery was the fiction that Black people are not the equals of white people—that they are less evolved, less human, less capable, less worthy, and less deserving (Chotiner, 2020). The ideology of white supremacy was necessary to justify enslavement. In Stevenson's view, slavery did not end in 1865; it evolved. Immediately after 1865 and the Thirteenth Amendment, violence broke out. The ideology of white supremacy and the presumption of African American dangerousness resulted in horrendous violence during Reconstruction through terror and intimidation, lynching, and Jim Crow laws.

Convict Leasing

The Thirteenth Amendment ostensibly ended slavery but made an exception for those convicted of crimes (Stevenson, 2019). The provisional governor of South Carolina declared in 1865 that Black people needed to be restrained from theft, idleness, vagrancy, and crime. Laws governing slavery were replaced with Black Codes governing free Black people; the criminal justice system was central to strategies of racial control. Whenever Black people asserted their independence or achieved any measure of success, strategies intensified. Anything that challenged the racial hierarchy could be seen as a crime punishable by law. The emergence of Black elected officials and entrepreneurs during Reconstruction was countered by *convict leasing*.

Convict leasing was introduced throughout the South because "free" Blacks represented a threat to white supremacy. Convict leasing was another form of chattel slavery that functioned to keep Blacks in a subordinate position. The subjugation of African Americans became common throughout the South after the war. Laws were passed (and sometimes old ones were reinstituted) to control the African American population—

vagrancy, loitering, disturbing the peace, and Jim Crow laws, to name just a few examples.

> Convict leasing was introduced at the end of the nineteenth century to criminalize former slaves and convict them of nonsensical offenses so that freed men, women, and children could be "leased" to businesses and effectively forced back into slave labor. Private industries through-out the country made millions of dollars with free convict labor, while thousands of African Americans died in horrific work conditions. (Stevenson, 2014, p. 299)

Before the Civil War, few people were sentenced to the penitentiary, but that changed. Convict leasing increased prison populations and shifted the composition to primarily African Americans. In Georgia, there was a tenfold increase in prison populations during a four-decade period (1868–1908). In Florida, the population went from 125 in 1881 to 1,071 in 1904. In Mississippi, the population quadrupled between 1871 and 1879. In Alabama, it went from 374 in 1869 to 1,878 in 1903 and to 2,453 in 1919 (Mancini, 1978). In Tennessee in October 1865, African Americans represented 33% of the population at the main prison in Nashville (Shelden, 1979). By November 1867, the percentage had increased to 58.3; by 1869 it had increased to 64%, and it reached 67% by 1877. Other states were similar. In 1888, the prison in Baton Rouge, Louisiana, held 85 whites and 212 African Americans. In 1875 in North Carolina 569 African Americans and 78 whites were sentenced to prison (Sellin, 2016).

Convict leasing involved leasing out prisoners to private companies that paid the state a fee. The convicts worked for the companies during the day outside the prison and returned to their cells at night. The sole aim of convict leasing "was financial profit to the lessees who exploited the labor of the prisoners to the fullest, and to the government which sold the convicts to the lessees" (Sellin, 2016, p. 144). One example was a lease system in Alabama, where in 1866 "the governor of Alabama leased the penitentiary to a contractor who was charged the sum of five dollars and given a sizable loan. The legislature granted him permission to work the prisoners outside the walls; they were soon found in the Ironton and New Castle mines" (p. 148).

In Tennessee by 1870, convicts were being leased from the main prison at Nashville to three separate railroad companies in Tennessee. Then, during the 1880s, the legislature appropriated about $14 million to relieve the railroad companies that had suffered great losses during the war. It is no exaggeration that convicts literally rebuilt Tennessee's railroads. In 1871, coal mining companies began to use convict labor; by 1882, more than half of the convicts at the Nashville prison were leased out. In 1884, the Tennessee Coal, Iron and Railway Company took complete control and leased the entire prison population (Shelden, 1979).

A notorious chain gang was called by one writer "The American Siberia" (Powell, 1891). This particular chain gang was a camp in Florida, where turpentine was extracted in a semi-tropical jungle atmosphere; the only labor that could be obtained was that of convicts. "Prisoners worked in gangs, chained together in filthy bunkhouses, exposed to dysentery and scurvy" (Barnes & Teeters, 1959, p. 625).

The convict lease system was cruel and inhumane. Deaths were common, as was sickness and suffering. In a coal mine in Georgia, convicts were routinely whipped if they did not produce the daily quota of coal (Mancini, 1978). In Alabama, inmates were punished by being placed in a "sweat box" during the day in the hot sun (Curtin, 2000). A Louisiana newspaper reported that "it would be more humane to impose the death sentence upon anyone sentenced to a term with the lessee in excess of six years, because the average convict lived no longer than that" (Sellin, 2016, p. 150). Indeed, the death rate in 1896 was 20%. The mortality rate for inmates in the South was 41.3 per thousand convicts, compared to a rate of 14.9 in the North (McKelvey, 1968).

The ideology of white supremacy dominated the entire leasing system. Lessees regarded Black labor as a commodity, similar to how slaveholders had regarded slaves (Hallett, 2006).

> The convict lease system perpetuated the *racialized* system of forced labor necessary for the survival of the agrarian planter class [precisely at the time it was to have legally ended], while also accommodating the industrial development of the New South. In short, owners of railroads, coal mines, and logging companies were equally interested in exploiting imprisoned African Americans as were plantation owners. (p. 46)

The convict lease system fit well with the emerging industrial capitalist system. It replaced and extended slavery, albeit in a new form and serving new interests. The control of the Black labor force was a constant goal of the southern punishment system after the Civil War.

Convict leasing was also widely supported because of its alleged success in controlling the "Black crime problem" (Blackmon, 2008; Freedman, 2013). As discussed earlier, the "Black crime problem" was an invention. The vast majority of Black prisoners were convicted of petty crimes, such as loitering, vagrancy, and trespassing (Ayers, 1984; Myers, 1998; Shelden, 1979)—and many were falsely accused (Carter, 1979; Patterson & Conrad, 1950). The convict lease system eventually disappeared. "The lease system was doomed by its decreasing usefulness to the state . . . , and it was not abandoned until profitable substitutes were perfected" (McKelvey, 1968, p. 185). These substitutes included plantations, industrial prisons, and chain gangs.

The Chain Gang Revisited

The chain gang developed alongside the convict lease system as one of the two major forms of convict labor. It was one of history's most degrading punishments; inmates were chained together in fetid bunkhouses, suffered malnutrition, and exposure to disease (Weiss, 1987). The vast majority of people on chain gangs were African Americans, often convicted merely for being Black. Over several decades, thousands of Black females convicted of misdemeanors worked on chain gangs building roads, harvesting turpentine, and laboring on various public works projects (LeFlouira, 2016). Chain gang operators ruthlessly enforced constant labor, subjecting women to illness and injury.

When the states changed from convict leasing (private) to chain gangs (public), the inmates fared no better (Glazer, 1996). Judges sent convicts to county chain gangs instead of state prison for two reasons: economics (the state needed cheap labor to build roads) and retribution (chain gangs were considered a more humiliating punishment than the penitentiary). The demise of chain gangs began in the 1930s as the unemployed sought jobs performed by prisoners; some forms survived until the 1960s when public pressure ended the practice (Burley, 1997).

Alabama was the first state to reinstate chain gangs in 1995 (Burley, 1997). The first year, prisoners were chained together. After an inmate died, Alabama settled a lawsuit and agreed to halt that practice. Florida, Iowa, Oklahoma, Tennessee, and Wisconsin soon followed Alabama in implementing chain gangs. In the 1990s iterations, inmates were shackled, but they were not chained to each other. "Chain gangs are uniquely designed to divest prisoners of their human dignity" (p. 154).

Historically chain gangs served as public spectacles for the embarrassment that they offered (Collier, 2017). When Alabama reinstated chain gangs, it was a visible symbol of humiliation and punishment (Staples, 1995). An elderly female spectator commented: "I love seeing 'em in chains. They ought to make them pick cotton" (p. 62).

> At the beginning of this century the chain gang was used to keep African Americans in servitude after Emancipation. Contract-enforcement laws—directed primarily at African American farm laborers—transformed contractual obligations into involuntary servitude by imposing criminal sanctions for a laborer's breach of an employment contract. These laborers had a choice: They could work out the contract or spend several months of forced, brutal labor on a chain gang, where death was not uncommon. The historical connection between chain gangs and slavery is well-entrenched in the minds of most Americans and probably all African Americans. (Meares, 1996)

Joe Arpaio, the notorious sheriff of Maricopa County, Arizona, required inmates to serve on chain gangs to perform various community services. When not working on the chain gang in uniforms with black and white stripes, four inmates were confined together in an 8- by 12-foot cell for 23 hours a day (Carter, 2010). Arpaio made inmates wear pink underwear (Mettler, 2017). More than 2,000 inmates were placed in tents outside the jail near Phoenix where temperatures average well over 100 degrees. He fed inmates only twice a day—serving them "Nutraloaf," served in other correctional institutions as a disciplinary measure (Johnson, 2019). In 2008 and 2010, a federal judge ruled that Arpaio violated the constitutional rights of inmates regarding medical care. As in other parts of the country, most of the 8,000 Maricopa inmates were in jail awaiting trial because they could not afford bail. Arpaio served 24 years as sheriff until he was defeated in 2016 after being charged with contempt of court for having ignored a federal judge's order to stop arresting immigrants solely on suspicion that they were in the country illegally. Convicted in July 2017, he was pardoned one month later by President Trump, who professed admiration for Arpaio protecting the public from the scourges of crime and illegal immigration. In the few other states that continued to utilize chain gangs (sometimes called work crews), inmates volunteered to participate. Sheriffs promoted the chain gangs as visible anti-crime campaigns (Ford, 2013). Civil rights activists challenged that portrayal, believing chain gangs, with their links to slavery and forced labor, send an inappropriate message.

Most of the arguments put forth by supporters of chain gangs have revolved around two issues, both of which ignore race: saving money and deterrence. Arguments are made that having work crews picking up trash, doing work at public parks, and for nonprofit organizations saves taxpayers' money. While individual jails and prisons cite as much as $200,000 in annual savings (PCSO, 2010), there is yet to be a large-scale economic analysis of the return on investment for the costs associated with jail and prison guards facilitating the movement of prisoners to work sites, use of work site equipment, and comparisons of the cost-savings to local municipalities who would otherwise pick up the litter on the side of the road.

Funneling African Americans into Prison

Groups targeted by the criminal justice system are disproportionately drawn from the most marginalized populations.

> Convict leasing, the practice of "selling" the labor of state and local prisoners to private interests for state profit, utilized the criminal justice system for the economic exploitation and political disempowerment of Black people. State legislatures passed discriminatory criminal laws, or "Black Codes," which created new criminal offenses such as "vagrancy" and "loitering." This led to the mass arrest and incarceration of Black people. Then, relying on language in the Thirteenth Amendment that prohibits slavery and involuntary servitude "except as punishment for crime," lawmakers empowered white-controlled governments to extract Black labor in private lease contracts or on state-owned farms. While a Black prisoner was a rarity during the slavery era (when slave masters were individually empowered to

administer "discipline" to their human property) the solution to the free Black population had become criminalization. (Stevenson, 2017, p. 11)

Black Incarceration

Blacks are far more likely to find themselves imprisoned than any other racial group (Hager, 2017; Pettit & Sykes, 2017). Central to understanding mass incarceration and excessive punishment is the legacy of slavery (Stevenson, 2019). The presumption of danger and criminality still follows Black people. The Black Codes are gone but have been replaced by new noncrimes: driving while Black, sleeping while Black, sitting in a coffee shop while Black. African Americans are arrested for conduct that would be ignored if engaged in by whites. Black children are suspended and expelled from school at rates that vastly exceed the punishment of white children for the same behavior; Black juveniles are more frequently tried as adults. There are racial disparities in sentencing for almost every crime category, and Black defendants are 22 times more likely to receive the death penalty for crimes in which the victims are white rather than Black—a type of bias the Supreme Court declared "inevitable" (*McCleskey v. Kemp*, 1987).

The demographics of US prisons look substantially different from nationwide demographics. Blacks constituted 33% of the sentenced prison population in 2018—and only 12% of the US population (Gramlich, 2020). Conversely, whites constituted 30% of prisoners—and 63% of the adult population. Hispanics constituted 16% of the adult population, and 23% of inmates. The racial differences in incarceration rates for state and federal prisons are stark. In 2019, there were 1,446 Black prisoners for every 100,000 Black adults compared to 263 white prisoners per 100,000 white adults, and 757 Hispanic prisoners per 100,000 Hispanic adults (Carson, 2020b). (The rates for all 3 groups declined substantially since 2009: a 32% decline for Blacks, 15% for whites, and 29% for Hispanics.) Imprisonment rates for Black men were significantly higher—2,203 inmates per 100,000 Black men. Black men ages 18 to 19 were 12 times as likely to be imprisoned as white men the same ages.

The Drug War, Minorities, and State-Organized Violence

President Nixon launched the war on drugs in 1971. As noted in chapter 1, Nixon's war on drugs was a political tool in response to groups who posed a threat—civil rights activists and opponents of the Vietnam War. The narrative linked Black communities and protesters with drug use (Pearl & Perez, 2018). Policy makers at all levels of government approved increased enforcement actions and passed harsh sentencing laws for low-level drug offenses. President Regan intensified the war on drugs started by Nixon. During his administration, Congress passed the Anti-Drug Abuse

Act of 1986 that introduced mandatory sentencing laws. The Act included disparate treatment of cocaine. Possession of 5 grams of crack cocaine (used by Blacks) received the same sentence as possession of 500 grams of cocaine (used by whites). Enforcement of the new drug laws focused on minority neighborhoods.

The evidence of racial disproportionality in the drug war was overwhelming. Arrest rates for minorities went from under 600 per 100,000 in 1980 to over 1500 in 1990, while for whites they essentially remained the same (Tonry, 1995). Prison sentences reflected the same disparity. In Pennsylvania, nonwhite males and females sentenced on drug offenses increased by 1613% and 1750% respectively. In Virginia commitments for drug offenses for minorities went from just under 40% in 1983 to about 65% in 1989, while for whites the percentage decreased from just over 60% in 1983 to about 30% in 1989. In North Carolina between 1980 and 1990, the rate of admissions to prison for nonwhites jumped from around 500 per 100,000 to almost 1,000 (Donziger, 1996).

From 1980 to 1996, drug offenses accounted for the greatest share of the increase in state and federal prisoners—33% (Blumstein & Beck, 1999). Drug offenses increased the incarceration rate for women and Blacks at a compounded rate of 20% annually over the 17-year period. Drug offenses accounted for 43% of the increase in women prisoners, 36% for Blacks, 32% for Hispanics, and 17% for whites.

In 1980, 33% of federal offenders committed a violent crime; in 1995, the percentage declined to 14 (Blumstein & Beck, 1999). In comparison, 25% of federal offenders in 1980 committed a drug offense compared to 60% in 1995. Two-thirds of the growth in the federal prison population from 1980 to 1995 was due to the increase in the numbers of drug offenders. The percentage of inmates in state prison for a drug crime also rose significantly—from 6% in 1980 to 23% in 1995. Drug offenses accounted for 30% of the increase in state prison populations during that time frame and 33% of the growth in the jail population. Sentences for new court commitments for a drug offense in 1980 averaged 26.7 months compared to 82 months in 1995.

The number of people in state prison for a drug offense in 2018 was more than 9 times greater than in 1980, accounting for 14.4% of state prisoners (Sentencing Project, 2020b). The federal system categorizes almost all new commitments for a drug offense as trafficking, but the definition of trafficking is not uniform. Sentence lengths are directly tied to mandatory minimum penalties. Nonviolent drug convictions remain a defining feature of the federal prison system (Sawyer & Wagner, 2020). In 2019 the percentages of federal prisoners convicted of a drug offense were: 47.6% white; 40.8% Black, and 59.8% Hispanic (Carson, 2020b).

As noted in chapter 1, Black Americans are nearly six times more likely to be incarcerated for drug-related offenses than their white counterparts, despite equal substance usage rates (Pearl, 2018). In state prisons, 60% of inmates serving time for drug charges are people of color. Almost 80% of inmates serving time for a federal drug offense are Black or Hispanic. The average Black defendant in the federal system convicted of a drug offense serves 58.7 months—almost the same amount of time as a white defendant convicted of a violent crime (61.7 months).

One might assume that the increase in the number of minorities incarcerated resulted from "unintended consequences" of the ongoing drug war, but the reasons may be more sinister than a failing drug war and disparate laws (e.g., crack v. powder cocaine). It may be plausible to argue that the "war on drugs" (and the "war on gangs") has actually been a "success" if the aim was to control the surplus population, especially Blacks (Chomsky, 1996; Shelden et al., 2013). Mona Lynch describes criminal law as a type of subterfuge—the government invents wars on crime, on drugs, and on gangs that are waged with harsh criminal statutes that barely disguise the target populations of poor African Americans (Natapoff, 2017). Institutional segregation and apartheid practices contribute to disproportionate incarceration (Currie, 1993; Reinarman & Levine, 1997).

Minorities are far more likely to be arrested and convicted for drug crimes than white Americans, despite using drugs at similar rates. One reason is the structural inequality built into the criminal justice system— the disparity in the criminalization of crack cocaine versus pure cocaine (Piaggio & Vidwans, 2019). The media frenzy in the 1990s over crack use and the alleged effect on babies born to mothers who used crack led to tremendous injustices against Black communities. As mentioned earlier, crack possession was punished far more severely (the 100:1 ratio). In 2012, the ratio was reduced to 18:1, but the punishment remains unequal for possession of the same substance in a different form.

As discussed in chapter 1, the war on drugs has also resulted in the police using militaristic tactics in drug crime cases. Judges can issue no-knock warrants for law enforcement officers (frequently Special Weapons and Tactics units) to enter a residence without notification. More than half (54%) of the people subjected to such searches between 2010 and 2016 were Black or Hispanic (Piaggio & Vidwans, 2019).

> The early association of drugs with minorities that led to the establishment of harsh crack punishments has also been translated into policing practices. Law enforcement devotes more resources and time to policing poverty-stricken areas in inner cities where the majority of the population is either Black or Hispanic. Drug laws, such as New York City's former "Stop and Frisk" law, give police offers an incentive to conduct drug searches on pedestrians and drivers in these overpoliced neighborhoods. As a result, Black Americans are arrested at far higher rates than white Americans. According to an extensive Human Rights Watch report, Black individuals in Manhattan were arrested at a rate of 3,309 per 100,000 people between 2010 and 2015, compared to

only 306 per 100,000 white people, making Black people 11 times more likely to be arrested for drugs than white people. (p. 49)

The war on drugs created "a harshly punitive set of practices that have deprived millions of individuals of their liberty simply for using drugs, even in cases where this use poses no threat to themselves or to others" (Piaggio & Vidwans, 2019, p. 49). Under federal law and in some states, drug possession is a felony. Individuals can lose their right to vote, custody of their children, and opportunities for housing, education, and employment—often leading them into a cycle of poverty. While disenfranchisement laws (see section below and chapter 9) are not necessarily a product of the drug war, the overcriminalization of drug offenses and its contribution to mass imprisonment "make it a significant threat to the health of American democracy" (p. 52).

The war on drugs has diminished judicial discretion and affects due process. Mandatory minimums for drug offenses give federal prosecutors more power in plea bargaining (Piaggio & Vidwans, 2019). By removing discretion from judges, defendants are not evaluated as individuals; rather, they are grouped depending on the offense with which they are charged. Mandatory minimums result in punitive sentences for nonviolent drug offenders. Severe punishment for nonviolent offenses endangers the core legal principle of proportionality. "All of these issues have had a questionable effect on due process and weaken the credibility of the judicial system in general" (p. 52).

Beyond the war on drugs and political expediency, a number of social scientists "see the growth of the punitive modern carceral state as the continuation of a familiar post-emancipation pattern" (Patterson, 2020, p. C-2). Sociologist Christopher Muller points out that imprisonment typically increases after periods when African Americans make significant economic, social, and political gains—most notably after Reconstruction and the civil rights movement.

Ruth Gilmore, Angela Davis, Beth Ritchie, and Michelle Alexander are leaders in the prison abolition movement (Kushner, 2019). Their leadership is part of a long history of abolitionist movements led by Black women. The word abolition intentionally echoes the movement to abolish slavery. Certain narratives attract attention and may facilitate policy changes, but Gilmore cautions that those changes address improvements to the current system; they do not question the existence of mass incarceration. She points to the narratives regarding people imprisoned for nonviolent drug convictions, prison as a modified continuation of slavery, and profits as the primary engine of incarceration. In this chapter, we have explored some of those narratives and the devastating consequences for the people involved.

In the United States, many people assume that prison is necessary for violent offenders. The narrative that focuses on the 20% of prison and jail inmates convicted of a drug offense omits the 80% convicted of violent crimes. The emphasis is on the injustice of the relatively innocent being subjected to state-organized violence—without addressing whether we need organized violence for any offenders (Kushner, 2019). The narrative of prisons as an extension of slavery for African Americans—slavery in the third millennium—offers two "crucial truths: that the struggles and suffering of Black people are central to the story of mass incarceration, and that prison, like slavery, is a human rights catastrophe" (p. 37). Gilmore points out that the reality of prison and of Black suffering is harrowing—we do not need the misconception of prison as slave labor to see the horror of it." Unlike Marx (see chapter 2), she characterizes prison as a government institution and not a business; prison does not function on a profit motive. Although others profit both financially and through employment from the existence of the prison system, as we outlined in chapter 2, Gilmore maps out the ways in which the California prison system is not based on profit motive but rather on the exercising of state violence against a segment of the population (Gilmore, 2007). The overwhelming problem for people in prison is minimally about their exploited labor. The predominant problem of mass incarceration is that it warehouses people in unsafe, degrading circumstances with nothing to do and no programs or resources to help them access non-incarceration futures once they leave prison.

Michelle Alexander's influential book, The New Jim Crow, focused on racial bias and the devastating effects of the war on drugs, fueling outrage over draconian laws that punish nonviolent minority offenders. Interviewed by a journalist, Alexander commented on Gilmore's guidance regarding violence.

> I think the failure of some academics like myself to squarely respond to the question of violence has created a situation in which it almost seems like we're approving of mass incarceration for violent people. Those of us who are committed to ending the system of mass criminalization have to begin talking more about violence. Not only the harm it causes, but the fact that building more cages will never solve it. (quoted in Kushner, 2019, p. 37)

Alexander credits Gilmore with being very clear that prison abolition is a theory of change involving more than the closing of prisons.

For more than 30 years, Gilmore has been active in the movement to abolish prisons, which are punitive, cruel, and life-annihilating—a symbol of vengeance (Kushner, 2019). Discussions about closing prisons frequently degenerate into questions about how then to deal with violent people. Gilmore suggests those are the wrong questions. You can't solve a problem with state violence or with personal violence; rather, you need to change the conditions under which violence prevails. How do you resolve the inequalities that can lead to violence? She advocates for vital systems of support that many communities lack—investment in jobs, education, housing, and health care—all of which are essential elements for a productive and violence-free life. In this chapter, we engage this very conversation, linking prisons in the post-Civil War era to the continued oppression and segregation of the underclass.

The New American Apartheid

In the Afrikaans language, *apartheid* means separate. The term refers specifically to the former policy of segregation and political/economic discrimination against Blacks in the Republic of South Africa. Some have called the modern penal system a new form of *apartheid* or *petit apartheid* (the latter applying to the criminal justice system in general) (Georges-Abeyie, 1990). Many studies have demonstrated that US minorities segregated in destitute areas have seen drastically reduced incomes, access to quality schools, and other factors correlated to positive life outcomes (Bones & Hope, 2015; Roberts & Willits, 2015; Spruk & Kešeljević, 2018). Systematic segregation of African Americans created underclass communities and a geographic concentration of extreme poverty. Adapting to an increasingly harsh environment of racial isolation, residents evolve attitudes, behaviors, and practices that further marginalize their neighborhoods and undermine their chances of success in mainstream society (Massey & Denton, 1998).

> The higher rate of crime among a minority of urban Blacks, herded into overcrowded ghettos with limited job opportunities and dysfunctional schools, offers easy justification for heavy-handed profiling and harassment. (Patterson, 2020, p. C-2)

Corporate downsizing and deindustrialization eliminated millions of occupations that previously lifted minorities out of poverty. An argument could be made that Blacks, especially males, became superfluous and expendable in US society (that is, not really needed for corporate profits), resulting in a perceived need of some form of social control. The criminal justice system provided the control (Shelden & Vasiliev, 2018). While the "old" apartheid of residential segregation continued unabated (Massey & Denton, 1998), a "new" apartheid arose (Xidias, 2017). The criminal justice system engaged in a systematic attack on Blacks; going to jail or prison became a common event in the lives of millions of racial minorities.

Loïc Wacquant describes four iterations of the "peculiar institutions" that have governed and controlled American Blacks: slavery, Jim Crow, the ghetto, and mass incarceration (Natapoff, 2017). In the post-Civil Rights era, the penal system (including all the components of the criminal justice system) has taken the place of the ghetto (Wacquant, 2001). Moreover, Wacquant argues that "the increasing use of imprisonment" aims to "shore up" the caste divisions in society by "upsizing" the penal sector while "downsizing" the social welfare sector (p. 97). This trend (which Wacquant calls the government of poverty) represents a merging of the "invisible hand" of the market with an "iron fist" so that there is what he calls a *carceral-assistential complex* that engages in various methods to control the dispossessed and dishonored (p. 97).

The new hyperghetto appears more like a prison than ever before, as the economic basis of the ghetto has shifted from directly servicing the

Black community (as was done by Black professionals within the traditional ghetto) to service to the state (with growing jobs within *public* bureaucracies). "At best," Wacquant (2001) argues, "the hyperghetto now serves the *negative economic function of storage of a surplus population* devoid of market utility, in which respect it also increasingly resembles the prison system" (p. 105). The emerging social control bureaucracies are "largely staffed by the new Black middle class whose expansion hinges, not on its capacity to service its community, but on its willingness to assume the vexing role of *custodian* of the Black urban sub-proletariat on behalf of white society" (p. 106), via "on-the-ground extensions of the penal system" (e.g., probation and parole officers), along with "snitches" hired by the police (p. 107).

Further evidence that the ghetto resembles a prison is illustrated by a sort of "prisonization of public housing," plus retirement homes, homeless shelters, etc. all of which have methods of surveillance that are borrowed from the penal system. Indeed, "projects" have been fenced up with security guards, ID card checks, electronic monitoring, random searches, resident "counts" just like in prisons. Bentham's "panopticon" design for prisons has been applied here, along with many public schools in the ghetto which serve more to control than to educate. Such elaborate control mechanisms habituate "the children of the hyperghetto to the demeanor, tactics, and interactive style of the correctional officers many of them are bound to encounter shortly after their school days are over" (Wacquant, 2001, p. 108).

During the Great Migration (1916–1970), approximately 6 million Blacks moved from the South for job opportunities (Harshbarger & Perry, 2019). In the early twentieth century, discriminatory zoning policies were legal (Comen, 2019). Laws and housing policies segregated Black residents moving to major metropolitan areas. Even after the Supreme Court prohibited racist zoning policies, government officials excluded residents from neighborhoods through the federal Home Owners' Loan Corporation (HOLC). Loan officers, appraisers, and real estate agents utilized HOLC "residential security" maps that outlined investment risks in neighborhoods—frequently redlining Black neighborhoods as "hazardous areas. Today 64% of the neighborhoods designated as high risk by HOLC remain minority neighborhoods. Segregation persists in some of the largest cities in the United States more than 50 years after the Fair Housing Act of 1968 outlawed housing discrimination on the basis of race, sex, national origin, and religion.

As white families moved from inner cities to outlying suburbs, many of the most segregated cities experienced a period of economic decline (Comen, 2019). Inner city residents faced crumbling infrastructure and a depleted tax base when wealthier families moved. In 1990, 95% of Blacks in the Northeast, Midwest, and West lived in metropolitan areas. Across the nation, 57% of Blacks lived in central cities (Semuels, 2016).

> Segregation retains a key role in the maintenance of broader systems
> of stratification. Neighborhoods occupied by racial and ethnic groups

are not only geographically separate but qualitatively different, so that members of different groups face dramatically different life chances as a function of differential exposure to educational and employment opportunities, pollution and other physical threats, crime, and social disorganization. There is strong evidence that these racial disparities in neighborhood opportunity structures—all rooted in persistent segregation—contribute in substantial ways to sharp racial differences in education, income, wealth, health, and general well-being. (Krysan & Crowder, 2017, pp. 4–5)

Residential segregation perpetuates inequality in labor markets and schools (Stebbins & Comen, 2020). Because people are more likely to hire someone like themselves, residential segregation is linked to employment segregation. Substandard schools, in turn, contribute to disparities in income, unemployment, and incarceration. Neighborhoods are the entry points to schools, transportation, jobs, health care, parks, and other amenities (Schuetz, 2017). Where we live determines the classmates with whom we interact daily, our casual social interactions, and professional networks. Blacks live in more segregated enclaves, and those neighborhoods are more geographically distant from other neighborhoods.

Cities in which Blacks constitute a majority of the population are increasing (Harshbarger & Perry, 2019). In 1970, there were 460 Black-majority cities; in 2017, the number was 1,262 (with 114 added since 2010). The Black population increased only 1.5% since 1970. The increased number of Black-majority cities was due to shifts in the population, including a new migration of Blacks back to the South. Nationwide, 16.8% of Black Americans live in majority Black neighborhoods (Comen, 2019). In Detroit, the percentage is 52%, compared to 48% in Chicago, 41% in Baltimore, 39% in New Orleans, and 30% in Philadelphia.

In the 100 largest metropolitan areas in 2013–2017, the average Black resident lived in a neighborhood that was 45% Black—down from 52% in 2000 (Frey, 2018). Neighborhoods were more diverse than in 2000 primarily because of an increase in Hispanic residents (from 12% to 17%). Segregation levels are also measured by the index of dissimilarity, which measures the concentration of races within small geographic areas (typically census tracts of 5,000 residents) (Schuetz, 2017). Segregation within cities and neighborhoods provides a public illustration of segregation of the United States via jails and prisons. That is, the intentional work required to segregate cities and neighborhoods as well as to ensure the segregated life outcomes that are directly correlated to housing segregation is akin to the intentional work required to make the prison industrial complex serve as the slavery mechanism in the third millennium.

Further, the COVID-19 crisis hit segregated residential neighborhoods hard. Social distancing to slow the spread of infection was difficult in multi-unit dwellings where people shared common spaces (Gould & Wilson, 2020). About 55% of Black American households live in single-unit dwellings compared to 74% of white households; 29% of Black American households (more than double the rate of white households) live in multi-unit structures. In addition, Blacks are twice as likely as Whites to live in households with three or more generations.

> The disparate racial impact of the virus is deeply rooted in historic and ongoing social and economic injustices. Persistent racial disparities in health status, access to health care, wealth, employment, wages, housing, income, and poverty all contribute to greater susceptibility to the virus—both economically and physically. (p. 1)

To make matters worse, in August 2019, the Black unemployment rate was 5.4%, a historical low. After the COVID-19 pandemic, the rate in May 2020 was 16.8%. Historically, the unemployment rate of Black workers has been twice as high as that of white workers (Gould & Wilson, 2020).

Race and class are defining features of the penal process (Natapoff, 2017). The criminalization of marginality and the punitive containment of the poor serve as social policy at the lower end of the class spectrum.

> Wealthy and well-educated African American men may be discriminated against based on their skin color. But their class status, residence in wealthy neighborhoods, speech, dress, knowledge of their rights, and access to counsel buffers them against the harshest impact of systemic discrimination. Their class gives them more access to protective rules and the means to invoke a robust legal response. Conversely, poor, undereducated Black men, especially those without a high school diploma, are most likely to be swept up into the criminal system and treated lawlessly when they get there. (p. 83)

James Forman (2012) comments that the class aspects of mass incarceration distinguish it from previous forms of institutional race discrimination like Jim Crow. Mass incarceration does not have the same impact on middle- and upper-class African Americans as it does on lower-income African Americans.

> One of mass incarceration's defining features is that, unlike Jim Crow, its reach is largely confined to the poorest, least-educated segments of the African American community. High school dropouts account for most of the rise in African American incarceration rates. . . . For an African American man with some college education, the lifetime chance of going to prison actually decreased slightly between 1979 and 1999 (from 6% to 5%). A Black man born in the late 1960s who dropped out of high school has a 59% chance of going to prison in his lifetime whereas a Black man who attended college has only a 5% chance. (p. 132)

Researchers looked at the relationship of education and incarceration and the cumulative effect of the inequalities produced by incarceration (Western & Pettit, 2010). From 1980 to 2008, there was almost no change in incarceration rates for people with a college education. About 10% of African American men with a high school diploma were incarcerated in 2008 compared to 5% in 1980. In 2008, 37% of African American men who dropped out of high school were in prison or jail compared to 10% in 1980. The researchers calculated the cumulative chance of imprisonment for two birth cohorts: (1) people born from 1945 to 1949 and (2) people born from 1975–1979. The cumulative chances of imprisonment were calculated up to age 34. For group 1 (reaching age 34 at the end of the 1970s), about 1 in 10 African American men served time in prison. For group 2 (reaching age 34 around 2009), the lifetime risk of imprisonment for African American men increased to 1 in 4. Incarceration in prison became a normal life event for African American men who dropped out of high school—68% of the men in group 2 had prison records.

Racial and class disparities in incarceration "have produced a generation of social outliers whose collective experience is wholly different from the rest of American society" (Western & Pettit, 2010, p. 12). The penal system removes primarily the underclass from society; the inequality created by incarceration is often invisible to mainstream society. The criminal process functions as a powerful engine of social inequality, which Loïc Wacquant labels a self-perpetuating cycle of social and legal marginality (Dolovich & Natapoff, 2017). People with prison records are less likely to be employed and/or experience significant declines in earning. Imprisonment increases the likelihood of divorce. Children, to some degree, are "prisonized" by exposure to prison routines through visitation and the parole supervision of their parents. For most of society, this reality remains hidden from view. "Much of the political debate about crime policy ignores the contemporary scale of criminal punishment, its unequal distribution, and its negative social and economic effects" (p. 18). The inequalities produced by incarceration have three characteristics: (1) the inequality is invisible to standard methods for assessing the economic well-being of a population, (2) the inequality is cumulative, and (3) the inequality transmits the penalties of a prison record from one generation to the next. The inequalities are sustained over lifetimes and passed through families.

Having a criminal record, especially a prison record, has always been a barrier to seeking re-entry into society. Jeremy Travis (2002) noted that as prisons and community corrections expanded significantly with increasing numbers of people under its control, so did laws and regulations that diminished the rights and privileges of ex-offenders. The expansive reach of these punishments included denial of public housing, public assistance, and the right to vote—all instruments of social exclusion.

> When Congress dismantled the six-decades-old entitlement to a safety net for the poor, the poor with criminal histories were thought less deserving than others. . . . There was little hesitation in using federal benefits to enhance punishments or federal funds to encourage new criminal sanctions by the states. (p. 19)

What Travis doesn't say here—but says elsewhere along with contemporaries such as Christopher Bennett (2017)—is that the group of offenders that feels the heaviest brunt of this exclusion are racial minorities. Todd Clear (2002) and other researchers such as Cara Jardine (2018) have pointed out that as many as one-fourth of the adult male residents in many urban, poverty-stricken neighborhoods are either in prison or in jail at some time during the year, creating ripples of negative impact on the financial and familial wellbeing of these areas.

Among the methods of controlling the surplus population is legislation that defines what a "crime" is and sentencing structures that define what crimes are "serious." Many sentencing structures have a built-in class and racial bias (Reiman & Leighton, 2020). This is especially the case with drug laws, which throughout history have targeted mainly the drugs used by minorities and the poor (Dollar, 2018; Helmer, 1975).

More Evidence of Slavery in the New Millennium: Disenfranchisement

The disenfranchisement of felons is not a new phenomenon. This course of action dates back to Ancient Greece, a time in which criminals and convicts were pronounced "infamous" and stripped of their right to vote and other rights as well (Harvard Law Review, 1989). This tradition and others informed the rationale behind current disenfranchisement laws. A primary belief is that disenfranchising felons is necessary to maintain the "purity of the ballot box." Ex-offenders are believed to be impure because of committing the crime that led to their incarceration. They are, therefore, incapable of voting with the rest of society and contributing to the "common good." In 1978, the Fifth Circuit Court argued that the state could exclude ex-offenders because (like insane persons) they have raised questions about their ability to vote responsibly.

About 2.5%—1 of every 40—of the voting age population is disenfranchised because of a current or previous felony conviction (Uggen et al., 2016; see also chapter 9). African Americans have been affected disproportionately—2.2 million Black citizens are banned from voting (Chung, 2019). Blacks of voting age are four times more likely to lose their voting rights than the rest of the adult population; 1 of every 13 Black adults is disenfranchised. In four states the number is more than 1 in 5: Florida (21%), Kentucky (26%), Tennessee (21%), and Virginia (22%). Felony disenfranchisement laws are antiquated and have a disgraceful past. These laws not only have a disproportionate impact on communities of color and low-income communities but also have no criminal deterrent or rehabilitative value (Bradford, 2019, p. 2).

In modern times felon disenfranchisement laws have had the greatest effect on African Americans due to the fact that this minority group is disproportionately represented in the criminal justice system. In 2002, all but two states had laws that deprived felons of the right to vote while serving a prison or jail sentence for a felony offense (Petersilia, 2009; Petersilia & Threatt, 2017). A mid-1990s study found that while 2% of *all* adults had been disenfranchised because of a felony conviction (mostly drug convictions as we discussed earlier), *about 13% of all Black men had been disenfranchised.* In six states the percentage of Black men disenfranchised was 25% or more, *going higher than 30% in Alabama and Florida during the 1990s* (Fellner, 1996; Fellner & Mauer, 1998). In 2004 about five million people were disenfranchised, with two million being African Americans (Manza & Uggen, 2006). The disenfranchisement rate for African American males was nearly twice that of whites. In some states that disenfranchised felons indefinitely, up to 40% of African American men permanently lost their right to vote (Wheelock, 2005). Disenfranchisement has no deterrent effect and does little but make the ex-offender experience second-class citizenship and even more isolation.

The impact of the high disenfranchisement rate for African Americans is especially felt during election seasons. The impact of mass incarceration and the attendant increases in felon disenfranchisement have had political consequences. One study found probable influence of disenfranchisement policies on seven U.S. Senate races from 1970 to 1998 in addition to the presidential election of 2000 (Chung, 2019). Prior to that election, a voter fraud law required Florida counties to purge voter registries of duplicate registrations, deceased voters, and felons. The office of the secretary of state circulated a list of 57,700 felons to be used in the computer-aided purging of centralized voter files (Palast, 2000). More than half (54%) of the people on the list were African Americans or Hispanics—many wrongly barred from voting because they were not felons. Bush won Florida by 537 votes.

> Although we have specified the political consequences of felon disenfranchisement, we have only touched on the origins of these laws and the mass incarceration phenomenon that gives such force to them today. These questions are important for situating felon disenfranchisement within a broader model of social control of dispossessed groups. Proponents of the "new penology" argue that the focus of criminological interest has recently shifted from the rehabilitation of individual offenders to the social control of aggregate groups. . . . Restricted access to the ballot box is but a piece of a larger pattern of social exclusion for America's vast correctional population. (Uggen & Manza, 2002, p. 796)

The right to vote is under assault from disenfranchisement laws to voter fraud laws to voter ID laws to closing polling places early to purging names from voter rolls (Anderson, 2018). A 3-judge federal appeals court in 2016 said of a 2013 North Carolina voting law that it targeted African Americans with almost surgical precision. Before passing the law, the legislature requested data by race on a number of voting practices. The resulting legislation restricted voting and registration in 5 areas that disproportionately affected African Americans. Across the entire country in 2016, the number of Black voters decreased by 66%; some states and cities saw even sharper declines.

In a 2018 ballot initiative, 65% of Florida voters approved Amendment 4 to restore voting rights to felons who completed their sentences, parole, and probation except for those convicted of felony sexual offenses or murder (Lockhart, 2019). Amendment 4 would have allowed 1.4 million Floridians to regain voting rights. However, legislation in 2019, SB 7066, required people with felony records to pay all fines and fees connected to their sentence before rights could be restored. Critics assert the measure is the equivalent of a poll tax. Estimates suggested that more than 500,000 people were affected—some of whom may never be able to clear their debts. Lawsuits filed claim SB 7066 is unconstitutional and disproportionately affects the poor and people of color.

It is important to emphasize that the right to vote has been one of the central and most important features of democratic societies. The importance of this right is demonstrated in the struggles for women, Blacks, and other marginalized groups to gain this right. It cannot be denied that one method of controlling a given population is by excluding them from participation in this most fundamental aspect of civil society. This was done for more than 100 years following the end of the Civil War; former slaves were prohibited from voting through various mechanisms such as the grandfather clause (i.e., an ex-slave could only vote if his grandfather was once a registered voter and various sorts of literacy tests that ex-slaves were subjected to (e.g., reading ability, knowledge of the Constitution, etc.).

The Fourteenth Amendment granted citizenship to formerly enslaved people, but it is also the basis for withholding voting rights if convicted of a crime. In *Richardson v. Ramirez* (1974), the Supreme Court held that the Fourteenth Amendment explicitly authorizes denying citizens' voting rights due to criminal conviction. Since the Constitution does not offer a path to reverse felony disenfranchisement, reform must come from the states (Taylor, 2018).

> Many states continue to disenfranchise individuals with felony drug convictions. . . . Legal scholar Michelle Alexander explains how criminal justice laws have worked to re-establish the structural inequalities that were supposedly undone by the repealing of Jim Crow laws during the civil rights movement. Domestic drug prohibition policies like criminalization and police militarization present a threat to the civil rights gains made in the past five decades for Black Americans. (Piaggio & Vidwans, 2019, p. 52)

Research has examined the impact of disenfranchisement on the participation of those eligible to vote (King & Erickson, 2016). Voting is a type of prosocial behavior; People empowered to vote feel as if they are part of a community. People denied voting rights are isolated, which can result in distrust in the democratic process (Bradford, 2019).

> The right to vote is a fundamental function of citizens in the democratic process. It gives each person a voice, a choice and a sense of belonging. For African Americans, it also represents a badge of freedom that many of their ancestors fought and died for. . . .
>
> Disenfranchisement after an individual has been released into society serves only as blanket over-punishment that disproportionately affects Black America by diluting its political power. If we are to believe that post-incarceration rehabilitation is truly a goal of America's justice system, stripping ex-felons of their right to vote seems to directly undermine that goal. By demoting ex-felons to second-class citizens, we are reminding them that they are not truly ever welcome back into the community. (Jackson, 2017, pp. 105–106)

Disenfranchisement is a literal "exile" from mainstream society (Travis, 2002).

Imprisonment and supervision have become a very common experience for racial minorities—a continuation of the deprivations of slavery that marked the early years of this country. Stevenson (2014) suggests many people are unaware of the legacy of particular institutional factors.

> I believe that there are four institutions in American history that have shaped our approach to race and justice but remain poorly understood. The first, of course, is slavery. This was followed by the reign of terror that shaped the lives of people of color following the collapse of Reconstruction until World War II. . . . The third institution, "Jim Crow," is the legalized racial segregation and suppression of basic rights that defined the American apartheid era. . . . The fourth institution is mass incarceration. Going into any prison is deeply confusing if you know anything about the racial demographics of America. The extreme over-representation of people of color, the disproportionate sentencing of racial minorities, the targeted prosecution of drug crimes in poor communities, the criminalization of new immigrants and undocumented people, the collateral consequences of voter disenfranchisement, and the barriers to re-entry can only be fully understood through the lens of our racial history. (pp. 299, 300, 301)

NOTE

[1] Stevenson founded the Equal Justice Initiative in 1989 to provide legal representation to people illegally convicted, unfairly sentenced, or abused in jails and prisons. He successfully argued the case of *Miller v. Alabama*, in which the Supreme Court ruled that juveniles cannot be sentenced to life in prison without the possibility of parole. He wrote *Just Mercy: A Story of Justice and Redemption*, which was a *New York Times* best seller and became a motion picture starring Michael B. Jordan and Jamie Foxx in 2019.

5

Legalized Homicide
The Death Penalty

In European and Indo-European societies, where the United States borrows its practices, the penalty of death for crimes ranging from petty to serious dates back to at least the eighteenth century BCE (see text box on the following page). It seems that every imaginable method of execution has been utilized—stoning, drawing and quartering, beheading, burning at the stake, crucifixion, drowning, burying alive, breaking on a wheel, garroting, gibbeting, disemboweling, etc. (Newman, 2008). Most executions and other forms of punishment were conducted in public as a form of general deterrence.

During the medieval period, executions became ceremonial rituals, especially during the Inquisition. On many occasions the planned execution would be "announced thirty days in advance and would be scheduled to coincide with such momentous events as the coronation or marriage of a king or the birth of a royal child. "The pageantry would but thinly disguise the raw violence of the executions with which it culminated" (Johnson, 1998, p. 15). Such a "pageant" would begin with a "grand procession" leading up to the location of the execution.

After the Middle Ages, public execution became less ritualistic, although often just as gruesome. The head of the executed would be prominently displayed following a beheading. Eventually public sensibilities changed; morbid rituals mostly disappeared. For example, in England many executions became "proper and dignified undertakings, marked by the ringing of church bells, special prayers for the condemned, and the final dropping of a handkerchief by the prisoner—if he was not overcome by fear—to signal his readiness to die" (Johnson, 1998, p. 17).

The Origins of the Death Penalty

Toward the end of his reign (around 1750 BC), King Hammurabi of Babylon created one of the earliest written legal codes. (Hammurabi is included in the carvings of historic lawgivers on the south wall of the Supreme Court.) The Code of Hammurabi prescribed the death penalty for 25 different crimes. The death penalty was also part of the Hittite Code (fourteenth century BC), the Draconian Code of Athens (seventh century BC), which made death the only punishment for all crimes, and the Roman Law of the Twelve Tablets (fifth century BC). Death sentences were carried out by such means as crucifixion, drowning, beating to death, burning alive, and impalement.

During the tenth century, hanging became the usual method of execution in Britain. In the following century, William the Conqueror would not allow persons to be hanged or otherwise executed for any crime except in times of war. By the sixteenth century, under the reign of Henry VIII, an estimated 72,000 people were executed. Some common methods of execution at that time were boiling, burning at the stake, hanging, beheading, and drawing and quartering. Executions were carried out for such capital offenses as marrying a Jew, not confessing to a crime, and treason.

The number of capital crimes in Britain continued to rise throughout the next two centuries. By the 1700s, 222 crimes were punishable by death, including stealing, cutting down a tree, and robbing a rabbit warren. Because of the severity of the death penalty, many juries would not convict defendants if the offense was not serious. This led to reforms of Britain's death penalty. From 1823 to 1837, the death penalty was eliminated for over 100 of the 222 crimes punishable by death.

Source: Death Penalty Information Center (DPIC, n.d.)

In Colonial America, a large number of crimes were theoretically punishable by death. In the Massachusetts Bay Colony, the crimes punishable by death included statutory rape, rebellion, adultery, buggery, idolatry, witchcraft, bestiality, man-stealing, and blasphemy (Costanzo, 1997). Despite the capital laws, these crimes were very rarely actually punished by an execution. One exception occurred during the Salem witchcraft trials, when 19 people (mostly women) were executed (Shelden & Vasiliev, 2018).

Executions in the colonies were public and carried out on scaffolds located in the central part of town. They were generally quite restrained displays. The first execution occurred in 1608 when Captain George Kendall was executed in Virginia (Costanzo, 1997). In 1612, Virginia passed the "Divine, Moral and Martial Laws," which applied the death penalty for such petty offenses as stealing grapes, killing chickens, and trading with Indians (DPIC, n.d.). Although there were always a few members of the nobility that met their death via a hanging, for the most part the vast

Table 5-1	**Executions in America, by Race: 1608–1972**	
White	41%	(5,902)
Black	49%	(7,084)
Hispanic	2%	(295)
Other (includes Asian Pacific and unknown)	8%	(1208)
Total Executions		**14,489**

Source: DPIC, 2019a

majority have always been outsiders to the mainstream society, such as foreigners, minorities, or the poor—people "for whom spectators might feel the least sympathy" (Masur, 1989, p. 39).

Lynching: Forerunner to the Death Chamber

Lynching was once a common form of punishment—part of what has been called *vigilantism*, a form of "frontier" or "street" justice. The term originated during the American Revolution and was named after Charles Lynch and his "Virginia associates," who took matters into their own hands when confronting Tories and other "criminal elements." In early American history, cattle rustlers, gamblers, horse thieves, and others were targeted. In the early years of westward expansion, there was an absence of any kind of legitimate legal authority in the form of law enforcement or courts; lynching became a common method of social control (Miethe & Lu, 2005).

From the 1830s to the 1850s, the majority of people lynched in the United States were whites (Gibson, 1979). Lynchings occurred across the United States (only Massachusetts, New Hampshire, Rhode Island, and Vermont had no deaths from lynchings). Shortly after the end of the Civil War, lynching took on racial and ethnic overtones. The most common targets were former slaves (Zangrando, 1991). During slavery, plantations maintained tight social control of slaves. After emancipation, lynching became the means of controlling Blacks.

From 1882 to 1951, there were 4,730 people lynched in the United States: 3,437 Blacks and 1,293 whites (Gibson, 1979). The largest number of lynchings (230) occurred in 1892: 161 Blacks and 69 whites. The number of Black lynching victims was more than 2.5 times the number of white victims. The majority of lynchings took place in the Southern states. Most lynchings took place in small towns in isolated rural communities of the South, with Mississippi leading the way, followed closely by Georgia, Texas, Louisiana, and Alabama. Others mainly took place in the border states of Maryland, West Virginia, Ohio, Indiana, Illinois, and Kansas. The majority of people participating in lynch law were poor and illiterate, similar to their African American victims. Black men were seen as economic

competitors and any progress made was bitterly resented. Racial antago-
nism made raising a mob a simple process, a macabre form of local amuse-
ment to break the monotony of rural life.

Fear was another driving force behind lynching—fear of African Americans achieving higher social status, fear of Black men associating with
white women, and fear of African Americans "taking over" (Freedman,
2013; Waldrep, 2006). Black people were lynched for a variety of reasons,
and often for no reason at all. Those involved in lynchings were rarely ever
indicted. Judges, prosecutors, jurors, and witnesses were all white. A
1930s study of one hundred lynchings found that in at least half of the
cases local police officers participated; officers condoned the mob action in
all of the cases (Raper, 1933).

The lynching of Black men accused of raping white women was notorious throughout this period (Costanzo, 1997). Blacks were subject to
lethal violence—whether extralegal through lynching or through legal
executions. One study looked at Georgia and North Carolina between
1882 and 1930 (Beck et al., 1989). The researchers found that rape was
the alleged behavior for 41% of Blacks lynched in Georgia compared to
12% of Blacks executed for the crime of rape. In North Carolina, 39% of
African Americans were lynched for an alleged rape, and 22% of executions of African Americans were for the crime of rape.

Lynching became one of the most gruesome methods of vigilantism in
American history.

> By the 1890s lynchers increasingly employed burning, torture, and dis-
> memberment to prolong suffering and excite a "festive atmosphere"
> among the killers and onlookers. White families brought small chil-
> dren to watch, newspapers sometimes carried advance notices, rail-
> road agents sold excursion tickets to announced lynching sites, and
> mobs cut off Black victims' fingers, toes, ears, or genitalia as souvenirs.
> Nor was it necessarily the handiwork of a local rabble; not infre-
> quently, the mob was encouraged or led by people prominent in the
> area's political and business circles. Lynching had become a ritual of
> interracial social control and recreation rather than simply a punish-
> ment for crime. (Zangrando, 1991, p. 685)

One source found 4,743 lynchings in the United States from 1882 until
1968; 1,297 whites were lynched, and 3,446 Blacks were lynched (Tuskegee Institute, 2010). From 1882–1886, 39% of the 776 people lynched
were Black. The number of lynchings peaked at 876 a decade later, when
the percentage of Black victims rose to 69%. Lynchings decreased steadily,
while the percentages of Black victims increased. Fifty years later (1933–
1937), there were 77 lynchings—73 of the victims were Black. The five
states with the most lynchings were Mississippi (581), Georgia (531),
Texas (493), Louisiana (391), and Alabama (347).

Several researchers have argued that there were a large number of un-
reported cases of lynching in the South, especially between 1865 and 1875.

Table 5-2	African American Lynching Victims by Southern State, 1877–1950	
	Alabama	361
	Arkansas	492
	Florida	311
	Georgia	589
	Kentucky	168
	Louisiana	549
	Mississippi	654
	North Carolina	123
	South Carolina	185
	Tennessee	233
	Texas	335
	Virginia	84
	Total	**4084**

Source: EJI, 2017.

This was a period when whites feared intervention by the federal government and therefore either buried or burned the bodies of the victims (Bowers et al., 1984; Wright, 1997). The Equal Justice Initiative (EJI, 2017) analyzed available data on lynching and conducted supplemental research of local newspapers, historical archives, and court records plus interviews with local historians, survivors, and descendants of victims. Between 1877 (the end of Reconstruction) and 1950, researchers documented 4,084 racial terror lynchings in 12 Southern states. The number is 800 higher than previous reports.

EJI also documented more than 300 racial terror lynchings in other states during the same time frame.

> Racial terror lynching was a tool used to enforce Jim Crow laws and racial segregation—a tactic for maintaining racial control by victimizing the entire African American community, not merely punishment of an alleged perpetrator for a crime. Our research confirms that many victims of terror lynchings were murdered without being accused of any crime; they were killed for minor social transgressions or for demanding basic rights and fair treatment. (p. 5)

Mississippi, Georgia, and Louisiana had the highest total *number* of African American lynching victims. Mississippi, Florida, and Arkansas had the highest per capita *rates* of lynching by *total* population. Arkansas, Florida, and Mississippi had the highest per capita *rates* of lynching by *African American population*.

Lynching "served to give dramatic warning to all Black inhabitants that the iron clad system of white supremacy was not to be challenged by deed, word or even thought" (Friedman, 1970, p. 191). Indeed, as Ralph Ellison (1986) noted, "the ultimate goal of lynchers is that of achieving ritual purification through destroying the lynchers' identification with the basic humanity of their victims. Hence their deafness to cries of pain, their stoniness before the sight and stench of burning flesh, their exhilarated and grotesque self-righteousness" (p. 178). Lynchings sent a strong message of fear into the hearts and minds of African Americans in the South. Lynchings enabled the white south to maintain a caste society, not unlike slavery, for decades to come (Shelden, 1979). The terror generated also contributed significantly to the Great Migration (EJI, 2017). Within a single decade, the Black populations of Georgia and South Carolina declined by 22% and 24%. The United States Department of Labor observed that one of the reasons for the exodus was insecurity due to mob violence and lynchings.

Shortly after the end of the Civil War, an anti-lynching campaign began. Eventually organizations such as the National Association of Colored Women (NACW), the National Association for the Advancement of Colored People (NAACP), the Council for Interracial Cooperation (CIC), and the Association of Southern Women for the Prevention of Lynching participated (Barber, 1973; Rable, 1985; Reed, 1968). By the 1930s, the effects of these campaigns had an impact; the number of lynchings began to drop significantly. In the early 1930s, the Costigan-Wagner Act called for federal trials "for any law enforcement officers who failed to exercise their responsibilities during a lynching incident." Congress did not pass the bill despite overwhelming public support. A national poll taken in 1937 found that "65 per cent of all southerners supported legislation that would have made lynching a federal crime" (Tolnay & Beck, 1995, p. 202).

Lynching soon became a relic from a severely violent past, but the decline of lynching was replaced by capital punishment. "Southern legislatures looked to shift to capital punishment as a means of using ostensibly legal and unbiased court proceedings to reach the same goal as vigilante violence: satisfying the lust for revenge" Stevenson, 2017, p. 17). There is considerable evidence that at roughly the same time lynchings declined, legal executions began to increase. In the 1890s, the number of lynchings exceeded legal executions by a ratio of about 1.5: 1 (Miethe & Lu, 2005). By the second decade of the twentieth century the numbers were about the same. By the 1930s legal executions far exceeded lynchings. (See figure 5-1.)

Throughout the history of the death penalty in the United States, African Americans have been proportionately far more likely to receive the death penalty. It has become, in short, a form of *legalized lynching.* "More than eight in ten American lynchings between 1889 and 1918 occurred in the South, and more than eight in ten of the more than 1,400 legal executions carried out in this country since 1976 have been in the South" (Stevenson, 2017, p. 20).

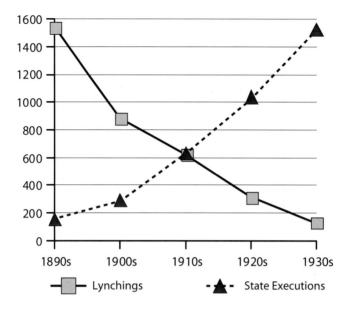

Figure 5-1   Lynchings and State-Based Executions

Source: Miethe & Lu, 2005, p. 98

Capital Punishment

There has been a long history of attempts to abolish punishment by death. The roots of the movement to abolish capital punishment are firmly implanted in the writings of classical European writers such Montesquieu, Voltaire, and Bentham, in addition to English prison reformer John Howard. In 1764, Cesare Beccaria made perhaps the strongest anti-death penalty statement in his book *On Crimes and Punishment.* He argued that the death penalty was "an act of war on the part of society" as it "is not useful because of the example of savagery it gives to men" (cited in Ishay, 1997, pp. 125–126). In America, the first attempt to reform capital punishment was Thomas Jefferson's bill to revise Virginia's death penalty. The bill proposed that the death penalty be applied for just two crimes (murder and treason), but it was defeated by one vote. Benjamin Rush, one of the signatories of the Declaration of Independence and a founder of the Pennsylvania Prison Society, was probably the first to challenge the belief that the death penalty was a deterrent. In fact, Rush may have been the first to introduce the concept of the "brutalization effect," suggesting that the death penalty actually causes an increase in homicides. Largely due to the efforts of Rush, along with Benjamin Franklin and William Bradford, Pennsylvania in 1794 repealed the death penalty for all offenses except first-degree murder (DPIC, n.d.).

Michigan became the first state to abolish the death penalty for all crimes except treason in 1846. Later in the century, Rhode Island and Wisconsin abolished the death penalty for all crimes. The abolitionist movement picked up steam through the Progressive Era (1900–1920). Six states completely outlawed the death penalty, and three limited it to treason and first-degree murder of a law enforcement officer. Five of the six abolitionist states reinstated their death penalty by 1920. In the 1920s, there were 1,289 executions (Wilson, 2017).

By the 1950s, the abolitionist movement again began to gather momentum, supported by a growing change in public opinion. Many nations around the world abolished the death penalty, while in the United States the number of executions dropped from 1,684 in the 1930s to 1,296 in the 1940s to 724 in the 1950s, and to 191 in the 1960s (Wilson, 2017). There were no executions after February 6, 1967, until 1977.

Two landmark Supreme Court decisions in the 1970s rekindled the controversy surrounding the death penalty: *Furman v. Georgia* (1972) and *Gregg v. Georgia* (1976). In *Furman* the nine justices each wrote separate opinions. The Court did not rule that the death penalty *in and of itself* constituted cruel and unusual punishment; rather, it ruled that the punishment *as it was administered* constituted cruel and unusual punishment, in violation of the Eighth and Fourteenth Amendments of the Constitution.

The response by the states was almost immediate; appeals began flowing into the court system. Within four years of *Furman,* the Supreme Court made perhaps its most significant ruling on the matter. In *Gregg v. Georgia* on July 2, 1976, the Court upheld the Georgia statute calling for the death penalty for murder. The Court ruled: "A punishment must not be excessive, but this does not mean that the states must seek the minimal standards available. The imposition of the death penalty for the crime of murder does not violate the Constitution." On January 17, 1977, Gary Gilmore was executed by a firing squad in Utah.

Several United States Supreme Court rulings in the twenty-first century have narrowed the application of the death penalty, finding it unconstitutional and violating cruel and unusual punishment for some offenders (NCSL, 2020b). The court abolished the death penalty for mentally disabled offenders (*Atkins v. Virginia,* 2002), juvenile offenders (*Roper v. Simmons,* 2005), and for the rape of a child where death was not intended (*Kennedy v. Louisiana,* 2008). The Court also ruled on procedures in capital punishment cases.

Lockett v. Ohio (1978) held that a range of mitigating factors (including aspects of a defendant's character, his or her record, and circumstances of the offense that suggested a reason for a sentence less than death) must be considered before imposing the death penalty. *Lockett* made individualized consideration of the background and character of the accused an indispensable part of the process of deciding a sentence of death. In *Eddings v. Oklahoma* (1982), the Court ruled that the trial court erred when it did not consider the mitigating circumstances of the defendant's unhappy childhood and emotional disturbance. In *McKinney v. Arizona* (2020), the question was whether a state appellate court could reweigh aggravating and mitigating circumstances or whether a jury would have to resentence the defendant. The Court ruled 5–4 that after the finding of a capital sentencing error, a state appellate court rather than a jury may assess aggravating and mitigating evidence.

The court also ruled that juries not judges must determine whether to impose a sentence of death. *Ring v. Arizona* (2002) established that the Sixth Amendment provides the right to a jury determination of all facts necessary to impose a death sentence. In *Hurst v. Florida* (2016), the Court struck down Florida's death-penalty statute for violating that constitutional guarantee. Prior to *Hurst*, three states (Alabama, Delaware, and Florida) permitted judges to impose death sentences when jury recommendations for death were not unanimous and to override jury recommendations for life. Arizona and Florida refused to apply *Ring* to cases that had already completed the direct appeal stage of judicial review by 2002 when *Ring* was decided. There are 99 men and one woman on death row in eight states who were condemned to death by judges without authorization of a jury (Radelet & Cohn, 2019). Since the resumption of capital punishment in 1976, there have been 18 executions following judicial overrides. Alabama has executed 11 men whom judges sentenced to death despite jury recommendations for life, followed by Florida with four jury-override executions. Missouri has executed three prisoners who were sentenced to death in judge-only sentences. In January 2020, the Florida Supreme Court overturned a 2016 ruling that had required jury unanimity in capital punishment cases (Sarat, 2020).

Since 2015, 25 states enacted 65 laws addressing capital punishment (NCSL, 2020b). Legislation included expanding or limiting aggravating factors, modifying execution methods and procedures, changing trial and appellate procedures, modifying laws to comply with litigation outcomes, and repealing capital punishment.

Modern Era of the Death Penalty

Since 1976 more than 8,000 people have been sentenced to death; 1,527 have been executed (DPIC, 2020a). There were 3 executions from 1977–1979; 117 executions in the 1980s; 478 executions in the 1990s; 590 executions from 2000–2009; 324 executions from 2010–2019; 15 executions through November 30, 2020. The number of death sentences per year has declined dramatically—from 295 in 1998 to 34 in 2019; the number of executions decreased from 98 in 1999 to 22 in 2019. Texas leads the country in executions since 1976 with 572; Virginia is a distant second with 113. The South accounts for almost 82% of all executions since 1976 (1,246); it also has consistently had the highest murder rate in the country.

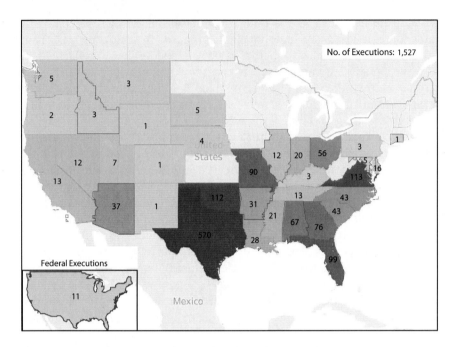

Figure 5-2   US Executions from 1977 through November 30, 2020

Source: DPIC, 2020c

Geographical differences are not limited to states and regions of the country. The likelihood of a death sentence or execution depends more on the county in which the crime takes place than on the severity of the offense (EJI, 2020). Only 2% of all the counties in the United States have been responsible for the majority of cases leading to executions since 1976. Harris County (TX) has been the site of 129 executions; Dallas County (TX) is second with 62 (DPIC, 2020b). Of the 10 counties with the most executions, 7 are in Texas; 2 of the others are in Oklahoma, and 1 is in Missouri. Death sentences are more frequent in urban, densely populous counties, counties with large Black populations, and counties with more white homicide victims (Shelden & Vasiliev, 2018). Justice Stephen Breyer voiced his concern in his dissent to *Reed v. Louisiana*, (2017): "The arbitrary role that geography plays in the imposition of the death penalty, along with the other serious problems I have previously described, has led me to conclude that the Court should consider the basic question of the death penalty's constitutionality."

As of July 2020, there were 2,591 people on death row (DPIC, 2020a). California led the way with 724 on death row, followed by Florida (346), Texas (214), Alabama (172), North Carolina (145), and Pennsylvania (142). In the modern era of the death penalty (i.e., from 1976 onwards),

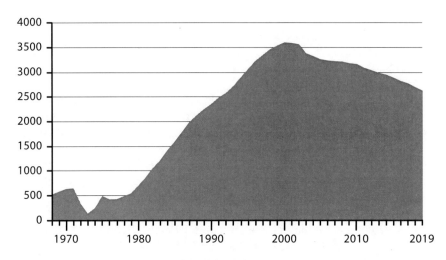

Figure 5-3   Death Row Inmate Population by Year

Source: DPIC, 2020e

the size of death row peaked in 2000 with 3,593 prisoners; the number has been slowly decreasing ever since.

In 2020, there were 28 death penalty states plus the federal government; 22 states have abolished the death penalty, and 3 others (California in 2019, Oregon in 2011, and Pennsylvania in 2015) declared moratoriums (EJI, 2020). In 16 states without the death penalty, the last execution took place before 1976 (DPIC, 2020f). Of death penalty states, Kansas has not executed anyone since before 1976. The federal government reinstated the death penalty in 1988; until 2020, it executed 3 people (2 in 2001, 1 in 2003). In June, there were 60 federal prisoners on death row.

In 2019, the attorney general announced the resumption of federal executions, saying the government owed it to the victims and their families to carry out the sentences imposed by the justice system (DPIC, 2019b). Legal actions delayed the four federal executions scheduled for that year. Earlene Peterson, whose daughter, son-in-law, and 8-year-old granddaughter were murdered, had asked the president to commute the death sentence of Daniel Lewis Lee to life without parole—the sentence received by his co-defendant. Addressing the president and the attorney general in letters, 175 relatives of victims asked that the government not schedule the executions, stating: the death penalty does not prevent violence; it does not solve crime; it exacerbates the trauma of losing a loved one and creates another grieving family; it wastes millions of dollars that would be better invested in programs to reduce crime and violence (Schwartz, 2020).

On July 14, 2020, the federal government carried out its first execution since 2003. The execution of Lee, age 47, followed legal delays. Relatives of Lee's victims sued to try to halt the execution, citing concerns about the coronavirus pandemic; they wanted to be present to counter the contention that the execution was held on their behalf. Lee's lawyers filed multiple appeals to halt the execution. One day before the execution, a US district judge ruled in favor of death row inmates who contested the drug used in the execution, and an appeals court upheld the ruling. Hours before Lee's execution, the Supreme Court ruled 5–4 that it could take place as scheduled. The federal government in 2020 executed three people in July, two in August, two in September, and one in November.

In 2017 the number of countries that abolished the death penalty for all crimes reached 106; 7 countries had abolished the death penalty for ordinary crimes. Another 29 countries had stopped using the death penalty in practice, bringing the total of non-death penalty countries to 142, versus 56 countries that retained the punishment (DPIC, 2017). While more than 70% of the nations in the world have abolished the death penalty, the United States remains in the company of primarily third-world countries with authoritative regimes.

The Race Factor

Race figures prominently in the imposition of the death penalty. Of the 1,527 people executed from 1976 to November 2020, the racial breakdown was 55.9% white, 34.0% Black, 8.5% Hispanic, and 1.7% other races (DPIC, 2020a). The race of victims is also a factor in punishment by death. Three-quarters of the victims of executed prisoners were white, whereas about 50% of the victims of *all* homicides were African American.

After the death penalty was reinstated, researchers began examining the impact of the defendant's and/or victim's race on death penalty decisions. Baldus, Woodworth, and Pulaski (1990) conducted one of the most significant studies. The researchers found that the race of the victim played a key role in the prosecutor's decision to seek the death penalty and the jury's decision to impose it. Race was the most significant contributor even after controlling for an astounding 200 variables. In 1990, the General Accounting Office reviewed 28 race studies including the Baldus study. The report concluded that in 82% of the studies reviewed, the race of victim influenced the likelihood of receiving the death penalty (Pierce et al., 2017).

In 2003, Baldus and Woodworth reviewed 18 studies on race and death sentencing published or released after 1990. Again, there was a consistent pattern of white-victim disparities, although they were not apparent in all jurisdictions or at all stages of charging and sentencing (Pierce et al., 2017). The studies displayed four clear patterns: (1) the defendant's race was not a significant correlate of death sentencing, (2) offenders who killed whites were significantly more likely to be sentenced to death, primarily because of prosecutorial charging decisions (3) cases in which Afri-

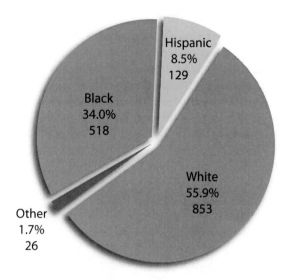

Figure 5-4   Race of Defendants Executed through October 2, 2020

Source: DPIC, 2020a

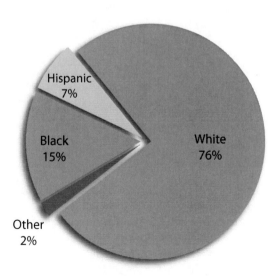

Figure 5-5   Race of Victims in Death Penalty Cases through October 2, 2020

Source: DPIC, 2020a

can American defendants killed white victims were treated more punitively, and (4) counties with large numbers of cases with African American defendants or white victims had particularly strong death sentencing rates for African American offenders. Another team of researchers in 2014 looked at 36 studies completed after the GAO report. Four of the studies found no race effects. Four other studies found effects regarding the race of the defendant, while 24 studies in 15 jurisdictions found significant race-of-victim effects. Nine studies found that Black defendants with white victims were more harshly treated than other homicide defendants.

One study reviewed executions after the resumption of the death penalty through 2013 (Baumgartner et al., 2015). The researchers found that the race of the victim was the single most reliable predictor of whether a defendant in the United States would be executed. Despite the fact that Black males are the most likely victims of homicide, capital punishment is very rarely applied. Blacks make up about 47% of all murder victims, but in cases resulting in an execution 17% of the victims were Black males. There were 534 white defendants executed for the murder of a single victim; 9 involved the murder of a Black male. The researchers also reviewed other studies published since 1972 and found that the vast majority of death sentences were applied when the victims were white.

Research in Oklahoma found that the race, as well as the gender, of the victim was highly correlated with the imposition of the death penalty (Pierce et al., 2017). The researchers did not find a correlation of the defendant's race with a death sentence, but they did find a strong correlation with the race of the victim. Cases with white female victims were 9.59 times more likely to end with a death sentence than cases with minority male victims. Defendants who killed minority females were 8.68 times more likely to receive a death sentence than defendants who killed minority males. Homicides with white male victims were 3.22 times higher than homicides with minority male victims to be capital punishment cases.

Another study confirmed that the race of the victim weighs most heavily in determining capital cases (Medwed, 2020). The tendency of decision makers to place a higher value on white crime victims has ripple effects throughout the capital punishment process. Perpetrators who kill whites are more likely to face capital charges, to receive a death sentence, and to be executed. The race of the defendant also affects decisions. Blacks who kill whites are the most likely offenders to receive the death penalty, followed by white offenders who kill white victims.

More than any other crime, the use of the death penalty for rape demonstrates the racially discriminatory nature of capital punishment in the United States. The overtly racist underpinnings were an outgrowth of slavery and lynching (DPIC, 2020d). Overwhelmingly, death sentences for rape were a Southern phenomenon applied to Black defendants in cases with a white woman or child victim. In most slave states, the attempted rape of a white woman was a capital offense for Blacks but not for whites. There were 455 executions for rape between 1930 and 1972; 443 (97.4%) took place in the South; 405 (89.1%) of the people executed were Black. In *Coker v. Georgia* (1977), the Supreme Court ruled that the death penalty was a disproportionate punishment for the crime of rape of an adult.

Wolfgang and Reidel (1973) studied 3,000 rape convictions in eleven southern states between 1945 and 1965. "Among 1,265 cases in which the race of the defendant and the sentence are known, nearly seven times as many Blacks were sentenced to death as whites" (p. 129). They also found that 36% of the African Americans who raped whites were sentenced to death, while all other racial combinations resulted in only 2% being sentenced to death. These relationships held true even when the researchers held constant such other factors as prior record and contemporaneous offenses (e.g., murder while committing robbery).

Research documenting racial bias in the death penalty has a long history. Bias begins with the charging process; African Americans are more likely than whites to be charged with capital crimes and sentenced to death (Harries & Cheatwood, 1997; International Commission of Jurists, 1997). Juries are often prejudiced; they are more likely to convict minorities than they are to convict whites in capital cases (Barkan & Cohen, 1994). Of the more than 15,000 executions between 1608 and 1986, there were 30 cases (about 0.2%) in which a white person was executed for killing a Black person (Radelet, 1989).

In *Batson v. Kentucky* (1986), the Supreme Court ruled that it is unconstitutional for prosecutors to use peremptory challenges to exclude jurors based solely on their race. Justice Thurgood Marshall, however, warned that the decision was insufficient to eliminate discrimination. He believed prosecutors would assert race-neutral reasons for their peremptory challenges, and judges would accept the explanations. He cautioned that even if all parties approached Batson's requirements with good intentions, he was not confident that the parties could confront and overcome their own conscious or unconscious racism. Many legal scholars argue that cases decided after *Batson*—as predicted by Marshall—significantly weakened its protections (Kappeler & Potter, 2018). Since *Batson v. Kentucky* (1986), the Supreme Court has overturned the convictions of four capital defendants (Roberts, 2019).

McCleskey v. Kemp

Many older studies were featured in one of the most significant Supreme Court cases concerning the death penalty—*McCleskey v. Kemp* (1987). Like *Furman* and *Gregg,* the case originated in Georgia. Warren McCleskey, an African American, had been convicted of killing a white police officer. In the appeal, the defense referenced the Baldus study.

Despite the overwhelming evidence in support of the importance of the race of the victim, the Supreme Court rejected the appeal. While accepting the validity of findings and statistical correlations of the Baldus study, the Court nevertheless ruled that in the case of McCleskey, there was no evidence that *"any of the decisionmakers in McCleskey's case acted with discriminatory purpose"* (emphasis added). The Court also suggested that *at best*, all that could be shown was a "discrepancy that appears to correlate with race."

What is perhaps most interesting about this ruling is that the Court appeared to be afraid of what the "logical conclusions" of such evidence might be. Justice Powell, writing for the majority, noted that such evidence "throws into serious question the principles that underlie our entire criminal justice system . . . if we accepted McCleskey's claim that racial bias impermissibly tainted the capital sentencing decision, we would soon be faced with similar claims as to other types of penalty." The ruling was immediately attacked in the four dissenting opinions by Justices Blackmun, Marshall, Brennan, and Stevens. Heaven forbid, the justices suggested, that others might challenge such obvious biases. Most critics voiced the opinion that this ruling sent a message that racial bias is perfectly constitutional. McCleskey was eventually executed in the electric chair on September 26, 1991. Justice Thurgood Marshall, who with two other justices was outvoted in granting a stay of execution, stated: "the court values expediency over human life" (Walker et al., 2018, p. 397).

Cole (1999) has argued that it would be nearly impossible to prove that a prosecutor and a jury have imposed the death penalty in a particular case because of the defendant's race. He notes that there are long-standing rules that prohibit defendants from obtaining discovery from the prosecution; therefore, without an admission of acting for racially biased reasons, it would be difficult to prove discrimination by the prosecutor. In short, "defendants are precluded from discovering evidence of intent from the two actors whose discriminatory intent the *McCleskey* Court required them to establish" (p. 135). Indeed, *Foster v. Chatman* (2016) illustrates Cole's point. The Court found for the defendant and remanded the case for a new trial but only because defense attorneys obtained the prosecution's notes—that marked each Black prospective juror with the letter "B."

The Supreme Court concluded that "discrimination is inevitable," a "natural by-product of discretion" and hence "constitutionally acceptable" (Cole, 1999, p. 137). Some members of Congress responded to the *McCleskey* decision by adding a "Racial Justice Act" to the Omnibus Crime Bill of 1994. By a slim majority, the House voted for this provision, which would have allowed those on death row to challenge their sentence based on statistical evidence of race discrimination in capital cases. The Senate defeated the provision, which was dropped from the 1994 bill. Senator Orin Hatch remarked that this "so-called Racial Justice Act has nothing to do with racial justice and everything to do with abolishing the death penalty. . . . It would convert every death penalty case into a massive sideshow of statistical squabbles and quota quarrels" (Kennedy, 1997, p. 346). African Americans and other minorities continue to receive the death penalty in numbers far greater than their proportion in the general population. Almost without exception, the executed are drawn from the ranks of minorities and the underclass (Shelden & Vasiliev, 2018).

Deterrence

Much of the confidence Americans have in the death penalty revolves around the perception that punishment alters behavior. It is commonsensical to believe that offenders will not want to die and that the threat of capital punishment will have a general deterrent effect. Unfortunately, there is no credible evidence that the death penalty deters homicide or any other felony offenses. The simplest test of deterrence relates to the idea that states or countries with the death penalty should have lower homicide rates than those without capital punishment. There is no evidence to indicate that this is true. The United States is the only Western democracy that retains capital punishment; it is also the country with the highest homicide rate in the industrialized world. Comparative analyses of regions within the United States reveal the same pattern. Southern states, which are the most active death penalty states, have consistently had the highest homicide rates (DPIC, 2020a). While the South accounts for about 80% of all executions, it is the only region with a homicide rate above the national average. Similarly, comparisons of states with the death penalty to those without reveal that the homicide rate for states with the death penalty in 2018 was 5.4 compared to the homicide rate of 4.1 in non-death penalty states (a 44% difference).

Numerous studies of the deterrent effect of the death penalty have been conducted using diverse methodologies. There have been comparisons between contiguous states; studies of jurisdictions that abolished and reinstated capital punishment; research on homicides committed by prisoners and parolees; and studies of the murders of police officers. None of the studies found that capital punishment reduced homicides. Police officers and prison inmates are no safer in death penalty states than in non-death penalty states. Individually and collectively these studies reveal that the death penalty has no general deterrent effect on homicides or other felonies.

Specific deterrence is commonly cited as a reason to retain capital punishment. While it is certainly true that an executed offender will not recidivate, research reveals that recidivism is unlikely without executions. When the *Furman* decision declared existing death penalty statutes unconstitutional in 1972, James Marquart and Jon Sorensen (1988) compared the behavior of the 47 Texas inmates whose sentences were commuted to 156 inmates serving life sentences for similar crimes. Three-quarters of the *Furman*-commuted inmates and 70% of the comparison group did not commit a serious violation of prison rules; there were no prison homicides

committed by any of the inmates studied. Marquart and Sorensen concluded that the former death row inmates did not pose a disproportionate
threat to society. Another study tracked the behavior of 185 *Furman*-com-
muted inmates who were paroled (Vito et al., 1991). Eight committed a
violent crime—including 3 homicides. The homicide recidivism rate for all
parolees was 1.6%.

Beginning with Robert Dann's (1935) study of the homicide rate in
Philadelphia 60 days before and 60 days after 5 highly publicized executions of Philadelphia murderers, researchers have explored the possibility
that executions have a brutalization effect. Some researchers have determined that the number of homicides increases during the period immediately before and after an execution. For example, William Bailey (1998)
found a significant increase in stranger homicides following Oklahoma's
resumption of executions in 1990 after a 25-year hiatus. Ernie Thomson
(1997) found an increase in gun-related and spontaneous stranger homicides following executions in Arizona. A California study found that more
murders occurred in the days before, on the day of, and in the weeks following an execution (Bowers et al., 1984). The findings from other studies
confirm the brutalization effect (Cloninger & Marchesini, 2009; Dezhbakhsh & Rubin, 2011; Land et al., 2012).

There has been criticism of research showing that the death penalty is
not a deterrent and that it contributes to an increase in homicides. After
Jeffrey Fagan (2006) conducted a thorough review of studies finding a
deterrent effect of the death penalty, he reached the following conclusion.

> New deterrence studies are fraught with numerous technical and con-
> ceptual errors: inappropriate methods of statistical analysis, failures to
> consider several relevant factors that drive murder rates such as drug
> epidemics, missing data on key variables in key states, the tyranny of a
> few outlier states and years, weak to nonexistent tests of concurrent
> effects of incarceration, statistical confounding of murder rates with
> death sentences, failure to consider the general performance of the
> criminal justice system, artifactual results from truncated time frames,
> and the absence of any direct test of the components of contemporary
> theoretical constructions of deterrence. Social scientists have failed to
> replicate several of these studies, and in some cases have produced
> contradictory or unstable results with the same data, suggesting that
> the original findings are unreliable and perhaps inaccurate. The cen-
> tral mistake in this enterprise is one of causal reasoning: the attempt
> to draw causal inferences from a flawed and limited set of observa-
> tional data, and the failure to address important competing influences
> on murder. (pp. 260–261)

Noting correctly that murder is a very complex phenomenon that goes
through many cycles—not unlike epidemics of contagious diseases, Fagan
stated: "There is no reliable, scientifically sound evidence that pits execution against a robust set of competing explanations to identify whether it

can exert a deterrent effect that is uniquely and sufficiently powerful to overwhelm these consistent and recurring epidemic patterns" (p. 261).

Another problem with research about deterrence is that it usually treats homicides as a homogeneous group of crime, making little or no distinction between various kinds of homicides depending on the context (e.g., carefully planned vs. spur of the moment, crimes of passion, etc.). "The only scientifically and ethically acceptable conclusion from the complete body of existing social science literature on deterrence and the death penalty is that it impossible to tell whether deterrent effects are strong or weak, or whether they exist at all" (Fagan, 2006, p. 315).

A report by the National Research Council on deterrence and the death penalty characterized studies claiming that the death penalty has a deterrent effect on murder as fundamentally flawed and cautioned against using them when making policy decisions (DPIC, 2020a). A survey of former and current presidents of academic criminological societies found that 88% rejected the idea that the death penalty deters murder.

Juveniles and the Death Penalty

Critics of the death penalty consistently argued that the punishment was inappropriate for individuals who had not attained full physical or emotional maturity at the time of their actions. The majority of countries that retain the death penalty had abolished it for juvenile offenders, but there were juveniles on death row in Bangladesh, Iran, Maldives, Pakistan and Saudi Arabia in 2017 (Amnesty International, 2018). Until March 1, 2005, the United States was alone as a Western, democratic nation that imposed the death penalty on those who committed their crimes as juveniles.

Since 1642, at least 366 juvenile offenders have been executed (Streib, 2004). Before 1972, most were sentenced to death and executed while still teenagers. Twenty-two of the executions were carried out from 1977–2004, constituting 2.4% of the total executions during that period. Texas executed 13 of the juvenile offenders. One of the executed offenders was 16 at the time of the crime; the others were 17. At the time of the execution, the youngest offender was 23, and the oldest was 36. Perhaps the fact that it was not a child strapped down and killed made it easier for US society to continue this punishment for juveniles into the twenty-first century. The fact remains that the people executed were juveniles when they committed their crimes. Many were sentenced to death by juries that lacked an understanding of brain development and thus were unable to assess the mitigating aspects of youth.

Roper v. Simmons

The Supreme Court decided in *Thompson v. Oklahoma* (1988) that executing someone who was younger than 16 at the time of the crime was cruel and unusual punishment—it violated the "evolving standards of decency that mark the progress of a maturing society." At the time of *Roper v. Simmons* (2005), 38 states and the federal government had death penalty statutes. In 17 states, the minimum age for receiving the death penalty was 18; in 5 states the minimum age was 17, and in 20 states, the minimum age was 16 (Streib, 2004). There were 71 people on death row in 12 states for crimes committed at the age of 16 (18%) or 17 (82%). When *Roper* was decided, their ages ranged from 18 to 43; time spent on death row ranged from 6 months to 24 years. Imposing life without the possibility of parole on waived youth for crimes committed at 13 or 14 years of age and executing them for crimes committed at 16 or 17 challenged the social construction of adolescence and the idea that juveniles are less criminally responsible than adults (Feld, 1999).

In a 5–4 decision, the Court ruled in *Roper v. Simmons* (2005) that applying the death penalty to minors violated the Eighth Amendment to the Constitution. Writing for the majority, Justice Anthony Kennedy wrote: "The age of 18 is the point where society draws the line for many purposes between childhood and adulthood. It is, we conclude, the age at which the line for death eligibility ought to rest." Justice John Paul Stevens noted that the practice of executing juvenile offenders was a relic of the past and was inconsistent with evolving standards of decency in a civilized society. His opinion was shared by Justices David Souter, Ruth Bader Ginsburg, and Stephen Breyer. These views echoed the Court's stance in *Atkins v. Virginia* (2002) that found it unconstitutional to execute the mentally retarded; in both cases, the issue was the ability of defendants to understand their situation and their level of culpability.

The Court reasoned that a majority of states had rejected the death penalty for juveniles, and execution was infrequent even in the states where it was allowed (no juveniles had been executed since 1977 in 43 states). There was a consistent trend toward abolition of the juvenile death penalty—no juveniles were on death row in 38 states (Shelden & Troshynski, 2020). These facts demonstrated a national consensus against the practice. The Court also noted that the execution of juvenile offenders violated several international treaties, including the United Nations Convention on the Rights of the Child and the International Covenant on Civil and Political Rights. The ruling stated that the overwhelming weight of international opinion against the juvenile death penalty confirms the conclusion that the death penalty is a cruel and unusual punishment for offenders under 18.

Adolescent Brain Development

Roper also referenced the fact that juveniles are vulnerable to influence and that they are inclined toward immature and irresponsible behavior. Adolescent years are filled with trials and tribulations—storm and stress is sometimes the description. The term "juvenile delinquent" and the existence of a separate juvenile court reflect the recognition that kids are still growing up and have not yet matured. The term "juvenile" means "young, immature, redeemable, subject to change". We, as a society, have long recognized this, which is why we impose age restrictions on behaviors, such as voting, serving on a jury, entering into contracts, getting married, consuming alcohol and tobacco, and many more. We even limit what kinds of movies juveniles can see without an adult present.

Defense lawyers cited research on brain development during adolescence. Longitudinal neuroimaging studies show that the adolescent brain continues to mature until the mid-20s. The frontal lobes that include neural circuitry for planning and impulse control are among the last areas of the brain to mature (Johnson et al., 2009). The prefrontal cortex is responsible for prioritizing thoughts, thinking in the abstract, and anticipating consequences. Although teens are capable of thinking logically, the process is more easily derailed by emotions and other distractions than is the case for most adults (Shelden & Troshynski, 2020). During most of the teenage years, there is a release of hormones, starting around puberty, which cause areas of the brain, such as the amygdala (which governs emotional responses) to expand, thus causing irrational and impulsive behavior (Bowman, 2004).

An amicus curiae brief (2005) for the respondent in *Roper v. Simmons* filed jointly by several prominent organizations (American Medical Association, American Psychiatric Association, American Society for Adolescent Behavior, National Mental Health Association, among others) described the characteristics of juveniles that make them less culpable than adults.

> The average adolescent cannot be expected to act with the same control or foresight as a mature adult. . . . Cutting-edge brain imaging technology reveals that regions of the adolescent brain do not reach a fully mature state until after the age of 18. These regions are precisely those associated with impulse control, regulation of emotions, risk assessment, and moral reasoning. Critical developmental changes in these regions occur only after late adolescence.

The above factors do not suggest excusing the behavior; however, they *explain* the behavior. In all human behavior, there are *causes,* and often multiple causes. Despite the lack of brain development, a very small number of juveniles commit murder. The background characteristics of people on death row who committed their crimes when under the age of 18 reveal an assortment of childhood traumas. Chris Mallett found that about 75% experienced various kinds of family dysfunction; 60% were victims of abuse and/or neglect; 43% had a diagnosed psychiatric disorder; 38% were addicted to drugs; and 38% lived in poverty (Mallett, 2003). Almost one-third of the juvenile offenders experienced six or more childhood traumas, with an overall average of four such experiences; few adolescents experience even one of these traumas. Less than half of the juries who convicted the juveniles heard these mitigating circumstances.

In *Roper v. Simmons*, the Supreme Court barred the execution of juveniles for capital crimes committed when younger than 18. In *Graham v. Florida* (2010), the Court ruled that a sentence of life without the possibility of parole for a crime committed by a juvenile in which no one was killed is unconstitutional. The Court in *Miller v. Alabama* (2012) banned sentences to life without the possibility of parole for homicides committed by youth under the age of 18. These decisions set the stage for the next logical step—reviewing the certification of juveniles as adults. We predict a case will find its way to the Supreme Court that will challenge the constitutionality of certifying juveniles as adults.

The Death Penalty and the Mentally Disabled

Punishment by death is perceived as punishment reserved for the most culpable—the worst of the worst—but it is most frequently inflicted on the most vulnerable (EJI, 2020). At least 44 people with intellectual disabilities were executed before the Supreme Court banned such executions in *Atkins v. Virginia* (2002). Mental health experts estimate that at least 20% of people on death row have a serious mental illness.

In *Atkins v. Virginia* (2002), the Court ruled that people with mental disabilities categorically should be excluded from the death penalty

> *Gregg v. Georgia*, . . . identified retribution and deterrence of capital crimes by prospective offenders as the social purposes served by the death penalty. Unless the imposition of the death penalty on a mentally retarded person measurably contributes to one or both of these goals, it is nothing more than the purposeless and needless imposition of pain and suffering, and hence an unconstitutional punishment. . . . With respect to retribution—the interest in seeing that the offender gets his "just deserts"—the severity of the appropriate punishment necessarily depends on the culpability of the offender. Since *Gregg*, our jurisprudence has consistently confined the imposition of the death penalty to a narrow category of the most serious crimes. For example, in *Godfrey v. Georgia*. . . . we set aside a death sentence because the petitioner's crimes did not reflect a consciousness materially more depraved than that of any person guilty of murder. . . . the culpability of the average murderer is insufficient to justify the most extreme sanction available to the State, the lesser culpability of the mentally retarded offender surely does not merit that form of retribution. Thus, pursuant to our narrowing jurisprudence, *which seeks to ensure that only the most deserving of execution are put to death*, an exclusion for the mentally retarded is appropriate. [Emphasis added]

The Supreme Court twice ruled regarding the mental fitness of Bobby James Moore. In the first case (*Moore v. Texas*, 2017), the Court heard arguments regarding whether Texas used outdated medical standards to determine if intellectual disability renders a person exempt from execution under the Eighth Amendment's prohibition against cruel and unusual punishment and the precedent of *Atkins*. The Court vacated the judgment of the Texas Court of Criminal Appeals and remanded the case for additional proceedings. After the Texas Court of Criminal Appeals reconsidered the issue and reached the same conclusion, the Court again granted review in *Moore v. Texas* (2019). In a per curiam opinion issued without argument, the Court reversed the lower court, determining that Moore was intellectually disabled. Moore, no longer eligible for the death penalty, was resentenced to life in prison. Because he had already served 40 years after his conviction by a Harris County jury, he was immediately eligible for parole. He was released in June 2020; he was sixty years old.

In *Madison v. Alabama* (2019) the Court held that the Eighth Amendment does not prohibit a state from executing a prisoner who due to mental disability cannot remember committing his crime, but it does prohibit executing a prisoner who cannot rationally understand the reasons for his execution, whether that inability is due to psychosis or dementia.

In May 2020, the Florida Supreme Court allowed the state to proceed with its plan to execute Harry Franklin Phillips who was convicted of murdering a Miami parole officer in 1982 (Sarat, 2020). Phillips suffers from an intellectual disability and has an IQ of 70. In *Hall v. Florida* (2014), the Supreme Court found Florida's methods for identifying mental deficiencies violated the standards established in *Atkins v. Virginia* (2002). Justice Kennedy stated that intellectual disability is a condition, not a number and that Florida disregards established medical practice by utilizing an IQ score as final and conclusive evidence of a defendant's intellectual capacity. No bright-line rule captures the meaning and significance of intellectual disability (Sarat, 2020) Kennedy also stated that executing an intellectually disabled person violates his or her inherent dignity as a human being because the diminished capacity of the intellectually disabled lessens moral culpability and hence the retributive value of the punishment.

Wrongful Convictions

Rich and guilty offenders fare better in the death penalty system than the poor and innocent (EJI, 2020). The death penalty is imposed primarily on poor people who cannot afford to hire an effective lawyer. Receiving a death sentence typically depends on the quality of the defendant's legal team more than any other factor. Capital cases are complex, time consuming, and require substantial resources for investigation and expert assistance. Court-appointed attorneys for indigent capital defendants often have huge caseloads, inexperience in capital cases, and caps on fees. They frequently fail to investigate cases thoroughly, call witnesses, and/or challenge forensic evidence. By failing to object at trial, inadequate defense lawyers make it harder to correct errors on appeal. After the first appeal in capital cases, there is no right to counsel. Postconviction proceedings involve complicated procedural rules, and people sentenced to death have little hope for navigating the process successfully without assistance.

In *Strickland v. Washington* (1984), the Supreme Court held: (1) defense counsel's performance must be deficient; and (2) the deficient performance must have deprived the defendant of a fair trial. The defendant must demonstrate that defense counsel's representation fell below an "objective standard of reasonableness" and there was a "reasonable probability that the result would have been different except for the unprofessional errors. In his dissent, Justice Thurgood Marshall said the Court's attempt to create a uniform standard was so malleable as to be virtually useless.

Since 1973, 169 people on death row have been exonerated. For every 9 people executed, 1 person on death row has been exonerated (EJI, 2020). Perjury/false accusations and official misconduct are the leading causes of wrongful convictions in death penalty cases. In 2018, 111 exonerations involved witnesses who lied on the stand or falsely accused the defendant. In 50 of those cases, the defendant was falsely accused of a crime that never happened. Official misconduct by police or prosecutors (or both) is more common in death penalty cases. Of Black exonerees sentenced to death, 87% were victims of official misconduct compared to 67% of white death row exonerees. Wrongful death sentences are not limited to the innocent. The intense pressure to obtain a death sentence and the political stakes for police, prosecutors, and judges can cause serious legal errors that contribute to wrongful convictions. In Alabama, over 160 death sentences have been invalidated by state and federal courts, resulting in conviction of a lesser offense or a lesser sentence on retrial.

Over the last 30 years, the volume of research on wrongful capital convictions has increased. One detailed study found that about 400 death-sentenced defendants from 1900 through the summer of 1991 were not guilty (Radelet et al., 1992). About two dozen people who were innocent were executed, and many more spent countless years in prison before gaining their release. A disproportionate number of the wrongfully convicted were African Americans. In a study of 4,578 capital cases between 1973 and 1995, researchers found that there were serious reversible errors in almost 70% of capital cases (Liebman et al., 2000). Death sentences were overturned in two-thirds of the appeals, with 95 death row prisoners having been *completely exonerated*.

The risk of the state executing an innocent person has a significant impact on the use of the death penalty. Illinois, for example, declared a moratorium on executions in 2000, four years after the exoneration of five death row inmates; it abolished capital punishment in 2011. Since 1989, the National Registry of Exonerations (2020) has attempted to find every exoneration in the United States. From 1989 to mid-year 2020, there have been 2,631 exonerations. There were 24 exonerations in 1989; 419 in the 1990s; 762 from 2000–2009; 1,372 from 2010–2019; and 54 through June 2020. Of those exonerated, 47% were Black, 12% Hispanic, and 37% white. Most (91%) exonerees were male; 9% were female. Contributing factors to the wrongful convictions were: Mistaken identification, false confessions, bad forensic evidence, perjury/false accusations, and official misconduct.

Appellate courts reverse convictions based on legal errors; innocence is not grounds for reversal. In a 6–3 opinion, *Herrera v. Collins* (1993), the Supreme Court ruled that a lawfully convicted defendant cannot appeal solely on a claim of innocence—the claim must be based on a constitutional violation. Chief Justice Rehnquist wrote the opinion.

> Where, as here, a defendant has been afforded a fair trial and convicted of the offense for which he was charged, the constitutional presumption of innocence disappears. Federal habeas courts do not sit to correct errors of fact, but to ensure that individuals are not imprisoned in violation of the Constitution. Thus, claims of actual innocence based on newly discovered evidence have never been held to state a ground for federal habeas relief absent an independent constitutional violation occurring in the course of the underlying state criminal proceedings. . . .
>
> Herrera is not left without a forum to raise his actual innocence claim. He may file a request for clemency under Texas law, which contains specific guidelines for pardons on the ground of innocence. History shows that executive clemency is the traditional "fail-safe" remedy for claims of innocence based on new evidence, discovered too late in the day to file a new trial motion.

The rate of exonerations for death row inmates is much higher than for any other category of wrongful convictions. Death sentences represent less than 0.001 of all prison sentences but account for about 12% of known exonerations (Kappeler & Potter, 2018). Capital defendants sentenced to life imprisonment receive much less attention than defendants who face execution. Some argue that exonerations are proof that the system and the appeals process work, but most releases result from meticulous investigation by innocence resource centers and journalists.

In his lone dissent to the Supreme Court's 8–1 decision denying review in a Texas death penalty case, *Callins v. Collins* (1994), Justice Harry Blackmun stated:

> From this day forward, I no longer shall tinker with the machinery of death. For more than 20 years I have endeavored—indeed, I have struggled—along with a majority of this Court, to develop procedural and substantive rules that would lend more than the mere appearance of fairness to the death penalty endeavor. Rather than continue to coddle the Court's delusion that the desired level of fairness has been achieved and the need for regulation eviscerated, I feel morally and intellectually obligated simply to concede that the death penalty experiment has failed. It is virtually self-evident to me now that no

combination of procedural rules or substantive regulations ever can save the death penalty from its inherent constitutional deficiencies. The basic question—does the system accurately and consistently determine which defendants "deserve" to die?—cannot be answered in the affirmative. It is not simply that this Court has allowed vague aggravating circumstances to be employed, relevant mitigating evidence to be disregarded, and vital judicial review to be blocked. The problem is that the inevitability of factual, legal, and moral error gives us a system that we know must wrongly kill some defendants, a system that fails to deliver the fair, consistent, and reliable sentences of death required by the Constitution.

The Machinery of Death

There have been 1,337 lethal injections since 1976 (Stunson, 2020). Death penalty states and the federal government generally used a three-drug protocol developed by Oklahoma in 1977 (Kappeler & Potter, 2018). The three drugs were: (1) a short-acting sedative or anesthetic, usually sodium thiopental; (2) a neuromuscular blocking drug that paralyzes the muscles, usually pancuronium bromide; and (3) a lethal dose of potassium chloride to stop the heart. People administering the drugs had little knowledge about their properties or what to do if the execution did not proceed as expected. The second step created the appearance of a peaceful death. However, if the sedative in step one did not work, the inmate would not convulse or cry out because muscle movement was inhibited. If not completely sedated, the final step was excruciatingly painful. States designed their procedures with primary attention on executioner anonymity and the experiences of witnesses—not the potential agonies of the person being executed.

Baze v. Rees (2008) challenged Kentucky's four-drug protocol. In a 7–2 decision, the Court ruled that Kentucky's protocol did not violate the Eighth Amendment's prohibition of cruel and unusual punishment. Under the ruling, challenges to lethal injection procedures must address two issues: the procedure poses a substantial risk of severe pain. and the state has refused to adopt a feasible alternative reducing that risk. A state's refusal to alter its execution protocol violates the Eighth Amendment only if an inmate identifies a feasible alternative procedure that would reduce substantially the risk of severe pain and also demonstrates that the state has refused to adopt the alternative method without a legitimate penological reason. The Court stated that while the Eighth Amendment forbids "cruel and unusual" methods of capital punishment, it does not guarantee a prisoner a painless death.

In 2009, death penalty states were unable to obtain sodium thiopental (Kappeler & Potter, 2018). The only US supplier stopped production. It planned to produce the drug at a facility in Italy, but the Italian Parliament demanded the drug be used only for medical purposes. Great Britain was a source for several states until officials there banned the exportation of the drug for executions. States began experimenting with types of drugs and dosages. Some states substituted midazolam as the first drug, with disastrous results in 2014. Ohio used midazolam and hydromorphone, a combination of drugs that had never been used previously; Dennis McGuire died a painful death after 24 minutes. In Oklahoma, midazolam was administered as the first drug to Clayton Lockett. The drug went into tissue rather than a vein, and Lockett died in excruciating pain 43 minutes later. Attorneys for Joseph Wood in Arizona sought information about the drugs that would be used and the qualifications of his executioners. The Ninth Circuit federal appeals court ordered Arizona to provide the information or delay the execution; the Supreme Court overruled the Ninth Circuit. It took 2 hours for Wood to die after receiving 15 times the amounts of midazolam and hydromorphone specified in the state's protocol. The lack of transparency regarding procedures has become more pronounced with the shortage of drugs and the use of unregulated compounding pharmacies to create them.

In *Glossip v. Gross* (2015), inmates petitioned the Court because Oklahoma planned to execute them using midazolam, the same initial drug used in Lockett's execution. The Court ruled that there was insufficient evidence that the use of midazolam entailed a substantial risk of severe pain. Because some risk of pain is inherent in execution, the Eighth Amendment does not require that a constitutional method of execution be free of any risk of pain. The Court found that the petitioners in the case were unable to identify a reasonable alternative that presented a significantly lower risk of pain. The Court also stated that the district court is entitled to a high degree of deference in its determination and that the petitioners did not prove that the district court's factual findings were erroneous.

Both *Baze* and *Glossip* asserted that the Constitution affords a measure of deference to a state's choice of execution procedures. The Constitution does not authorize courts to serve as boards of inquiry to determine best practices for executions—and previous methods of execution are not necessarily unconstitutional once an arguably more humane method becomes available. In *Bucklew v. Precythe* (2019), the Court reiterated that the *Baze-Glossip* test governs all Eighth Amendment challenges alleging that a method of execution inflicts unconstitutionally cruel pain. Bucklew challenged Missouri's single-drug execution protocol as causing excruciating pain due to his rare medical condition. The Court ruled he failed to meet the requirements of *Baze-Glossip* and accused him of gamesmanship and delay.

After lethal injection drugs became difficult to obtain, death penalty states stockpiled supplies. Several pharmaceutical companies filed a lawsuit against Nevada in 2018 for illegally obtaining supplies of the drugs; the lawsuit was dismissed in 2020 after Nevada agreed to return its supplies to the companies, leaving the state without any drugs to carry out executions (Lozano, 2020). When the lawsuit was filed, 15 states (including Florida, Oklahoma and Texas) referred to it as guerrilla warfare waged by activists opposed to the death penalty and by criminal defense attorneys to stop lawful executions.

When the COVID-19 pandemic hit, hospitals reported shortages of sedatives, painkillers, and paralytics used in the treatment of coronavirus patients on ventilators (Lozano, 2020). Lethal injection drugs—like fentanyl, midazolam, vecuronium bromide, and rocuronium bromide were needed to treat seriously ill patients. Hospitals use midazolam and fentanyl to sedate patients on ventilators; they use vecuronium bromide and rocuronium bromide for both ventilation and intubation. In April 2020, seven leading anesthesiologists, pharmacists, and medical academics wrote an open letter to the corrections departments of death penalty states asking that they send the needed medications to health-care facilities. Alabama and Florida did not respond to inquiries from journalists about the letter. Arkansas, Texas, and Utah said they did not have any of the drugs listed. Tennessee would not confirm whether it possessed the drug but indicated it had no plans to give the medications to hospitals. Oklahoma said state hospitals had not requested the medications. Thirteen states since 2011 enacted statutes that protect states from revealing their death penalty procedures and protocols. COVID-19 affected the administration of capital punishment; the Texas Court of Criminal Appeals stayed three executions because of the health crisis and the enormous resources needed to address the emergency. Planned executions in Tennessee and Ohio were also placed on hold.

The Expense of Executions

A common assumption is that executions are less expensive than incarceration. However, putting people to death is *more* expensive than life without parole. (Greenblatt, 2019). Costs are higher at every stage (Kappeler & Potter, 2018).; because of the finality of the sentence. Capital cases are bifurcated: first a jury determines guilt or innocence; if found guilty, the trial moves to the penalty phase in which the jury hears mitigating circumstances and decides whether to impose a sentence of death.

Appeals are filed as a matter of course in capital cases. Relatively few of them result in sentences of death. The history of Curtis Flowers illustrates the process. In 1996 in Winona, Mississippi, four employees of a furniture store were killed during an armed robbery. Curtis Flowers was tried for the murder of one of the employees; he was convicted and sentenced to death. The Mississippi Supreme Court reversed and remanded the case for a new trial on the grounds that admitting evidence of the other three murder victims violated Flowers's right to a fair trial. Flowers was tried and convicted for the murder of a second victim, and the Mississippi

Supreme Court reversed and remanded on the same grounds. In a third trial, Flowers was tried for all four murders; a jury found him guilty and sentenced him to death. The Mississippi Supreme Court again reversed and remanded on the grounds that the prosecutor engaged in racial discrimination during jury selection. The fourth and fifth trials were on all four counts of capital murder; both resulted in mistrials when the jury was unable to reach a unanimous verdict during the guilt phase. In the sixth trial, Flowers was convicted of all four murders. The Mississippi Supreme Court rejected Flowers's arguments that the prosecution exercised its peremptory strikes in a racially discriminatory way when it struck five African American prospective jurors. The Supreme Court ordered reconsideration in light of its ruling in *Foster v. Chatman* (2016). On remand the Mississippi Supreme Court again upheld the ruling for the state. In *Flowers v. Mississippi* (2019), the Supreme Court ruled 7–2 that the trial court committed clear error in concluding that the peremptory strikes were not motivated in substantial part by discriminatory intent.

The expense of capital trials and appeals decimated budgets; prosecutors stopped seeking the death penalty (Von Drehle, 2019). One study found that capital punishment cost California $5 billion since the 1970s. Ernest Goss, an economics professor at Creighton University, found that each death penalty prosecution in Nebraska cost $1.5 million more than prosecutions that sought a sentence of life without parole (Liptak, 2019).

Brandon Garrett (2017), a law professor at Duke University and author of *End of Its Rope: How Killing the Death Penalty Can Revive Criminal Justice* collected and analyzed national data on the death penalty. When Henry McCollum was condemned to death in 1984 in rural North Carolina, death sentences were commonplace. In 2014, DNA tests set McCollum free after 30 years on death row. By then, the number of death sentences dropped dramatically, as did executions. Georgia, once a leading death penalty state, last imposed a death sentence in 2014. Virginia has not sentenced anyone to death since 2011. The death penalty has essentially disappeared from rural counties, in part due to the costs associated with capital cases. As discussed earlier, fewer than 2% of the counties in the nation are responsible for half the death row convictions. Until recently, jurisdictions like Philadelphia County, Los Angeles County, and Harris County imposed 10 or more death sentences apiece per year (Greenblatt, 2019). For years, if Harris County were a country, it would have ranked among the world's top 10 for death sentences. Experts suggest one of the reasons for the change in Texas is the availability of a sentence to life without parole, legislated in 2005. Prior to that time, juries did not trust that the system would keep violent criminals imprisoned. In many large counties, including Harris and Philadelphia, voters have elected reform-minded prosecutors less likely or unwilling to seek execution as a punishment.

Politics and the Death Penalty

Daniel LaChance (2016), an Emory University historian and author of *Executing Freedom: The Cultural Life of Capital Punishment in the United States,* notes that the death penalty was historically a local, populist punishment. The legal requirements and professional standards surrounding the death penalty post-*Furman* weakened the connection between capital punishment and a racist past. The development of an elaborate federal jurisprudence to standardize the death penalty disassociated executions from lynchings. Lengthy appeals separated government imposition of death from the behavior of a lynch mob. Lethal injections made executions appear as medical procedures rather than a violent expression of communal rage. LaChance refers to the contradictory coexistence of a *fiery rhetoric* of retribution with an *icy reality* of sober restraint as a cultural reservoir from which to secure support for capital punishment.

In the 1980s and 1990s, the death penalty was a significant influence on political careers. Michael Dukakis lost the presidency in 1988; a contributing factor was his response in a debate that he would oppose an execution even if his wife were murdered (Arango, 2019). Bill Clinton learned from the example. He returned to Arkansas in the middle of his presidential campaign in 1992 to preside over the execution of Ricky Ray Rector, a mentally impaired prisoner who said he was saving part of his last meal for later. Stephen Bright, a professor at Yale Law School, said the issue of capital punishment was toxic; many state judges were removed from office for opposing the death penalty.

Violent crime rates peaked in the early 1990s; legislators embraced a tough-on-crime response. The Violent Crime Control and Law Enforcement Act of 1994 (known as the 1994 Crime Law) made dozens of federal crimes punishable by death (Greenblatt, 2019). The bill provided federal funding for states and localities to build more jails and prisons and to pass mandatory sentencing laws and other punitive measures that accelerated mass incarceration. Death sentences peaked in 1996, with 315 people condemned to die. By the time the crime bill passed, crime rates began to fall. Violent crime rates plummeted by 49% between 1993 and 2017. The steep national decline in violent crime and murders have facilitated politicians seeking something other than the maximum possible sentence—including reexamining the ultimate punishment.

Politics have shifted. In 2019 the governor of California issued an executive moratorium on the execution of any of the 737 death-sentenced inmates at San Quentin State Prison. Governor Newsom said that—by any measure—the death penalty system has been a failure with no public safety benefit or deterrent value that has wasted billions of taxpayer dollars. He emphasized that the death penalty is absolute, irreversible, and irreparable in the event of human error (Shafer & Lagos, 2019). His executive order argued that capital punishment is inherently unfair, applied more often to people of color and those with mental disabilities. He ordered the execution chamber (upgraded at an expense of $853,000 in 2010 but never used; the last execution in California was in 1976) closed and rescinded the state's protocol for lethal injection. Newsom took the action despite California voters having narrowly rejected a 2016 ballot initiative to end the death penalty and narrowly approved an initiative to expedite executions by shortening the appeals process.

A 1966 survey found that 42% of Americans were in favor of the death penalty; 47% were opposed—the only time more people expressed opposition than support (Jones, 2019). At least 60% of Americans favored the death penalty from 1976 through 2016, peaking at 80% in 1994, when crime was a top concern. In October 2019, the percentage in favor dropped to 56, with 42% opposed. When the question was phrased as a choice between the death penalty and life without parole, 36% supported the death penalty (a decrease from 50% in 2014) compared to 60% in support of life without parole (an increase from 45% in 2014). Two-thirds of women versus 53% of men advocate punishing convicted murderers by means of life imprisonment rather than the death penalty. Gallup began polling beliefs about the moral acceptability of the death penalty in May 2001; the highest percentage of people expressing the view that the death penalty was morally acceptable was 71% in both 2006 and 2007. By 2020, the percentage dropped to 54%, and 40% of US adults thought the death penalty was morally wrong—the highest percentage in 20 years.

An Arbitrary and Flawed Policy

We have reviewed discrimination, geography, and other factors contributing to the arbitrariness of the death penalty. Examples exist even in the last moments of the ultimate punishment—whether the issue is the free exercise of religion or the timeliness of appeals. In *Dunn v. Ray* (2019), a Muslim inmate requested that an imam be present at his execution, which Alabama denied. Ray claimed his First Amendment right to the free exercise of religion, as expanded by the Religious Land Use and Institutionalized Persons Act (RLUIPA), rendered unconstitutional an Alabama election protocol that placed a Christian minister on the prison team that entered the execution chamber but barred, even upon request, ministers of all other faiths (Greenblatt, 2019). His execution date was February 7, 2019; he sought relief January 28, 2019. The Supreme Court ruled 5–4 in *Dunn v. Ray* that the inmate had waited too long to object. One month later in *Murphy v. Collier* (2019), the Court granted a stay of execution to Patrick Murphy who wanted his Buddhist advisor in the execution room. At that time, Texas allowed only Christian or Muslim advisors in the execution room. An asterisk at the end of the ruling stated that the plaintiff made his request in a sufficiently timely manner, one month before the scheduled execution.

Ruben Gutierrez argued his religious rights were violated because Texas does not allow a chaplain in the execution chamber. After the ruling in *Murphy*, Texas had changed its policy to allow only prison security staff in the execution chamber. On June 12, 2020, the U.S. Court of Appeals overturned a stay of execution for Gutierrez; his lawyers sought relief from the Supreme Court. On June 16, 2020, the Supreme Court issued the stay approximately one hour before the scheduled execution.

In addition to arbitrariness in the application of the death penalty, critics argue that the punishment violates human dignity. Justice Anthony Kennedy again referenced dignity in *Kennedy v. Louisiana* (2009), as he had in *Atkins*.

> Evolving standards of decency must embrace and express respect for the dignity of the person, and the punishment of criminals must conform to that rule. . . . As we shall discuss, punishment is justified under one or more of three principal rationales: rehabilitation, deterrence, and retribution. . . . It is the last of these, retribution, that most often can contradict the law's own ends. This is of particular concern when the Court interprets the meaning of the Eighth Amendment in capital cases. When the law punishes by death, it risks its own sudden descent into brutality, transgressing the constitutional commitment to decency and restraint. For these reasons we have explained that capital punishment must be limited to those offenders who commit a narrow category of the most serious crimes and whose extreme culpability makes them the most deserving of execution.

Arbitrariness, discrimination, dehumanization, and violence are inherent in death sentencing (Hoag, 2020).

Justice Stephen Breyer in his dissent to *Glossip v. Gross* (2015) argued that the constitutionality of a punishment must be evaluated based on currently prevailing social and legal standards. He pointed to studies showing that the exoneration rate is disproportionately high with capital crimes—both in cases in which the defendant was innocent and in cases with procedural errors. The death penalty is not reliably applied even in cases in which the defendant has been convicted of crimes that society harshly condemns. Studies have shown factors other than the egregiousness of the crime influence the imposition of the death penalty—whether the races and genders of defendants and victims, the location of the crime, and/or political pressures. The arbitrariness results in the punishment being unconstitutionally cruel.

> Thus, whether one looks at research indicating that irrelevant or improper factors—such as race, gender, local geography, and resources—do significantly determine who receives the death penalty, or whether one looks at research indicating that proper factors—such as "egregiousness"—do not determine who receives the death penalty, the legal conclusion must be the same: The research strongly suggests that the death penalty is imposed arbitrarily. (p. 14)

Breyer also noted the imposition of the death penalty requires procedural safeguards, resulting in long delays between sentencing and execution—if the execution happens at all. The process itself is cruel and also divorces the punishment from the punitive purposes of deterrence and retribution. The nation has consistently been moving away from the use of the death penalty; it is used so rarely that it is demonstrably unusual for the purpose of the Eighth Amendment.

Public support for the death penalty is declining; new death sentences have remained near record lows since 2015; executions have declined significantly over the past two decades. The death penalty is an expensive policy defined by bias and error. The arbitrary, discriminatory application corrupts the integrity of our criminal justice system and does not make us safer (EJI, 2020).

6

Punishing Women

Throughout world history women offenders have been subjected to differential forms of punishment reflecting their subservient position. In the Middle Ages, a pregnant woman might receive lenient punishment if she were to "plead her belly," yet she could be burned at the stake for adultery. Prior to the rise of imprisonment in the nineteenth century, daughters and wives who were unwanted were often forced into convents and similar institutions, along with political prisoners, the mentally defective, and other outcast persons (Dobash et al., 1986).

Since ancient Greece and Rome, states were organized as patriarchies; the earliest law codes established the subordination of women to men (Shelden & Vasiliev, 2018). Much of Roman law was eventually incorporated into the English common law, which subsequently formed the basis of law in the colonies. For several years, the only law book used was Blackstone's *Commentaries on the Laws in England*, originally published in 1765. Family law incorporated Blackstone's famous dictum that the husband and wife are as one and that one is the husband (Eisenstein, 1988). Women had no separate identity; they were defined by their relationship with their fathers or later with their husbands. The husband had rights over his wife that resembled in many ways the rights of masters over their slaves. Even if a man killed his wife, he would be treated under the law with far more leniency than if his wife killed him. In fact, a man killing his wife was treated almost the same as if he had killed an animal or a servant.

Colonial law was often very specific about women; some crimes were, in effect, women's crimes and were severely punished (Shelden & Vasiliev, 2018). For instance, a woman who berated her husband or was too vocal in public settings could be charged with the crime of being a "common scold." The "ducking stool" was used to punish scolding. The female offender was placed in a chair and plunged underwater several times "to cool her immoderate heat" (Mays, 2004, p. 366).

In colonial America, women were singled out for committing various "crimes" related to religion. For instance, Anne Hutchinson was persecuted for expressing alternative religious views and eventually was banished from Massachusetts in the 1630s. Perhaps the most famous case was that of Mary Dyer, a friend of Anne Hutchinson, who became a Quaker (a religion strongly resisted by the Puritans). Dyer was convicted in 1658 of preaching Quakerism, a crime punishable by death; the governor, a friend of her husband, banished her instead. In 1660, she returned to Boston, continued preaching, was arrested, and was again sentenced to death. She was hanged the next day (Knappman, 1994). Two centuries later, the state of Massachusetts constructed a statue of her in front of the state capitol— ironically across the street from Boston Common where 100 years after her hanging patriots gathered to drill to fight for freedom. The inscription on her statue reads "Witness for Religious Freedom."

The witch hunts in the American colonies stand as classic examples of the use of the legal system to punish women who dared challenge the male power structure. In New England, during the 1600s, at least 36 women were executed for witchcraft. The "crime" of witchcraft was one among many religious-based laws on the books during colonial times. Women who were unattached—not wives, sisters, and daughters of men— received the most severe treatment. Most of those labeled witches were women who were outspoken in their views or had a great deal of informal power either as healers or as community leaders (Pollock, 1996).

The continued unequal treatment of women is perhaps nowhere better demonstrated than in the criminal justice system and the use of imprisonment as a method of control. In the next section, we review the historical development of women's prisons. The sordid history not only illustrates the brutal treatment of women as a group but also the class and racial dimensions of such treatment.

A Brief History of Women's Prisons

In Colonial America, incarceration was rare. White women who committed crimes were primarily of the servant class and were usually arrested for petty violations of religious and secular laws (Collins, 2010). After arrest, women were held in local jails for trial; the standard punishment was often a humiliating public reprimand, such as the stocks or the pillory.

For African American women, the situation was quite different; the majority were legally slaves, and those who were not were indentured servants (Sellin, 2016). Most violations of laws were handled on the plantation. Slave owners dominated the legislatures in the South; they protected their property rights by laws. Crimes by slaves were subject to public punishments not applicable to whites. If owners preferred not to punish on the plantation, they created special "Negro Courts" consisting of county justices acting without a jury. Death and incarceration were rarely imposed because they would deprive owners of labor. Crimes punishable by death included "knowingly buying or receiving a stolen horse" and striking a "master, a member of the master's family, or the overseer, so as to cause a contusion, or effusion or shedding of blood" (pp. 135–136).

As discussed in chapter 4, it was not until after the Civil War that African Americans were sent to penal institutions in large numbers, largely as a result of Jim Crow laws and the Black Codes (Shelden, 1979). Black women over eighteen years of age without lawful employment could be declared vagrant and fined up to fifty dollars and imprisoned for 10 days. If unable to pay, the sheriff would hire the women out to anyone who paid the fine (Ritchie, 2017). Before and after the Black codes were struck down by the Civil Rights Act of 1866, Black women were subject to arrest for actual or perceived transgressions reported by their employers. Larceny was the most prevalent offense charged against freedwomen. Once incarcerated, many Blacks were subjected to the convict lease system.

As discussed in chapter 3, early American jails were often mere extensions of the earlier workhouses and almshouses. Newgate prison (New York), opened in 1797, was the first institution for felons only; women offenders were housed in an area separate from men (Rafter, 1990). When Newgate Prison closed in the 1820s, the men were transferred to Auburn, but the women were sent to Bellevue Penitentiary in New York City. There was no classification of prisoners and no supervision. The food was poor quality and in short supply; there were no sanitary or security precautions. Eight women died during a cholera epidemic, and 11 escaped. Sing Sing prison opened in 1826; both Sing Sing and Auburn resisted housing women prisoners.

Women were first admitted to Auburn in 1825; they were housed in the third-floor attic over the kitchen (Rafter, 1990). There was little interest in the women offenders, who were viewed with particular distaste. Neglect of women prisoners between 1820 and 1870 included patterns of overcrowding, harsh treatment, and sexual abuse. The difficulty of housing and supervising women in facilities that were not designed for them created terrible conditions. No matron was hired until 1832. At one time there were 70 women inmates housed together in the unventilated attic. In 1826, a woman named Rachel Welch became pregnant while in solitary confinement and died shortly after childbirth from the flogging received from a prison guard. Conditions were so bad that the prison chaplain once remarked that it was bad enough for male prisoners, "but to be a female convict, for any protracted period, would be worse than death" (Freedman, 1981, p. 16).

Auburn and Bellevue women prisoners were transferred to the Mount Pleasant Female Prison on the grounds of Sing Sing in 1839. Little changed for the female prisoners, and they rioted in 1843 (Freedman, 1981). Elizabeth Farnham was appointed matron after the riot. She ended the silence rule, set up a library and school, classified prisoners, implemented incentives for good behavior, and introduced music, handcrafts, and entertainment to discourage criminal tendencies. She left in 1848 after state officials complained that there was nothing masculine in the prison routine.

A women's annex was built on the grounds of the Ohio Penitentiary in 1837. At this time, it was widely believed that women offenders should be treated more harshly than their male counterparts. The argument was that female offenders were more depraved than men because, having been born pure, they had fallen further from grace. Indeed, women were often blamed for the crimes of men (Freedman, 1981). Women prisoners who had been sexually promiscuous were pariahs. One nineteenth-century prison official stated that prevailing opinion held that female convicts were beyond the reach of reformation. Punishment consisting of turning "them loose within the pen of the prison and there leave them to feed upon and destroy each other" would be sufficient (p. 17). The chaplain at the Ohio Penitentiary said: "As woman falls from a higher point of perfection, so she sinks to a profounder depth of misery than a man" (p. 18).

Women entered prison reform during different decades. The first steps in the 1820s were taken by religious women (Freedman, 1981). The majority of women working for prison reform were from the middle and upper-middle classes. Many had been teachers or nurses, such as Clara Barton (1821–1912). Of thirty women active in reform, one-third were Quakers, including Elizabeth Fry (1780–1845); most were abolitionists. By the 1890s, women's prison reform changed from private, voluntary efforts to public, professional work. For example, Margaret Fuller, an editor at the *New York Tribune*, focused on women victimized by social forces; she questioned the predominant view that women were hopelessly fallen. She campaigned for a home for discharged women prisoners and reported in 1845 on the shocking sight of mothers and infants in city almshouses. Dorothea Dix (1802–1887) and Josephine Shaw Lowell (1843–1905) advocated for separate facilities for women and classification of offenders by age and offense, as well as other reforms. Lowell's family was deeply involved in anti-slavery. She lost a husband and brother in the Civil War and helped establish schools for Blacks in the South.

Separate facilities for women gradually began to emerge following the 1870 meeting of the National Congress on Penitentiary and Reformatory Discipline in Cincinnati. One of the resolutions of this conference was that the goal of prisons should be *rehabilitation* rather than punishment. Reformers argued that women prisoners would be treated more fairly and would stand a better chance of being reformed if they were confined in separate institutions controlled by women. Reformers countered male resistance by arguing that "the shield of a pure woman's presence" would enable them "to govern the depraved and desperate of her own sex" (Freedman, 1981, p. 61).

The Indiana Women's Prison, the first totally separate prison for women, opened in 1873. Female prisoners were previously held at Indiana State Prison, where officials were eager to get rid of them (Rafter, 1990). The warden said they were an expense, and their labor was unproductive. The Indiana Women's Prison was run entirely by female staff and was the first reformatory in the nation. One section of the prison was for adult offenders; a separate section housed juveniles.

> It embraced the revolutionary notion that women criminals should be *rehabilitated* rather than punished. Young girls from the age of sixteen who "habitually associate with dissolute persons" and other uneducated and indigent women were ushered into the model prison apart from men and isolated from the "corruption and chaos" of the outside world. The essential ingredient of their rehabilitative treatment would be to bring discipline and regularity into their lives. Obedience and systematic religious education would, it was felt, help the women form orderly habits and moral values. (Watterson, 1996, p. 198)

In its early days, the prison primarily provided domestic training. Although run by women, the prison was under the administrative authority of a board of managers appointed by the governor. Originally all three managers were men. Conflicts surfaced; in 1877 the policy changed to require all managers be women (Rafter, 1990).

Several other women's prisons were opened over the next 40 years, including the Massachusetts Prison at Framington (1877), the New York Reformatory for Women at Westfield Farm (1901), the District of Columbia Reformatory for Women (1910), and the New Jersey Reformatory for Women at Clinton (1913). These institutions would be separate, home-like institutions where women "would have an opportunity, with as much time as they needed, to 'mend their criminal ways' and learn to be good housewives, helpmates and mothers" (Watterson, 1996, p. 198).

There was a flurry of women's prison reform activities between 1870 and 1900. Four major factors contributed to the rise of the women's prison movement: (1) an apparent increase in female crime after the war and an increase in women prisoners; (2) the women's Civil War social service movement; (3) the emergence of charity and prison reform movements in general, many of them emphasizing the problem of crime and the notion of rehabilitation; and (4) the beginnings of a feminist movement that emphasized a separatist approach and a reinterpretation of the notion of the "fallen woman" (Freedman, 1981).

The alleged crime wave among women following the war primarily involved the wives and daughters of men who had died in the war. The large number of deaths during the war created a class of poor women arrested primarily for public order offenses and offenses against morality (Freedman, 1981). Several reformers placed the blame of the rise of fcmale criminality on the attitudes and sexist practices of men. Josephine Lowell complained that many women "from early girlhood have been tossed from poorhouse to jail, and from jail to poorhouse, until the last trace of womanhood in them has been destroyed" (p. 49). She condemned law officers who regarded women "as objects of derision and sport" and who "wantonly assaulted and degraded numerous young women prisoners" (p. 59). Many specifically blamed a sexual double standard whereby men condemned female sexual activity while condoning their own and, moreover, arrested and imprisoned prostitutes but not the men who enjoyed their services. Finally, reformers campaigned against male guards in prisons where women were confined. Investigations found that women "may be forced to minister to the lust of the officers, or if they refuse, submit to the inflection of the lash until they do" (p. 60).

The Reformatory

Two major types of prisons emerged during the nineteenth century (Rafter, 1990). One type was the *custodial prison*, which resembled the classic penitentiary originally designed for male prisoners. As the name implies, these institutions emphasized custody and security as the main goals; in the modern vernacular, custodial prisons incapacitated and warehoused prisoners. There were three main types of custodial prisons for women: (1) those that were either within or attached to male prisons; (2) prison farms in the South; (3) totally independent prisons. In custodial prisons, Black women labored in the fields, while white women sewed, gardened, and cared for chickens. Quarters for Black women were inferior to those for white women.

Reformatories were supposed to be more treatment oriented. The first reformatories relied on enforcing domestic routines; after release, women were placed in private homes as housekeepers. These institutions, and most to follow, were all designed according to the cottage plan. Separate housing facilities resembled, as nearly as possible, an average family home to teach women to become good homemakers. While the women reformers often claimed to be staunch feminists, the organization of prison life they created was perfectly suited to relegate women to a traditional role. In fact, the design won the approval of many skeptical men, one of whom commented that: "Girls and women should be trained to adorn homes with the virtues which make their lives noble and ennobling. *It is only in this province, that they may most fittingly fill their mission*" (Freedman, 1981, p. 62, emphasis added). The end result, of course, would perpetuate women's traditional roles of dependency as housewives and maids.

The Role of Racism

The early prison system reflected the segregation in the general society. African American women were housed in prisons where there was little or no hope of any sort of rehabilitation (i.e., custodial prisons), while white women were most likely to be sentenced to reformatories where there was at least a formal commitment to rehabilitation (Rafter, 1990). In 1923, almost two-thirds (64.5%) of the women inmates in custodial prisons were African American, compared to only 11.9% in reformatory institutions. For African American women prisoners, the custodial prisons represented a continuation of their slave status prior to the Emancipation Proclamation. African American women prisoners were often, like their male counterparts, leased out to local businesses such as farms, mines, and railroads to work on various kinds of chain gangs. According to the 1880 census, more than one-third of the 220 African American female prisoners in Alabama, Louisiana, Mississippi, North Carolina, Tennessee, and Texas were leased out, compared to only 1 of the 40 white women prisoners.

The overrepresentation of African American women varied widely by region (Rafter, 1990). In New York, for instance, 44% of the women inmates were African American, compared to a percentage of only 20 for African American men. In 1868 in Tennessee, *every female inmate was African American*, compared to around 60% of the male prisoners. In 1880, the percentage of women prisoners who were African American were significantly higher than the percentages of Black men in the Midwest and the South (see table 6-1). By 1904, the pattern appeared in all regions. By 1923, only the South had a large discrepancy.

Table 6-1 **Percent Black in State Prison Population, by Sex and Region, 1880, 1904, 1923**

	Total State Prisoners % Black	Males in Prison % Black	Females in Prison % Black	General Population % Black
1880				
Northeast	8.1	8.2	7.0	1.6
Midwest	12.2	11.8	29.0	2.2
South	73.0	72.4	85.8	36.0
West	18.0	18.0	20.0	0.7
1904				
Northeast	12.6	12.2	18.2	1.8
Midwest	22.5	22.0	48.4	1.9
South	72.7	73.0	90.2	32.3
West	9.1	8.9	26.1	0.7
1923				
Northeast	15.2	15.1	15.4	2.3
Midwest	19.7	19.6	22.0	2.3
South	60.3	59.6	79.6	26.9
West	7.1	7.0	10.0	0.9

Source: Rafter (1990, p. 142)

Women in the Criminal Justice System

Over the last four decades, the involvement of women with the criminal justice system has increased—the result of more expansive law enforcement efforts, stiffer drug sentencing laws, and post-conviction barriers to reentry that uniquely affect women (Sentencing Project, 2019a).

Jails have been labelled the "front door" to the criminal justice system. However, contact with the police is the initial component in entry to the system. In 2018, women accounted for 27% of all arrests compared to 21% in 1997 and 16% in 1980 (Prison Policy Initiative, 2019a). For every woman arrested, five more women experienced non-voluntary interactions with police officers. Women made up 44% of all police-initiated contacts, 41% of traffic stops, and 36% of street stops. Twelve million women per year experience police-initiated contacts.

The full scope of racial discrimination in policing is unknown. Narratives constructed during slavery, reconstruction, and Jim Crow shape reactions—conscious and unconscious—of police to Black women. Black women who are not submissive and do not show deference are framed as subhuman, deserving of punishment (Ritchie, 2017). Pretext stops use traffic laws to uncover more serious crime (Forman, 2018). When executing a pretext stop, police are more than twice as likely to stop Black women than white women. Black women are also more likely than white men to be stopped—yet, white men carry guns and commit violent crimes at much higher rates than do Black women. The most destructive aspect of the pretext-stop is that it propels disparities in the rest of the criminal justice system. These disparities illuminate the need to make policing more transparent, accountable, effective, and just.

Arrests

From 1997 to 2017, arrests of men decreased 30%; arrests of women decreased 6% (Prison Policy Initiative, 2019a). In 2019, more than 1.9 million women were arrested (FBI, 2020a). From 2010 to 2019, arrests of women decreased 15.1% while arrests of men decreased 23.1%. The only increases in arrests of males were 2.7% for murder/manslaughter and 14% for motor vehicle theft. Arrests of women increased in 6 categories: 1.3% increase for all other offenses; 7.5% for stolen property; 10.3% for murder/manslaughter; 21.3% for weapons charges; 26.3% for drug abuse violations; and 56.4% for motor vehicle theft.

Police reforms that resulted in fewer arrests of men have not been of equal benefit to women (Kajstura, 2019). The upward trajectory of women's incarceration was affected by policing practices. Women face a widening net from overcriminalization of drug use and prostitution and from policy changes in domestic violence that have increased arrests (Sawyer, 2018). After arrest, there are fewer diversion programs available for women.

Community Supervision

The 884,988 women on probation comprise 25% of the probation population, and the 114,134 women on parole comprise 13% of the parole population (Kaeble & Alper, 2020). In 1990, there were 520,000 women under community supervision; the number almost doubled in less than three decades. (Pew Charitable Trusts, 2018). One of every 124 women is under community supervision.

Almost three out of four women under control of the US correctional system are on probation. Probation is ideally an alternative to incarceration, but its unrealistic conditions too frequently undermine the goal of keeping people from being locked up (Kajstura, 2019). Steep fees are often involved in meeting the conditions of probation. Most women do not have the income to pay the fees, leaving them vulnerable to being incarcerated because they fail to meet the obligations of their community supervision. Responsibilities of caring for children complicate probation requirements such as meeting with probation officers. Women often lack the money to pay a babysitter or to secure reliable transportation. Very few post-release programs are available for the two million women released from jails and prisons each year. Formerly incarcerated women are more likely than formerly incarcerated men to be homeless—a severe complication for complying with probation or parole requirements.

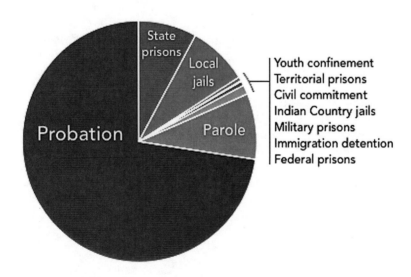

Figure 6-1   Women under Correctional Control

Source: Kajstura, 2019

Women in Jail

In 1970, 8,000 women were jailed (Swavola et al., 2016). In 2018, there were more than 13 times that number (Zeng, 2020). Men account for 84% of the people in jail—685,900 in 2018. The US jail population tripled over three decades, as local justice systems increasingly detained people too poor to make bail (Aiken, 2017). From 2008 to 2018, the number of men in jail *decreased* by 9%. The number of women *increased* from 99,700 to 115,100—a 15% increase (Zeng, 2020). From 2005 to 2018, the jail incarceration rate for men decreased 14% from 448 to 387 per 100,000 male U.S. residents. The jail incarceration rate for women increased 10%, from 63 to 69 inmates per 100,000 female U.S. residents. The following factors or combination of factors provide possible explanations for the increase in the number of women in jail: more arrests, frequent pretrial detention, longer case processing times, punishment for probation or parole violations, or lengthier jail sentences (Kajstura, 2019).

Local jails are particularly significant in the mass incarceration of women. There are twice as many men in state prisons than in local jails. Incarcerated women are divided almost equally between local jails and state prisons. Half of all jailed women are in small counties (Swavola et al., 2016). Most are jailed for nonviolent, low-level offenses—including failure to appear after receiving a citation, failing a drug test, or missing a scheduled appointment with a probation or parole officer.

Sixty percent of women in jails have not been convicted of a crime; they are detained because they cannot afford bail (Kajstura, 2019). Women in pretrial detention had median annual incomes below the poverty line—about 30% lower than men who could not afford bail. Typical bail amounts are often an entire year's income for women. Pretrial detention of even a few days can be life-altering for women and their families, putting jobs and housing at risk. If convicted, women generally serve jail sentences of one year or less. Although jail sentences are shorter than prison sentences, it is harder to stay in touch with family. Jail phone calls are three times more expensive than calls from prison, and there are more restrictions on other forms of communication. Eighty percent of women in jails are mothers, and most are the primary caretakers of their children—subjecting the family to the collateral consequences of incarceration.

Most of the women are in jail because of efforts to cope with poverty, unemployment, and challenges related to past histories of trauma, mental illness, or substance use (Swavola et al., 2016).

> Among a sample of nearly 500 women in jails across various regions of the country, 82 percent had experienced drug or alcohol abuse or dependence in their lifetime. Older research shows that at the time of the offense, incarcerated women were more likely than men to have been using drugs. Additionally, 60 percent of women in jail did not have full-time employment prior to their arrest—in contrast to incarcerated men, 40 percent of whom lacked full-time employment. And

nearly 30 percent of incarcerated women receive public assistance, compared to just under 8 percent of men. (pp. 9–10)

Women in jails are more likely to have mental health problems and to experience serious psychological distress than are men (Kajstura, 2019). Almost a third of the women in jails have a serious mental illness—six times the rate among women in the general population and twice the rate of men in jail (Prison Policy Initiative, 2019a). Jails rarely have the resources to provide mental health care.

Since 1978, jail populations grew in tandem with state prison populations in all states (Aiken, 2017). Three-quarters of the population live in states where both the state prison and the local jail incarceration rates doubled. Crime rates have fallen dramatically over 35 years, but "tough on-crime" attitudes continue to shape local and state policies regarding punishment. Incarcerating people for low-level crimes results in more and more Americans with criminal and arrest records. Jails are increasingly filled with people who are marginalized and poor. Spending time in jail has numerous collateral consequences, many of which are roadblocks to successful reentry, resulting in higher recidivism rates.

Women in Prison

During the last four decades, women have been the fastest rising group in US prisons. In 1980, there were 13,420 women in state and federal prison; the numbers peaked at 114,612 in 2008—a 854% increase. After 2008, there were some fluctuations up and down. By 2018, 110,845 women were incarcerated, the lowest number since 2005. Male prisoners

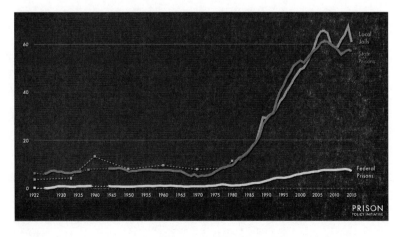

Figure 6-2   Growth in Women's Rate of Incarceration (per 100,000 female residents)

Source: Sawyer, 2018

comprised 92.4% of the total prison population in 2018; the number of male prisoners sentenced to more than one year decreased by 23,500 (down 1.7%) from 2017 (Carson 2020b). Women made up 7.6% of the total prison population; the number of female prisoners sentenced to more than one year decreased by 530 (down 0.5%).

The incarceration rate for women remained fairly stable for most of the twentieth century, ranging from 6 per 100,000 population in 1925 to 8 in 1975. After 1975 the rates changed dramatically, doubling to 17 in 1985, reaching 45 by 1994, and peaking at 69 in 2008 (Carson, 2015). Imprisonment rates based on female sentenced prisoners under state and federal jurisdictions per 100,000 female residents in 2019 was 61 (Carson 2020b). There is wide variation among the states. Oklahoma had the highest imprisonment rate (155 sentenced prisoners per 100,000 female state residents); it imprisoned 3,081 women. Massachusetts had the lowest imprisonment rate (10); it imprisoned 293 women. Texas incarcerated the most sentenced women (13,204; imprisonment rate 91); Rhode Island incarcerated the fewest (59; imprisonment rate 11).

The imprisonment rate for Black women in 2019 was 83; for Hispanic women 63, and for white women 48 (Carson 2020b). The imprisonment rate of Black females was 1.3 times higher than that of Hispanic females (see table 6-2). The imprisonment rate of Black females was 1.7 times the

Table 6-2   Imprisonment Rates for Women by Demographic Characteristics

| Age | Per 100,000 U.S. residents in a given category | | | | |
| | Female | | | | |
	All female	White	Black	Hispanic	Other
Total	61	48	83	63	109
18-19	10	6	20	12	11
20-24	71	49	116	78	118
25-29	149	120	186	150	239
30-34	178	156	199	178	276
35-39	169	148	187	164	270
40-44	126	110	151	114	201
45-49	95	83	128	82	144
50-54	70	54	110	64	123
55-59	42	32	68	42	83
60-64	20	14	32	20	48
65 or older	5	4	9	6	15
Number of sentenced prisoners	101,348	47,900	17,800	19,000	16,600

Source: Carson, 2020b

rate of white females, while the imprisonment rate of Hispanic females was 1.3 times the rate of white females. The rate of imprisonment for African American women has been declining since 2000, while the rate of imprisonment for white and Hispanic women has increased (Sentencing Project, 2019a).

Table 6-3 compares incarceration rates for men and women from 1980 through 2019 (data on Hispanics was not available until 2000). Between 2000 and 2017, the rate of imprisonment in state and federal prisons declined by 55% for Black women (and 32% for Black men). The rate of imprisonment for white women rose by 44% (the rate for white men *decreased* 12%). The rate of imprisonment for Hispanic women increased 10% (versus a 14% decrease for Hispanic men).

More than half (57.9%) of the men in prison in 2018 were convicted of a violent crime, compared to 38% of incarcerated women (Carson, 2020b). Women who commit violent acts often do so in self-defense, examples include intimate partner violence (National Resource Center, 2016). Violent offenses committed by women usually occur against family members or intimates in domestic settings. Women in state prisons are more likely than men to be incarcerated for a drug, property, or larceny/theft offense (Carson, 2020b). More than one-quarter (25.7%) of the women in prison were convicted of a drug offense, compared to 13.4% of

Table 6-3	Rate of Sentenced Prisoners in State and Federal Prisons, by Race and Gender, 1980–2019					
Gender and Race	1980	1990	2000	2010	2019	Percent change Incarceration Rate 1980–2019 (Hispanic 2000–2019)
Males						
White	168	339	449	459	385	129
Black	1,111	2,376	3,457	3,074	2,203	98
Hispanic			1,220	1,258	979	−20
Females						
White	6	19	34	47	48	700
Black	45	125	205	133	83	84
Hispanic			60	77	63	5
Black/White Ratio						
Males	6.6:1	7.0:1	7.7:1	6.7:1	5.8:1	
Females	7.5:1	6.6:1	6.0:1	2.8:1	1.8:1	

Source: Beck & Dilliard, 1995, table 11; Guerino et al., 2011, appendix table 14; Carson, 2020b, table 10.

incarcerated men; 24.4% of incarcerated women were convicted of a property offense, compared to 15.6% of men; 7.6% of women were convicted
of larceny/theft versus 2.8% of men.

Characteristics of Incarcerated Women

As noted previously, the increasing rates of female incarceration
reflect disturbing social trends. The inclination to punish through incarceration ignores the social and psychological forces that often underlie female
offending. Over the last three decades, research in the fields of health,
mental health, substance abuse, and violence against women has found
that women offenders face challenges that not only differ from those of
male offenders but also greatly influence their involvement in the criminal
justice system (Hope Rises, 2020).

Demographics

There are differences between male and female offenders in terms of
offending histories, risk factors, and life circumstances (National Resource
Center, 2016). Some factors are significant for both men and women but
are observed with greater frequency among women. Other factors are seen
with about equal frequency for both genders, but there are distinct physical, personal, and social effects for women. Other factors occur with
women but typically not with men.

Women's pathways to criminal justice differ from those of men.
Women are much more likely to have experienced poverty, intimate partner violence, sexual abuse, and/or other forms of victimization often
linked to their offending behavior. Dysfunctional and abusive relationships
can lead to involvement in crime. Research has found that women's identities and self-worth are defined by relationships with others (National
Resource Center, 2016). Criminal experiences of women are often linked
to unhealthy relationships that encourage criminal behavior. An estimated
80%–85% of women in prison are incarcerated for crimes that directly
result from their relationships with an abusive partner (Law, 2019).
Research on women's criminal histories has found that motivations to
commit crime often have to do with survival, providing for children, coping with early trauma, and unhealthy relationships with chronic offender
partners (Jessie, 2020).

Women have higher-than-average rates of exposure to cumulative
trauma. Trauma such as sexual victimization contributes to criminal pathways for women; it is inked to mental health, substance abuse to manage
distress, and relationship difficulties (Cowan, 2019). Compared to male
inmates, women report higher rates of physical and sexual abuse as children and adults. At least 50% of women entering prison reported physical

and/or sexual abuse prior to their incarceration (Briefing Report, 2020). As many as 90% of women in prison experienced traumatic events— among the most common were interpersonal or sexual violence. The risk of abuse for males generally drops after childhood, but the risk for females continues throughout their adolescence and adulthood.

Society's emphasis on law enforcement and punishment has resulted in throw-away attitudes toward people with serious mental illness (Cowan, 2019). About 73% of state women prisoners exhibit mental health problems compared to 55% of men (National Resource Center, 2016). About 33% of justice involved women have PTSD. Women (40.5%) are twice as likely as men (22.9%) to have co-occurring substance abuse disorders and mental illness.

Women's behavioral choices can be affected by economic disparities. More women (37%) than men (28%) report incomes of less than $600 per month prior to their conviction (National Resource Center, 2016). Two-thirds of incarcerated women earned a maximum wage of $6.50 per hour; most were employed in entry-level positions. Researchers found that in California, only 37% of the incarcerated women interviewed listed a legitimate job as their primary source of income; 22% said their primary source was public assistance, while 16% reported selling drugs to provide for themselves and their children.

Table 6-4 lists the major offenses committed by women incarcerated in state prisons plus ethnicity and age.

Table 6-4 **Characteristics of Women in State Prison**

Characteristic	Percent
Major Offense	
Violent	38%
Property	24.4%
Drug	25.7%
Public Order	11.1%
Race/Ethnicity	
White	47.3%
Black	17.6%
Hispanic	18.7%
Other	16.3%
Age	
18–24	7.8%
25–34	36.5%
35–44	30.6%
45–54	16.7%
55+	8.3%

Source: Carson, 2020b, Tables 9, 13

Incarcerated Mothers

Over 60% of imprisoned women are mothers with children under the age 18 (Cowan, 2019). Most of these women were the sole caregivers prior to incarceration. Children of incarcerated mothers are at high risk of being placed in foster care. The Adoption and Safe Families Act of 1997 requires termination of parental rights when a child has been in foster care for 15 of the past 22 months.

> In the era of mass incarceration and mandatory minimum sentencing laws that leave the majority of incarcerated people behind bars for well over twenty-two months, this provision leads to increasing numbers of incarcerated parents losing their parental rights. In part because people of color are disproportionately policed and incarcerated, and because children with incarcerated mothers are disproportionately likely to be placed in foster care, Black children and other children of color are especially impacted by this policy. (Rippey, 2020, p. 532)

Transportation to hearings regarding their children may not be provided for incarcerated women. Also, there is no right to counsel, and women may not know how to navigate the legal process (Briefing Report, 2020). There is a higher rate of permanent custody loss for incarcerated parents than for nonincarcerated parents who neglected or abused their children.

As mentioned above, Texas incarcerates the most women—four of every five female inmates are mothers. The average sentence is nine years for a drug conviction and more than eight years for theft offenses, a significant portion of a child's life (Levin, 2019). After a series of inmate deaths and scandals involving the treatment of imprisoned women, Texas in 2019 passed legislation, known as dignity laws, addressing needs of female prisoners. One measure directs the Texas Department of Criminal Justice to study the effects of its visitation policies on the relationships between inmates and their children. The department has a program that allows mothers to bond with their newborn children for several weeks after their birth. Since 2016, parental incarceration has played a role in nearly 20,000 children entering the foster care system.

The federal government has 29 facilities for housing women—less than one facility per state. The distance of institutions from families make visitations and maintenance of familial relationships difficult. The Bureau of Prisons requires that its inmates be housed within 500 miles of home, but most women are from impoverished communities. Relatives (usually grandparents) who may have taken over the role of primary caregiver for children of the incarcerated woman often cannot afford the cost of travel and lodging for visitation. Most federal facilities are in rural areas without access to public transportation.

There are long-lasting consequences of imprisonment on the maternal-child bond. Many incarcerated mothers lose contact with their children because of the hardships of visitation (Cowan, 2019). The location of facilities, the design, and the rules and policies of prisons make it difficult to parent from behind bars (Briefing Report, 2020). Researchers at the University of Chicago interviewed incarcerated mothers at a correctional center in Illinois (Stevens, 2020). The interviewees had spent an average of four years in prison, with another 8.5 years left before their release date. Their children ranged in age from infants to 17. The women wanted to stay connected to their children during their time in prison but cited numerous obstacles. Only 1 in 3 mothers reported that their children lived within two hours of the prison. Many of the children lived with relatives who could not make the drive for visitation. Mothers worried that the children who did visit might be traumatized or physically harmed by conditions in the prison: pervasive mold, broken toilets, pest infestations, and lead paint. Many of the phones in the facility were broken; there were two-hour waits to call home on the remaining functioning phones. Phone times were allotted and the assigned times often did not align with children's schedules. Prisoners paid for their phone calls out of a $10 per month allowance (a 15-minute call costs about $7); the same allowance covered mail supplies (envelopes, stamps), snacks and toiletries.

Asked about their response to unsympathetic readers who might believe people who do the crime should be able to do the time, the researchers suggested reminding them that the children did nothing wrong (Stevens, 2020). The researchers suggested the need to reflect on moral and ethical concerns regarding criminal justice system: "Do we feel as though we have to punish people every single minute of their time in prison in order to feel some sense of justice has been served?" (p. 3). Parental incarceration means their children share the repercussions of the punishment. The toll is often more severe when the inmate is their mother (Levin, 2019).

More than 5 million children in the United States have had a parent incarcerated at some point in their life (Cramer et al., 2017). Black children and children from economically disadvantaged families are more likely to experience parental incarceration. One in 9 Black have experienced the incarceration of a parent who lived with them compared to 1 in 17 white children and 1 in 16 Hispanic children. A child living in poverty is more than 3 times more likely to have experienced parental incarceration (1 in 8) than a child whose household income is at least twice the federal poverty level (1 in 26). Most studies have measured the number of parents in prison; less is known about how many parents have been jailed—which means there are probably many more children affected by parental incarceration than available estimates.

Negative outcomes for children as a consequence of parental incarceration range from depression and anxiety to aggression and delinquency, depending on the child's age and the length of a parent's incarceration (Gotsch, 2018). Having an incarcerated parent and/or placement in foster care significantly increases the chances that a child will eventually become involved in the criminal justice system plus the chances of substance abuse and/or homelessness across the lifespan (Cowan, 2019). The generational effects are devastating.

The complications of criminal justice involvement do not end with the release of a mother from prison. Federal and state laws create obstacles to securing employment, housing, food stamps, and financial assistance. The stress of repairing frayed relationships with families and children after a prolonged absence (or living with the termination of parental rights) exacerbate the challenges of reentry (Gotsch, 2018).

Pregnancy

About 3.8% of women entering prison and 5% of women entering jail are pregnant. Prisons and jails are required to provide prenatal care, but there are no detailed standards to ensure that women receive the care they need (Daniel, 2019). Policies for local jails are more variable, inaccessible, and incomplete than policy for state prisons. For example, in August 2019 a woman told Denver County Jail deputies that she was in labor; the staff failed to take action, and she gave birth without medical aid or assistance. This was not an isolated case, but data about pregnancy in state prisons and local jails is scarce. Carolyn Sufrin, a researcher at Johns Hopkins School of Medicine, commented that any available data is old; we do not the number of incarcerated women or what happens during their pregnancies (Briefing Report, 2020).

> Women who don't count don't get counted. That is, the lack of any comprehensive or updated statistics about pregnancy among women behind bars signals the systematic disregard in the carceral system, and indeed our country, for incarcerated pregnant people. (p. 101)

There are multiple complexities regarding birth while in custody—including the medically unsafe practices of placing pregnant women in solitary confinement, shackling women in labor, providing proper pregnancy and postpartum care, and determining who will care for the infants born to mothers in custody (Briefing Report, 2020). Pregnant women generally face abrupt separation from their newborn babies.

The First Step Act of 2018 prohibits shackling during pregnancy in federal prisons (although the 2 exceptions for flight risk and security have been criticized as overly broad and subject to abuse), and the practice is prohibited in 26 states (Briefing Report, 2020). The use of restraints (shackling) exacerbates pain, inhibits diagnosis of complications, and limits movement during the birthing process.

Incarcerated pregnant women are at higher risk for pregnancy complications because of substance use disorders, sexually-transmitted infections, and poor nutrition. Thirty-one states lack any policy on nutrition for incarcerated pregnant women (Daniel, 2019). In some states, more than 20% of prison pregnancies result in miscarriages; in others, preterm birth rates exceed the national average of 10%.

Institutional Life

A substantial amount of research on the sociology of punishment documents and explains societal shifts toward coercive control that accompanied mass incarceration (Kreager & Kruttschnitt, 2018). Interrelated political, cultural, and criminological responses to social change created the overarching emphasis on exclusion and control to solve perceived issues of crime and insecurity. Mass incarceration focused on controlling and excluding stigmatized offenders—replacing the rehabilitative emphasis of the penal-welfare era.

Society's focus on punitiveness has consequences for inmate-staff relationships. Societal views that emphasize punishment and the incarceration of incorrigible offenders affect prison personnel and changes the experiences of female prisoners (Kreager & Kruttschnitt, 2018) Some of the consequences include weakened inmate-staff trust, cessation of rehabilitation programming, and inmates retreating from one another. The political contexts of penal policy fractured inmate cohesion.

Early research on the inmate society in women's prisons was an outgrowth of the classic studies of men's institutions (Kreager & Kruttschnitt, 2018). Researchers focused primarily on whether women's adaptations to prison were similar to men's in terms of deprivation and importation. In the late 1990s scholars began studying how women's carceral lives were changing. Crowding became a defining feature of women's institutions. Some research found that crowding resulted in more self-reported physical assaults, but a wide range of research suggests that physical violence is rare in women's prisons, although verbal and emotional aggression is common. The general absence of gangs in female institutions and the absence of race as a significant determinant in women's inmate social structure or adaptations to prison life contribute to relatively low levels of serious physical aggression in women's prisons. Race can surface in interpersonal relationships and competition over scarce resources, particularly when conditions of confinement are more severe.

Age and aging are important in understanding women's prison experiences. Younger inmates' experiences are more varied than those of older inmates (Kreager & Kruttschnitt, 2018). Newly admitted young women may find the experience isolating and frightening. Older inmates are generally a stabilizing presence in the prison. Most of the research on aging prisoners focuses on health care needs.

Correctional practices were developed through the lens of managing men. Classification, screening, and risk assessment were not adapted to women, generally resulting in women being classified at a security level higher than warranted. Women rarely exhibit violent behavior when incarcerated (National Resource Center, 2016). For women with a history of trauma and mental health issues, institutional misconduct is more closely linked to the lack of services to address these needs than to offense severity and criminal history typically assessed by classification tools.

Recall the discussion in the history section about prisons preferring not to house women. In 1845, there were very few women in Illinois prisons, but state auditors claimed one female prisoner was more trouble than twenty males (Shapiro et al., 2018). Historical attitudes were in clear evidence when Logan Correctional Center in Lincoln, Illinois, changed from housing men to housing women in 2013. The corrections officers who worked at the men's facility remained after the change to the largest Illinois institution for women. Logan was a chaotic, overcrowded place with six different wardens in three years. Suicide attempts increased from 1 a month to 10. Officers overused solitary confinement and force to control the women prisoners; they routinely used racial and homophobic slurs. Women were punished twice as often as men in other state prisons—and at almost five times the rate of men for "minor insolence." After an audit revealed the practices, Illinois passed legislation requiring specific programming for women in prison and mandating officer training in gender responsive corrections.

NPR and the Medill School of Journalism at Northwestern University collected data from prisons housing women and from prisons housing men (Shapiro et al., 2018). In 13 of the 15 states analyzed, women were disciplined at higher rates than men, with the largest discrepancies for minor infractions of prison rules. In California, women received more than twice the disciplinary tickets for "disrespect." In Vermont, women were more than three times as likely as men to be disciplined for "derogatory comments" about a corrections officer or another inmate. In Rhode Island, women received more than three times the tickets for "disobedience." In Iowa, female prisoners were nearly three times as likely as men to be disciplined for being "disruptive." In Illinois, an inmate was playing Scrabble in her cell when a guard asked what she was doing. She replied, "What does it look like I'm doing?" She was disciplined for contraband (the Scrabble set) and for "insolence." Another inmate made a face when a corrections officer gave her an order. She was disciplined with solitary confinement for "reckless eye-balling." In Idaho and Rhode Island, women were more likely than men to end up in solitary confinement for violations like disobedience. In California in a 25-month period, women had the equivalent of 1,483 years added to their sentences through good-credit revocations. Discipline for small infractions can also result in the loss of privileges, including access to the prison commissary or visitation and phone privileges.

The NPR/Medill investigators visited five women's prisons around the country, interviewing current and former prisoners, wardens, prison officials, academics, and other experts (Shapiro et al., 2018). They asked why women were disciplined more frequently and more severely for minor infractions. Respondents said prison rules were set up to control men, especially violent ones. That system of control is problematic for female prisoners. Women are more likely than men to be convicted of drug and property crimes; they are also less likely to be violent in prison. Women are more likely than men to have significant problems with substance abuse, to have mental health problems, to be the caregiving parent of a minor child, and to have been victims of sexual or physical violence. When a corrections officer—the majority of whom are men—yells an order, a woman with a history of abuse might shut down, ignore the officer, or yell back. All those responses can result in a disciplinary ticket.

Maggie Burke served as warden of Logan; she had worked for 29 years as a corrections officer in both men's and women's prisons (Shapiro et al., 2018). She began training corrections officers to understand differences between male and female prisoners. A logical starting point was the question of whether a facility is safer by putting a woman in solitary confinement because she talked back to someone. She explained discrepant attitudes by noting that when guards tell a male inmate to do something, he either does or does not comply; he doesn't talk back. Those sentiments were echoed in other interviews. Women in prison are more communicative; they want to talk. If they see an injustice or a problematic situation, they want to engage in a conversation. But most corrections officers resent the questions. They perceive women who want to talk and don't take no for an answer as difficult, aggressive, and problematic—and they react with punishment.

Correctional facilities infrequently provide rehabilitation or substance abuse and mental health treatment services, exacerbating the vulnerabilities of female inmates (Cowan, 2019). Women report higher rates than males of physical and sexual victimization perpetrated by fellow inmates during incarceration. Few correctional settings have the resources or specially trained staff to address the unique needs of female offenders. The harsh rules and regulations of correctional facilities, and the preexisting vulnerabilities of women place them at greater risk of distress. For some, acting out behaviors result in infractions and greater restrictions, including solitary confinement.

Solitary confinement or restrictive housing includes what some systems term segregation, isolation, room confinement, special housing units (SHU), control units, or special management units that separate prisoners from the general population in cells for an average of 22 or more hours per day for 15 or more continuous days. Research has found that minor infractions such as being disrespectful are sometimes punished with solitary confinement (Briefing Report, 2020).

> The limited treatment options in many prison settings are directly reflected in the greater number of disciplinary problems, rule violations, and physical assaults among those who have mental health disorders, often compounded by the resulting solitary confinement as punishment for these behaviors. (p. 125)

One study looked at women in solitary confinement in six states in 2018. The percent of women in restrictive housing was 12.1% in Louisiana, 4.8% in Nebraska, 5.7% in Nevada, 5% in North Carolina, 3.4% in Oregon, and 4% in Utah (Briefing Report, 2020). Women of color and women who identify as lesbian, gay, and bisexual face discipline disparities, especially regarding solitary confinement. Prolonged periods of isolation can have severe psychological and physical effects. It also limits access to rehabilitative opportunities to earn good time credit.

The majority of women in prison experienced more trauma than their male counterparts prior to their incarceration. The routine practices of prisons (e.g., strip searches, or solitary confinement) and the physical environment (e.g., limited light, loud noises, clanking metal doors, and often extreme temperatures) can trigger memories of traumatic experiences. Some women cope with these triggers by talking back to prison staff or engaging in behaviors that lead to disciplinary infractions. Crowded living quarters, lack of privacy, increased risk of victimization, and solitary confinement present challenges for adaptation and serve as strong correlates for self-harm for those with mental health conditions.

Sentencing Patterns

As noted in previous chapters, there is no way we can separate the phenomenal growth in prison populations from the war on drugs, a war that has adversely affected women.

Mandatory Sentencing

When New York City experienced a spike in heroin use in the 1970s, a fearful public's mood became increasingly punitive. Governor Nelson Rockefeller had previously viewed drugs as a social rather than a criminal problem, favoring rehabilitation over punishment. In 1973, he changed course and launched a campaign for 15-year mandatory sentences for possession of four ounces of narcotics (Kappeler & Potter, 2018). The New York legislature passed statutes that became known as the Rockefeller Drug Laws, which became a model for the national trend toward punitive sentences and sowed the seeds for mass incarceration. Judges in New York were required to sentence offenders to mandatory minimums that were more severe than the federal minimums. The amount of the illegal drug possessed or sold determined the sentence. The possession of four ounces or sale of two ounces carried a sentence of 15 years to life compared to a federal sentence of five years for a first offense of selling 500 grams (almost 18 ounces). The majority of people convicted under these laws had no prior criminal convictions, but their sentences were more severe than those of felons convicted of rape, manslaughter, and robbery.

The number of drug convictions increased dramatically, but there was no corresponding decrease in drug use or crime. Although whites used substantial amounts of drugs in the 1970s, the people arrested and sent to prison under the Rockefeller laws were primarily from poor Black and Hispanic neighborhoods (Kappeler & Potter, 2018). A commission appointed by the New York Bar Association found that the state had spent $32 million in implementing the laws, but the net effect of three years of intensive enforcement was negligible. There was no reduction in drug-related crime or in heroin usage—and drugs were readily available. The commission declared the law an expensive failure. Critics argued that the laws criminalized a public health problem, incarcerated nonviolent felons, increased recidivism rates, and eliminated judicial discretion in sentencing. New York reduced some mandatory minimum sentences in 2004 and the New York legislature in 2009 repealed many of the mandatory minimum prison sentences for lower-level drug felons. David Paterson (then governor) expressed the opinion that no criminal justice strategy had ever been less successful than the Rockefeller Drug Laws.

A tragic event in June 1986 cemented public support for punitive drug laws. Len Bias, an All-American basketball star at the University of Maryland, was drafted second by the Boston Celtics. Two days later, he was dead of a cocaine overdose, wrongly attributed to crack cocaine. House Speaker Tip O'Neill observed his constituents' reaction to the death of Bias and saw drugs as the path to victory for his party in the upcoming elections (Schuppe, 2016). Four months later, the Anti-Drug Abuse Act of 1986 became law. The lasting legacy was mandatory minimum sentences for drug crimes, which Congress had repealed in 1970. Once drug crimes opened the door for mandatory minimums, similar penalties for other crimes soon followed.

There was little research into the implications of the bill. Lawmakers believed drugs were an epidemic and that crack cocaine was the most dangerous. After Bias died, more than 1,000 stories appeared on crack cocaine in the national press; there was also extensive television coverage (Shelden & Vasiliev, 2018). Heated rhetoric about widespread use and abuse of crack cocaine included assertions—instant addiction, violent behavior, lifetime damage to babies born to mothers addicted to crack—unsupported by scientific data about the psychopharmacological and behavioral effects of the substance. As discussed in chapter 4, the Anti-Drug Abuse Act established a mandatory minimum sentence of 5 years imprisonment for drug offenses involving 5 grams of crack, 500 grams of cocaine, 100 grams of heroin plus penalties for other illicit drugs. The minimum mandatory sentence for 50 grams of crack, 5,000 grams of cocaine, and 1,000 grams of heroin was 10 years. The goal may have been to imprison high-level dealers, but the amounts specified were far below the amounts trafficked by kingpins (Schuppe, 2016). The average drug seller holds a low-wage job and sells drugs part-time to fund his or her own drug use. Police and prosecutors used the laws against street-level dealers; poor residents in inner cities were the most prominent targets. The laws resulted in decades of soaring prison populations and disproportionate prison sentences for Blacks and Hispanics (Kappeler & Potter, 2018). In July 2010 the disparity in sentencing between crack and cocaine was reduced to 18 to 1—despite the reduction, the legacy of erroneous assumptions about crack cocaine remains.

Sentencing Commission Guidelines

Sentencing is a pipeline in which decisions upstream greatly influence punishment determinations downstream. If sentencing is going to be equal, there must also be equality in arrests by the police and charges by prosecutors. "Equalizing outcomes at sentencing locks in earlier unequal decisions to arrest, charge, and plea bargain" (Bierschbach & Bibas, 2016, p. 1497). Removing discretion at sentencing may make the system more unequal.

Congress created the US Sentencing Commission, a bipartisan, independent agency of the judicial branch of government, in 1984 to reduce sentencing disparities and to promote transparency and proportionality in sentencing. The Commission establishes sentencing policies and practices for the federal courts, including guidelines for the appropriate form and severity of punishment for offenders convicted of federal crimes. The Supreme Court in *United States v. Booker* (2005) invalidated provisions that made the sentencing guidelines mandatory and ruled that the guidelines would be advisory. In April 2014, the US Sentencing Commission reduced the base offense levels assigned to drug offenses. The changes were retroactive. In November 2015, the Bureau of Prisons (BOP) released approximately 6,000 federal inmates convicted of drug trafficking offenses. Twenty-nine states have scaled back sentencing policies, but the scale of change has been small. Most of the changes have been relatively minor: exceptions to mandatory minimum sentence laws for some first offenders and expanded parole release of people convicted of drug crimes. Although an improvement, the changes do not alter the structure of sentencing (Kappeler & Potter, 2018).

Nancy Gertner served as a federal judge from 1994 to 2011. Prior to *Booker*, she was required to issue 10-, 15-, and 20-year sentences for drug offenses—sentences which she described as making no sense under any rational social policy (Kappeler & Potter, 2018). Gertner (2020) notes that few judges take advantage of the discretion *Booker* gave them because decisions made within the guidelines typically survive review. "Thus, even in an advisory regime, the Guidelines—imperfect and ill-considered as they are—still hold sway" (p. 1410).

In 2017, the US Sentencing Commission issued a report, "Demographic Differences in Sentencing," that said judges were more lenient with women and that they received shorter sentences than men. Gertner (2020) believes that if there is a disparity between men's and women's sentencing, further analysis is required. Has there been a women's crime wave that justifies the increase in imprisonment of women, or has it occurred because of political decisions made by the Sentencing Commission and Congress? Rather than disparity in sentencing being unwarranted, it may be critical to reflect the differences between women and men offenders.

Sentencing guidelines emphasize the quantity of drugs involved; they underestimate role in the offense. Women codefendants are rarely in leadership roles; they are usually partners of male leaders and may have been subject to coercion, intimidation, and abuse. Women most often play subordinating roles to their partners or codefendants. Women are significantly more likely than their male counterparts to appear at sentencing with no arrests, but the guidelines group such defendants with someone with multiple arrests but no convictions. The guidelines devalue substance abuse; addiction is not relevant to sentencing. The guidelines do not address family circumstances. Women offenders are more likely than men to be single parents; there is a disproportionate impact on their children. Family ties play a significant role in the chances of rehabilitation and the probability of recidivism. A study of probationers found that gender has a statistically significant effect on recidivism. Because the guidelines do not account for this factor, women may be overclassified in terms of risk.

Life Sentences

Nationwide, 1 in 15 women are serving life sentences; one-third are not eligible for parole. Between 2008 and 2016 there was a 2% increase in the number of imprisoned women for a violent crime and a 20% increase in the number of women serving life sentences (Sentencing Project, 2019b). The increase for men during the same time frame was 15%. States with highest number of women serving life sentences are: California (1 in 4); Louisiana (1 in 7); Georgia (1 in 8); Massachusetts (1 in 8); Utah (1 in 8); Maryland (1 in 9). Almost 300 women were under the age of 18 at the time of the crime; three states hold half of these women: California (80), Georgia, (23) and Texas (42). The number of women serving life without parole sentences increased by 41% compared to 29% for men.

Women serving life sentences have the same characteristics as those discussed earlier. Compared to men, women report higher levels of psychiatric disorders, histories of physical and sexual violence, and previous suicide attempts (Sentencing Project, 2019b). Over one-third of women serving life sentences have attempted suicide. Of the women serving life without parole sentences for offenses committed as youth, 80% had experienced physical abuse, 77% sexual abuse, and 84% witnessed violence at home.

Cyntoia Brown was a victim of sex trafficking; in 2004 at age 16 she killed and robbed a man who solicited her for sex. She claimed self-defense but was convicted and received a life sentence, which required serving 51 years before her first parole hearing (Allyn, 2019). Celebrities including Amy Shumer, Ashley Judd, and Rihanna brought national attention to her case through social media. Her case inspired legislation to protect minors who are victims of sex trafficking. The governor commuted her sentence in 2019.

To summarize the sentencing section, we return to the assessment by Gertner (2020) that the results of the advisory sentencing guidelines can be unfair and disproportionate, especially for women offenders.

As long as the Guidelines hold sway over sentencing decisions, judges are more likely to sentence women to the same—or perhaps slightly lower—thoughtless and disproportionate sentences as men. In our fixation about unwarranted disparity in sentencing, we have enforced an unwarranted uniformity: treating women and men alike when they are not, ignoring criminogenic differences between men and women, and trivializing the factors that define women's crimes and predict women's recidivism. (p. 1410)

Criminalizing Pregnancy

Loren Siegel (1997) revealed the extent to which repressive measures were taken to criminalize pregnant women during the panic over crack cocaine. Overzealous prosecutors stretched the limits of legal reasoning in more than 200 prosecutions of women for endangering a fetus. Jennifer Johnson, a Florida woman with no prior criminal convictions, was the first to be charged—for delivering drugs to her infant through the umbilical cord. She had sought treatment for her cocaine addiction but could find no program that would accept her. Routine tests revealed cocaine in her system after the birth of her baby. The hospital notified authorities; Johnson was arrested, convicted, and sentenced to one year of house arrest (during which she was subject to random urine tests and warrantless searches of her home) and 14 years of probation. If she became pregnant during the 14 years' probation, she would have to follow a court-approved pregnancy care program. Black women and poor women were disproportionately targeted for prosecutions. Eventually, careful research revealed that less than 2% of all newborns were exposed to cocaine and that such exposure rarely had any effect on the baby's health.

The crack epidemic helped popularize the idea of fetal rights (Editorial, 2018b). Fanned by racism, many Americans erroneously feared that crack-addicted mothers in inner cities were giving birth to a generation of damaged and possibly vicious children. The sentiment was that any woman who would endanger her child forfeited society's protection. A series of editorials in *The New York Times* argue that these laws are creating a system of social control that polices pregnancy.

Women coping with the heartbreak of losing an unborn child have been charged with a variety of violations, including manslaughter (Editorial, 2018b). In the 1850s, women were put to death for the crimes of "abusing a corpse" or "concealing a birth." Similar laws remain on the books today; they are felonies in Arkansas and Virginia and misdemeanors in other states. The laws were originally intended to make it easier to prosecute women who killed their babies. Fetal homicide laws treat the fetus as a potential crime victim separate from the mother.

In 2016, a 25-year-old Virginia woman wrapped the remains of her stillborn fetus in a bath mat before placing it in a garbage bag and then sought medical care (Editorial, 2018b). Her father, unaware of the contents, disposed of the bag in a public dumpster. The local prosecutor convicted the woman of concealing a dead body. She was sentenced to five months in jail. A woman in Arkansas gave birth to twins, both of which were stillborn. Panicked, she placed the bodies in a suitcase that she disposed of near a rural highway. After the bodies were found, she was arrested and charged with two counts of abuse of a corpse. Her bail was set at $50,000, almost twice the per capita income of most members of her community. Even if the fetus does not die, women can be charged with endangering their children. Pregnant women have found themselves stripped of the right to consent to surgery or the right to receive treatment for a medical condition.

These cases are rare, but there have been several hundred since 1973. The concept that a fetus in the womb has the same rights as a fully formed person has worked its way into federal and state regulations (Editorial, 2018b). It extends the rights of fetuses while eroding the rights of women. The involvement of law enforcement in pregnancy loss compounds the trauma. It may deter pregnant women from seeking medical help, and it forces health care providers to collect evidence rather than caring for their patients. Other children suffer collateral damage if their mothers are jailed.

In 2004, Congress passed the first federal statute to give victim status to fertilized eggs, embryos, and fetuses in cases of violent crime against pregnant women. Pregnant women addicted to drugs, women who miscarried at home, or those who went about their lives in ways that were perceived to harm their pregnancies have been detained and jailed for a variety of crimes—murder, manslaughter, neglect, criminal recklessness, and chemical endangerment (Editorial, 2018b). Indiana was the first state to convict a pregnant woman of feticide. In 2018, the state expanded its 1979 feticide law to include fetuses that would not survive outside of the womb. Many feticide laws use carefully chosen language to legitimize fetal rights, providing grounds for the state to intervene and control pregnant women for the sake of the fetus. Twenty-nine states have feticide laws that recognize the ending of any stage of pregnancy, from fertilization onward, as equivalent to murder, except in cases of legal abortion. Nine states recognize feticide only in later periods of development.

Women charged with pregnancy-related crimes are often poor and nonwhite, without adequate access to education, health care, and job opportunities (Editorial, 2018b). About 7 out of 10 women charged cannot afford a lawyer. The punitive response to pregnant Black women who used cocaine set a standard for treating addiction while pregnant as a criminal matter, rather than a public health concern. In recent years, the methamphetamine and opioid epidemics began to change the racial makeup of those arrested.

The doctrine of fetal personhood significantly breaks Western law traditions that protect the individual from the power of the state. The doctrine allows police, prosecutors, and the courts to scrutinize decisions made by a pregnant woman that might affect the fetus (Editorial, 2018b). The womb of a pregnant woman becomes a legal battleground completely separate from the woman herself. In 2018, a 26-year-old Alabama woman was five months pregnant. She started a fight with another woman, was shot in the stomach, lost her fetus, and was arrested. In Alabama, all felony arrests go before a grand jury, which indicted her for manslaughter. The prosecutor declined to pursue the case, preserving the woman's rights—but not before she was arrested, indicted, and posted bail.

Women in at least 45 states have faced criminal charges for drug use during pregnancy. In almost every state, expectant mothers with a history or suspicion of drug use face assaults on their civil rights: nonconsensual drug testing; arbitrary family separations; court supervision; and compulsory treatment (Editorial, 2018b). The criminalization of certain drugs for controlling minorities has been extended to controlling pregnancy. Decades of research revealed that most drugs, including cocaine and methamphetamine, are less harmful to fetuses than originally believed. Researchers continue to work to discover the long-term effects of prenatal opioid exposure, but babies seem to recover fully within the first few months of life. Alcohol and nicotine can be more damaging than illegal drugs to a developing fetus. Incarcerating addicted mothers, separating them from their children, and relegating them to subhuman status may satisfy an impulse to punish, but those measures do not address the source of the problem. Brown University psychiatry professor Barry Lester specializes in opioid addiction; he notes that society loves to hate addicted pregnant women, but the hatred accomplishes nothing.

Fear of prosecution or family separation often prevents addicted women from seeking medical care. Tennessee passed a fetal assault law in 2014. The intent may have been to curb drug use and promote treatment by threatening jail time, but the result was pregnant women fleeing the state or giving birth at home to avoid the public hospital (Editorial, 2018b). The law was allowed to expire because it drove people away from treatment. Criminalization also affects the quality of treatment. Assertions that pregnant women who struggle with addiction are terrible people affects interactions with doctors, social workers, and judges. Sarah Wakeman, medical director of the Massachusetts General Hospital substance use program, argues that when we criminalize women, we make them scapegoats for the large structural forces and societal failures that create poverty and give rise to addiction.

Criminalizing women for prenatal drug use ignores the context of their lives. Many women face "economic disadvantage, abuse, domestic violence, and unsupported parenting, and are best dealt with away from the criminal justice system" (Du Rose, 2015, p. 84). Hundreds of pregnant women and new mothers have been accused of child abuse or other crimes when they or their newborns test positive for controlled substances

(Miranda et al., 2015). Minorities (especially Blacks) are far more likely to be arrested and prosecuted (Paltrow & Flavin, 2013).

Twenty-three states and the District of Columbia consider substance abuse during pregnancy to be child abuse under civil child-welfare statutes. (Guttmacher Institute, 2019). Alabama leads the country in prosecuting cases like these (Al.com, 2019). The Alabama Supreme Court held that drug use while pregnant is considered chemical endangerment of a child. Nineteen states have drug treatment programs targeted to pregnant women, and 17 states give priority access to state-funded programs to pregnant women. Ten states prohibit publicly funded drug treatment programs from discriminating against pregnant women (Guttmacher Institute, 2019).

Women prisoners in California were subjected to the cruelty of a revised eugenics movement. Between 1909 and 1964, California compulsory sterilization laws targeted minorities, the poor, the disabled, the mentally ill and criminals; 20,000 women and men were sterilized (Johnson, 2014). In 1979. Lawmakers banned forced sterilization, but California prison doctors continued procedures through a loophole that permitted payment through state funds. Although lawful consent was required under law, it was not always obtained. Prison medical staff pressured women into the procedures, targeting inmates with numerous children or perceived as likely to return to prison in the future. Thirty-nine women over a six-year period between 2005 and 2013 were sterilized illegally (Schwartz, 2014). California passed legislation in September 2014 banning coerced sterilization. Like the criminalization of pregnancy, forced sterilization is another egregious example of the attempt to control women's bodies and, in particular, to control the *dangerous classes*.

Violence Against Women

Millions of women in the United States experience some form of victimization each year. During their lifetimes, 1 in 5 women are victims of completed or attempted rape; 1 in 4 women suffer sexual or physical violence; 1 in 6 women experience stalking (Smith et al., 2018). Men are also victimized, but at much lower rates.

The consequences of violence have been well documented and range from short- and long-term physical, psychological, and sexual problems (World Health Organization, 2013). Specifically, violence has been linked to increased rates of depression, anxiety, post-traumatic stress disorder (PTSD), suicidal behavior, sexually transmitted diseases including HIV/AIDS, abortions, and eating disorders among others (Campbell, 2002). Victims of violence are also more likely to be addicted to alcohol, prescription medication, tobacco, or other types of drugs (World Health Organization, 2013). There are also economic and societal costs associated with victimization. For instance, the Centers for Disease Control and Prevention (2019) estimate that the lifetime per-victim cost is $103,767 for women and $23,414 for men, costs which cover medical, social, and legal expenses.

Violence against women can also have deadly consequences. In 2017, there were 1,948 murders of women by men (Violence Policy Center, 2019). For homicides in which the victim to offender relationship was determined, 92% of female victims were murdered by a man they knew. Women are more likely to be murdered by an intimate partner such as a former or current spouse or boyfriend. The homicide rate for women killed by men was 1.290 per 100,000 residents, a 7.5% increase over 2016. Figure 6-3 charts the homicides that occurred between 1996 and 2017.

Black females were disproportionately affected by homicides—a rate of 2.55 per 100,000 compared to 1.13 per 100,000 for white women (Violence Policy Center 2019). States with the highest homicide rates per 100,000 females, in order, were: Alaska, Louisiana, Arkansas, Nevada, Tennessee, South Carolina, Arizona, Montana, Vermont, and Georgia. Most murders took place during an argument (rather than during the commission of another crime) and were committed with a firearm.

Homicide is one of the leading causes of death for women younger than 45 (Petrosky et al., 2017). While women of all ages and ethnicities may be victims of homicides, young minority women are disproportionately affected. Several strategies have been offered to combat violence against women. State statutes that limit the access to firearms for people under a domestic violence restraining order is one preventive measure.

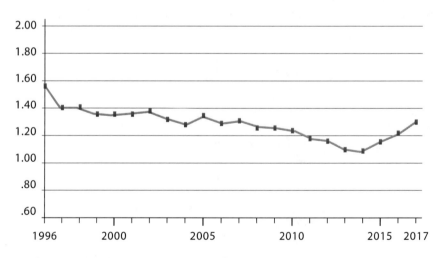

Figure 6-3   Rate of Women Murdered by Men in Single Victim/Single Offender Incidents 1996–2017

Source: Violence Policy Center, 2019

There are bystander programs (Green Dot is one) that teach participants how to recognize situations or behaviors that might become violent and how to intervene safely to reduce the likelihood of assault. Connecting women with services such as crisis intervention, medical and legal advocacy, and access to community resources also helps stem intimate partner violence. The World Health Organization (2013) emphasizes the need "for continued multidisciplinary research and analysis on the causes of, and cost and risk factors for, violence against women and girls, in order to inform laws, policies and strategies and support awareness-raising efforts" (p. 4).

Relationships, family history, economic circumstances, trauma, and mental health form a complex social reality that can contribute to women committing crime. The majority of people in the criminal justice system are men, and most punishments and procedures were established based on male offenders. However, long-standing beliefs about the place of women in society and how they should behave have created a different type of punishment, even criminalizing pregnancy. Gender responsive approaches by police, courts, and corrections is a critical component to address fair and relevant treatment of women in our punitive society.

7

Criminalizing
LGBTQ Lives

This chapter explores the LGBTQ[1] experiences within the criminal justice system. The historical and contemporary state sanctioned violence against the LGBTQ community creates unique experiences important to any discussion of our punitive culture. The Fifth and Fourteenth Amendments frame our understanding of equal protections for all citizens. While the courts continue to interpret the Equal Protection Clause in the Fourteenth Amendment as prohibiting discrimination on the basis of gender, religion, and disability, sexual orientation has not received the same protections (Magliocca et al., 2013). Government policies and employees directly and indirectly perpetrate terror against the LGBTQ community. This chapter illustrates the measurable and diverse ways that terror is enacted through the government, particularly the criminal justice system, against the LGBTQ community.

State-Sanctioned Violence

It is important to use the lens of *state sanctioned violence* when exploring the experiences of the LGBTQ community with the criminal justice system. State sanctioned violence can be defined as "violence inflicted by the system itself" (Shay & Strader, 2012, p. 181). Several disciplines, including anthropology, criminology, and sociology illustrate the variation in how state sanctioned violence occurs across legal, social, and educational institutions, to name a few (Murch, 2015; Schnabel, 2018). The evidence of state sanctioned violence in the criminal justice system is sobering; "law enforcement officers were the third largest category of perpetrators of anti-LGBT violence" in criminological data (Mogul et al., 2011, p. 47). Another study showed that 23% of anti-LGBT violence offenders unknown to the victim were police officers (Mallory et al., 2015).

There are four layers to state sanctioned violence. First, the very existence of LGBTQ identities has been criminalized historically (Eskridge, 1999). The modern gay rights movement was birthed from the need to socially and legally resist the government after decades of overt discrimination in employment, social, housing, and legal contexts (Morlock, 2017). For example, the Supreme Court in *United States v. Windsor* (2013) struck down the 1996 Defense of Marriage Act that declared the terms *marriage* and *spouse* referred to the legal union between one man and one woman. In a brief to the Court, the Department of Justice summarized the chronic discrimination faced by the LGBTQ community (Mallory et al., 2015).

> Perhaps most stark is the history of criminal prohibition on the sexual intimacy of gay and lesbian people: that history ranges from colonial laws ordering the death of "any man [that] shall lie with mankind, as he lieth with womankind," to state laws that, until very recently, "demean[ed] the existence" of gay and lesbian people "by making their private sexual conduct a crime." [T]hat declaration in and of itself [wa]s an invitation to subject homosexual persons to discrimination both in the public and in the private spheres. The federal government, state and local governments, and private parties all have contributed to a regrettable history of discrimination against gay and lesbian people in a variety of contexts. (p. 5)

Second, minority sexualities have a long history of being scrutinized and monitored by criminal justice professionals. While in the early twentieth century, publications existed that challenged heteronormative beliefs (Kinsey et al., 1948), it wasn't until 1961 that the first state (Illinois) removed sodomy laws from its criminal code (ACLU, 2020a). Connecticut became the second state in 1971, and 19 more states repealed sodomy laws in the 1970s. Nonetheless, the predominant experience for the LGBTQ community regarding sexual orientation has been and continues to be harassment and arrest.

Third, building on the previous two layers, progress made in terms of legal revisions to equal protection legislation has gotten a lot of attention in the mainstream press but without attention to the constant oppressive experiences when the LGBTQ community comes into contact with the criminal justice system. Below, we further examine arrest practices that disproportionately target the LGBTQ community (Nussbaum, 2010).

Fourth, involvement in the criminal justice system is typically involuntary and increasingly falls along the intersections of race/ethnicity and class—as other chapters in this book have discussed. Other chapters are not intended to be heteronormative in exploring the criminal justice system; instead, this separate chapter is geared to specifically honor LGBTQ experiences. We define the category of LGBTQ as including lesbian, gay, bisexual, transgender, queer, and questioning (Shay & Strader, 2012). Additionally, when we use the phrase *LGBTQ community*, this refers to diverse groups within a broad category of persons who carry non-culturally dominant gender and sexual identities. The LGBTQ community is disproportionately represented in arrests and incarceration along race/ethnicity and class lines (Eskridge, 1999; Shay & Strader, 2012). LGBTQ persons of color face greater risk within the criminal justice system (Mogul et al., 2011).

Targeting the LGBTQ Community

Research shows the extent to which criminal justice professionals target the LGBTQ community in public and institutional settings. This targeting unfolds disproportionately in arrest and incarceration as well as bias in the courtroom and violence during incarceration. In this section, we explore *indirect* state oppression through disproportionate arrest. We also examine the widespread direct use of violence by criminal justice professionals against the LGBTQ community—an overt, state-driven form of oppression.

Arrest

Phrases such as *queer penalties* (Russell, 2017) and *walking while trans* were coined to convey the subjectivities of disproportionately arresting transgender persons for noncriminal, criminal, and unknown behaviors. Researchers illustrate the widespread misuse of statutes, ordinances, and laws targeting trans persons ranging from public displays of affection (Nussbaum, 2010), to walking in parks, to sex trafficking (Mogul et al., 2011). The LGBTQ community has disproportionate face-to-face contact with police. For example, in a study of 2,376 transgender or gender nonconforming people age 18 or older, 73% had a face-to-face encounter with the police in the past five-years (Lambda Legal, 2015). Survey studies also show that as much as 57% of arrests of persons with LGBTQ identities are unjustified, resulting from biased use of the law and discretionary power against noncriminal acts (Waters, 2016).

Entrapment is illegal. A common theme in arrests is the police practice of stalking and excessively prompting an LGBTQ person to commit a crime. Police wait for a crime to be committed—or contribute to and encourage the crime to occur—for the purpose of an arrest. It can be difficult to prove entrapment, even if arresting officers use threats, harassment, or fraud to coerce defendants to commit crimes. Whether or not a crime occurs, studies illustrate that arrests, bookings, fines, and court appearances are constant (Mogul et al., 2011). These types of arrests are complimented by the frequent use of excessive force with LGBTQ persons. Nearly 33% of people experience excessive force by the arresting officers

(Waters, 2016). We argue that such situations are overt mechanisms for exercising state sanctioned violence.

In recent years, for example, communities in New York City (NYC) have experienced both a ramping-up of prosecutions for sex work and for the purchase of sex work. NYC police officers target trans women, assuming they are engaged in sex work and attempting to entrap them. Many community-based organizations track the consequences for the trans community. For example, a 23-year-old college student and trans woman, Raquel, was prompted three times for sex acts by an unknown male while she was walking through a neighborhood to meet her sister (Whitford, 2016). Each time she attempted to move past the man, he asked her for sex work and continued to follow her. Her verbal refusals did not dissuade him, eventually landing her in handcuffs and ushered into an unmarked police car. Her first arrest was emblematic of the "walking while trans" experience of the LGBTQ community.

Adults are not the only targets of "walking while trans" and other arrest strategies that disproportionately impact the LGBTQ community. Youth also face these circumstances. In schools and community spaces, youth with LGBTQ identities are targeted by school security guards and police. In fact, 23% of LGBTQ youth in schools with security guards or police hear those officers use anti-LGBTQ slurs such as "fag" or "dyke" on the school premises; 31% of youth of color reported hearing this language (Lambda Legal, 2015). The percentage increased to 45 for Latino youth compared to 19% of those who do not identify as youth of color.

Qualitative studies with youth show similar findings to large survey studies with adults. Youth who engage in public displays of affection and are perceived as violating gender norms are sent to the principal's office, suspended, and expelled while their heteronormative peers are not (Snapp et al., 2014). Importantly, multiple studies show that when youth with LGBTQ identities fight to protect themselves or respond to anti-LGBTQ bullying with violence, they are quickly punished as well as blamed for bringing on their own victimization (Cianciotto & Cahill, 2012; Mountz, 2016).

Finally, and unique to the youth context, students who are open about their LGBTQ identities face significant rejection by their families and are overrepresented in the youth homeless population (Mountz, 2016). "Walking while trans," being expelled from school (which increases the likelihood of involvement in delinquent activities), and being arrested for status offenses like homelessness usher many LGBTQ youth into the juvenile and criminal justice systems. Anti-homelessness ordinances that make homelessness a crime disproportionately impact LGBTQ youth (Marksamer & Tobin, 2014).

Prosecuted Victims of Hate Crimes

Investigations of violent crimes committed by LGBTQ persons often neglect consideration of the use of violence as self-protection from hate-fueled assaults or attempted assaults (Yacka, 2014). Similar to LGBTQ youth often being blamed for school violence, adults in the LGBTQ community are also vulnerable to this bias. On August 18, 2006, seven gay Black women from Newark (NJ) visited New York City. Dwayne Buckle, 28, catcalled Patreese Johnson, 19 (Pasulka, 2016). She replied that she was gay. Buckle responded by calling the women "dyke bitches" and threatened to rape them until they turned straight. Renata Hill and Venice Brown defended the group (Black, 2018). Buckle yanked hair from Brown's head and choked Hill. Johnson pulled a knife and swung at Buckle. Onlookers joined the skirmish to defend the women. The encounter was captured on a surveillance camera at a nearby movie theater. When the fight ended, everyone started to walk away—but the police had been called. Buckle, stabbed, claimed he was the victim of a hate crime against a straight man (Pasulka, 2015). The women claimed Buckle threw the first punch and they were defending themselves. The women were arrested on felony charges, including gang assault.

The media reported the women as savage aggressors, labelling them "killer lesbians" and "wolf pack." Three of the young women pled guilty and were sentenced to 6 months. Four of the women—Venice Brown, Terrain Dandridge, Patreese Johnson, and Renata Hill—went to trial and were found guilty by an all-white jury. Dandridge was sentenced to 3.5 years, but her conviction was overturned and she was released with no criminal record. Brown (sentenced to 5 years) and Hill (sentenced to 8 years) were granted retrials. Hill decided to plead guilty so that she could be released after serving 3.5 years. Johnson was sentenced to 11 years; her sentence was reduced to 8 and she was released in 2013.

Public opinion about the New Jersey 4, as the women were called, coalesced around gender, race, and sexuality (McClain, 2015). Dandridge's mother said she was apprehensive about the trial precisely because her daughter was a gay Black woman. Rutgers historian Kali Nicole Gross (2015) writes about the historical experiences of Black women and the exclusionary politics of protection.

> Exclusionary notions of protection have created a need for Black women to trade in extralegal violence for personal security. Historical accounts are replete with examples of otherwise-law-abiding Black women found carrying small knives and other weapons to guard against daily assaults and violations at home and in the workplace—behaviors gesturing toward their often-overlooked vulnerability. . . . Long-standing barriers to protection play central roles in the relationship among race, gender, violence against Black women, and Black female criminalization. Acknowledging this not only will enhance future scholarship on the carceral state but will also begin to upend those historic forces that have pushed Black women to the margins of justice. (pp. 32–33)

Angela Davis suggested imagining that the assailant was Black and the seven young women were white (Black, 2018). If young white women resisted, the public could well have had a different reaction, but there is no institutional mode of resisting homophobic street attacks. Victims have no place to turn; they either assent to the homophobia of everyday culture by smiling and moving on, or they try to speak out and resist. At the intersection of queerness and Blackness, the act of self-defense by the seven women was demonized—their voices were silenced.

In 2008, Blair Dorash-Walther began research on the New Jersey 4 for her documentary, *Out in the Night*, released in 2014. She said she first became interested in the plight of the women when she noticed that a *New York Times* article written by two female journalists stated that a man was stabbed after "admiring" a stranger (Pasulka, 2015). Dorash-Walther wanted to learn the women's side of the story. In the documentary, journalist Reva McEachern states that the only people who were considered the villains—because of deeply ingrained assumptions linking race, sexual orientation, gender, and violence—were the women who were harassed and attacked (Pasulka, 2016). McEachern says the bias creates an environment where people are on guard because others perceive you as a threat before they know anything about you. Three of the New Jersey 4 have criminal records because their self-defense was perceived as aggression.

Another example of self-defense by a Black woman, reframed as an attack, occurred in Minneapolis on June 5, 2011. CeCe McDonald, a 23-year-old Black transgender woman, and four African American friends went on a late-night grocery run (Erdely, 2014). As they passed a tavern, two patrons were drinking outside. Molly Flaherty (age 40) and Dean Schmitz (age 48) yelled "bitches with dicks," "faggot-lovers," "niggers," and other insults. McDonald replied, "Excuse me. We are people, and you need to respect us. We're just trying to walk to the store." More patrons came out of the tavern to watch the confrontation. Flaherty hit McDonald in the face with a cocktail glass, slicing open her check. A street brawl followed. When the fight ended, CeCe realized she was bleeding and headed toward the grocery store. Dean Schmitz pursued her. She pulled scissors from her purse that she had for a sewing course; Schmitz lunged toward her and landed on the scissors. He died in the ambulance on the way to the hospital.

All of the witnesses corroborated CeCe's account of the events. When she refused to accept a plea deal of first-degree manslaughter, she was charged with second-degree murder, which can carry a sentence of 40 years. As the jury was being selected, she accepted a plea offer of 41 months (the minimum sentence) for second-degree manslaughter but had to give up her claim of self-defense/accidental injury. She served 19 months in two male prisons (her nine months in jail counted toward the sentence plus she earned good behavior time reductions). Molly Flaherty was charged with second-degree assault; she pled guilty to third-degree assault and served 6 months in jail.

Director Jac Gares and actress Laverne Cox collaborated on *Free CeCe!*, a documentary. Production began in August 2013 before CeCe was released in January 2014 (Anderson, 2016). At the premier of the documentary in 2016, McDonald said she wanted people to decolonize their minds from being conditioned to accept only certain kinds of people in society as legitimate. She asked that people challenge their ideas of gender identity and sexual orientation and give other people a chance to live. Cox, who is also transgender, added that we need a culture that doesn't stigmatize, criminalize, and try to erase LGBTQ people through various forms of violence by the state and by individuals. These incidents illustrate the overzealous prosecution of LGBTQ hate-crime victims systematically prosecuted for trying to protect their own lives.

Hate crime legislation for the protection of the LGBTQ community is a recent, twenty-first century invention. Prior to the headline generating murders of Matthew Shepard and James Byrd, Jr., there was no legislation that included sexual orientation as a hate crime type. The names of those two victims are featured in a 2009 federal law. In 1998 in Wyoming—a state that still has no hate crime laws—Matthew Shepard, a college student, was lured by two men from a local bar. The men ultimately pistol-whipped Matthew so severely they broke his brain stem. The men also tied Matthew to a fence in freezing temperatures and left him to die, which he did several days later in the hospital. The attackers were found guilty and are serving two life sentences. Another grizzly hate crime occurred in Texas in 1998. Three white men kidnapped James Byrd, Jr, a Black man. They assaulted James and then tied him to the back of a truck, dragging him for three and a half miles; James was decapitated from the dragging. The three attackers were found guilty of capital murder. Lawrence Russell Brewer was executed September 21, 2011—the first time in Texas history that a white person was sentenced to death for killing a Black person (Editors, 2020). John William King was executed April 24, 2019. Shawn Allen Berry received a life sentence; he must serve 40 years before being eligible for parole.

Despite the historic change to hate crime legislation, the violence continues. LGBTQ individuals comprise about 4.5% of the US population but are 18.5% of hate crime victims (Fitzsimons, 2019). The Uniform Crime Reporting program collects hate crime statistics. In 2019, there were 7,314 incidents: 1,395 were based on sexual orientation bias and 224 on gender identity bias (FBI, 2020b). About 62% targeted gay men; 25% targeted a mixed group of LGBTQ people; 10% targeted lesbians; 2% targeted bisexuals; and 1% targeted heterosexuals. Transgender and gender-nonconforming people were the targets in approximately 3% of reported hate crime incidents. Hate crimes target people more frequently than property. In 2019, 62% of hate crimes targeted people compared to 38% targeting property. Hate crimes stemming from anti-LGBTQ bias increased 19% from 2015. The number of incidents involving transgender and gender-nonconforming people increased 68%.

Some states have laws that require the collection of hate crime data but have not legislated increased punishment for hate crimes; some states have enacted both types of legislation. Under the federal Matthew Shepard and James Byrd, Jr., Hate Crimes Prevention Act of 2009, states can request the Department of Justice to participate in the prosecution of hate crimes.

> The Shepard-Byrd Act makes it a federal crime to willfully cause bodily injury, or attempt to do so using a dangerous weapon, because of the victim's actual or perceived race, color, religion, or national origin. The Act also extends federal hate crime prohibitions to crimes committed because of the actual or perceived religion, national origin, gender, sexual orientation, gender identity, or disability of any person, only where the crime affected interstate or foreign commerce or occurred within federal special maritime and territorial jurisdiction. The Shepard-Byrd Act is the first statute allowing federal criminal prosecution of hate crimes motivated by the victim's actual or perceived sexual orientation or gender identity. (DOJ, 2019)

The experiences of Venice Brown, Terrain Dandridge, Patreese Johnson, Renata Hill, and CeCe McDonald show that even when hate crimes occur, federal and state laws do not ensure that protections are afforded to LGBTQ victims and increased penalties applied to attackers. Official hate crime statistics are based on crimes deemed hate crimes by authorities, creating gaps in a more accurate representation of the frequency of anti-LGBTQ crimes.

Anti-Sodomy Laws

Sodomy laws were derived from church law and targeted nonprocreative sexuality and sexuality outside of marriage. In the late 1960s, opponents of the gay rights movement that had made some strides in weakening social condemnation began invoking sodomy laws to justify discrimination (ACLU, 2020b). In 1969, Kansas became the first state to rewrite its sodomy laws to apply only to gay people. Arkansas, Kentucky, Missouri, Montana, Nevada, Tennessee, and Texas followed suit in the 1970s. Courts in Maryland and Oklahoma ruled that sodomy laws could not be applied to private heterosexual conduct but did not provide the same protection to same-sex conduct. In many other states where the laws ostensibly covered all couples, they were applied only to gay individuals.

The laws were rarely enforced for sexual conduct, especially in homes because the police generally have no access without a warrant (Platoff & Greene, 2018). However, the laws criminalized behavior ascribed to LGBTQ people. The assumption of criminal activity was used to restrict rights against LGBTQ individuals in three primary ways (ACLU, 2020b). First, they restricted the ability to raise children by denying custody of natural-born children (Alabama, Arkansas, Mississippi, Missouri, North Carolina, North Dakota, Pennsylvania, South Dakota, Virginia), adoption (Florida, Mississippi), and foster parenting (Arkansas, Missouri). Second, the laws were used to deny employment. Georgia's attorney general used the state's sodomy law as a justification for refusing to hire a lesbian. Third, the laws were used in public debate to deny LGBTQ individuals equal treatment and to discredit their voices. Utah used its sodomy law to justify not protecting gay people from hate crimes.

Prior to 1961, every state had laws prohibiting sodomy. By 1986 as attitudes about sexual behavior became more liberated, twenty-six states had abolished their sodomy laws. Prejudice about homosexual behavior, however, continued to exist. The gay rights movement made homosexual culture more visible, with the unintended consequence of strengthening the link between sodomy laws and gay individuals. Some states amended their laws to apply only to same-sex intimacy; others interpreted gender-neutral statutes as if they applied only to LGBTQ people. *Bowers v. Hardwick* emphasized negative attitudes toward homosexuality and illustrated the use of sodomy laws as a means of legal discrimination.

For example, in Atlanta police officer knocked on the door of Michael Hardwick's house in August 1982, planning to question him about his failure to appear in court on a public drunkenness charge (Naeger, 2004). A house guest answered and directed the officer to Hardwick's bedroom. The door was partially open, and the officer arrested Hardwick and another man for violating Georgia's sodomy law. Hardwick challenged the constitutionality of the statute, claiming that it violated his due process right to privacy, basing his argument on privacy cases decided by the Supreme Court that recognized that the government, without a compelling justification, cannot violate the fundamental right to form intimate personal relationships within the protective shelter of the home.

In *Bowers v. Hardwick* (1986) the Supreme Court ruled 5–4 that

> The Constitution does not confer a fundamental right upon homosexuals to engage in sodomy. None of the fundamental rights announced in this Court's prior cases involving family relationships, marriage, or procreation bear any resemblance to the right asserted in this case. And any claim that those cases stand for the proposition that any kind of private sexual conduct between consenting adults is constitutionally insulated from state proscription is unsupportable. (pp. 190–191)

The ruling allowed courts to justify discrimination against LGBTQ employees and job applicants, to separate children from their LGBTQ parents by denying custody or restricting visitation, to uphold the removal of competent homosexuals from military service, and to suppress gay people from publicly exercising their First Amendment rights (Naeger, 2004). The backlash from gay rights activists was zealous. By 2003 when *Lawrence v. Texas* reached the Supreme Court, half of the states that had sodomy statutes when *Bowers* was decided no longer had such laws, including Georgia itself.

A very distinctive combination of events occurred on September 17, 1998—events that resulted in a landmark case for the rights of LGBTQ individuals that came to the attention of the criminal justice system because of a lie about Black violence that the fabricator knew would result in police response (James, 2020). Robert Eubanks (a white gay man in Harris, Texas) became enraged when he thought Tyron Garner (a Black, on-and-off again lover of Eubanks, age 31) was flirting with John Geddes Lawrence, Jr. (a white, gay man, age 53). Eubanks was jealous and left Lawrence's apartment to call the police. He said he was reporting a gun crime—a Black male going crazy with a gun. When the sheriff's deputies arrived, he directed them into the apartment. The officers found Garner and Lawrence engaging in sex and arrested them under Texas's anti-sodomy law.

The arrests of Lawrence and Garner became a vehicle for challenging anti-sodomy laws that were used solely to shame and stigmatize gay couples (Lithwick, 2012). Their case unfolded unconventionally. That is, a closeted gay file clerk saw the arrest report. At a gay bar, he mentioned the arrests for sodomy, which was so rare there was not an assigned code for the charge, to the bartender. As a gay activist, the bartender recognized the potential importance of the case (Lithwick, 2012). Civil rights attorneys had learned that challenges to existing laws fared better if defendants elicited sympathy from juries. However, the biases against interracial, lower-middle to lower-class defendants hooking up in a seedy apartment in a marginal neighborhood were not ideal plaintiffs. However, no other test case had emerged since *Bowers* in which someone was actually arrested for violating a state sodomy law. The unusual circumstances of the false claim about a gun being brandished—an all too often claim against Black men in America—allowed deputies to enter the apartment, where they found Lawrence and Garner.

National gay-rights groups had been challenging state sodomy laws on the potential harm to gay citizens by making them look like presumptive criminals, but that strategy wasn't working. The Supreme Court, in *Romer v. Evans* (1996), had struck down a Colorado initiative excluding gays from anti-discrimination protection (see discussion later in this chapter). Activists thought the time was optimal for another challenge to sodomy statutes, but they needed to find plaintiffs who would not suffer custody losses or other collateral harms from admitting that they had violated criminal sodomy laws. Lawrence and Garner had pled guilty before a justice of the peace, and their experience was central to building a test case.

Lawrence and Garner became plaintiffs in a suit challenging the constitutionality of the Texas sodomy statute. The Texas State Court of Appeals held that the statute was not unconstitutional under the due process clause of the Fourteenth Amendment, relying on *Bowers v. Hardwick* (1986) as precedent. The Supreme Court agreed to hear the case to determine whether criminal convictions for adult consensual sexual intimacy in the home violated vital interests in liberty and privacy protected by the due process clause of the Fourteenth Amendment. The 6–3 decision was delivered by Justice Anthony Kennedy, who wrote that due process gives people the right to engage in conduct without intervention of the government. "The Texas statute furthers no legitimate state interest which can justify its intrusion into the personal and private life of the individual." After the Court's ruling, a law professor commented that the case removed the reflexive assumption of the inferiority of LGBTQ individuals and laid the legal precedent for same-sex marriage (Platoff & Greene, 2018). *Lawrence* removed the presumptive criminal charge against LGBTQ people and opened new opportunities for jobs and freedoms. However, the Texas antisodomy laws (albeit unenforceable) remain on the books, as do similar laws in 16 states (Wakefield, 2020).

Incarcerated LGBTQ Individuals

The incarceration of LGBTQ people is a long-established practice in the US criminal justice system. The on-ramping of the LGBTQ community into jails and prisons has not slowed. We have discussed mass incarceration elsewhere in this book. Here it is vital to understand the factors specific to the LGBTQ community. The rate of sexual, physical, and verbal abuses as well as denial of health services experienced while in custody in jails and prisons is striking. Persons from the LGBTQ community suffer disproportionate sexual assaults by peers and correctional officers (Beck et al., 2013). Specifically, 12.2% of LGBTQ individuals in prison (111,500) were assaulted by another inmate compared to 1.2% of heterosexual inmates (1,298,000). The percentages in jails were 8.5% for LGBTQ inmates (50,100) compared to 1.2% for heterosexual inmates (654,500). The percentage of LGBTQ inmates sexually assaulted by correctional staff in prisons was 5.4% compared to 2.1% of heterosexual inmate. In jails, 4.3% of LGBTQ inmates were sexually assaulted by correctional staff compared to 1.7% of heterosexual inmates.

LGBTQ prison and jail inmates reported higher rates of inmate-on-inmate sexual victimization than heterosexual inmates in every measured subgroup: gender, ethnicity, age, education, and mental health problems. Rates of sexual victimization by other inmates against LGBTQ inmates were at least 10 times greater than that of heterosexual inmates when the victim was male, Black, Hispanic, or had less than a high school education (Beck et al., 2013). For LGBTQ female inmates, the differences were 2.5 times larger. For whites, the differences were 6 times larger. For high school graduates, the differences were 8 times larger. Staff-on-inmate victimization rates were at least double for LGBTQ inmates compared to heterosexual inmates. Rates of staff sexual misconduct were the highest for inmates ages 18 to 24 (6.7%), Blacks (6.2%), and males (6.1%).

The National Center for Transgender Equality (NCTE) was founded in 2003 as a national social justice organization devoted to ending discrimination and violence against transgender people (Grant et al., 2011). In 2008, NCTE and the National LGBTQ Task Force formed a research partnership and launched a comprehensive national transgender discrimination study (NTDS). In 2011, the results of interviews with 6,450 transgender and gender non-conforming people were released. Sixteen percent of respondents reported being sent to jail or prison (Grant et al., 2011). Incarcerated respondents reported harassment by correctional officers (37%) more often than harassment by peers (35%). Sixteen percent experienced physical assaults, and 15% reported sexual assaults by correctional staff or fellow inmates. Health care denial was another form of abuse in prison, with 17% reporting denial of hormones.

In 2016, NCTE released the second iteration of the NTDS that measured the current experiences of 27,715 respondents (James et al., 2016). Of incarcerated respondents, 23% reported physical assaults by staff or other inmates, and 20% reported sexual assaults. Incarcerated transgender respondents were 5 to 6 times more likely to be sexually assaulted by facility staff than the general incarcerated population and nine to ten times more likely to be sexually assaulted by another inmate. Sexual assaults by staff were reported by 11% of respondents compared to 17% of respondents sexually assaulted by another inmate. Physical assaults by staff were reported by 18% of respondents compared to 16% of respondents physically assaulted by other inmates. More than half (58%) of respondents had been on hormone therapy before incarceration; 37% were denied hormones while imprisoned.

Rebecca Stotzer (2014) points out the immediacy in which abuses begin for the LGBTQ community. As soon as transgender people begin the booking process, explicit acts of aggression from correctional staff arise, including being exhibited for others to see, called names, sexually groped, purposely injured, and damage to property. One study found that 49.2% of transgender and gender nonconforming respondents were laughed at during the search process, 47.5% were "put on display", 45.8% were called names, 33.9% were groped, 11.9% were physically hurt, and 1.7% had property damaged (Emmer et al., 2011).

The federal government designed standards to ensure the constitutional right to safety for all incarcerated persons, which theoretically address the safety needs of LGBTQ persons while in jails and prisons. The Prison Rape Elimination Act (PREA) of 2003 outlines 12 areas for reducing sexual violence in all incarceration settings (i.e., city and county jails, state and federal prisons, immigration prisons, juvenile facilities, and halfway houses). While requirements differ for each type of setting, all settings must ensure that staff are in compliance with the standards for screening and classification, housing, protective custody, segregation units, searches, minors in adult facilities, staff training, reporting abuses, support for survivors, consensual sex versus sexual abuse, grievances and access to courts, and compliance with standards (National Center, 2012).

While PREA was designed to address a significant problem, its implementation has been sporadic (Stotzer, 2014); in fact, compliance is nearly voluntary. The only incentive offered for implementation is financial. If a facility fails to report compliance, it loses 5% of federal funding. In addition, there is no oversight to insure the accuracy of reported compliance (Palacios, 2017; Sullivan, 2017a, 2017b).

PREA was partially inspired by the tragedy of Rodney Hulin, Jr., who committed suicide (Chammah, 2015). In 1996, Rodney, a 17-year-old Texan first-time offender, was transferred from adult jail to prison to serve a three-year sentence. After being raped and beaten, Rodney asked to be placed in protective custody, but his request was denied. He was subjected to constant rape. After his death from hanging, major news networks covered the story. Hulin became a symbol of problems created by sending young people to adult prisons for nonviolent crimes where prison rape is so well known. Prison reform advocates pointed out the long history of vulnerable persons (e.g., youth, LGBTQ persons, persons with disabilities, and those with small statures) preyed upon in prisons with the knowledge and/or participation of correctional staff.

As mentioned above, the transgender segment of the LGBTQ community is frequently denied hormonal replacement therapy. In addition 12% were denied routine health care (Grant et al., 2011). Even when medical needs were obvious, transgender people were less likely to receive medical attention from the facilities. Denial of medical support is a long-time mechanism used around the world to exercise state oppression (Wildeman, 2015).

As part of the landscape of incarceration experiences for the LGBTQ community, 57.1% of transgender persons serve their entire sentence without any conditional release compared to 18% of the general incarceration population (Emmer et al., 2011). That is, transgender people are consistently required to serve the maximum sentence where their cisgender (personal identity and gender corresponds with one's birth sex) counterparts are not. Hence, incarcerated LGBTQ individuals endure sexual, physical, and verbal abuses as well as denial of health services for the maximum amount of time.

Jailing of LGBTQ youth is also riddled with discrimination. In addition to the earlier discussion of youth in school settings who are disproportionately suspended, expelled, and arrested for school-based infractions, LGBTQ youth experience multiple avenues of justice system bias outside the school setting. For example, "Romeo and Juliet" exceptions to statutory rape laws are often applied only to opposite-sex couples. Most states make an exception to statutory rape laws for sexual acts involving a victim below the age of consent if the age difference of the defendant is no more than three or four years. Because of heterosexual bias, LGBTQ youth cannot easily invoke "Romeo and Juliet" provisions to offer evidence of a consensual relationship (Mogul et al., 2011). The provisions in some states protect minors from registration as sex offenders, but LGBTQ youth who participate in the same conduct as their straight counterparts often receive lengthy sentences and lifelong registration as a sex offenders. *Lawrence* included language that some courts have interpreted to mean that the decision does not apply to minors (Shay & Strader, 2012). The supreme court in one state upheld a law criminalizing oral and anal sex among teenagers on the grounds that the statute properly promoted morality among the state's youth. Heteronormative views of morality continue to affect the enforcement of criminal laws—even after *Lawrence* specifically held that the morality of the majority should not form the basis for a criminal law.

The link between LGBTQ youths and health services are also a major feature to understanding the youth incarceration context. The youths score high on mental health needs often linked to stress from homelessness, violence, and abuse from family, peers, and correctional staff (Barnert et al., 2017). Yet, juvenile detention centers and prisons have minimal mental health services, few trauma-informed practices, and sparse practices for appropriately serving the needs of LGBTQ youths (Barnert et al., 2016; White, 2016).

While little is known about whether LGBTQ youth serve longer sentences than their cisgender peers, as in the case of LGBTQ adults, significant amounts of research show the disproportionate incarceration of LGBTQ youth (Snapp et al., 2014). For example, LGBTQ identifying youth are incarcerated two to three times more than their cisgender peers with adjudications lasting a year or more (B. Wilson et al., 2017). These lengthy incarcerations expose the youth to the chronic stressors and trauma that are fundamental components of the U.S. juvenile system (Barnert et al., 2017).

State Leadership and Oppression

It is useful to inquire into who is involved in the state sanctioned oppression of LGBTQ persons. "In terms of crime enforcement, LGBTQ people face discrimination by police and prosecutors on an ongoing basis. And as victims of crime, LGBTQ people face police indifference, even hostility, when confronted with crimes such as domestic abuse" (Shay & Strader, 2012, p. 174). While sexual, physical, and verbal abuse is a constant feature of the LGBTQ experience in the criminal justice system, some may wonder if these abuses are perpetrated by "a few bad apples." Chief Norman Stamper (2016), former Chief of Police of Seattle, offers some insight on this question.

> The "few bad apples" theory is not enough to explain police misconduct. The kind of behavior widely questioned and condemned today is,

in reality, a moldering orchard, or, if you prefer, a rotten barrel. A fresh, healthy apple will quickly turn in such an environment. (p. xvi)

Chief Stamper's analysis of the police profession is useful in considering the chronic violence against the LGBTQ community directly and indirectly perpetrated by the criminal justice system. In the sections below, we explore the roles of criminal justice personnel in legitimizing the widespread oppression of the LGBTQ community. Before doing so, we discuss two examples of voters denying equal treatment of the LGBTQ community.

The Electorate

Colorado voters approved (53% to 46%) a ballot initiative to add Amendment 2 to the state constitution that prohibited the enactment of antidiscrimination protections for gays, lesbians, and bisexuals. The Supreme Court struck down Amendment 2 in *Romer v. Evans* (1996) which voided the voter-sanctioned discrimination against LGBTQ persons. Justice Anthony Kennedy wrote the majority opinion, and he noted that even if a law disadvantages a specific group, it could be sustained under the equal protection clause to advance a legitimate government interest— Amendment 2 did not qualify. He noted that if the constitutional conception of equal protection under the law means anything, it must—at the very least—mean that the desire to harm a politically unpopular group cannot constitute a legitimate governmental interest. While the Amendment was ruled unconstitutional and was the first to do so, it was an example of the public's overt disdain for the LGBTQ community.

Even landmark cases do not necessarily remove discrimination against LGBTQ individuals. *Obergefell v. Hodges* (2015) granted same-sex couples the right to marry (13 states did not allow same-sex marriage in 2015) and led to the enactment of benefits policies for married same-sex couples (Platoff & Greene, 2018). Two taxpayers in Houston challenged the extension of benefits by the city of Houston. They argued that the right to marry does not extend to employee fringe benefits. The Texas Supreme Court in June 2017 vacated a lower court ruling that spouses of LGBTQ public employees are entitled to government-subsidized same-sex marriage benefits (Ura, 2017). The lawyer representing opponents of the Houston policy argued that marriage benefits are not a fundamental right and that *Obergefell* did not resolve such policy questions. The unanimous decision ordered a trial court to reconsider the case. Justice Jeffrey Boyd wrote the court's opinion and stated there was room for state courts to explore the reach and ramifications of Obergefell v. Hodges. In December 2017, The Supreme Court declined to review the June decision by the Texas Supreme Court.

Chiefs and Sheriffs

Some sheriffs and police chiefs engage in anti-gay rhetoric and actions. For example, several audio recordings and first-hand testimony in one lawsuit against Jackson County Sheriff Steven Rand revealed his sexist, racist, anti-disability, and anti-LGBTQ rhetoric. In another lawsuit, a former deputy claimed the sheriff's office was an "incubator for egregious racism and bigotry" and "Sheriff Rand is a bigot, with a known animus against, amongst others, African Americans" (Salisbury, 2019). The lawsuit describes Rand using expletives to refer to Black officers and members of the community. The other lawsuit brought by a lieutenant in the sheriff's office described chronic hostility coming from the leader. Rand is described as "a multi-faceted bigot" who insulted Blacks, women, gays and Hispanics. He repeatedly mocked the lieutenant for his work-related hearing loss" (Clark, 2018).

Some sheriffs become infamous for their careers going south in the age of cell phone recordings and social media tracking. For example, in March 2018, the former Milwaukee County Sheriff David Clarke tweeted an anti-gay joke at former Vice President Joe Biden. The former sheriff simultaneously accused Biden of a gay lifestyle while denigrating such a lifestyle (*Wisconsin Gazette*, 2018). Clarke resigned in 2017 after a series of scandals, including a man dying in his county jail cell of dehydration (West, 2017).

Chiefs are active participants in anti-LGBTQ rhetoric and actions toward the community as well as toward LGBTQ officers. After reporting to internal affairs about the abuses he and community members experienced from his peers and the chief, Jeremy LeMire was dismissed from the police department weeks before the end of his probationary period (McGraw, 2017; Smith, 2017). He filed a lawsuit against former Elk Grove Police Chief Robert Lehner and the city.

While in many ways police organizations incubate cultures that reflect white, heteronormative, and patriarchal priorities, law enforcement leadership affects rank-and-file officers (Cockcroft, 2014; Fitz-Gibbon & Walklate, 2018). LGBTQ individuals endure homophobic attitudes from law enforcement personnel (Dario et al., 2020). Police culture can foster these beliefs, which result in the under policing of LGBTQ victims but over policing of behavior. The intersectional effect of gender and sexual orientation exacerbates the discrimination. Historically police organizations foster hegemonic masculinity, reifying the dominant position of heterosexual men and subordinating women and LGBT people. Hostility to homosexuality and LGBTQ equality increases tensions between the police and LGBTQ individuals—and legitimizes anti-LGBTQ attitudes in the general public.

For example, a police officer followed a vehicle with two passengers leaving a known LGBTQ center (Braunstein, 2017). When the vehicle pulled into a nearby gas station, the officer turned on his lightbar and approached the vehicle. He mockingly referred to the mixed-race woman passenger as a "white male" and asked the driver how she could be gay if she had kids. He arrested the passenger. At the station, a male officer refused to allow a female officer to search the woman and conducted the search himself. Police officers laughed at her and took photos with their cell phones while she cried in the holding cell.

Discriminatory police practices are a form of violence against LGBTQ people (Braunstein, 2017). The continued existence and utilization of statutes to police LGBTQ-related activities can be tragic for those targeted. A high school football player, Marcus Wayman, was drinking with another male in a vehicle when police approached. The officers told the boys to empty their pockets and found condoms. They arrested the boys for underage drinking and suspected the boys intended to engage in homosexual activity. After taking them to the police station, the officers lectured the boys on religious prohibitions against homosexuality and threatened to inform Wayman's grandfather that he was gay. After release, Wayman told his friend he was going to kill himself—and did so several hours later.

Judges and Prosecutors

Several studies have found that the majority of gay and lesbian defendants experience courthouses as hostile and threatening environments (Braunstein, 2017). Discrimination is revealed in the insensitive language used by judges, prosecutors, jury members, and sometimes defense attorneys. A prosecutor in a homicide case described the defendant as a "hardcore" lesbian and alleged that murdering the victim was a "natural response" for a lesbian. Another prosecutor in the sentencing portion of a case in which the defendant had been convicted of killing his lover argued for the death penalty on the grounds that sending a homosexual to prison would be a reward—only death would be an appropriate punishment.

Jury members also discriminate. In surveys, 39% of LGBTQ witnesses believed their sexual orientation was used to devalue their credibility. One respondent said jurors discredited the testimony of a gay witness saying he had probably been out at a club before he witnessed the accident. Another respondent said "jury members suggested that a witness was gay and therefore his testimony could not be trusted" (Braunstein, 2017, p. 13).

Lambda Legal (2015) conducted a national study to explore government misconduct by the police, courts, prisons and school security against the LGBTQ community. Of the 2,376 survey respondents, 43% had been involved in the court system as an attorney (19%), juror (44%), witness (21%) or a party to a legal case (61%) in the previous five years. Respondents in every category heard negative comments about the sexual orientation, gender identity, gender expression or HIV status of individuals in the court proceedings.

Overt transphobia by judges, attorneys and other court employees is common (Lambda Legal, 2015). A judge in a Georgia drug court told a trans woman not to come back to the courtroom unless she was dressed as a man. A judge in New York would not issue visitation/custody rights to a transgender parent unless she agreed not to follow through with her plans for gender transition surgery. A chief justice of the Alabama Supreme Court in a child custody case cited scripture referring to gay partners as "immoral," "detestable," "an inherent evil," and "inherently destructive to the natural order of society." After a formal complaint, the Judicial Inquiry Commission in the State of Alabama found "no reasonable basis" to find that the judge had violated of the Alabama Canons of Judicial Ethics.

Some judges and prosecutors have public agendas that include explicit homophobic stances. The language used by judges and prosecutors, powerful players in the criminal justice system, is quoted in newspapers and other media outlets. The language can normalize oppression. For example, when Calvin Burdine was tried and sentenced to death in Texas in 1984, the prosecutor's argument for a death sentence included the following: "Sending a homosexual to the penitentiary certainly isn't a very bad punishment (Mogul, 2011). Fifteen years later, the case was overturned, but the very language permitted in the courtroom to emphasize that prison rape is qualitatively equivalent to same-sex consensual sex demeaned the behavior of consenting adults. The well documented disproportionate arrest, incarceration, and violence against the LGBTQ community, perpetrated in part by criminal justice professions, mirrors the boldness of courtroom leadership to normalize these forms of oppression through their rhetoric.

Reform Voices

Many advocates pursue policy reforms to address the long-standing state oppression against the LGBTQ community. The emphasis on legislative reform has played an important role in advancing equality for the LGBTQ community. In fact, some innovations show that shifts in policy and legislation have the potential to mitigate the daily violence experienced by LGBTQ persons at the hands of criminal justice professionals and in criminal justice settings. For example, some jails maintain housing units for non-gender conforming persons (e.g., Los Angeles County) (Phillips, 2014; Potter et al., 2011), though with arguable flaws (Robinson, 2011).

Some reformers emphasize the importance of context-specific policies and oversight bodies needed for protecting incarcerated persons from assault behind bars. Further, emphasis has been given to formal checks-and-balances that hold facility administrators accountable for violence taking place in the settings that they oversee (Mogul et al., 2011). Relatedly, researchers highlight the importance of not using solitary confinement for the LGBTQ inmates as the sole safety mechanism against sexual assault in prisons (McCauley et al., 2018). The serious and long-term health consequences of solitary confinement (Kaba et al., 2014; Shalev, 2017) are internationally recognized as cruel and unusual punishment (Amnesty International, 2014).

Some view the approach of grafting policy and legislative reforms onto a fundamentally biased and oppressive criminal justice system as ineffective. While there have been major reforms for de-normalizing legal and social attacks on the LGBTQ community, legislation cannot remove the bias embedded in criminal justice professionals and the culture of the criminal justice system. Many critiques of criminal justice reform efforts make this same argument regarding racism embedded within the criminal justice system (Walker et al., 2018) The calls for caution direct attention to reducing the number of behaviors that constitute a crime so that fewer people come into contact with police officers (Reynolds, 2018). Relatedly, these calls also include consideration for screening and punishing predatorial criminal justice professionals (Bacigal, 2013; Hanna, 2015) and systematically closing prisons as outdated, ineffective, and overused public safety approaches (McLeod, 2015).

The US cultural inclinations to punish and punish severely are exercised most often on historically marginalized populations such as the LGBTQ community, women, persons of color, poor communities, and persons with disabilities. These stigmatized groups—framed as inferior to the white, male, middle class standard—are funneled into the criminal justice system.

NOTE

[1] For a good discussion of what LGBTQ means see Petrow (2014).

8

Punishing Kids

Imprisoning children has been a dominant form of punishment in the United States for about 200 years. Educational (Vélez Young et al., 2010), workforce (Vuori et al., 2015), and health (Barnert et al., 2017) barriers arise as a result of having lived inside a youth prison. Conditions within the walls of "total institutions" have been well documented. The power differential between correctional officers and prisoners threaten basic constitutional rights and are counterproductive to rehabilitation.

Houses of Refuge

The roots of the juvenile justice system can be traced to a legal doctrine known as *parens patriae*, which originated in medieval England's chancery courts. *Parens patriae* established that the king, in his presumed role as the "father" of his country, had the legal authority to take care of his people, especially those who were unable (for various reasons including age) to take care of themselves (Sutton, 1988). By the nineteenth century this legal doctrine had evolved into the practice of the state assuming wardship over a minor child and, in effect, playing the role of parent if the child had no parents or their parents had been declared unfit.

In the American colonies, for example, officials could "bind out" as apprentices "children of parents who were poor, not providing good breeding, neglecting their formal education, not teaching a trade, or were idle, dissolute, unchristian or incapable" (Rendleman, 1979, p. 63). Later, during the nineteenth century, *parens patriae* supplied (as it still does to some extent), the legal basis for court intervention into the relationship between children and their families (Teitelbaum & Harris, 1977). Another legal legacy of the colonial era that relates to the state's involvement in the lives of

195

youth is the *stubborn child law*. Passed in Massachusetts in 1646, it established a clear legal relationship between children and parents and made it a capital offense for a child to disobey his or her parents.

Interest in the state regulation of youth was directly tied to explosive immigration and population growth. Between 1750 and 1850 the population of the United States went from 1.25 million to 23 million. The four-fold increase in immigrants between 1830 and 1840 was in large part a product of the economic hardships faced by the Irish during the potato famine (Brenzel, 1983). The social controls in small communities were overwhelmed by the influx of newcomers.

Prominent citizens in the cities of the East began to notice the poor, especially the children of the poor. The parents were declared unfit because their children wandered the streets unsupervised, committing various crimes to survive. Many believed uncontrolled youths were the source of social problems that, unchecked, would result in even greater problems in the future. Poor and immigrant children, their lifestyles, and social positions would soon be associated with crime and juvenile delinquency.

A number of philanthropic associations emerged in eastern cities to deal with these problems. One of the most notable was the *Society for the Reformation of Juvenile Delinquents* (SRJD), founded in the 1820s (Pickett, 1969). Importantly, the SRJD group was formerly called the Society for the Prevention of *Pauperism*, illustrating the portrayal of the poor as criminals in need of supervision and control. The SRJD, composed primarily of wealthy businessmen and professional people, convinced the New York legislature to pass a bill in 1824 that established the *New York House of Refuge*, the first correctional institution for young offenders in the United States.

The general aims of the New York House of Refuge, including a definition of "delinquents," are reflected in the following extract from the SRJD:

> The design of the proposed institution is, to furnish, in the first place, an asylum, in which boys under a certain age, who become subject to the notice of our police, either as vagrants, or homeless, or charged with petty crimes, may be received, judiciously classed according to their degree of depravity or innocence, put to work at such employments as will tend to encourage industry and ingenuity, taught reading, writing, and arithmetic, and most carefully instructed in the nature of their moral and religious obligations, while at the same time, they are subjected to a course of treatment, that will afford a prompt and energetic corrective of their vicious propensities, and hold out every possible inducement to reformation and good conduct. (Abbott, 1938, p. 348)

The statute contained vague descriptions of behaviors and lifestyles which were synonymous with the characteristics of the urban poor. Being homeless, begging, vagrancy, and coming from an "unfit" home (as defined from a middle-class viewpoint) were examples. The legislation also established specific procedures for identifying the type of youths requiring intervention and the means for the legal handling of cases.

According to law, the state, or a representative agency or individual, could intervene in the life of a child if it was determined that he or she needed "care and treatment," the definition of which was left entirely in the hands of the agency or individual who intervened.

Immigrants received the brunt of enforcement of these laws, especially children of Irish parents. At the time, Irish immigrants were viewed as corrupt and unsuitable as parents. Robert Pickett (1969) notes that one superintendent accounted for a boy's delinquency because "the lad's parents are Irish and intemperate and that tells the whole story" (p. 15). Stereotyped beliefs were evident in the percentage of children of Irish heritage committed to the refuge between 1825 and 1855, which reached 63%.

Children confined in the New York House of Refuge were subjected to strict discipline and control. A former army colonel working at the institution said: "He [the delinquent] is taught that prompt unquestioning obedience is a fundamental military principle" (Mennel, 1973, p. 103). It was strongly believed that rigid discipline would add to a youth's training in self-control (specifically to avoid the temptations of evil surroundings) and respect for authority (which was a basic requirement of a disciplined labor force). Corporal punishments (including hanging children from their thumbs, the use of the "ducking stool" for girls, and severe beatings), solitary confinement, handcuffs, the "ball and chain," uniform dress, the "silent system," and other practices were commonly used in houses of refuge (Pisciotta, 1982).

Following the lead of New York, other cities soon constructed houses of refuge. Within a few years, there were refuges in Boston, Philadelphia, and Baltimore. In the refuges, protests, riots, escape attempts, and other disturbances were almost daily occurrences (Pisciotta, 1982). While at first limited to housing first-time youthful offenders and pre-delinquents, the refuges eventually confined more hardened offenders (most of whom had been hardened by the experiences of confinement); overcrowding became a problem. The cycle would repeat itself in institutions of confinement throughout the nineteenth and twentieth centuries—and continues today.

The rhetoric of the founders and managers of houses of refuge about the best interests of the child fell far short of the reality experienced by the youths held in these facilities. Legislation establishing houses of refuge had little impact on delinquency, but it did establish methods of controlling children of the poor and their parents (Shelden & Vasiliev, 2018). Legislators gave little thought to the rights of children or their parents—nor did justices in a case where a father tried to assert those rights.

Court Decisions and Effects

Ex Parte Crouse

Argued in 1838, *Ex Parte Crouse* arose from a petition of *habeas corpus* filed by the father of Mary Ann Crouse. Without her father's knowledge,

Crouse had been committed to the Philadelphia House of Refuge by her mother on the grounds that she was "incorrigible." Her father argued that the incarceration was illegal because she had not been given a jury trial. The Pennsylvania Supreme Court rejected his claim, stating that the Bill of Rights did not apply to juveniles and referenced *parens patriae* in its ruling.

> The House of Refuge is not a prison, but a school. Where reformation, and not punishment, is the end, it may indeed be used as a prison for juvenile convicts who would else be committed to a common jail, and in respect to these, the constitutionality of the act which incorporated it, stands clear of controversy. . . . The object of the charity is reformation, by training its inmates to industry; by imbuing their minds with principles of morality and religion; by furnishing them with means to earn a living; and, above all, by separating them from the corrupting influence of improper associates. To this end may not the natural parents, when unequal to the task of education, or unworthy of it, be superseded by the *parens patriae*, or common guardian of the community? It is to be remembered that the public has a paramount interest in the virtue and knowledge of its members, and that of strict right, the business of education belongs to it. . . . The infant has been snatched from a course which must have ended in confirmed depravity; and, not only is the restraint of her person lawful, but it would be an act of extreme cruelty to release her from it. (*Ex Parte Crouse*, 1838)

Note that the court ignored the fact that Crouse's father had filed the suit, clearly an indication that he felt "equal to the task" of his daughter's education. Barry Krisberg (2005) notes, "It is important to recognize the significance of both social class and hostility toward Irish immigrants in the legal determination of the Crouse case" (p. 29). The court predicted future behavior based on vague criteria—a practice that became quite common and continues today. The ruling assumed that the Philadelphia House of Refuge (and presumably all other houses of refuge) had a beneficial effect on residents and, as a school rather than a prison, was not subject to procedural constraints.

What evidence did the justices consult to support their conclusion that the Philadelphia House of Refuge was not a prison but a school? They solicited testimony only from those who managed the institution. The justices of the court came from the same general class background as those who supported the houses of refuge. They believed the promises rather than the actions of the reformers. A more objective review of the treatment of youths housed in the refuges, however, might have led the justices to a very different conclusion.

Subsequent investigations found that there was an enormous amount of abuse within these institutions. The strict military regimen, the use of corporal punishment, solitary confinement, and the silent system were examples of punishment with deleterious rather than beneficial effects. Work training was practically nonexistent, and outside companies contracted for cheap labor. Religious instruction was often little more than Protestant indoctrination (many of the youngsters were Catholic). Education, in the conventional meaning of the word, was almost nonexistent.

People v. Turner

For thirty-two years, state courts followed the paradigm of state intervention in *Crouse* (DiFonzo, 1995). *People v. Turner* (1870) provided an intriguing contrast to the *Crouse* case. Daniel O'Connell was incarcerated in the Chicago House of Refuge, where Robert Turner was the superintendent—not because he had committed a criminal offense but because he was "in danger of growing up to become a pauper." Michael O'Connell filed a writ of *habeas corpus* for his son, charging that his incarceration was illegal.

Although the facts were almost identical to the *Crouse* case, the outcome was the exact opposite. The Illinois Supreme Court characterized juvenile confinement that was not based on a criminal conviction as a restraint on liberty constituting tyranny and oppression.

> This boy is deprived of a father's care; bereft of home influences; has no freedom of action; is committed for an uncertain time; is branded as a prisoner; made subject to the will of others, and thus feels that he is a slave. Nothing could more contribute to paralyze the youthful energies, crush all noble aspirations, and unfit him for the duties of manhood. (quoted in DiFonzo, 1995, p. 894)

The Illinois Supreme Court concluded that Daniel was being *punished*—not treated or helped by incarceration in the house of refuge. The court also examined the realities of reform schools and contrasted that with presumed good intentions of the parents—whereas the Pennsylvania court harshly criticized the parents and extolled the promises of the house of refuge (Bernard & Kurlychek, 2010). Illinois rejected the *parens patriae* doctrine. They reasoned that the outcome for Daniel was the same as imprisonment and subject to *due process* safeguards in the criminal law. In short, while the Pennsylvania court viewed the house of refuge uncritically in the Crouse case, the Illinois court viewed it in a much more negative light in the O'Connell case, addressing its cruelty and harshness of treatment.

Isaac Redfield, a former chief justice of the Vermont Supreme Court, pointed out that the class-neutral terms of "ignorance, idleness, and vice" (the behaviors the reformers purported to correct) disguised an anti-immigrant and anti-Catholic bias.

> We do not indeed suppose that the persons mainly instrumental in getting up these [reforms] in the country really intend them for their own children, or indeed in the present case for the children of Protestant parents, to any large extent. We cannot disguise to ourselves that these things do have an ominous squint towards the children of Roman Catholic parents, and of the multitudes of poor emigrants yearly coming to our shores, most of whom are of that faith. (quoted in DiFonzo, 1995, p. 895)

Redfield's hope that *Turner* would halt the use of state intrusion into the lives of minorities by upper-class social reformers was not realized. In the nineteenth century, cases continued to mirror the *Crouse* decision; only two state supreme courts rendered decisions consistent with *Turner* (DiFonzo, 1995). Indeed, the Pennsylvania Supreme Court reiterated the *Crouse* stance in 1905.

> To save a child from becoming a criminal, or continuing in a career of crime, to end in maturer years in public punishment and disgrace, the legislatures surely may provide for the salvation of such a child, if its parents or guardians be unwilling or unable to do so, by bringing it into one of the courts of the state without any process at all, for the purpose of subjecting it to the state's guardianship and protection. (*Commonwealth v. Fisher,* 1905)

This case would not be overturned until 1967. Even the Illinois Supreme Court in 1882 upheld a commitment to an industrial school saying that the ruling in *Turner* was based on the reform school being a place of confinement and punishment, while the current case was a school (DiFonzo, 1995). The O'Connell case played a major role in the movement to establish the juvenile court in Chicago in 1899. The founders of the juvenile court, in part, were attempting to get around the argument in *People v. Turner.*

Challenges to the Punitive Nature of Juvenile Justice

Despite the obvious failures of the houses of refuge, reformers continued to respond to juvenile offenders by building institutions. The "edifice complex" (see chapter 3) that endorses enforcement of the law through coercion extends to juvenile facilities, whether reform schools, training schools, or youth correctional centers. The problems found within the houses of refuge continued unabated throughout the twentieth century and into the twenty-first. While there were occasional "voices in the wilderness" calling attention to abuses within institutions, they mostly fell on deaf ears until the 1960s. At that time, the U.S. Supreme Court began to hear cases that extended due process rights to juveniles.

The two most significant cases were *Kent v. United States* (1966) and *In re Gault* (1967). In September 1961 in Washington, DC, an intruder entered the apartment of a woman, robbed her, and raped her. Police found the fingerprints of Morris Kent, age 16 and on probation, in the apartment. Kent was arrested, taken into custody, and admitted his involvement in the crime. His mother hired an attorney, who filed a motion requesting a hearing on jurisdiction and access to his client's file established with his first contact with the juvenile court at age 14. The juvenile court judge waived Kent to the jurisdiction of the adult court without conferring with the attorney or Kent's mother and without holding a hearing on the jurisdiction motion. Kent was convicted and sentenced in adult court to 30–90 years in prison.

The Supreme Court ruled that when a judge considers transferring a case from juvenile to adult court, the juvenile is entitled to a hearing and has the right to counsel. The court must provide a written statement giving the reasons for the waiver, and the defense counsel must have access to all records and reports used in reaching the decision to waive. Justice Abe Fortas issued a strong indictment of the juvenile court.

> There is no place in our system of law for reaching a result of such tremendous consequences without ceremony—without hearing, without effective assistance of counsel, without a statement of reasons. It is inconceivable that a court of justice dealing with adults, with respect to a similar issue, would proceed in this manner. . . . There is much evidence that some juvenile courts . . . [lack] the personnel, facilities and techniques to perform adequately as representatives of the State in a *parens patriae* capacity, at least with respect to children charged with law violation. There is evidence, in fact, that there may be grounds for concern that the child receives the worst of both worlds; that he gets neither the protection accorded to adults nor the solicitous care and regenerative treatment postulated for children. (*Kent v. United States*, 1966)

The ruling in *Kent* focused on the rights of juveniles to due process protections in hearings to determine transfers from juvenile court. The Court signaled its concern about the absence of due process protections for juveniles in other court proceedings. One year later it heard another landmark case. The circumstances of the *Gault* case involved an overly punitive response to a crank call. A neighbor alleged that Gerald Gault, 15, had made a lewd telephone call. The sheriff placed Gault, who was on probation for a previous delinquent act, in a detention home without notifying his parents. Gault did not receive notification of the charges, was not advised that he could be represented by counsel, and his accuser did not appear in court. He was sentenced to a six-year term in a state training school in Arizona. An adult charged with the same crime would have been fined $50 and sentenced to two months in jail (Shelden & Vasiliev, 2018).

The Supreme Court ruled that at the adjudicatory hearing stage, juvenile court procedures must include adequate written notice of charges, the right to counsel, privilege against self-incrimination, the right to cross-examine accusers, and safeguards against self-incrimination. Fortas once again provided the concise critique, stating that "the condition of being a boy does not justify a kangaroo court" (*In re Gault*, 1967). While there are legitimate reasons for treating juveniles and adults differently, the adjudicatory hearing must include the essentials of due process and fair treatment. As in *Kent*, the Court criticized the assertion based on *parens patriae* that juvenile proceedings are civil in nature and not subject to constitutional safeguards that restrict the state when depriving someone of liberty (claiming that a child has a right only to custody not liberty). Most observers thought that such a critique was long overdue and anticipated significant improvements within the juvenile justice system.

In 1970, the Supreme Court addressed the standard of evidence to adjudicate delinquency. Samuel Winship, age 12, was arrested after breaking into a locker and stealing $112. The family court acknowledged that the evidence did not establish Winship's guilt beyond a reasonable doubt but found him guilty using the "preponderance of the evidence" standard that applies in civil cases. *In re Winship* (1970) looked at whether proof beyond a reasonable doubt was among the essentials of due process and fair treatment required when a juvenile is charged with an act that would be a crime if committed by an adult. The Court ruled that the strict reasonable doubt standard must be applied to both juveniles and adults to establish guilt in criminal charges. Any charge that could result in the loss of liberty must be resolved by the higher standard.

In *McKeiver v. Pennsylvania* (1971), the Supreme Court ruled that states are not required to provide jury trials in the juvenile justice system but that such trials were permitted. Ten states grant juveniles the right to a jury trial if requested; 8 states allow a jury trial in limited circumstances; and 32 states do not provide the right to a jury trial (Shelden & Troshynski, 2020). *Breed v. Jones* (1975) specified that jeopardy applies at the adjudication hearing; waiver cannot occur after jeopardy attaches. Juvenile courts must hold transfer hearings prior to adjudication. *Schall v. Martin* (1984) was a setback to juvenile rights. The Supreme Court ruled that courts can hold youths in preventive detention if judges determine the youths pose a serious risk to the community. Three justices dissented, saying the standard of serious risk was too vague, that it is not possible to predict if a juvenile will commit future crimes, and that government objectives did not outweigh the adverse effects of incarceration on juveniles.

The Court eliminated some of the most glaring injustices, but abuses continue (see discussion of Pennsylvania scandal below). Despite the guarantees in *Gault*, 50% to 90% of juveniles waive their rights to counsel. The limited understanding of juveniles combined with their vulnerability requires greater procedural protections, such as a nonwaivable right to counsel.

Unreasonable Searches and Seizures

In 1985, the Supreme Court addressed the application of the Fourth Amendment's protection against unreasonable searches to students. In 1980, a teacher at Piscataway High School in New Jersey found two girls smoking in a restroom, a violation of school rules. She brought the girls, both 14, to the vice principal, who questioned them. One girl admitted smoking cigarettes; T.L.O. denied she had been smoking and claimed she did not smoke at all. The administrator demanded to see her purse, in which he found cigarettes, cigarette rolling papers, a small amount of marihuana, a pipe, a number of empty plastic bags, a substantial quantity of money in one-dollar bills, an index card that listing students who owed T.L.O. money, and two letters implicating T.L.O. in marihuana dealing. The vice principal notified T.L.O.'s mother and the police. At police headquarters,

T.L.O. confessed that she had been selling marihuana at the high school. The state brought delinquency charges in juvenile court. T.L.O. moved to suppress the evidence found in her purse under the Fourth Amendment protection against unreasonable searches, but the court ruled the search reasonable, found her delinquent, and sentenced her to a year's probation.

The case made its way through the New Jersey courts and eventually to the Supreme Court, which ruled in *New Jersey v. T.L.O.* (1985) that the search was reasonable. Students have legitimate expectations of privacy but schools have equally legitimate needs for searching students if there are reasonable grounds for suspecting that the search will turn up evidence that the student has violated the law or the rules of the school. A search must be reasonable at its inception; the scope must be reasonably related to the infraction; and the search must not be excessively intrusive given the age and gender of the student. Three justices dissented.

> Today's decision sanctions school officials to conduct full-scale searches on a "reasonableness" standard whose only definite content is that it is not the same test as the "probable cause" standard found in the text of the Fourth Amendment. In adopting this unclear, unprecedented, and unnecessary departure from generally applicable Fourth Amendment standards, the Court carves out a broad exception to standards that this Court has developed over years of considering Fourth Amendment problems. Its decision is supported neither by precedent nor even by a fair application of the "balancing test" it proclaims in this very opinion.

The desire to deter student drug use influenced Supreme Court rulings in 1995 (*Vernonia School District v. Acton*) and 2002 (*Board of Education of Independent School District No. 92 v. Earls*). In both cases, the Supreme Court upheld a specific type of search—drug testing of urine—for students involved in athletics and other extracurricular activities. In *Vernonia*, a divided Court upheld an Oregon school district policy that required students participating in interscholastic athletics to consent to random drug testing. Balancing expectations of privacy against the government's interest in drug-free schools, the Court held that the drug policy did not violate the Fourth Amendment. They cited the relatively low expectation of privacy for athletes—communal undress and preseason physical exams. They also noted that athletes were leaders in the school's drug culture, which was "in a state of rebellion" and that drug use increases the risk of sports related injury (*Vernonia School District v. Acton*, 1995).

In the *Earls* case, the Court held 5 to 4 that an Oklahoma school policy of randomly drug testing students who participate in competitive, nonathletic extracurricular activities was constitutional. The decision reversed a federal court ruling. The majority opinion found the school's policy "a reasonably effective means of addressing the school district's legitimate concerns in preventing, deterring and detecting drug use." Justice Ginsburg dissented: "The particular testing program upheld . . . is not reasonable, it is capricious, even perverse" (ACLU, 2019). One commentator said the decision would make high school more like prison, saying the court's decision allows "public schools to treat their students—future citizens—as though they're likely to commit a drug crime" (Lithwick, 2002).

The intersection of policies about preventing drug abuse and the rights of students from unreasonable searches were starkly at issue in *Safford United School District v. April Redding* (2009). Safford Middle School is located in a small, eastern Arizona mining town, about 100 miles from Tucson. In 2003, the assistant principal escorted 13-year-old Savana Redding from her middle school classroom to his office. He said a student had reported that she was giving pills to other students and showed her four prescription-strength pain relief pills. She denied knowing anything about the pills and agreed to let him search her belongings. He found nothing in her backpack. Despite being an honor-roll student and having no history of disciplinary problems, she was escorted to the school nurse's office and told to strip to her undergarments in front of the nurse and the assistant principal's female assistant. She was then required to pull open the underwear so that two female officials could determine if she had hidden pills. No pills were found.

When Savana's mother arrived at the school, a student called out asking her what she was going to do about the strip search of Savana. After meetings with both the principal and the superintendent, neither of whom apologized, April Redding, with the help of the American Civil Liberties Union, sued the school district for damages. A federal magistrate held that the search was reasonable because the assistant principal was relying on the tip from another student. In a 2–1 decision, the U.S. 9th Circuit Court of Appeals agreed. The full 9th Circuit Court heard the case in 2008 and ruled 6 to 5 for the Reddings. "Common sense informs us that directing a 13-year-old girl to remove her clothes, partially revealing her breasts and pelvic area, for allegedly possessing ibuprofen . . . was excessively intrusive. . . . The overzealousness of school administrators in efforts to protect students has the tragic impact of traumatizing those they claim to serve" (Mears, 2009).

The school appealed to the Supreme Court to preserve the flexibility of administrators to deal with problems to protect campus safety, arguing that requiring probable cause to conduct student searches would be a roadblock to the swift response required to protect students from the threats posed by drugs and weapons (Mears, 2009). The Court ruled that the search was unreasonable and unconstitutional, saying that a strip search at school is categorically distinct from other inspections for drugs. The Court also rejected the suit against the school employees because the law had not been clear. They sent the case back to Arizona to consider whether the district should face liability. Justices Stevens and Ginsburg dissented on the issue of qualified immunity, writing that the search was unreasonable and excessive under *T.L.O.*

Capital Punishment and Life without Parole (LWP)

Supreme Court cases addressed issues beyond due process rights for juveniles and their rights regarding searches and seizures. Although infrequent, juveniles do commit serious violent crimes, and the Court considered cases regarding whether sentences to death or LWP sentences were appropriate punishments for juveniles. Contemporary decency standards in terms of what amounts to "cruel and unusual punishment" played a significant role in the deliberations.

Chapter 5 discusses the reasoning behind the Court's decision in *Roper v. Simmons* (2005) that the death penalty for juvenile defendants under 18 years of age at the time of their crime is cruel and unusual punishment. In September 1993, when Christopher Simmons was 17 years old, he and an accomplice (age 15) abducted and murdered Shirley Crook by throwing her off a bridge. On several occasions prior to the crime, Simmons had talked about his plan to find someone to burglarize and murder, telling his friends they would get away with it because they were juveniles. In 1994, Simmons was sentenced to death. In 2002, the Missouri Supreme Court stayed the execution of Simmons while the U.S. Supreme Court decided *Atkins v. Virginia*. The ruling, which referenced a majority of Americans finding the punishment cruel and unusual, forbid the execution of the mentally disabled, The Missouri Supreme Court decided to reconsider Simmons's case. That court, relying on *Atkins*, reasoned that *Stanford v. Kentucky* (1989), which had found that executing juveniles under the age of 18 was constitutional because a majority of Americans did not consider the sentence cruel and unusual, was no longer valid—citing numerous laws passed since 1989 that limited the scope of the death penalty, indicating that national opinion had changed. The Missouri Supreme Court ruled the death sentence of Simmons unconstitutional and resentenced him to LWP. The state of Missouri appealed the decision to the US Supreme Court. Missouri argued that allowing a state court to overturn a Supreme Court decision by looking at "evolving standards" was a dangerous precedent; state courts could just as easily decide that executions prohibited by the Supreme Court were now permissible due to a change in the beliefs of the American people. The US Supreme Court affirmed the decision of the Missouri Supreme Court; the Eighth and Fourteenth Amendments forbid the imposition of the death penalty on offenders under the age of 18.

Another landmark Supreme Court case, *Graham v. Florida* (2010), established that LWP sentences for juveniles who commit crimes in which no one is killed are cruel and unusual. In 2003, 16-year-old Terrance Graham and three accomplices attempted to rob a restaurant in Jacksonville. One of the accomplices struck the manager twice in the head with a metal bar; when the manager yelled, the youths ran out without taking any money. In Florida, the prosecutor decided whether to charge juveniles aged 16 and 17 as juveniles or adults. Graham was charged as an adult with a first-degree felony (maximum sentence LWP) and a second-degree felony (maximum sentence 15 years). He accepted a plea agreement for a one-year sentence to jail and three years probation. The trial court accepted the plea agreement but withheld adjudication of guilt on the two felony charges. He was released from jail at the end of June 2004. In December 2004, he was arrested for a home invasion. His probation officer filed a report with the trial court that Graham had violated the conditions of his probation by possessing a firearm, committing crimes, and associating with persons engaged in criminal activity. Revocation hearings on the probation violations took place in December 2005 and January 2006. Under Florida law, the minimum sentence without a downward departure by the judge was 5 years in prison; the maximum was life imprisonment. Graham's attorney requested the minimum (presentence report recommended a 4-year sentence), and prosecutors asked for 30 years on the first-degree felony and 15 years on the second-degree felony. The presiding judge (not the same judge who had accepted the plea agreement) sentenced Graham to LWP, saying that his escalating pattern of criminal conduct indicated that the only recourse was to protect the community from his behavior. *Graham v. Florida* entitled juveniles sentenced prior to 2010 to a resentencing hearing. The ruling applied to at least 123 prisoners; 77 had been sentenced in Florida, and the others were sentenced in 10 other states (Rovner, 2020). Terrance Graham appeared for resentencing in 2013; he was sentenced to 25 years.

In 2012, the Supreme Court settled two cases jointly; both involved boys age 14 at the time of their crimes. The landmark cases (*Miller v. Alabama* and *Jackson v. Hobbs*) found mandatory LWP sentences unconstitutional for juveniles convicted of homicide. The ruling affected approximately 2,500 juveniles (Rovner, 2020).

Kuntrell Jackson was 14 in November 1999 when he and two other teens attempted to rob a video store in Blytheville, Arkansas. One of Jackson's companions fatally shot Laurie Troup, the store clerk, with a sawed-off shotgun he pulled from his jacket. The teens fled without taking any money. Prosecutors in Arkansas had the discretion to try juveniles as adults for certain offenses. Jackson had a juvenile record of car theft and shoplifting; he was tried as an adult and convicted of murder and aggravated robbery. Capital murder in Arkansas carries a mandatory minimum LWP sentence.

In 2003, 14-year-old Evan Miller and Colby Smith (16) were drinking and smoking marijuana with Cole Canon (52), a neighbor. When Canon passed out, the boys took $300 from his wallet. He woke up and grabbed Miller by the throat. Smith hit Canon with a baseball bat; Miller then grabbed the bat and struck Canon multiple times. The boys left but returned and set fire to Canon's trailer to cover up the crime. Cannon died from the assault injuries and smoke inhalation. Alabama law required that Miller be charged as a juvenile initially but allowed the district attorney to seek transfer to adult court. Evan was convicted in adult court of murder in the course of arson, which carried a mandatory minimum LWP punishment. The Alabama Court of Criminal Appeals affirmed, holding that Miller's sentence was not overly harsh when compared to his crime.

In a 5–4 vote, the Supreme Court said the Eighth Amendment's prohibition against cruel and unusual punishment forbids the mandatory LWP sentencing for juvenile homicide offenders (*Miller v. Alabama*, 2012). Mandatory sentencing is an unconstitutionally disproportionate sentence for juveniles. Justice Elena Kagan wrote the majority opinion and noted that sentencing authorities in both cases had no discretion to impose a different punishment. State law prohibited considerations of the lessened culpability of juveniles and their greater capacity for change. Adolescence is marked by transient rashness, proclivity for risk, and inability to assess consequences—all factors that should mitigate the punishment of juvenile defendants. The ruling did not prohibit the LWP sentences, but Kagan noted that the Court believed appropriate occasions for the harshest possible penalty would be uncommon.

The ruling struck down statutes in 29 states. The decision requires lower courts to resentence juveniles, taking into consideration life circumstances, individual characters, age, and the circumstances of the crime. An Arkansas judge resentenced Jackson to 20 years in prison (AP, 2017). Disciplinary violations made him ineligible to come before the state parole board until 2016. His first request for parole was denied; he appeared again on February 21, 2017, and was conditionally released on parole. There was a resentencing hearing for Miller in March 2017; his lawyers cited his abusive upbringing and the lack of brain development at age 14. Prosecutors argued Miller should remain behind bars the rest of his life. Under a 2016 Alabama law, the judge can resentence Miller to LWP or allow parole hearings after serving 30 years (Janos, 2019).

The *Miller* ruling affected the mandatory sentencing laws of the federal government and 28 states (Rovner, 2020). Supreme Courts in 14 states ruled that *Miller* applied retroactively; 7 other states decided the ruling was not retroactive, and 6 states passed legislation that made juvenile sentencing retroactive. The Supreme Court ended the inconsistency with its ruling in *Montgomery v. Louisiana* (2016) making *Miller's* finding retroactive. Henry Montgomery was 17 when he killed a sheriff's deputy in Louisiana. He was 68 years old and had been imprisoned since 1963 when the Supreme Court made its ruling.

States can address the unconstitutionality of mandatory juvenile LWP sentences by granting parole hearings rather than resentencing the approximately 2,100 people affected by the ruling (Rovner, 2020). Henry Montgomery went before the parole board in 2018, which denied parole in a 2–1 decision because he had failed to take enough classes. In Louisiana, parole applications are only granted every two years, but an appeal allowed him to appear again in 2019. This time parole was approved 2–1, but the approval must be unanimous. He remains imprisoned.

States have found workarounds to maintain past practices and to continue life sentences for youth. For example, a court in Idaho denied the appeal of Sarah M. Johnson, convicted of killing her parents in 2003 because the judge *did* consider her age as a mitigating factor before issuing a LWP sentence (Bevan, 2014). The Supreme Court of Idaho affirmed the district court's ruling that the sentencing court met the substantive requirements in *Miller* and *Montgomery*.

Punishing Youths: Abuses Inside

Americans avoid discussing how young offenders are punished. The plain and simple truth is that juvenile "correctional institutions" are prisons circumscribed by strip searches, shackles, jumpsuits, and cells. In Orwellian fashion, we obfuscate the reality through the use of euphemistic terminology. Adjudication is the juvenile court process that determines if the juvenile committed the act with which he or she is charged—*adjudicated* is the equivalent of *convicted* in adult court. *Disposed* and *disposition* are the equivalent of *sentenced*. Juveniles are sometimes confined in a facility as part of a *diversion* agreement without going through the adjudication process. *Detained* indicates the status of being held in custody until the completion of the adjudication hearing before the juvenile court. Many juveniles are detained before their adjudication as well as before being transferred to criminal court if processed as an adult. *Committed* is used to indicate that the juvenile will be incarcerated in a facility by the court-ordered disposition. Committed juveniles include those convicted and sentenced in juvenile and criminal courts.

The commitment of juveniles to prisons represents the "end of the line" in the juvenile justice system. Committed juveniles may never recover from the pains of their imprisonment. Conditions in many juvenile institutions have improved very little since the houses of refuge. Any rehabilitation programs are the exception rather than the rule; punishment is the hallmark of these institutions.

There are several different prisons to which a youth can be committed. Some are public (i.e., run by state or local governments), and others are privately funded. Prisons for young offenders can be further subdivided into short-term (usually ranging from a few days to a couple of months) and long-term confinement (ranging from three or four months to one or two years). Each of these examples has had its share of scandals associated with abuse.

In 1997, there were 105,055 youths in residential placement. The number declined 59% to 43,580 in 2017 (Hockenberry, 2020). The numbers of committed youths decreased 64% from 75,406 in 1997 to 26,972 in 2017; the number of detained youths decreased 44% (28,040 to 15,660). A small number of youth were in placement as part of a diversion

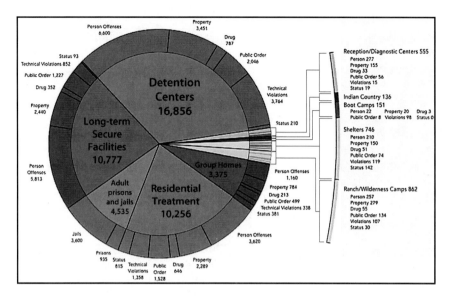

Figure 8-1   Youth Confinement Facilities

Source: Sawyer, 2019

agreement. Delinquency offenses accounted for 96% of those in placement, with status offenses accounting for the remaining 4%. Approximately 40% were held for a person offense.

While there has been a 60% decrease in the practice of incarcerating
youth since 2000, the disproportionality for youth of color, youth with disabilities, and LGBTQ youth remains (Sawyer, 2019). While 14% of all
youth under 18 in the United States are Black, 42% of boys and 35% of
girls in juvenile facilities are Black. The national detention rate for Black
youth was 6 times the rate for white youth, and the commitment rate was
4 times the rate for white youth. When considering the total population,
33% of juveniles in residential placement were white, 41% were African
American, 21% were Hispanic, 2% Native American, 1% Asian, and 2%
other groups (Hockenberry, 2020).

In 2018 there were 1,510 juvenile facilities in the United States; 60%
of the facilities were publicly operated and held 73% of juvenile offenders
(OJJDP, 2020). About two-thirds of youths in residential placement are
held in facilities restricted by locked doors, gates, or fences (Sawyer,
2019). Detention centers, reception/diagnostic centers, and long-term
secure facilities are the most restrictive facilities. More than 15,000 youth
are placed in facilities with variable restrictions, ranging from secure, mili-
tary-style boot camps to group homes where youth may leave to attend
school or go to work. More than three quarters (78%) of these youth are in
locked facilities where conditions sometimes are worse than in prisons.

Almost 9 out of 10 youth in residential placement are in group homes or residential treatment facilities. Other facilities include ranch/wilderness camps and shelters.

The type of facility where a child is confined can affect their health, safety, access to services, and outcomes upon reentry (Sawyer, 2019). Adult prisons and jails are at the worst end of the continuum for youth. Youth under the age of 18 may be placed in solitary confinement to comply with the PREA safety standard of "sight and sound" separation from incarcerated adults. Yearly, 76,000 juveniles are prosecuted as adults; on any night approximately, 4,600 youth are in adult jails or prisons (Campaign for Youth Justice, 2018). More than half (51.9%) of the youth transferred to adult court are Black. In California, Latino youth are direct filed at 3.3 times the rate of white youth (compared to 2.4 times ten years earlier). Youth are more likely to be traumatized by the harsh realities of imprisonment than adults. Youth in adult facilities are 5 times more likely to commit suicide than those in juvenile facilities. Youth who are prosecuted in the adult system are 34% more likely to recidivate and to commit more violent offenses than those handled by the juvenile system.

Detention Centers

The largest percentage of confined youth are held in detention centers, the functional equivalent of a jail (Sawyer, 2019). Detention centers are usually operated by local authorities and are generally used for the temporary restrictive custody of defendants. Sixty percent of youth in detention centers are awaiting a hearing or disposition. Federal guidelines suggest only youth who are serious, violent, or chronic offenders should be held in pretrial detention, but judges order pretrial detention in 26% of delinquency cases. Almost 4,000 status offenders and youths who have committed technical violations of their probation (low-level offenses) are held in detention centers. Youths in pretrial detention are isolated from their families and communities and exposed to the risk of victimization. In 2017, over 40% of detained youth had been held more than 30 days; almost 500 had been detained for over a year. Person offense cases were the most likely to involve detention (37%), followed by public order offense cases (26%), property offense cases (20%), and drug offense cases (8%) (Hockenberry & Puzzanchera, 2020).

It has been repeatedly determined that most youths do not need to be placed in detention, that far too many have been charged with minor offenses, and that there are many negative consequences of being in detention. Dan Macallair and Mike Males (2004) identified the following harms of detention:

- promotes further delinquency through association with delinquent peers;
- stigmatizes and reinforces a delinquent identity;

- results in harsher treatment by decision makers throughout the process;
- accelerates further involvement in the juvenile justice system;
- diverts resources from comprehensive community-based interventions;
- reduces involvement and interaction with community-based services;
- increases rejection by local public institutions such as schools;
- promotes isolation, lethargy, and ineffectiveness;
- results in overcrowding, punitive custody, and abusive conditions.

The ultimate negative consequence is that youths in custody are at greater risk of death. One study tracked a sample of 1,829 youths processed through the Cook County Juvenile Court with a 3-year follow-up period (Teplin et al., 2005). Youths entering the juvenile justice system were 4 times more likely than the general population to die, with 90% of the deaths attributed to homicide. The mortality rate for female youth was nearly 8 times the general-population rate. The death rate for Black youths was the highest, followed closely by Hispanics (of the 65 who died, 23 were Black and 21 were Hispanic). A follow-up study in 2015 found that these rates remain extremely high as "the mortality rate for delinquent youth (806 deaths per 100,000 person-years) is approximately 4.4 times that for general-population youth (184 deaths per 100,000 person-years)" (Teplin et al., 2015).

Two-thirds of juvenile detention facilities hold youths waiting for mental health treatment (McCormick et al., 2017). Thousands of mentally ill youths (about 7% of all detainees) are held in juvenile detention centers. In 33 states, detained mentally ill youths have not been charged with a crime. Youths awaiting mental health treatment average 23.4 days in detention, compared with an average of 17.2 days for all detainees. Detention places such youths at high risk of suicide or aggressive behavior (Abram et al., 2008).

Similar to the lack of services for youth with mental health needs, detention centers are deficient in education and rehabilitation programs. School activities typically entail filling-out work packets and reading quietly. The poor quality of schooling in juvenile facilities is well documented. About two thirds of youth in-custody have low academic performance and school connection (Vélez Young et al., n.d.). Many facilities operate schooling on a one-room schoolhouse basis structurally and/or in terms of curriculum and instruction (Vélez Young et al., 2010). For example, juveniles are housed based on factors such as offense type and age and the size of the population in the facility. In facilities where classrooms are built into the living unit or bunk room space, youth attend school with their cohorts in the housing unit. Thus, youth with diverse academic standing attend school together. Even in juvenile facilities with classrooms located separate from living units, young people are assigned classrooms based on factors found during adjudication. The end result is that most young people complete work packets and textbook exercises independently rather than receiving aggregate curriculum and learning activities.

Studies show that academic success in facilities is unlikely (Vélez Young et al., n.d.). Only 16% of youth facilities provide the same education and vocations programming that is available in the community context, and only 20% of facilities have a formal process for bridging youth to school in the community once released (Council of State Governments, 2015). More than half (56%) never return to school after their release (Cavendish, 2013). Youth in detention centers receive the fewest education services, such as GED preparation and job training. About 2,000 youths serve their dispositions in detention centers despite those facilities offering fewer programs and services (Sawyer, 2019).

Reception and Diagnostic Centers

Psychologists or social workers in reception/diagnostic centers evaluate youth committed by the courts (Shelden & Troshynski, 2020). These centers are often located adjacent to long-term facilities. "Diagnostic" can be a lucrative tool for those more interested in enriching themselves than in helping children. Charlie Balasavage, 16, was sentenced to a private secure detention facility by Mark Ciavarella—a facility for which the judge helped secure more than $30 million in county contracts (see discussion of Kids for Cash scandal below). Charlie's parents had wanted him to see a doctor covered by their medical insurance, but the county said no. The psychologist who evaluated him was the brother-in-law of Michael Conahan, the other corrupt judge in the scandal. The Balasavages were charged $250 for the evaluation, and the state of Pennsylvania eventually paid the psychologist $836,636 for such exams (Sullivan, 2009).

Reception/diagnostic centers are intended to be temporary, transitional placements, but more than half the youth they hold are there longer than 90 days; more than 1 in 7 are held more than a year (Sawyer, 2019). In 43% of reception/diagnostic centers, mechanical restraints such as handcuffs, leg cuffs, restraining chairs, and strait jackets are used.

Long-Term Secure Facilities

Youths who have been committed are most commonly placed in long-term facilities, often called training schools (Sawyer, 2019). These facilities are usually large and old; the conditions of confinement are similar to prisons. Hundreds of youths are imprisoned behind razor wire fences and may be subjected to pepper spray, mechanical restraints, and solitary confinement. While most detained youth are held in detention centers, almost 1,000 youth who have not yet been committed are held in long-term secure facilities—and less than half are accused of violent offenses. Confinement is a traumatizing punishment for youth who often have a history of trauma and victimization.

Conditions of Confinement

Child advocates nationwide have deplored the operational practices and conditions of confinement for young offenders in state-run facilities—from the days of houses of refuge through today. The Civil Rights of Institutionalized Persons Act (CRIPA) passed in 1997 authorizes the attorney general of the United States to conduct investigations and litigation relating to conditions of confinement in state or locally operated institutions (the statute does not cover private facilities).[1] The Special Litigation Section of the Civil Rights Division of the U.S. Department of Justice investigates facilities to determine whether there is a pattern or practice of violations of federal rights. Investigations have looked at medical care, mental health care, protection from staff-on-youth or youth-on-youth violence and exploitation, equal treatment for minority youth, fair court procedures, adequate educational services, and programs to encourage juveniles to manage their behavior (Shelden & Troshynski, 2020).

In February 2020, the DOJ filed a notice letter with the state of South Carolina about deficiencies at its Broad River Road Complex (BRRC), a long-term, juvenile commitment facility. BRRC houses about 100 youth age 17 or younger. The average length of stay is 7 months, while others spend almost 3 years. Many youth are nonviolent offenders, and 28% of all commitments were from probation violations. The facility is supposed to identify youth with serious mental illness and transfer them to a psychiatric residential facility. Of the 117 people who entered the facility with serious mental illness in 2017, 75 were never transferred.

The DOJ investigation found that BRRC failed to keep youth reasonably safe from youth-on-youth violence and that the facility harmed youth by using punitive, prolonged isolation (Civil Rights Division, 2020). The violations were exacerbated by failure to train staff, to implement effective behavior management tools, and to establish key safety features in the physical structure. The DOJ's investigation of the facility's failure to protect youth from physical abuse by staff was ongoing. The Department determined that South Carolina had not violated the Americans with Disabilities Act in its use of secure presentencing residential evaluation centers. Among the recommendations from the DOJ were: improve the physical plant to ensure adequate surveillance and retain video that enables investigation of allegations of abuse; eliminate the use of isolation for minor misbehavior, protective custody, and mental health observation; replace long-term isolation with a short-term cool-down room in each housing unit for youth who are a threat to safety; develop admissions screening protocols to identify youth who are vulnerable to victimization by other youth in the facility.

The Manson Youth Institute (MYI) in Connecticut houses offenders whose cases were transferred from juvenile to adult court (Lyons, 2019). A DOJ investigation found that youth with the most complex mental and behavioral health needs were the most likely to be subject to repeated and prolonged physical and social isolation—putting them at risk of mental health deterioration and suicide. They were locked in their cells 23.5 hours per day; they were handcuffed when they left the cell. They had no access to education or rehabilitative programming. Even youth not in isolation did not have meaningful access to school, rehabilitative services, visits with family, or the opportunity to purchase hygiene products or extra food if they were deemed a risk to the general youth prison population.

What counts as minimal standards for the operations of youth prisons is typically established through lawsuits. For example, the ACLU of Washington filed a lawsuit in March 2017 on behalf of a mother whose son was repeatedly placed in solitary for minor infractions, such as talking back (Haviland, 2017). In a settlement approved by the U.S. District Court for Western Washington, Grays Harbor County agreed to use solitary confinement only as a temporary measure to address an immediate threat of harm, escape, or substantial disruption.

Many confined youth grapple with post-traumatic stress from abuse and maltreatment (e.g., withholding food) within facilities. Even when researchers account for pre-incarceration post-traumatic stress, the abuse and hostile conditions behind bars leaves significant trauma for youth (Dierkhising et al., 2014). Young people who spend time behind bars face significant crises in medical and mental health (Barnert et al., 2017).

Confining youth in isolation continues to be used in correctional facilities for punitive or administrative reasons despite evidence of substantial and lasting damage (Clark, 2017). Human rights organizations have characterized the practice as a form of psychological torture, and mental health professionals have condemned the practice. Solitary confinement is a form of extended sensory and social isolation. It typically involves placement alone in a small cell for 22 to 24 hours a day; restricted contact with staff and peers; suspension or restriction of family visits; and the absence or minimization of reading material, radio, or television. Some facility administrators believe solitary confinement is necessary to maintain discipline and to curb disruptive behaviors. Staff who rely on solitary confinement as a primary behavioral management technique resist limitations on its use. Critics see it as an indicator of inadequacies in correctional settings, including deficient screening and identification of mental illness. States that have reduced reliance on juvenile solitary confinement, have done so by setting rehabilitative goals, developing new policies, monitoring data, and training staff.

In 2018, an estimated 7.1% of youth in juvenile facilities reported being sexually victimized during the prior 12 months (Smith & Stroop, 2019). Sexual misconduct by facility staff was reported by 5.8% of youth, and an estimated 2.1% reported force or coercion in staff misconduct. Incidents are probably considerably more frequent than reported—whether because of fear of retaliation, the belief by juveniles that no one will believe them, or differences in perception. Some youths regard sexual relationships with staff members as consensual rather than as adults in positions of authority abusing their power.

The failure of youth prisons to protect youth and improve their outcomes plus the institutional model's stubborn resistance to transformation argues for the replacement of youth prisons (McCarthy et al., 2016).

> The harmful effects of incarceration are embedded in the physical facilities themselves and the nature of institutionalization. Changes in leadership, training, or enriched programming ultimately are trumped by correctional physical plants, the great distance most facilities are from families and oversight mechanisms, and the bureaucratization and institutionalization such facilities engender. Large, institutional structures, surrounded by razor wire and filled with noise and harsh lighting, create a toxic environment. The staff and kids are inevitably caught in their roles of guard and prisoner, locking both into a struggle of power and resistance. Life in these places is about violence and control, submission, and defiance, leaving little room for the guidance, learning, role-modeling, and caring relationships that young people need. (p. 10)

Funneling Youth into the "Pipeline" to Prison

There is a disturbing intersection of schools and juvenile justice known as the school-to-prison pipeline. Schools can indirectly push students into the criminal justice system through suspensions and expulsions (Shelden & Troshynski, 2020). They can directly funnel students into the system through zero tolerance policies that rely on police officers to maintain order through arrests. The daily presence of school resource officers (SROs) became widespread in the 1990s amid concerns mass shootings, drug abuse, and juvenile crime (Goldstein, 2020). Federal and state officials offered local districts money to hire officers and to purchase law enforcement equipment, such as metal detectors. Eventually two-thirds of high school students, 45% of middle schoolers, and 19% of elementary school students attended schools with police officers.[2]

> Their power to legally use physical force, arrest and handcuff students, and bring the full weight of the criminal justice system to bear on misbehaving children is often obscured until an act of violence, captured by a student's cell phone, breaks through to the public. Police in schools are first and foremost there to enforce criminal laws, and virtually every violation of a school rule can be considered a criminal act if viewed through a police-first lens. Schools offer an ideal entry point for the criminal justice system to gather intelligence, surveil young people, and exercise strong-arm policing tactics to instill fear and compliance. The capacity for school policing to turn against students instead of protecting them has always existed, and it continues to pose a first-line threat to the civil rights and civil liberties of young people. (French-Marcelin & Hinger, 2017, p. 2)

Extending policing into schools and relying on law enforcement for classroom management transforms school administrators, teachers, guidance counselors, and other members of the school community into agents of the criminal justice system.

The criminalization of education has a disproportionate impact on: the poor and minority offenders; students in special education; and LGBTQ adolescents who are more likely to be punished harshly for ordinary misbehavior (Mallett, 2016). Pipeline research illustrates the ways that the school and juvenile justice systems are deeply tied to inequities in the larger society (Vélez Young, 2017). More than ten years of studies show that suspensions, expulsions (Wallace et al., 2008), and arrests (Rodriguez, 2013) from schools are disproportionately applied to students of color and with disabilities. Youth are tracked into the pipeline not because of their behavior but because of the power of the biases present in youth-specific institutions. The presence of police in schools makes arrests and referrals more likely. Black students are the most likely to attend schools with SROs. When police are consistently present in minority communities, they criminalize behavior that they would overlook in other places (Blad & Harwin, 2017). Once in the pipeline, systemic bias further disadvantages minorities, as evidenced by the statistics earlier in the chapter.

When students are referred to the juvenile court for school infractions, they may face adjudication. If the pipeline is not disrupted, offenders are placed in juvenile facilities. An egregious corruption scandal involving the juvenile justice system in a central Pennsylvania county provided an alarming example of the school-to-prison pipeline.

Judge Michael Conahan oversaw the budget for the court in Luzerne County, and Judge Mark Ciavarella oversaw the juvenile courts. The two judges instituted a kickback scheme in December 2002 (the scheme was eventually labeled *Kids for Cash*). Conahan shut down the county-run juvenile detention center and helped secure contracts worth tens of millions of dollars for two private detention centers (Chen, 2009). Between 2003 and 2008, Ciavarella presided over more than 6,500 cases.

Approximately half of the juveniles appeared in Luzerne County Juvenile Court without benefit of counsel, almost ten times the state average (Juvenile Law Center, 2010). Ciavarella ignored the Pennsylvania rules for juvenile court procedure that said juveniles could not waive their right to an attorney unless the decision was made knowingly, intelligently, and voluntarily. He failed to ask if youth understood the consequences of waiving their rights (Woolard, 2019).

> Virtually all of these unrepresented juveniles were adjudicated delinquent, many for acts so minor and trivial that in most counties these charges would never have even made it to juvenile court. Of those youth without counsel who were adjudicated delinquent, nearly 60 percent were sent to out-of-home placements . . . leaving thousands of children and parents feeling bewildered, violated and traumatized. Luzerne County was a toxic combination of for-profit facilities, corrupt judges, and professional indifference. (Juvenile Law Center, 2010, p. i)

For years, court personnel witnessed juveniles shackled and sent to juvenile facilities and never spoke up about the denial of constitutional protections to children (Shelden & Troshynski, 2020). Marsha Levick, deputy director of the Juvenile Law Center, asserted there was an internal conspiracy of silence in Luzerne County. She alluded to the familiarity and coziness that happens in small-town courtrooms where the same lawyers consistently appear before the same judge. The cocoon of silence accompanies a go-along-to-get-along situation where no one wants to challenge the judge.

The nonprofit Juvenile Law Center in Philadelphia received calls from alarmed parents in 2007. The Center investigated and petitioned the Pennsylvania Supreme Court in 2008 to vacate the adjudications of delinquency and expunge the records. The first request was denied. The U.S. Attorney's Office brought charges against the two judges in January 2009. In October, the Pennsylvania Supreme Court vacated Ciavarella's adjudications of delinquency. Three months later, the special master ordered all Ciavarella's cases dismissed. Ciavarella was convicted in 2011 and sentenced to 28 years in prison. Michael Conahan pleaded guilty to racketeering and was sentenced to 17.5 years.[3] The co-owner of the two private juvenile justice facilities served 18 months in prison and settled a class-action suit for $4.75 million. The developer was sentenced to a year in prison after pleading guilty to failure to tell federal agents about more than $2 million in payments to the judges.

The system failed at numerous levels. From corrupt judges to district attorneys to public defenders to juvenile probation officers to the state Judicial Conduct Board to private attorneys and to other court personnel, everyone connected to the juvenile justice system in Luzerne County contributed to the enormous harm done to children (Juvenile Law Center, 2010). Ciavarella had been elected to a 10-year term in 1996 after running on a platform of being tough on juvenile crime; he was reelected in 2006 (Shelden & Troshynski, 2020). In the documentary, *Kids for Cash* (May, 2014), he asserts he never took bribes—describing the money he took as finder's fees and saying the facilities needed to be built because parents didn't know how to be parents. The schools in Luzerne called the police for incidents such as a student mocking an assistant principal on social media, a 14-year-old girl having a minor fight with another girl in the school gymnasium, and a 12-year-old arguing with the mother of another child at a bus stop. School authorities outsourced discipline to the police and courts, pushing low-performing students out of school.

Scandals like this one do irreparable harm to youths. They suffer collateral consequences in addition to the pains of being imprisoned and separated from family and friends. One mother whose son was sentenced by Ciavarella said: "What do these kids see of the legal system and of authority figures? These kids see people who abuse their power. Now, we have a whole county and generation of children who have lost trust in the system" (Chen, 2009).

The school-to-prison pipeline is expanding at alarming rates. Exclusionary school discipline practices funnel increasing numbers of students from educational facilities to carceral institutions. "Researchers have determined that students are more likely to be arrested on days they are suspended from school, and that suspensions are connected to higher dropout rates and increased risk of contact with the juvenile justice system" (Epstein et al., 2017, p. 9). School discipline increases the links to criminalization and feeds the commitment to mass incarceration of people deemed threatening and disposable (Annamma et al., 2019).

Young men of color were first identified as victims of school discipline and criminality, and recent research has focused on Black girls. Black girls receive disproportionate referrals for infractions such as disruptive behavior, dress code violations, disobedience, and aggressive behavior—infractions that are subjective and influenced by gendered interpretations (Morris & Perry, 2017). School discipline penalizes African American girls for behaviors perceived to transgress normative standards of femininity. Black girls are nearly 6 times more likely to be suspended than white girls (Epstein et al., 2017). Being suspended or expelled affects the probability of being incarcerated. Black girls, while only 17% of the overall student population, represent 31% of girls referred to law enforcement by school officials and 43% of those arrested on school grounds.

Black girls tend to receive harsher sentences than other girls for the same offenses (Epstein et al., 2017).

> The differential treatment of Black girls in public systems extends beyond the classroom and into the juvenile justice system. Broad discretion is granted to decision-makers across the juvenile justice system, including police officers, probation officers, defense attorneys, prosecutors, and judges. And from arrests to prosecutions, Black girls face more punitive treatment compared to their peers. (p. 12)

All of these factors are linked with lower achievement later in life (Annamma et al., 2019).

Research has identified *adultification bias* as a form of prejudice that can lead authority figures to assess Black girls (and boys) as more mature than they actually are and to punish them more harshly. Adultification contributes to beliefs that the transgressions of Black youths are intentional and malicious rather than the result of immature decision making that is a key characteristic childhood (Epstein et al., 2017).

> If authorities in public systems view Black girls as less innocent, less needing of protection, and generally more like adults, it appears likely that they would also view Black girls as more culpable for their actions and, on that basis, punish them more harshly despite their status as children. Thus, adultification may serve as a contributing cause of the disproportionality in school discipline outcomes, harsher treatment by law enforcement, and the differentiated exercise of discretion by officials across the spectrum of the juvenile justice system. (p. 8)

If young people are not allowed to mature out of indiscretions without getting entangled in the justice system, the long-term consequences can be extreme.

> Concentrated in low-income areas of color, the use of extreme police tactics in schools has continued despite evidence that demonstrates the significant, disparate, and sometimes lifelong consequences of school policing on young people. Studies have also found that emphasizing a positive school climate—in which students feel safe, welcomed, and nurtured—decreases suspensions and expulsions while increasing student attainment. Creating equitable school climates—that is, schools that nurture and protect the rights and capacities of every student—will mean ending our reliance on school policing and recognizing how the criminalization of youth of color has denied students access to equitable education. (French-Marcelin & Hinger, 2017, p. 32)

LGBTQ Youth in the Juvenile Justice System

LGBTQ youth face several systemic challenges in their interactions with the juvenile justice system (Marrett, 2015). At least 13% of youth involved in the juvenile justice system are LGBTQ, totaling around 300,000 per year (Development Services Group, 2014). Layered with the disproportionate representation of LGBTQ youth in the system is the overrepresentation of LGBTQ youth of color who comprise 60% to 85% of the LGBTQ youth who are arrested and incarcerated (Poteat et al., 2016).

LGBTQ youth face a hostile climate in schools. School-based peer bullying (including violence) and adult biases lead to heightened levels of depression and suicidal ideation for LGBTQ youth (Hatchel et al., 2017). Adults in schools contribute to the hostile climate through their actions or inactions—ranging from the enforcement of biased school policies regarding dress to gender biases such as regulations against same-sex students holding hands (Mitchum & Moodie-Mills, 2014). Research is still developing an understanding of the rate at which LGBTQ youth are entering the juvenile justice system via school truancy (i.e., not wanting to be at school) and school fights (e.g., assault charges), both of which can carry incarceration time.

The intersection of systematic discrimination and economic hardship place transgender youth at risk. One quarter to 37% of LGBTQ high school students are or have recently been homeless (Hussey, 2015). "A safe and consistent place to live is a critical prerequisite for academic achievement, good physical and mental health, and career development" (p. 29). Of homeless youth, nearly 40% are LGBTQ. LGBTQ youth are four times as likely to be arrested for sex trafficking. Perhaps even more troubling, LGBTQ youth are likely to be charged with sexual assault crimes—accused of assault in age-appropriate consensual same-sex relationships by overzealous parents, school administrators, and juvenile court prosecutors and judges (Majd et al., 2009).

Transgender young people face violence and unequal treatment in juvenile facilities. In studies of New York and California juvenile detention centers, hostile school settings were recreated in the incarceration settings. Juvenile justice professionals report witnessing their colleagues and youth verbally and physically assaulting LGBTQ youth. Facility data show that LGBTQ youth are disproportionately impacted by peer assaults, physical and sexual, while incarcerated (Heaton et al., 2016).

Alternatives to Punishing Children

At the beginning of the chapter, we noted that imprisonment has been a dominant form of punishment for children in the United States. While legislation purports to control delinquent behavior, it most frequently controls children of the poor and their parents. We apply various labels to the unwanted behavior. As Jerome Miller (1998) noted, we began with *possessed* youths in the seventeenth century, moved to the *dangerous classes* in the eighteenth and late nineteenth centuries. We continued in the twentieth century with the *psychopath* of the 1940s, the *sociopath* of the 1950s, the *compulsive* delinquent, the *unsocialized aggressive,* and finally the *bored* delinquent. "With the growth of professionalism, the number of labels has multiplied exponentially" (p. 234).

Miller (1998) asserts that the problem with these labels is that they maintain the existing order, buffering it from threats that might arise from its own internal contradictions. They reassure

> that the fault lies in the warped offender and takes everyone else off the hook. Moreover, it enables the professional diagnostician to enter the scene or withdraw at will, wearing success like a halo and placing failure around the neck of the client like a noose. (p. 234)

More importantly, the labels reinforce the belief that harsh punishment works, especially the kind of punishment that includes some form of incarceration, so that the offender is placed out of sight and, not coincidentally, out of mind. There are alternatives to punishing children through incarceration.

The Missouri Model

Like most other states, Missouri had a history of confining young offenders in large institutions. Starting in the 1980s they began experimenting with regionally based smaller, facilities. An editorial (2007) in *The New York Times* stated:

> With the prisons filled to bursting, state governments are desperate for ways to keep more people from committing crimes and ending up behind bars. Part of the problem lies in the juvenile justice system, which is doing a frighteningly effective job of turning nonviolent childhood offenders into mature, hardened criminals. States that want to

change that are increasingly looking to Missouri, which has turned its juvenile justice system into a nationally recognized model of how to deal effectively with troubled children.

Missouri has an agency-wide commitment to helping troubled youth change their antisocial, self-destructive behaviors and preparing them to return to their communities. Youths are confined in small facilities located near their homes and families. Each has four levels of programs: community (nonresidential) care for the least serious offenders; group homes housing 10–12 less serious offenders; moderate security facilities with 20–50 youths; and secure facilities with 36 or fewer residents. Youths eat together, study together, exercise together, and attend daily treatment sessions together. The treatment process is enhanced by remaining with the same group by encouraging members to trust and feel responsible toward one another. The rooms at all levels are carpeted and resemble those in college dormitories—no concrete cells.

The Missouri program emphasizes keeping youths safe physically and emotionally. It eliminates ridicule and emotional abuse through constant staff supervision and positive peer relationships. Coercion and demeaning treatment are not part of the process. The youths spend 6 hours each day on education; each group has its own teacher. Staff members work to help youths develop self-awareness and communication skills—critical to future success. Missouri recruits family members as partners in the treatment process and for success after release—rather than treating them as the source of the delinquency. There is intensive support and supervision to help youths transition to life outside the facility. There is intensive aftercare planning before release and close monitoring and mentoring after release. The core philosophy is that every young person wants to—and can—succeed. The hunger for approval, acceptance, and achievement is universal.

> Delinquent youth can't be reformed through a military-style treatment, and few will be deterred from crime by fear of punishment. Rather, change can only result from internal choices made by the young people themselves—choices to adopt more positive behaviors, seek out more positive peers, and embrace more positive goals. (Mendel, 2010, p. 37)

Detention Diversion Advocacy Project

The Center on Juvenile and Criminal Justice (CJCJ) in San Francisco, California, developed the original Detention Diversion Advocacy Project (DDAP) in 1993. The program's major goals were to reduce the number of youth in court-ordered detention and to provide them with culturally relevant community-based services and supervision. Youths selected for the program would likely have been detained pending their adjudication—youths destined for what Jerome Miller (1998) calls the "deep end" of the juvenile justice system. By focusing on *detained* youth, the project ensures that it is a true diversion alternative—*not* an example of widening the net to ensnare lower-level offenders. Youths are screened by DDAP staff to determine if they are likely to be detained and whether they present an acceptable risk to the community. The program has been replicated in Washington, DC and Montgomery County, Maryland.

DDAP was designed to accomplish the following goals: (1) provide multilevel interventions to divert youth from secure detention facilities; (2) demonstrate that community-based interventions are an effective alternative to secure custody and that the needs of both the youths and the community can be met at a cost savings to the public; and (3) reduce disproportionate minority incarceration.

Juvenile Collaborative Reentry Unit (JCRU)

In 2011 a new program was established as part of the Second Chance Act; it followed some of the basic principles of DDAP. The *Juvenile Collaborative Reentry Unit (JCRU)*, addressed historically high recidivism and failure rates of youth exiting out-of-home placements in San Francisco. The program provided case planning and aftercare services for recently released youth (Center on Juvenile and Criminal Justice, 2020). The program targeted low-income minority youth. Not unlike other large cities, youth living in San Francisco's poorest neighborhoods accounted for 76% of youth referrals. Long-term out-of-home commitments can distance youth from destructive local influences, but they also disconnect them from potentially beneficial community, family, and educational supports. Reentry and aftercare services for high-risk youth returning from placement are essential components for successful exits from the justice system.

After a disposition, a JCRU representative meets with the offender to begin the process of preparing for release. Both the youth and family members are involved in every decision about the services that will be provided (e.g., education, and vocational opportunities) in a comprehensive reentry plan. Once released, both the youth and their family meet with all the groups involved in JCRU to coordinate implementation and delivery of services. The JCRU consists of members from the San Francisco Juvenile Probation Department, the San Francisco Superior Court, the San Francisco Public Defenders Office and representatives from the Center on Juvenile and Criminal Justice. The team works with a judge to ensure that they assist the youth in a reintegration process that addresses their needs. The average length of enrollment in JCRU is 6–24 months.

California

California's approach to juveniles has undergone revolutionary reform since 2007 when it began implementing the realignment of responsibilities for youth from the state's Division of Juvenile Justice (DJJ) to the counties (Shelden & Troshynski, 2020). It has gone from one of the most repressive state systems to one at the forefront of reform. A series of laws reduced the number of incarcerated youth from almost 10,000 in 1996 to 1,700 in 2008. Policy makers then banned commitments of all but the most serious juvenile offenders. By 2012, California had closed 8 of its 11 large facilities. In 2020, the DJJ housed about 750 youth. It operated a fire camp, 2 large institutions for males, and a reception center/clinic for males and females at an annual cost of almost $300—$336,00 per youth in custody.

In October 2018, California became the first state to forbid the transfer of children younger than 16 to adult court for any crime, including homicide (Shelden & Troshynski, 2020). Other legislation bars children younger than 12 from the jurisdiction of the juvenile court; makes individuals sentenced to LWOP as minors eligible for release after reaching their twenty-fifth year of incarceration; and limits the amount of time youths deemed mentally incompetent can be detained in juvenile facilities—they must be given supportive mental health services or released to other placement.

In May 2020, California Governor Gavin Newsom proposed shuttering the four remaining facilities and transferring the responsibilities for the remaining juveniles to the counties by the end of the year (Boyer, 2020). The 59 county probation departments have a capacity of 11,200 beds and currently hold 3,100 youth. Moving the juveniles would bring high-needs youth closer to home and curb the trauma and violence endemic to large state facilities. The population of confined youth fell 73% since 1999, yet the capacity of county juvenile justice facilities grew by 14% (Shelden & Troshynski, 2020). California invested $300 million in the construction and renovation of county facilities, and counties received hundreds of millions of dollars in state grant funding to develop alternatives to state confinement.

Vincent Schiraldi, co-director of the Columbia University Justice Lab, characterized the closing of state facilities as astonishing (Boyer, 2020). In 2012, New York's close to home law removed all New York City children (about 500) from the state's system of youth incarceration after closing many state youth prisons. Vermont and Connecticut have also moved to end state-run youth incarceration. Other states continue to operate detention facilities; indeed, raise the age efforts in some states have increased the populations of state-run juvenile systems. North Carolina operates seven juvenile detention facilities and four youth development centers, and it plans to build a new youth development center to house post-adjudication youth. Since the nineteenth century, reforming juvenile justice has always centered on replacing old facilities with new structures—the nicer institution syndrome. Once built, the new institutions quickly revert to conventional methods, and the same problems occur (Shelden & Troshynski, 2020).

Dan Macallair (2015) refers to reliance on institutionalization as path dependency—the practice of continuing a traditional practice even when more effective alternatives have been identified. People with economic, professional, and/or political dependence on existing institutions campaign to maintain the existing system. Primary interest groups are those with a direct financial interest—the staff employed at the institutions and the companies that supply the facilities. Secondary interest groups are those who benefit from the option of transferring responsibility for the most challenging youths to the state (county probation departments, for example). A community-oriented approach means counties must spend resources on juvenile justice, and politicians may be reluctant to ask taxpayers for the necessary funds. The combination of these interest groups and the tendency of reform efforts to lose momentum create a natural inclination to return to old practices. Confinement is the option of convenience since it represents an established path and carries fewer political risks.

Problems don't disappear with the transfer of responsibilities to counties. Los Angeles County is one of the worst local juvenile justice systems in the country; its institutions are as brutal as any of those administered by the state (Shelden & Troshynski, 2020). However, innovations in other counties are models of what can be done when local resources are utilized properly. Santa Cruz County established community partnerships and became one of the best local juvenile justice systems in the country. San Francisco relies on the local nonprofit sector to deliver community-based programs.

At the end of 2021, San Francisco will become the first major US city to shut down its juvenile detention center (Ho, 2019). The push to close the detention center came as youth crime and juvenile felony arrests dropped throughout the state. Despite the decrease, it cost San Francisco $13 million a year to maintain a facility that was three-quarters empty— about $300,000 per youth. One of the sponsors of the legislation said it makes no sense given current understanding of the youth brain to keep using outdated, extremely expensive methods. A member of the San Francisco board of supervisors who voted to close the facility had been confined there 27 years earlier. When he returned to the detention center, he realized that nothing had changed after almost 3 decades. He learned nothing during his confinement to help him change his behavior. He hopes that an emphasis on rehabilitation rather than punishment will end the cycle of criminality that too often results from punitive sanctions.

NOTES

[1] This is just the latest in a long line of abuses dating back to houses of refuge. It's been almost 200 years since the refuges were opened. Note that invariably the victims are minorities or the poor in general. They are treated as if their lives don't matter. The senior author has been teaching, writing, and speaking about this for 40+ years, and he wonders if it will ever change.

[2] In concert with 2020 demonstrations over police violence, some school districts (including Minneapolis, Seattle, Portland, and Denver) discontinued contracts with police departments for officers in the schools.

[3] In June 2020, Conahan (age 68) was furloughed from a federal correctional institution because he has medical conditions that put him at a high risk if he contracts coronavirus. The furlough could lead to home confinement for the remaining six years of his sentence.

9

Community Supervision
Punishment without Walls

Community supervision is the largest component of the corrections system. The 4.4 million people on probation and parole are double the number in prisons and jails combined. The sheer size of the population means that failure rates contribute significantly to the nation's volume of arrests and incarceration. Prison reform has been the focus of a broad national conversation, but community corrections has received less attention, despite the large numbers of people under supervision (Phelps, 2020).

> Over time, the sprawling size of the community supervision system has begun to undermine its effectiveness as an alternative to incarceration and a tool to help people convicted of crimes stabilize their lives and avoid further involvement in the criminal justice system. Recidivism rates for people on supervision are high, and probation and parole revocation has become a leading driver of jail and prison admissions in many states. (PEW Charitable Trusts, 2020, p. 57)

Probation and parole were conceived to divert people from incarceration. However, overly punitive supervision regimes have instead fueled mass incarceration by funneling people back to jail and prison. Supervision in some states has become a system to control and warehouse those who are struggling with an array of economic and health-related challenges stemming from poverty (Frankel, 2020). Incarceration is a grossly disproportionate response that further upends their lives.

History of Probation and Parole

Community supervision today focuses on fines, penalties, and incarceration for minor noncriminal infractions. There has been a radical departure from the original rehabilitative philosophy of probation and parole (Rodriguez, 2019). John Augustus, the father of probation, in the 1840s began posting bail for people before sentencing and worked with them to change their behavior. Zebulon Brockway is credited as the architect of parole. As warden of the Elmira Correctional Facility in 1876, he voiced the opinion that inmates who observed the rules in prison should earn conditional release earlier than inmates who were less cooperative.

In the late nineteenth century, courts began sentencing people convicted of low-level crime (often related to alcohol use) to probation for rehabilitation (Frankel, 2020). A community sponsor watched over and guided the individual. The sponsor reported back to the court after a few weeks. If the judge agreed the person was reformed, probation ended; failure to reform could result in a prison sentence. Prisons began releasing people from prison early for good behavior. For about six months, a community member monitored the parolee, set rules, and helped with reintegration. If all conditions were met, the individual was released from parole; if not the penalty was reincarceration. Supervision was endorsed as a tool of rehabilitation through the 1960s when nearly half of the people convicted of crimes were sentenced to probation.

As noted in previous chapters, the war on drugs combined with tough-on-crime policies reflected far more punitive attitudes. The Comprehensive Crime Control Act of 1984 created the Sentencing Commission that established determinate sentences for the federal courts and abolished parole. The Anti-Drug Abuse Act of 1986 established five-year mandatory minimum sentences for offenses involving low-quantity drug possession (Rodriguez, 2019). States passed "three strikes laws" in the 1990s, sentencing people with two prior convictions to life without parole. Probation and parole were characterized as too lenient. Legislatures, courts, and supervision agencies lengthened supervision terms, increased monitoring, and implemented severe sanctions for violations (Frankel, 2020). States began imposing supervision *in addition to* rather than *instead of* prison or jail terms. Twenty states in the 1980s either eliminated parole or dramatically reduced early release. States implemented mandatory supervision for people released after completing their prison sentences.

Parole and probation followed the punitive lead, taking on characteristics of the prisons for which they once functioned as an alternative. Agents who previously characterized themselves as counselors helping clients now saw themselves as officers monitoring offenders, and they began carrying guns. Probation and parole agencies opened boot camps, implemented electronic monitoring, and imposed multiple requirements on people under their supervision (Rodriguez, 2019). Probation and parole became add-ons to prison—continuing to punish former inmates and far too frequently denying them successful reentry. In the late 1970s, 16% of prison admissions resulted from violations of parole and some types of probation; the percentage climbed to 36 in 2008 before declining to 28% in 2018 (Frankel, 2020). The percentage for probation violations feeding state prison populations was 45%. These statistics do not include people jailed for supervision violations, for which there is little nationwide data available.

At year-end 2018, an estimated 1 in 58 adults were under community supervision (Kaeble & Alper, 2020). The numbers and percentages of people under community supervision have declined for a decade (see figure 1-3, p. 18). Despite the reduction, the United States maintains high rates of community supervision compared to historic rates and to European rates (Bradner et al., 2020). Adjusted for population growth, there were more than twice as many people under community supervision in 2018 as there were in 1980. Nationwide, the 1,726 people under community supervision for every 100,000 adults in the United States is 8.5 times higher than the European average of 202. More than half (54%) of the reduced number of people under supervision from 2016 to 2018 took place in four states (Illinois, California, Washington, and Massachusetts). Seventeen states experienced an *increase* in the number of people under community supervision.

Probation

Probation is a criminal sentence to community supervision imposed in misdemeanor and felony cases. Critics have charged that probation has been used to widen the net. In Georgia for example, courts routinely sentence people to probation for traffic infractions if they cannot pay the required fines and fees on their court date (Frankel, 2020). At least 40% of probationers are supervised for a misdemeanor offense (the ratio is probably higher but there is a lack of data from agencies supervising only misdemeanants) (PEW, 2018).

Sentences to probation require people to comply with stipulated conditions that may include reporting to a government agency, undergoing electronic monitoring, or taking classes (Brett et al., 2020). Many people on probation also owe fines, fees, and/or restitution as part of their sentence; the combination of probation and financial sanctions has grown the last several decades. When probation and financial sanctions are combined, the result is a more punitive system that disproportionately burdens people who cannot afford to pay. Failure to meet payment conditions is a probation violation that can result in additional sanctions, extensions of probation, and incarceration. Probation is extended until all the debt is paid.

> As financial sanctions continue to be imposed at rates far beyond what people can afford, and as courts continue to rely on probation as a sentence for many misdemeanors and certain felonies, more and more people are trapped in the criminal legal system under probation supervision simply because they cannot pay. (p. 1)

Probation often lacks centralized control, resulting in a patchwork of policies and practices (Brett et al., 2020). In many states, there are separate systems for felony probation (generally run by a statewide executive or judicial branch agency) and misdemeanor probation (usually run locally by a municipal or county agency or outsourced to private companies, as discussed in chapter 2). Despite the variations by state and counties, there are some common elements of probation supervision. All jurisdictions require probationers to satisfy specified conditions of supervision, and 48 states charge supervision fees. Some states establish levels of probation with varying requirements, including unsupervised. Judges may specify nonreporting supervision, or people may be moved to that level if all conditions other than financial sanctions have been satisfied.

All states provide probation departments with the authority to address violations of conditions, although permissible responses vary from state to state (Brett et al., 2020). Statutes and judicial deference in most states give the probation entity significant discretion in determining conditions, fees, consequences for noncompliance, and administering graduated sanctions (additional punishments). There is very little transparency about probation policies and how key decisions are made.

Probation is distinct from parole; together the two designations form community corrections. In 2018, 80% of the people under community supervision were on probation, while 20% were on parole (Kaeble & Alper, 2020). The 3,540,000 people on probation represented a decline of 17% since 2008. However, the decrease was less than the decline in arrests (26%)—meaning there was an increase in the rate of probation per arrest (Bradner et al., 2020).

Parole

The term *parole* describes both release from prison by a parole board and supervision by a parole agency after release (Bradner & Schiraldi, 2020). Parole is a conditional release of offenders from a correctional institution after they have served a portion of a court-imposed sentence to incarceration. The state retains legal control of parolees until they fulfill the conditions of parole; if the terms of parole are violated, the parolee can be reincarcerated. In 2018, 878,000 people were on parole, an increase of 6% since 2008 (Kaeble & Alper, 2020).

Members of parole boards usually are appointed by the governor of a state. Many boards are autonomous units; others are located in the state's department of corrections. Parole boards work very closely with institutional officials in making their decisions. They rely on the information and recommendations of prison staff, and they place a heavy emphasis on an inmate's behavior while in prison. Paroling authorities occupy an influential, low visibility position in the landscape of corrections (Rhine et al., 2019). In the 34 states with discretionary parole, they decide the release dates for most incarcerated individuals; they also control the amount of time served through revocation and rerelease authority These back-end officials have vast discretion over the length of incarceration, sometimes more than sentencing courts. Under both indeterminate and determinate sentencing structures, corrections officials have leverage through their decisions about good time credits. Sixteen states do not have discretionary parole.

State parole systems operate in secret; their decisions about whom to consider for parole are inconsistent and bewildering (Renaud, 2019). Most states do not have face-to-face hearings. A staff person interviews the prospective parolee and sends a report to the parole board members. Incarcerated individuals do not have the opportunity to refute erroneous information or to present their views; however, many states allow prosecutors and victims to voice their opinions. Parole denials are often based on static factors beyond the control of the incarcerated, such as the nature of the offense. These denials signal that the parole board does not recognize or reward transformation. Some states allow up to ten years to elapse before the next review. A number of critics have called for states to adopt transparent policies about when records are reviewed, the identification of who receives parole, and the parole conditions attached. Harmful factors associated with conditions of parole included prohibiting parolees from associating with others under supervision or anyone with a criminal record, extending the period of supervision beyond the length of the imposed sentence, and requiring the payment of supervision or drug-testing fees.

The national rate of parole supervision is 349 per 100,000 adult residents. Although New York's rate is lower (285), the state sends more people back to prison for noncriminal, technical parole violations (missing an appointment, being out past curfew, or testing positive for alcohol) than any state except Illinois (Bradner & Schiraldi, 2020). Six times as many people are reincarcerated in state prisons for technical violations as are reincarcerated for new criminal convictions. People on parole violation detainers are the only population whose numbers are increasing in New York jails (Editorial, 2018a). Costs for the incarceration of people for technical violations exceed $600 million annually in New York. Harmful parole policies fall disproportionately on minority communities. Blacks and Hispanics are significantly more likely than white people to be under supervision, to be jailed pending a violation hearing, and to be incarcerated in New York State prisons for a parole violation.

Overly restrictive supervision practices of parolees create a self-perpetuating prison population—a revolving door releasing people from prison only to return them for violations of their conditions of parole. One study in Michigan compared the outcomes of people convicted of felonies and sentenced to either prison or probation; researchers looked at multiple indicators of recidivism, including future prison admissions and felony convictions (Harding et al., 2017). There was no difference in the likelihood of being convicted of a future felony, but parolees had almost a 20%

higher chance than probationers of being returned to prison within five years because of technical violations of parole. Although both probationers and parolees are under strict supervision, post-prison supervision is even more stringent. Technical violations of parole account for almost 30% of prison admissions nationwide because of detection and punishment of low-level offending or violation behavior—behavior that would not result in imprisonment for someone who was not on parole.

Feeding Mass Incarceration

Recall from the introduction that David Garland included the shift from social work practices and rehabilitation to surveillance in departments of probation and parole in his twelve indices of change in penal policy. Probation and parole revocations account for a significant percentage of prison and jail admissions.

> Historically, probation and parole were intended to provide a less punitive, more constructive alternative to incarceration, but a growing body of evidence suggests that a frequent emphasis on surveillance and monitoring of people under supervision rather than on promoting their success, along with the resource demands of ever-larger caseloads, has transformed community supervision into a primary driver of incarceration. (PEW Charitable Trusts, 2020, p. 4)

Almost half (45%) of state prison admissions are due to violations of probation or parole for technical violations or new offenses (Council of State Governments, 2019). Almost 1 in 4 people (280,000) are incarcerated in state prison for supervision violations, costing states more than $9.3 billion annually—$2.8 billion for probation violations and $6.5 for parole violations. In 13 states, the ratio of people in prison for supervision violations is 1 in 3.

In six states (Utah, Montana, Wisconsin, Idaho, Kansas, and South Dakota) violations accounted for more than two-thirds of state prison admissions (Frankel, 2020). In many states, admissions for supervision violations are increasing while admissions for other reasons are decreasing. From 2008 to 2018, prison admissions from parole violations grew by 40% in Pennsylvania, while prison admissions for other conduct decreased by 21%. About one-third of prisoners in the state are incarcerated for probation or parole violations (Rodriguez, 2019). Probation revocations made up 55% of prison admissions in Georgia and 61% in Rhode Island. Parole revocations accounted for 54% of prison admissions in Arkansas.

Other states had significantly lower proportions. In Massachusetts, probation revocations accounted for 19% of admissions, and parole revocations accounted for 7% (PEW, 2018). In Nebraska, those figures were 8% and 17%. Policy makers in some states are adopting reforms that prioritize scarce resources for higher-risk individuals while removing lower risk individuals from supervision. Changes include shorter terms, earned compliance credits, and reduced or inactive supervision. Some states also reduced revocations for technical violations and provided a range of options for addressing noncompliance. After reforms, compliance revocations in South Carolina decreased 46%. Louisiana implemented a 90-day cap on jail or prison terms for first-time technical violations. Length of incarceration declined by 281 days, and new-crime revocations fell 22%. Missouri adopted earned discharge (probationers and parolees accrue time off their sentences for compliance). Supervision terms decreased by 14 months; the supervised population fell 18%; and average caseloads decreased 16%.

Governments can choose to break the supervision-to-incarceration pipeline by diverting the money spent on supervision and confinement to education, employment opportunities, substance use treatment, and other resources that help steer vulnerable populations away from the criminal justice system (Frankel, 2020). Eliminating petty violations, implementing incentives for good behavior, and changing the culture of community corrections to a system that offers a helping hand rather than a punitive one—would aid offenders in the successful completion of probation or parole (Rodriguez, 2019).

Set Up to Fail

A Bureau of Justice Statistics report tracked the recidivism of 401,288 state prisoners released in 30 states; approximately 45% were arrested within one year of release (Alper et al., 2018). Is it any wonder that most parolees, with little going for them prior to their prison sentence, find it almost impossible to survive through legitimate means after release? Is this by design? Jeffrey Reiman and Paul Leighton (2020) said of crime control in America: "nothing succeeds like failure" (p. 11). Is that phrase part of the mission statement of the parole system? We believe it is. Rather than helping ex-prisoners adjust to life outside, the parole system is designed to catch parolees and return them to prison (Austin & Irwin, 2012, p. 177). Despite the consistently high recidivism rate, the failure of the parole system has not been recognized by those in charge.

Loic Wacquant (2010) argues that this is part of prisoner reentry as myth and ceremony. Parole supervision does not help releasees reenter society; rather, it maintains a ceremonial façade, cloaking the "nefarious consequences of hyperincarceration" (p. 613). Rehabilitation is resurrected "after custody to help stage the resolve of the state to tackle the crime question on an individual, case-by-case basis" (p. 613). However, that resolve is a myth—a symbolic approach without substance and with no more than a marginal impact on the endless recycling of people through the criminal justice system. Reentry "is but a minor bureaucratic adaptation to the glaring contradictions of the punitive regulation of poverty" (p. 614). Wacquant argues that if authorities were serious about reentry, there are a number of changes they could implement.

> They would start by reestablishing the previously existing web of programs that build a bridge back to civilian life—furloughs, educational release, work release, and half-way houses—which has atrophied over the past two decades and avoid locating "reentry services" in decrepit facilities located in dangerous and dilapidated inner-city districts rife with crime and vice. They would restore the prison college programs that had made the United States an international leader in higher education behind bars, until convicts were denied eligibility for Pell Grants in 1994 to feed the vengeful fantasies of the electorate, even as government studies showed that a college degree is the most efficacious and cost-effective antidote to reoffending. They would end the myriad rules that extend penal sanction far beyond prison walls and long after sentences have been served—such as the statutes barring "ex-cons" from access to public housing, welfare support, educational grants, and voting—and curtail the legal disabilities inflicted on their families and intimates. . . . They would stop the costly and self-defeating policy of returning parolees to custody for technical violations of the administrative conditions of their release. (p. 614)

Released prisoners struggle to reach a minimal level of economic viability. They must find affordable housing, clothes, food, and employment—all with extremely limited resources. Most prisoners were poorly educated with few vocational skills and limited work experience when they entered prison, which usually worsens rather than improves their preparation for work on the outside (Austin & Irwin, 2012). Parolees leave imprisonment no better equipped to succeed in society than when they were admitted.

The emphasis of the parole system is social control. Rather than trying to assist a parolee in making positive adjustments to life outside the prison, the role of the parole agent emphasizes punishment. "The institution of parole has shifted from treating parole agents as providers of services to emphasizing surveillance; the kind of training parole officers now receive is more akin to law enforcement than social work—stressing monitoring and arrests, for example, rather than service referrals" (Herbert et al., 2016). A study of 79,082 parolees in California found that parole violations are influenced by parolee behaviors, the amount of attention parole agents pay to those behaviors, and the assessment of dangerousness attached to the parolee (Grattet & Lin, 2014). The researchers in Michigan noted: "Postprison parole supervision surveilles and punishes, and in so doing increases incarceration. In other words, the rise in incarceration was in part a self-perpetuating process resulting from the workings of the criminal justice system itself" (Harding et al., 2017, p. 5).

Conditions of probation and parole require people to comply with an array of rules often difficult to complete: steep fines and fees, attendance at frequent meetings, abstinence from drugs and alcohol, reports of any change in housing or employment. People under supervision are subject to: violations for minor omissions; incarceration while alleged violations are adjudicated; flawed procedures; and harsh sentences for violations. A Georgia defense attorney described probation as a prison sentence outside of jail. "You walk around with a rope tied around your leg to the prison door. Anything can lead to revocation" (Frankel, 2020, p. 1).

Fines, Fees, and Restitution

Criminal sentences often impose fines, fees, and restitution. Payments of these legal financial obligations (LFOs) are included in the conditions of supervision (PEW Charitable Trusts, 2020). Many community corrections agencies fund their operations by charging fees for required programs and processes. The costs to operate a system that supervises 4.4 million people strains budgets. States implement new fees, increase existing fines, and deploy law enforcement in debt collection strategies to avoid job cuts (Martin et al., 2017).

> We must consider what perverse incentives we create by tying the solvency of major institutions to criminal justice enforcement. Essentially, the basic conflict that emerges when a public institution is both the originator and the beneficiary of financial obligations is that resources are directed away from other critical, but less lucrative, law-enforcing or adjudicating tasks (e.g., clearing backlogs of DNA analysis or testing rape kits). (p. 6)

LFOs are significant barriers to supervision success; they impose economic burdens on people least able to afford them. One critic calls these fees the new peonage.

> Like peonage in the late nineteenth century, the new peonage marginalizes large segments of the community, segregates them physically in jails, prisons, and ghettos, and then authorizes discrimination against them in the judicial system, with collateral consequences in areas such as employment, voting, and public benefits. (Birckhead, 2015, p. 1677)

In 48 states (the exceptions are Alaska and South Dakota), statutes authorize the imposition of probation supervision fees (Brett et al., 2020). Most are assessed monthly and range from $10 to $150 per month; a person on probation for five years would pay $600 to $9,000. Every probation system allows the imposition of conditions (i.e., drug testing, electronic monitoring, specialized classes) that carry fees. In some Colorado jurisdictions, a probation officer can require a drug test every two weeks during a two-year probation term. Each drug test costs between $9 and $11. The probationer must spend $468 to $572 to satisfy the condition. If the probationer does not have the fee for the test and skips a visit, the probation officer can file a petition stating a violation of probation conditions, which could lead to additional punishment. If the additional punishment is electronic monitoring, the probationer incurs another $15 per month fee. Failure to make the payments can lead to incarceration.

In California "16 different statutes codify 269 separate court fines, fees, forfeitures, surcharges and penalty assessments that, depending on the type of offense, may now be assessed" (Martin et al., 2017, p. 4). Forty-three states charge a fee to cover some of the costs of court appointed lawyers; the fees range from $10 in California to $500 in Georgia (Frankel, 2020). In Pennsylvania, the median court costs were $1,110 in addition to any fines and restitution required. Georgia has 36,000 people on "pay only" probation—which means the courts placed them on probation because they could not pay their fines and surcharges. In 43 states, unpaid court costs can result in a suspended driver's license. Without a driver's license, an individual may have trouble reporting for work or supervision meetings.

The expansion of criminal justice financial obligations—deployed at every stage of criminal case processing—is that some 10 million people owe more than $50 billion from contact with the criminal justice system (Martin et al., 2017).

> This form of sanction can, if left unchecked, have long-term effects that significantly harm the efforts of formerly incarcerated people to rehabilitate and reintegrate, thus compromising key principles of fairness in the administration of justice in a democratic society and engendering deep distrust of the criminal justice system among those overburdened by them. (p. 2)

Length of Time Under Supervision

Research indicates that long supervision sentences do not deter crime (PEW Charitable Trusts, 2020). Practices that emphasize adherence to rules rather than addressing the risks and needs of people under supervision often lead to failure. Numerous experts agree that supervision terms should last only several years. About 62% of the states limit probation terms for most offenses to five years (Frankel, 2020). California, Georgia, Minnesota, Pennsylvania, and Wisconsin place no ceiling on probation sentences; judges can impose probation terms for the length of the maximum sentence for the underlying crime. Repeat shoplifting in Georgia carries up to 10 years of probation. In Wisconsin, possessing 40 grams of cocaine with intent to distribute can trigger 40 years of probation. Judges in some states, including Pennsylvania and Georgia, can sentence people who commit multiple offenses to separate probation terms for each offense that run consecutively. Most states allow early termination of supervision, but state law often requires that people pay all court costs, fines, supervision fees, and restitution before release. At least 13 states can extend the supervision term for failure to pay.

Some states require parolees to serve the remainder of their original sentence under parole supervision. Pennsylvania uses indeterminate sentencing. For example, a particular crime might have a minimum sentence of 10 years and a maximum sentence of 20 years. People released after serving 10 years then serve the remaining 10 years under parole supervision. Under Wisconsin law, a judge is required to impose a period of extended supervision that is at least 25% the length of the prison term (Frankel, 2020).

Adhering to stringent requirements over a long period of time is difficult if not impossible without monetary resources, reliable transportation, stable housing, and access to health services Very few people under supervision have the necessary resources. Two-thirds of those on probation make less than $20,000 a year, and 2 in 5 make under $10,000 a year—far below the poverty line (Frankel, 2020).

Array of Requirements

Lengthy supervision terms, strict conditions, and intense surveillance of probation and parole combine to make successful completion of community supervision unlikely (Jones, 2018). Only about half of the people on probation or parole succeed in completing their supervision. Those who don't are subject to revocation, which can lead to incarceration. Each year, almost 350,000 people are removed from the community and returned to jail or prison—a revolving door that affects housing stability, caring for children, employment, and other collateral consequences. Vincent Schiraldi, co-director of the Columbia Justice Lab, advises that if we want ex-offenders to succeed, we need a watershed rethinking of community supervision that abandons the unnecessarily punitive aspects of the system and embraces a more rehabilitative methodology (Rodriguez, 2019).

Failure to satisfy any of the conditions of supervision is a technical violation. Even if the failure does not involve criminal conduct, the technical violation can result in jail or prison time. People under supervision can be incarcerated for actions that are not criminal and would not carry criminal punishment for someone not under supervision (Bradner & Schiraldi, 2020). The intense scrutiny of people under community supervision often leads to the detection of low-level offending (such as drug use) or technical violations (breaking curfew, possession of alcohol, and absconding—which conjures images of fleeing the jurisdiction but more frequently indicates failure to report a change of address or to appear at a designated time at the parole office). Even minimal time in jail can create serious hardships—loss of employment, lost wages, housing insecurity, and family instability (PEW Charitable Trusts, 2020). Research indicates that subjecting low-risk individuals to intensive supervision or treatment leads to worse outcomes than no intervention.

Many of the conditions are ordered arbitrarily rather than addressing specific needs and capabilities. For example, someone with no history of substance abuse on probation for nonpayment of parking fines may be required to submit to weekly or monthly drug tests (Rodriguez, 2019). Many states apply a general list of conditions regardless of the offense committed. Conditions may be vague. Wisconsin, for example, states: "avoid all conduct . . . which is not in the best interest of the public welfare or your rehabilitation" (Frankel, 2020. p. 45). Georgia requires people on probation to "avoid injurious and vicious habits." Standard rules in Wisconsin and Pennsylvania prohibit people from drinking alcohol or entering bars even if their offense did not involve alcohol. Courts in Georgia can impose banishment provisions requiring people to stay out of particular counties.

Individuals may be required to complete specific programs—often with fees they cannot afford. An anger management course in Bucks County (PA) costs $45 per class plus a $100 intake fee; a violence prevention program in Lehigh county costs $240 (Frankel, 2020). If people cannot pay the fees, they face failure-to-pay violations. Programs also have rules, and program violations count as supervision violations. At a Pennsylvania drug treatment program, rules prohibit "coarse joking or gesturing," wearing torn clothing, and watching television outside of specified hours. In a Milwaukee cognitive-behavioral program, people must "actively participate in groups, satisfactorily complete all homework assignments, and demonstrate they have acquired the specific skills taught in the program"—all subjective assessments (p. 47). Studies have shown that people who participate in programs are more likely to have their supervision revoked than people who do not because they are watched more closely, and authorities have more opportunities to detect violations.

There may be conflicting conditions. For example, people may be required to attend frequent meetings or programs typically held during working hours—and to maintain a job. People are required to report to the supervising officer, whether weekly, biweekly, or monthly. Some may need to travel long distances and to rely on public transportation—sometimes spending an hour or more to reach the office. A requirement to report regularly for years can be an overwhelming task. Probation and parole policies ignore the realities of unemployment, homelessness, and drug addiction relapse, effectively criminalizing marginalized populations who struggle daily with such challenges (Rodriguez, 2019).

> Conditions of supervision are both vague and comprehensive; it is almost impossible not to violate some of them. Indeed, in order to fulfill certain requirements of everyday living, some rules must be broken. For instance, in some jurisdictions a parolee must obtain permission to drive a car and must also have a driver's license. To register a car, one must have insurance. But before the parolee can afford insurance (and thus drive), the parolee must find a job, which usually requires driving to the place of employment. Another rule specifies that the parolee

must not associate with ex-inmates or with people with "bad reputations." For most parolees, this is virtually impossible. In disadvantaged neighborhoods, it is common to know many people with an arrest record. Another condition is not to drink alcoholic beverages "in excess." The definition is vague enough to catch almost every person in a violation.

Technical violations are costly—to the offender and to the system. A quarter of admissions to state prisons in 2017 were for noncriminal, technical violations of probation and parole at a cost of $2.8 billion, as mentioned earlier (Council of State Governments, 2019). The figure does not include the cost of incarcerating people for technical supervision violations in local jails, which would increase the total significantly (Bradner et al., 2020). Money spent on technical violators could be redirected to help ex-offenders with employment, housing, mental health issues, substance abuse, and education (Rodriquez, 2019).

Few Procedural Rights

Prior to *Morrissey v. Brewer* (1972), courts had taken a hands-off position regarding the due process rights of parolees, concluding that parole boards were administrative in function. It was commonly held that parole was a *privilege* rather than a *right* and that a contract existed between the parolee and the parole board. Violating a parole condition constituted a violation of the contract. The ruling in *Morrissey* found that parole revocation inflicted a grievous loss of liberty. "It is hardly useful any longer to try to deal with this problem in terms of whether the parolee's liberty is a "right" or a "privilege." By whatever name, the liberty is valuable and must be seen as within the protection of the Fourteenth amendment." Parolees are entitled to six constitutional protections: (1) an informal hearing to determine if there is reasonable evidence of violating a parole condition; (2) notice of the charges; (3) the opportunity to be heard, present evidence, and call witnesses; (4) opportunity to confront and cross-examine adverse witnesses; (5) the hearing board must be neutral and detached; (6) a written statement of the findings and the reasons.

In *Gagnon v. Scarpelli* (1973), the Court considered whether a probationer was entitled to a hearing before revocation of the probation. The Court reasoned again that the substantial loss of liberty through revocation entitles probationers to the same due process protections of preliminary and final revocation hearings under the conditions specified in *Morrissey*. The Court also said the Constitution does not require that the defendant be provided representation. Those decisions should be decided on a case-by-case basis. Despite these rulings, probationers and parolees have few procedural rights.

Supervision officers generally have vast discretion in addressing violations of probation and parole (Frankel, 2020). They can ignore violations, issue informal warnings, or impose sanctions that include electronic monitoring, mandatory treatment, and jail confinement. They can also pursue revocation, which can result in substantial prison time. If the choice is revocation, the officer files a detainer, and the supervisee is detained until the revocation proceeding. Detainers override any other pretrial release, as mentioned in chapter 3. If a detainer were filed against someone who had been arrested for a criminal offense and a judge authorized pretrial release, the detainer keeps the person in jail until at the revocation proceeding. The length of detention can be weeks or months. Detention may be in an overcrowded, unsanitary jail, pressuring people to admit to violations in the hope of being released. Even if probation or parole is not revoked, individuals can be sentenced to additional supervision and mandated attendance in programs that can add years to the term of correctional control.

Revocation hearings determine whether someone violated supervision conditions and the punishment for doing so. There is no presumption of innocence; many jurisdictions limit access to lawyers for revocation proceedings. Due process rights, such as the exclusion of illegally obtained evidence or hearsay evidence generally do not apply. Indeed, parole officers do not need a warrant to search the home or person of someone under supervision. While criminal charges must be proven beyond a reasonable doubt, most states only require supervision violations to be proven by a preponderance of the evidence (Frankel, 2020). People have faced revocation of their supervision for committing new offenses even if a judge dismissed the charges in criminal court. The government thus secures incarceration for alleged crimes without having to prove the charges beyond a reasonable doubt in criminal court.

Disproportionate Sanctions

Inequities in supervision rates between Blacks and whites declined between 2008 and 2018, but Blacks were still 2.6 times as likely to be on probation and nearly 4 times as likely to be on parole (Bradner et al., 2020). Blacks made up roughly 12% of the general population in both 2008 and 2018; they comprised approximately 30% of people on probation and approximately 38% of people on parole in both years. The disparities are greater in specific counties. In the Pennsylvania county that includes Pittsburg, Blacks are 13% of the population but 42% of the supervision population (Frankel, 2020). In the Georgia county that contains Savannah, Blacks are 39% of the population but 67% of the population on felony probation. In Wisconsin, 1 in 8 Black men were under supervision, which was more than 5 times the rate for white men.

There is a smaller body of research on racial disparities in supervision violation charges and outcomes (Bradner et al., 2020). Research on disparities in parole violation charges found that Black people were between 50% and 100% more likely to be charged with violations. Blacks were more likely to be returned to prison for a parole violation. Research on probation practices found similar disparities in probation violation charges, as well as higher rates of revocation for both Blacks and Hispanics. Research has also found that minorities remain on probation and parole for longer terms than white people, which increases the chances of being charged with violations.

Because minority communities often experience concentrated disadvantage (elevated poverty rates, concentrated policing activities, substandard education, lack of access to health care and transportation), supervision requirements that appear race neutral can have disproportionately negative impacts for minorities under supervision (Bradner & Schiraldi, 2020). For example, a requirement not to associate with people who have a felony conviction may be extremely difficult. One in 12 people in the United States— and one in three Black men—have a felony conviction. People on supervision may be forced to choose between obeying the rules or risking a technical violation for associating with relatives and friends with a criminal record. The lack of access to transportation in disadvantaged communities impacts requirements to report for meetings with parole officers. Requirements to obtain employment and to pay supervision fees is more difficult for people living in areas with limited employment options.

As discussed throughout the book, minority populations are disproportionately represented at every stage of the criminal justice process, leaving them particularly vulnerable to the revolving door caused by onerous conditions of supervision. In addition, many states use risk assessment tools to set conditions and sanctions Studies show these instruments disproportionately label minorities "high risk," resulting in more stringent levels of supervision and enforcement. Risk assessment instruments potentially exacerbate racial disparities in jurisdictions where minorities have disproportionate contact with the justice system (Picard-Fritsche et al., 2017).

Caseloads

The soaring number of people under supervision over the last half century has created average caseloads of more than 100 supervisees per office (Frankel, 2020). Supervision agencies are often understaffed; officers are undertrained, underpaid, and assigned excessively large caseloads. About half of a probation officer's time is spent collecting fees and checking with treatment providers, drug testing labs, the courts, child protective services, and/or clients—and then recording the findings in the file (Rodriguez, 2019). The administrative work leaves little time to engage clients and improve outcomes. Workers must deal with fewer resources, higher caseloads, a shrinking social safety net, society's more punitive attitudes, and an environment less welcoming to people who have committed crimes.

When responsible for enforcing rules, authorities predictably impose revocations. Experts on supervision practices note that high caseloads contribute to prioritizing the enforcement of conditions over providing resources (Frankel, 2020). Enforcement is less time consuming than finding the services needed by a particular individual. Changing the culture of supervision from one of punishing failure to one promoting success could cut spending and reduce recidivism (PEW, 2018). Helping people become self-sufficient should be the goal of supervision rather than catching violations and imposing penalties, including incarceration.

Collateral Punishments

About 70 million people have criminal records that harm their chances of finding a job, securing housing, or attending college—key elements for a stable life. Individuals with felony convictions face significant ongoing punishments in the loss of benefits, the loss of civil rights, and the lack of relief from unsealed criminal records (Love & Schlussel, 2020). For much of the public, the collateral punishments are invisible, but the approximately 48,000 prohibitions on ex-felons imposed by the states and the federal government have been characterized by one reporter as "everlasting retribution" (Davidson, 2016).

About 600,000 people leave federal and state prisons every year; added to those numbers reentering society are the estimated 10 million people churning through local jail systems. Whether individuals return to their communities after incarceration for a few days or several decades, they face multiple challenges (Johnson & Beletsky, 2020). Individuals must acclimate to a different environment and altered relationships with family and friends in addition to a litany of probation and parole rules including work requirements, drug testing, and scheduled check-ins—with very few resources. The penalty for failure to meet the requirements can set in motion the revolving door cycling people from communities to incarceration.

> The reentry process is extraordinarily difficult and emotionally taxing. Returning people are rarely truly free, as they typically must navigate a long list of onerous rules. This may include electronic monitoring, housing restrictions, and curfews. They must also struggle against the sanctioned stigma of a criminal record, restricting education, employment, and housing opportunities. Since healthcare, substance use treatment, and other support services are utterly lacking behind bars, reentry is a time of extreme physical and mental health risk. This includes the odds of fatal overdose, which is up to 130 times more likely for those in the first two weeks post-release than in the general population.
>
> But these are not normal times. The coronavirus pandemic is drastically compounding the challenges of reentry. With the economy in free-fall, some requirements of supervised release—like obtaining housing and employment—are virtually unattainable. People reentering society are facing increased risk of homelessness, as halfway housing is unavailable and their own families may be reluctant to take them in if they come from facilities with COVID-19 infections. (p. 2)

People with criminal records face routine and often legal discrimination. Only eight cities protect the formerly incarcerated from housing discrimination; no state provides the same protection (Johnson & Beletsky, 2020). Individuals with criminal records face employment discrimination despite some legal protections. Many returning offenders have mental, emotional, and physical problems after incarceration, including post-traumatic stress, social alienation, and long-term health conditions that were untreated during confinement.

Restrictions on offenders vary by state and can include: revocation or suspension of driver's licenses; prohibitions from employment in certain professions such as teaching or child care; restrictions on the right to vote; termination of parental rights; and restrictions on the right to hold public office. These collateral punishments harm the life prospects of people long after they have served their sentences. Margaret Love of the Collateral Consequences Resource Center, a nonprofit focusing on relieving the legal restrictions and societal stigma that burden people with a criminal record, believes there is a growing recognition that society has gone too far in imposing additional, endless penalties (Ewing, 2017).

Denial of Welfare Benefits

The 1996 Personal Responsibility and Work Opportunity Reconciliation Act included a provision that denied Supplemental Nutrition Assistance Program (SNAP) and Temporary Assistance for Needy Families (TANF) benefits to individuals with drug felony convictions—a lifetime ban regardless of the nonviolent or minor nature of the offense. As a result, tens of thousands of people were ineligible for the anti-poverty programs (Polkey, 2019). Congress granted states the ability to opt out of enforcing the ban or modifying it. By 2019, South Carolina was the only state that imposed the lifetime ban on SNAP benefits; 25 states have modified restrictions, and 24 states have no ban. Most states modified the TANF restrictions. Researchers at Harvard University found that released felons who have full public benefit access are less likely to return to prison within a year. The coronavirus pandemic created an urgent need to expand food assistance and to reduce TANF restrictions.

Housing Instability

Housing is a basic necessity, but it is often unavailable for people released from prison, adding a significant barrier to rebuilding one's life (Couloute, 2018). Before parolees can learn new skills, find a job, and address health problems, they need a place to live. Stable housing is the foundation of successful reentry from prison.

> Without a stable, affordable and supportive place to call home, every aspect of a person's life becomes problematic. Imagine trying to apply for a job without a permanent address, going to school without know-

ing where you will take a shower in the morning, or waking up on time for therapy without an alarm clock. . . . [Attempting to reintegrate without a home leads to] relapse, more illegal activity and, eventually, another incarceration. (Monocchio & Burns, 2019, p. 14)

People returning from prison face a housing crisis. There is a lack of affordable housing in many cities, restrictions may limit where parolees can live, there may be no public housing or eligibility may be restricted, and many landlords may be reluctant to rent to someone with a criminal record (Wiltz, 2019). If other family members have criminal records, parole conditions may bar former inmates from moving back home. Federal law prohibits two types of former offenders from living in public housing: people convicted of manufacturing methamphetamines and registered sex offenders. Individual authorities have broad discretion to bar other kinds of offenders: current drug users; people who abuse alcohol; anyone evicted from federal housing due to drug-related activity within the last three years; drug-related criminal activity; violent criminal activity; other criminal activity that interferes with the health, safety or right of peaceful enjoyment of the property by other tenants (Illinois Justice Project, 2019). Of the approximately 30,000 people exiting state prisons in Illinois annually, about 40% will return to prison within three years of being released (Illinois Justice Project, 2019). The failure to help people stay out of prison disrupts communities and costs Illinois taxpayers $100 million a year. A significant reason for the failure is the lack of stable housing.

There are substantial barriers for ex-offenders to rent an apartment. Landlords may not want to rent to a released prisoner or someone with an arrest record. The individual may not have the funds to pay a security deposit and the first month's rent. Often unemployed and without resources, people may end up homeless (Illinois Justice Project, 2019). The formerly incarcerated are 10 times more likely to experience homelessness, and the greatest risk of homelessness is in the first few months after leaving prison (Monocchio & Burns, 2019). Ex-offenders with mental illness have higher than average rates of homelessness and housing insecurity, about 20% (McKernan, 2017). Mental illness, drug and alcohol abuse, prior incarcerations, and prior experiences of homelessness were all predictive of residential instability.

Providing housing assistance has a significant positive effect on returning individuals (NIJ, 2018). Nationally, almost 50,000 people enter the shelter system, which provides temporary housing, directly upon release (Monocchio & Burns, 2019). Some states, cities and counties have taken steps to make it easier for former inmates to find housing and employment. In Cook County (IL), a problem-solving court assists nonviolent defendants with substance abuse, recovery, and readjustment to the community. The court and the Housing Authority of Cook County launched a pilot program to provide housing vouchers to graduates of the court's program. The Georgia Department of Corrections opened the Metro Reentry Facility in Atlanta—a transitional confinement for offenders scheduled for release within 18 months where they receive intensive counseling, vocational training, and housing support (Wiltz, 2019). Seattle and Washington, DC have barred landlords from asking about felony convictions on rental applications.

Employment Stigma

The COVID-19 pandemic created the highest unemployment rate since the Great Depression. Before the pandemic, the unemployment rate of the formerly incarcerated was 27% compared to 5% for the general public (Johnson & Beletsky, 2020). Finding employment has always been a struggle for justice-involved individuals, but the 2020 recession linked to the pandemic created even more competition for scarce jobs—adding to the burden faced by those with a criminal record (Amaning, 2020). If two people have similar qualifications, hiring favors the person who has never been arrested and/or convicted. Individuals who remain unemployed two months after reentry are twice as likely to recidivate as those who are employed.

Returning prisoners typically are not eligible for cash assistance or unemployment (Johnson & Beletsky, 2020). The only means of obtaining the funds to survive is a job, and a criminal record is a significant barrier, especially when unemployment rates are high. Without a place to live, reliable transportation, and phone service, individuals are further hampered in the search for employment. Most people looking for work have access to computers and cell phones; the formerly incarcerated most likely have neither.

Successful reintegration requires the removal of unjustifiable barriers. Laws formally disqualify people from certain types of jobs, depending on the offense committed. Informal barriers include employer aversion to risk and stereotypes linking individuals and criminality. There has been progress in limiting inquiries into criminal history in the early stages of the hiring process, especially in the public sector (Love & Schlussel, 2020). In 1998, Hawaii extended its Fair Employment Practices law to criminal records. It was the first state to address disqualification based on criminal background checks. Its prohibition on inquiries into an applicant's criminal record was a model for the "ban-the-box" (the box on job applications that asks about a criminal record) campaign that began several years later in California. By 2020, laws or ordinances prohibiting application-stage inquiries applied to public employment in 36 states and more than 150 cities and counties. Many of the regulations prohibit background checks until after a conditional offer of employment. Fourteen states and 18 cities and counties also regulate private sector employment. Effective at the beginning of 2021, the federal government's Fair Chance Act prohibits agency procurement officials from asking persons seeking federal contracts and grants about their criminal history.

Banning the box is a first step, but there also needs to be mechanisms to enforce standards and procedures in hiring (Love & Schlussel, 2020). In 2010, the District of Columbia was the first to enact a general fair employment law. It initially applied to public employment; a few years later, it applied to private organizations of more than 10 people. California and Nevada (for public employment only) passed similar laws in 2017. Illinois and Massachusetts legislated limited record-elated protections. Illinois prohibits consideration of nonconviction records, juvenile records, or expunged or sealed records; Massachusetts prohibits consideration of non-convictions and some misdemeanors.

Licensing agencies play a significant role in whether people with a criminal record secure employment. These agencies control access to about 20% of all available jobs (Love & Schlussel, 2020). All 50 states and the federal government limit occupational licensing for people with criminal records. Of the almost 14,000 legal provisions, more than 5,000 are mandatory bans on specific licenses for individuals who committed certain crimes (Bacon et al., 2020).

By 2020, more than 30 states had enacted legislation to ease the restrictions on people with a criminal record in qualifying for occupational licenses (Love & Schlussel, 2020). The procedural reforms hold licensing authorities accountable for decisions about who does and does not qualify for particular professions. For example, the standards listed must be objective, eliminating vague "good moral character" criteria. Minor offenses unrelated to job performance cannot disqualify an applicant; the offense committed must have a direct relationship to the duties and responsibilities of the position.

States with strong fair employment laws do not necessarily have similarly strong systems for regulating licensing agencies (Love & Schlussel, 2020). Two jurisdictions (Hawaii and DC) with strong employment regulations have poor occupational licensing systems. Four states (Iowa, Mississippi, New Hampshire, and North Carolina) with strong occupational licensing had no law regulating employment. Three states (Alaska, South Carolina, and South Dakota) had no regulation of either employment or occupational licensing.

More than 27,000 people left Illinois prisons in 2018, and more than 50,000 were released from Cook County Jail, many of them returning to impoverished neighborhoods. About 42% of the state's population have criminal records or arrest histories—including those not charged or convicted (Elejalde-Ruiz, 2019). JPMorgan Chase, the nation's largest bank by deposits, began actively recruiting ex-offenders in Illinois in 2019.

Prior to its efforts in Illinois, Chase worked to address the high unemployment among those with criminal records that can lead to recidivism and poverty (Elejalde-Ruiz, 2019). In 2018, 10% of new hires at Chase were people with criminal backgrounds. Federal rules prohibit banks from hiring individuals with certain convictions, but Chase and others lobbied for changes that were loosened modestly in 2018. The Federal Deposit Insurance Corporation, which requires banks to get approval to employ anyone whose crimes involved "dishonesty, breach of trust or money laundering," exempted more people from the restrictions. Chase created a unit to advocate for other policy changes and to educate companies on what they can do to be a part of the effort. Among the policy priorities are automatic record-clearing for certain misdemeanors or crimes committed as a juvenile, and reforming laws that suspend driver's licenses for failure to pay fines. Chase supports legislation that would allow access to federal Pell grants for people in prison to pay for higher education, including college classes and workforce training.

The hiring process at Chase holds candidates to high standards (Elejalde-Ruiz, 2019). The company believes ex-offenders are an underserved group and that hiring them benefits the community by reducing recidivism. A global security group assesses applicants for safety risks and to determine if the law prohibits their hiring. A team from human resources and employee engagement uses criteria including the length of time since the conviction, age at the time of the crime, the seriousness of the offense, and whether the crime relates to the job for which the applicant is being considered.

Education Barriers

The Federal Pell Grant Program was authorized in 1972 to provide low-income students—including those in prison—with financial support for education. By the early 1990s, there were more than 770 postsecondary programs in almost 1,300 prisons. The Violent Crime Control and Law Enforcement of 1994 revoked access to Pell Grants, as policy makers adopted more punitive approaches to the rising crime rate (Oakford et al., 2019). The absence of funding significantly reduced educational opportunities for incarcerated individuals, contributing to the profound challenges of finding a job without education and skills. Many of the formerly incarcerated are locked in a cycle of poverty and potential recidivism. State economies suffer from fewer skilled workers and increased incarceration costs because of high recidivism.

> People behind bars typically live in poverty even before they enter a jail or prison. Research shows that people's earnings at the time of incarceration are on average 41% less than the income of people of similar ages who are not incarcerated. Moreover, serving time only compounds a person's struggle against poverty. The hardships of cash bail and fines and fees—coupled with countless barriers to reentry, such as employment and housing restrictions—perpetuate an endless cycle that robs people of their dignity and upends entire families and communities. . . .
>
> This [denial of Pell Grants to the incarcerated] relic of the "tough-on-crime" era has resulted in long-term negative consequences for all of us, including high recidivism rates and intergenerational incarceration, as well as lost economic potential for individuals, families, and

communities. In recent years, some states have recognized the need to reverse many overly punitive criminal justice policies and have worked to implement evidence-based legislative reforms. But with 1.5 million people currently in prison—90% of whom will eventually be released—there is still much progress to be made. (p. iv)

Most people in prison have limited work experience and few marketable skills. More than two-thirds have a high school degree, but only 6% have a postsecondary degree (Bacon et al., 2020). A meta-analysis of more than 50 research studies found that providing incarcerated people with any form of education was associated with a 43% reduction in recidivism. People who participated in any educational programming were 13% more likely to find employment after incarceration than those who did not—the percentage increased to 28 for participation in vocational training. There has been bipartisan support for increased federal investments in career and technical education and for reinstating Pell Grant funding eligibility for people in prison. At the local level, nonprofits and institutions of higher education have partnered to expand postsecondary education opportunities, vocational training, record clearance, and reentry support services for the formerly incarcerated.

The incarcerated face hurdles other than cost in pursuing education. There are statutory and/or administrative restrictions in more than three-quarters of the states that limit access to postsecondary education for people currently and formerly incarcerated (Bacon et al., 2020). In only 10 states are postsecondary opportunities available for all incarcerated individuals. Five states restrict access through state statutes; most states impose restrictions through state correctional agency regulations. Sixteen states base participation restrictions on custody level; 25 states base restrictions on sentence length; 11 states base restrictions on the offense committed.

Research shows the benefits of education in reducing recidivism and in securing employment. It would seem advantageous for states to encourage participation in programming and for parole to recognize efforts regarding education (if the programming exists). Only 34 states allow incarcerated people to earn release time credits for participation in postsecondary education activities, while only 25 states policies that consider postsecondary education participation when making parole decisions. In terms of parole conditions (Bacon et al., 2020). After release, 34 states allow postsecondary education to substitute for parole requirements regarding employment. As a result, conditions of parole in the other states are a disincentive to participate in education. Less than half of parole-granting agencies have partnerships with universities, community colleges, trade schools, community-based organizations, and nonprofit service providers that could help the formerly incarcerated continue their education and develop their workforce skills. "Given the inherent challenges that incarcerated people face during the reentry process, it's critical that states don't actively restrict these individuals' ability to continue their postsecondary education and obtain employment in the community" (p. 10).

The policies of some state university systems also deter people with criminal records from college admission and participation. A significant barrier is inquiring about criminal convictions on college or university applications (Bacon et al., 2020). In 10 states, all four-year public universities inquire about criminal history. In 26 states, at least half of all four-year public universities inquire criminal history Only nine states do not require people to disclose their criminal history. Of the almost 200 public universities reviewed in one study, 59% asked applicants about their criminal history. There was significant variation in whether institutions asked applicants to disclose misdemeanors, arrests, traffic violations, drug charges, sex offenses, and/or juvenile offenses in addition to the felony/criminal conviction disclosure.

States oversee approximately 87% of all individuals in prison at a cost of $40 billion annually (Bacon et al, 2020). State policies have traditionally exacerbated the barriers faced by individuals returning to their communities. State policies, practices, and funding regarding postsecondary education could help people transition to crime-free, productive lives in the community. It is thus important to understand the extent to which states impose obstacles and barriers that "are stacking the odds against such individuals even further" (p. 2).

Disenfranchisement

Chapter 4 discussed historical roots of disenfranchisement and particularly its disproportionate effects on Black citizens. English colonists brought to North America the common law practice of "civil death" (Chung, 2019). Civic participation has been linked with lower recidivism rates. Felon disenfranchisement removes a prosocial behavior linked to desistance from crime. Restoring the vote to people who have served their sentence is one way to ease the transition from prison to the community. Conversely, revoking voting rights is yet another exclusion that isolates the formerly incarcerated.

In 2016, four states (Iowa, Florida, Kentucky, and Virginia) permanently disenfranchised people convicted of felonies. In 2020, Iowa was the lone state to do so until Governor Kim Reynolds issued an executive order on August 5 restoring the right to vote for those with nonhomicide felony convictions once they complete all terms of their sentence (Sentencing Project, 2020a). The order does not require the payment of outstanding fines, fees, or restitution as a condition of being able to vote (as does Florida). As discussed in chapter 4, felony disenfranchisement laws have a disproportionate impact on Blacks because of systemic racism in the criminal justice system. In 2016, more than 20% of potential Black voters in Florida, Kentucky, Tennessee, and Virginia could not vote (Lopez, 2020a).

The general trend has been toward reinstating rights. Since 1997, 25 states have modified felony disenfranchisement restrictions to expand voter eligibility and/or to inform people with felony convictions of their voting rights (Porter, 2020). During 2019, lawmakers in 8 states and Washington, DC, introduced legislation to expand voting rights to people in prison. Maine, Vermont, and the District of Columbia felons retain their right to vote, even while they are incarcerated (NCSL, 2020a). In 16 states, felons cannot vote while incarcerated. When released, prison officials automatically inform election officials that rights have been restored. The individual is responsible for re-registering to vote. In 21 states, felons lose their voting rights during incarceration and while on parole and/or probation; they may be required to pay outstanding fines, fees or restitution before rights are restored. In 11 states felons lose their voting rights indefinitely for some crimes, or require a governor's pardon, or face an additional waiting period after completion of sentence (including parole and probation), or require additional action before voting rights can be restored.

An estimated 6.1 million citizens have been disenfranchised because of a felony conviction (Uggen et al., 2016). In comparison, more than one million people were disenfranchised in 1976 and more than three million in 1996. More than half of those disenfranchised live in states where voting rights are restricted even after completion of prison, parole, and probation. About three-quarters of the individuals who have lost the right to vote live in their communities. In public opinion surveys, 80% of U.S. residents support voting rights for citizens who have completed their sentence; almost 66% support voting rights for those on probation or parole (Chung, 2019).

Advocacy organizations, academics, and lawmakers have worked to modify disenfranchisement laws for felons for years, but the de facto disenfranchisement of people in jails has received less attention (Porter, 2020). Two-thirds of individuals in jails are incarcerated pretrial because of the inability to post bail; they are eligible to vote. Most of the remaining people in jail are serving sentences for misdemeanor offenses that do not result in disenfranchisement. The problems with voting in jail disproportionately affect communities of color—almost half (48%) of the people incarcerated in jail are Black or Latino.

Some jurisdictions have expanded voting access for eligible incarcerated citizens. Individuals in California and Texas jails can submit a voter-registration form and absentee or vote-by-mail requests. In Massachusetts, people in jail do not have to register before completing an absentee ballot. Los Angeles County and the District of Columbia have in-person voting in their jails (Porter, 2020).

With the exception of Florida's SB 7066 (see p. 107), no state has passed legislation narrowing the access of convicted felons to voting for almost a decade (Love & Schlussel, 2020).

> The law in almost half the states now reflects an appreciation of the
> social and economic value of allowing all those who are living in the

community to participate in its governance. Restoring the vote may facilitate reintegration efforts and perhaps even improve public safety, providing benefits both to individuals with a record and more broadly to their communities. (p. 15)

Criminal Record Relief

Nine in 10 employers use criminal background checks, as do 4 in 5 landlords (Amaning, 2020). Two in 3 colleges and universities review an applicant's criminal history when deciding both admissions and funding. One mistake that results in a criminal record can mean a lifetime of poverty and stigma that affects not only ex-offenders but their families as well.

Digitized records and a heightened public appetite for access to information produced a virtually unregulated commerce in background screening and data aggregation. Employers, schools, landlords, and other authorities relied on digitized records, which also became a net-widening device for law enforcement (Love & Schlussel, 2020). There have been more than 250 million arrests over the past two decades, and modern technology makes those and other records easily accessible. In addition to the global pandemic, 2020 saw mass public protests against police violence and racism. Protestors were arrested—leaving a record that is hard to erase and creating long-term barriers to employment and housing. States have very diverse approaches to record relief. There is no consensus about how to manage dissemination of damaging information while also accommodating the public's interest in safety and in access to records.

When a person is arrested, the police generate a record, which is sent to the state's central repository (Love & Schlussel, 2020). All arrests do not result in charges. If charges are filed, they may be dismissed. Uncharged arrests remain in the state records repository if the police or prosecutor fail to indicate the dismissal. People—with or without a plea—may be placed in a diversion programs; completion of the specified requirements results in dismissal. Occasionally, the individual goes to trial and is acquitted. All these scenarios do not result in conviction, but each one produces a criminal record. Sometimes the records do not indicate how an arrest or charge was resolved. The record remains open—an employer (or landlord) may draw inaccurate conclusions. Despite some reform, significant challenges remain to neutralizing the malign effect of a criminal record. Many people are excluded by law from sealing or expunging their records. Even for those who are eligible, the path to relief can be burdensome, costly, and intimidating. If relief is inaccessible to the intended beneficiaries and unmanageable for administrators, it is both ineffective and unfair.

By 2021, 17 states will have laws to automatically expunge or seal most nonconviction records. Seven states expedite nonconviction relief through simplified procedures. But in 26 states and DC, individuals must file a court petition to obtain relief. Many of these jurisdictions unreasonably restrict eligibility and impose procedural hurdles such as filing fees.

Arizona does not have a nonconviction expungement law, nor does the federal government.

To reduce the impact of collateral consequences, advocates for criminal record relief have pushed for laws that expunge, seal, or set aside convictions (Love & Schlussel, 2020). Expungement and sealing laws restrict access to, and sometimes destroy, criminal records. Set-aside laws authorize a court to vacate a conviction to signal a person's rehabilitation. People whose records are sealed or set aside experience improved employment outcomes and low recidivism rates. In many states, eligibility is restrictive, and procedures are burdensome. Many who are eligible to petition the court are unaware of the option or do not have the resources (Amaning, 2020). A successful petition process can cost thousands of dollars for legal services and court fees. As a result, only 6.5% of people are able to clear their records within five years of eligibility.

The oldest means for relief from a criminal sentence is a pardon. "In theory and practice, pardon is the ultimate expression of forgiveness and reconciliation from the sovereign that secured the conviction" (Love & Schlussel, 2020, p. 26). The Constitution grants the president the power to pardon, and 48 state constitutions grant the power to governors. In Alabama and Connecticut, the power to pardon is regulated by the legislature. In the 16 states where courts have no authority to expunge or set aside convictions, pardon is the only source for record relief. In 18 states, pardons are an integral part of the justice system, and pardoning is shielded from politics through appointed boards that make the decisions. Standards are clear, procedures are relatively accessible, pardons are administered through a transparent public process, and a high percentage of applications are granted (i.e., 80% in Alabama and Connecticut). Until recently, a pardon supplemented (adding a certification of rehabilitation and good conduct) a person's record but did not revise it, as do sealing or set-asides. Today 19 states authorize sealing or expunging a pardoned conviction.

Thirteen states have broad felony and misdemeanor relief; 21 states have limited relief for felonies and misdemeanors; 4 states have relief only for misdemeanors and pardoned convictions; 4 states and Washington, DC have relief for misdemeanors; 8 states and the federal system have no general conviction record-revising relief (Love & Schlussel, 2020). Even if the court provides relief, people confront additional challenges in having records removed from the internet and commercial databases.

Many alternatives to incarceration widen the net of punishment and surveillance—extended probation, electronic monitoring, house arrest, mandated participation in programs, locked-down drug treatment centers (Schenwar & Law, 2020). Alternatives presented as cost-effective substitutes for incarceration bring people under state control who previously would not have been subject to sanctions. The narrative of reform obscures agendas of social control—promising change but replicating the status quo.

Punitive attitudes expanded surveillance, intrusion, and control in communities—an expansion of the conditions and burdens that count as punishment (Dolovich & Natapoff, 2017). For the people on whom it is imposed, punishment encompasses more than custodial terms, probation, and fines.

> It also includes such practical burdens and personal indignities as denial of the right to vote or serve on a jury, the unwillingness of private individuals to rent them an apartment, and the often insurmountable difficulty in getting a job. These experiences are not "collateral" to punishment. For those subjected to them, they are punishment. (p. 8)

Four principles should guide fair and just penal policies and practices: (1) proportionality—the punishment should fit the crime; (2) parsimony—the punishment should not exceed the minimum needed to achieve its legitimate purpose; (3) citizenship—the punishment should not compromise a formerly incarcerated person's chance to lead a fulfilling life; and (4) penal systems should not reproduce social inequalities (Martin et al., 2017). These principles have largely been ignored in the behemoth penal apparatus in the United States. At all levels of government, policy makers have produced a set of unintended and negative consequences that disproportionately harm the poor and people of color.

10

Is There a Better Way?

The recommendations for rethinking punishment in this concluding chapter address issues raised in the previous chapters, especially those centering on inequalities of class, race, and gender that show-up as differential treatment, life-long entanglement in the criminal justice system, and reifying inequalities as "natural." The suggestions are not exhaustive.

We cannot have equal and effective justice in an unequal society. For example, public safety will remain an elusive dream when some populations are targeted for punishment and street crimes are framed as the number one crime to fear. Violent crime is a concern, but the public tends to overlook the violence of white-collar crimes. There are many different types and causes of crime, as well as effective responses to crimes, that remain unattainable in the context of today's fixation on minority populations, inner cities, and punitive reactionary policies.

Social inequities refer to barriers and harms imposed on groups based on the socially constructed status of those groups. Social inequalities stare us in the face no matter where we look—that is, if we are looking. It is important to understand the underlying motivations for the policing and prosecuting of crimes in ways that fuel social inequities (refer to chapters 4 and 8 for particular examples). Before any meaningful reforms can be attempted and before there is any serious attempt to reduce crime and implement effective crime control, we must address the existence of social inequalities in our society—much of which came through the historical misappropriation of the justice system for race and class oppression.

Addressing the Problem of Social Inequality

One major consequence of social inequalities is crime. Research spanning more than a century has consistently demonstrated a close connection between specific types of crime and social inequality. Adolphe Quetelet, a Belgian astronomer and mathematician, and Michel Guerry, a French lawyer and statistician, in the mid-nineteenth century were the first to use statistical measures to document the correlation between crime and punishment and socioeconomic factors. They examined the residences of offenders, matching them with various socioeconomic variables, such as poverty, infant mortality, unemployment, and other social indicators. There was a strong correlation between poverty and unemployment and being policed for crimes. University of Chicago researchers pursued a similar line of investigation in the late nineteenth and early twentieth centuries; their findings were similar. More than 100 years later, researchers continue to show the correlation between various components of social inequality and crime (Krugman, 2007; Shelden & Troshynski, 2020).

Social inequality in the United States has reached its highest point since the start of the Great Depression. Technological changes, the emergence of a global economy, the flight of capital, and the shift from manufacturing to services have all contributed to economic disparity. The Gini index measures the extent to which the distribution of income deviates from perfectly equal (0) to perfect inequality (100). From 1947 to 1973, income inequality declined slightly. The Gini index was 39.4 in 1970 and grew to 47.7 in 2012 (Hutchison, 2017). In 2018, the index was 48.5 (Telford, 2019). No European nation was higher than 38. High levels of social inequality adversely affect the social health of a nation. Elizabeth Hutchison (2017) notes: "There is growing support for the idea that economic inequality is associated with a number of social ills, including low social cohesion, distrust, violence, poor health, and economic stagnation" (p. 271).

The nation's poverty and unemployment rates in 2019 were at historic lows. However, the divide between rich and poor was at a five-decade high (Telford, 2019). Since 2007, the number of households at $250,000 or more annually grew by more than 15%. After adjusting for inflation, the median household income ($63,000) has remained essentially the same for 20 years. Over the past 50 years, households in the top fifth of earnings have steadily increased their share of the country's total income (Schaeffer, 2020). In 2018, the top 20% of earners (incomes above $130,000) accounted for 52% of all earnings—more than the lower 80% combined. In comparison, the top 20% in 1968 accounted for 43% of the nation's income, while the lower 80% combined for 56%. The top 5% of households saw their share of all U.S. income increase from 16% in 1968 to 23% in 2018. From 1971 to 2019, the share of adults living in the lower-income tier increased from 25% to 29%; adults in middle-income households *decreased* from 61% to 51%; and adults in the upper-income tier increased from 14% to 20%.

In 2019, the median wealth of Black families was less than 15% of the net worth of white families—$24,100 compared to $188,200 for white households (Smialek, 2020). The median wealth of Hispanic families was $36,100. In the first quarter of 2020, the wealthiest 10% of Americans owned more than two-thirds of the nation's wealth; the top 1% owned 31% (Rugaber, 2020). White households owned almost 85% of total wealth, while Black households owned just 4.4% and Hispanics 3.2%.

Inequities could increase as workers at the bottom lose jobs and incomes. The COVID-19 pandemic raised unemployment rates to their highest levels since the Great Depression—12.4% for whites; 16.8% for Blacks, 17.6% for Hispanics; and 15% for Asians in May 2020 (Thorbecke & Mitropoulos, 2020). At least 45 million people filed for unemployment. Workers in communities of color were generally unable to work from home. People with the least advantages and the fewest economic opportunities bear the largest burdens during downturns, whether a recession or a public health crisis—and the pandemic was both.

> The disparate racial impact of the virus is deeply rooted in historic and ongoing social and economic injustices. Persistent racial disparities in health status, access to health care, wealth, employment, wages, housing, income, and poverty all contribute to greater susceptibility to the virus—both economically and physically. (Gould & Wilson, 2020, p. 1)

Even before the pandemic, the criminal justice, health, and employment data confirm that inequities are systemically experienced in our punitive society. The infant mortality rate for Blacks is 11.46 per 1,000 live births compared to 4.61 for whites and 5.35 for Hispanics (Kochanek et al., 2019). African American infants are 3.2 times as likely to die from complications related to low birth weight; they are twice as likely to die of sudden infant death syndrome (Office of Minority Health, 2017). African American mothers are 2.2 time more likely to receive late or no prenatal care. The lifespan of Black Americans is 3.5 years shorter than for white Americans (Arias & Xu, 2019).

The chapters in this book have discussed the increasing reliance on punishment to control crime and delinquency. The tendency is deeply rooted in the culture, economy, and race relations of the country, as evidenced by a shift from a welfare state to a penal state over the last four decades (Chesney-Lind, 2017). "Along with this shift, of course, come public attitudes about the crime problem and criminals that reinforce prison as a viable 'solution' to the many social problems associated with this nation's long history of racial injustice and increasing income inequality" (p. 106). Bruce Western and Becky Pettit (2010) suggest that addressing inequality provides an alternative path to public safety.

> Our perspective on inequality points to a broader view of public safety that is not produced by punishment alone. Robust public safety grows when people have order and predictability in their daily lives. Crime is

just one danger, joining unemployment, poor health, and family instability along a spectrum of threats to an orderly life. Public safety is
built as much on the everyday routines of work and family as it is on
police and prisons. Any retrenchment of the penal system therefore
must recognize how deeply the prison boom is embedded in the structure of American social inequality. Ameliorating these inequalities will
be necessary to set us on a path away from mass incarceration and
toward a robust, socially integrative public safety. (p. 18)

Jeremy Travis and Bruce Western (2017) suggest two goals to respond
to the injury inflicted on minority citizens by mass incarceration, which
grew out of and perpetuated poverty and violence.

The challenge, then, is one of social and political imagination—envi-
sioning how justice institutions might help extinguish rather than fan
the flames of poverty and violence in African American communities.
Two goals are central to this challenge: reimagining justice and promoting peace. Justice demands basic fairness in social and economic
life. Just communities ensure the wide distribution of social and economic opportunity and preserve full social membership for all, even
for those who have been involved in crime. Crime is exclusionary for
both victims and offenders, and indeed these are often revolving roles
in poor communities, where social contexts can be ripe with the potential for chaos and physical harm. Justice in this context should seek the
social reintegration of victims and offenders alike. Peace demands a
cessation of violence, most likely not through the force of interdiction
but, like any successful peace process, under conditions of trust and
consultation. Peaceful communities allow the development of routines
in everyday interaction, allowing citizens to plan for tomorrow, and
imagine a future. (p. 315)

Ending the War on Drugs

As noted in chapters 1 and 4, the negative consequences of drug policies have been far-reaching, including the exploding prison population,
the targeting of racial minorities (and their disenfranchisement), and the
enormous costs to taxpayers with little or no impact on drug use. We recommend a "cease-fire" in the war on drugs until other options are studied
and tried. The war on drugs was and is anchored in false beliefs about
dangerous drug dealers, the susceptibility of average Americans, and the
dangers to public safety.

Jeffrey Reiman and Paul Leighton (2020) have used the concept of the
criminal justice "mirror" that presents a distorted image of crime—namely
that the poor are primarily responsible for the crimes that threaten society.
They note that this viewpoint deflects the potential discontent of the middle class away from people in positions of power and toward the lower
classes. Their *Pyrrhic defeat theory* argues that the failure of the system to

reduce crime yields sufficient benefits to those in positions of power that it amounts to success. The drug war is one among many examples. It has been very beneficial to some groups, including law enforcement agencies that have received enormous sums of money to fight the "war." Companies that provide drug testing kits profit from the conditions of probation and parole. There would be money to be earned by ending the prohibition of drugs and regulating them as any other commodity.

The legal system is presented as ensuring equality, liberty, justice, and public safety, but the enforcement of laws is based on distributions of power. Punishment is applied to people who have no power (Karakatsanis, 2019).

> The punishment system would change overnight if the vast numbers of young, wealthy, and white drug criminals at private schools and famous universities were harassed and beaten by police in the streets, had their family homes raided at night, were sexually and physically assaulted in prisons, and were confined to live and die in cages. The human costs of the bureaucracy would be evaluated differently if drug searches by undercover police and SWAT teams were as common at Yale University as they are down the street in the low-income neighborhoods of New Haven. The brutality of separating tens of millions of families from their loved ones—with no empirical evidence of a benefit—would not be tolerated if it were happening to different people. Our culture would see it as widespread violence in need of serious justification, if not a human rights crisis demanding urgent and immediate action, rather than as a vague and impersonal aspect of the need for "law enforcement." (p. 857)

Evidence indicates that tax dollars are better spent on education and treatment services than on prohibition (Collins et al., 2015). Researchers warn that it is important to focus on changes to drug policy that address the inconsistencies and contradictions of prohibition to avoid minor reform that leaves underpinning principles unchanged (Taylor et al., 2016). What are the options for decriminalization? Do we legalize drugs with some regulations and restrictions (e.g., minors prohibited from using)? Do we legalize only some drugs (e.g., marijuana)? Do we "decriminalize" some or all drugs by limiting the penalties or some other options? Do we involve the criminal justice system in only indirect ways, such as having drug courts or drug treatment sentences instead of jail or prison? While legalizing all drugs in the U.S. could be the ultimate solution, it is not politically feasible, at least not for the foreseeable future.

We recommend four actions as a beginning. First, amend the Controlled substances Act to reclassify marijuana from a schedule I narcotic to schedule III or lower. The DEA has the authority to change the scheduling without input from Congress, but it has not changed the classification since it was put in place in 1970. The federal government defines schedule I drugs as having no currently accepted medical use and a high potential for abuse. Since 1968, only the University of Mississippi is legally approved to grow marijuana for research purposes—severely limiting medical research. The only path to providing evidence of the effectiveness of marijuana for medical use is through an application for clinical trials—controlled by the DEA. Similarly, the only way to overturn the DEA insistence that marijuana is so dangerous it must be classified like heroin is through research, which is currently prohibited. The insistence that marijuana is so dangerous it must be classified like heroin is a destructive lie (Pyke, 2019) that has affected law enforcement practices with far-reaching effects, including asset forfeiture (see chapter 4).

Second, legalize recreational marijuana use in all 50 states with age restrictions as there are for alcohol. The usual argument against legalizing marijuana is that such a policy equates to condoning the use of marijuana. We are tempted to reply with "so what?" Society condones the use of alcohol and, until recently, the use of tobacco (now taxed severely and prohibited in many public places but still legal). We can *discourage* use of marijuana—and other drugs as well—by using the methods that were so successful in reducing the demand for tobacco without the negative fallout of waging war against people's addictions or preferred recreational activity. Further, there is no evidence that marijuana use leads to the use of more serious drugs like opioids and cocaine (Biggar et al., 2016). Why criminalize it?

Third, eliminate drug testing for marijuana. The liberty of a large number of probationers and parolees is revoked for failing their urine tests (Hamilton & Campbell, 2013). Even states with legalized recreational use of marijuana, such as Colorado, do not allow recreational use of marijuana during probation and parole (*People*, 2012). Eliminating drug testing would help end the "catch and release" revolving door of incarceration.

Finally, for those addicted to drugs, treatment options would be a more effective alternative than incarceration. Treatment would help the individual overcome addiction and allow him or her to contribute to society rather than spending tax dollars on jails or prisons. *Treatment Alternatives to Street Crime (TASC),* which places drug offenders in drug treatment programs under community-based supervision rather than incarcerating them, is often coupled with additional treatments such as methadone maintenance therapy (MMT) (Clark et al., 2014). With such alternatives, there is a reduction in relapse as well as a delay to the onset of relapse. Similarly, *drug courts* oversee court-ordered treatment in community drug treatment programs. In most states, drug courts screen persons for their drug use histories, willingness to complete treatment, and so forth. If admitted to the drug court, offenders are assigned a primary counselor, a specific treatment plan is developed, and frequent appearances in drug court are required to help monitor progress.

Innovative individuals have developed alternatives to help communities ravaged by overt drug markets and law enforcement responses to the problem. David Kennedy is the cofounder and director of the National Network for Safe Communities at John Jay College of Criminal Justice. The alliance of more than 50 jurisdictions supports strategic interventions to reduce violence, minimize arrest and incarceration, and strengthen relationships between law enforcement and distressed communities.

High Point, North Carolina, had a population of 105,000 in 2004. Open-air drug dealing brought violence to a neighborhood known as West End. Overt drug markets destroy the quality of life and sense of community in neighborhoods by contributing to crime, shootings, prostitution, assaults, and robbery and adversely affecting local businesses and residential property values (Kennedy & Wong, 2012). Police sweeps, buy-bust operations, and the arrests and incarceration of drug dealers did not eliminate the drug markets. In fall 2003, the new police chief, James Fealy, began working with David Kennedy on a different approach. People in law enforcement, the community, social services, and academia designed the original West End operation. They set strong community and family standards against drug dealing; offered social services if dealing ceased; and addressed racial conflict between communities and law enforcement.

Call-ins were the central feature of the approach—face-to-face meetings of low-level drug dealers with community members, families, service providers, and law enforcement. Police presented the evidence they had gathered and an unsigned arrest warrant. If drug dealing continued, dealers would be arrested and prosecuted based on that evidence. If dealing stopped, job training, housing, and counseling was available. Authorities used the same strategy in High Point's three other drug markets. During the three-year implementation, overt drug activity was almost entirely eliminated, and crime was down (Kennedy & Wong, 2012). Chief Fealy commented on the strategy:

> It produces results that are so dramatic it's almost incredible. It is sustainable. It does not produce the community harms that our traditional street-sweeping, unfocused efforts of the past have. The most important benefit of this work by the people of High Point is the reconciliation that emerges from the dialog between the minority community and the police. In a 30-year law enforcement career, I have never seen an effort like this. It's nothing short of miraculous. (p. 5)

Targeted law enforcement attention too often treats dealers and other community members similarly (National Network, 2015). High levels of arrest, incarceration, and court supervision affect offenders directly and the community through collateral consequences. Traditional law enforcement does not eliminate the drug market or make the community safe.

> Law enforcement's willingness not to act on existing cases seemed to make a profound impression on the dealers' families and other community members. Dealers' mothers and grandmothers cheered both the community's and law enforcement's messages. Dealers were given

an opportunity to meet the social service coordinator to assess their various needs. Most dealers signed up for services the same day. The call-ins have been electrifying events with police officers being moved profoundly, drug dealers testifying to their gratitude for a second chance, community figures speaking of both accountability and redemption, and family members speaking strongly and plainly to their children. (Kennedy & Wong, 2012, p. 26)

High Point was the model for the Drug Market Intervention (DMI) launched by the Bureau of Justice Statistics in 2008 (Kennedy & Wong, 2012). DMI reduces the violence and disorder that accompany overt drug markets; it decreases incarceration and increases safety; it helps police do their work in a way that strengthens rather than harms the communities they serve; it improves relationships between law enforcement and minority communities; it supports communities in reclaiming their voices about the way they want to live (National Network, 2015).

Not only does crime go down—something the numbers can capture—but citizens also get their neighborhoods back, families get their yards and parks back, communities find their voice, and toxic relationships between neighborhoods and police are reset. The Drug Market Intervention (DMI) works for everybody because everybody moves and changes together. (p. vii)

There were almost 1.6 million arrests for drug violations in 2019 (FBI, 2020a). The rate of arrests for drug offenses (464.8 per 100,000) far exceeds the rate for other categories (the next highest rate was 286.8 for driving under the influence). The majority of drug arrests involve small quantities (see chapter 1). Almost every state imposes felony liability for the sale of any amount of illegal drugs and for simple possession of drugs such as cocaine, heroin, and methamphetamine. Joseph Kennedy, Isaac Unah, and Kasi Wahlers (2018) note: "Punishing those who sell illegal drugs or possess hard drugs in even the smallest amount as felons may seem natural because it has been done for so long and to so many" (p. 735). They suggest that amounts of one gram or less should be misdemeanor rather than felony offenses.

For comparison, Kennedy et al. (2018) describe other misdemeanor offenses. "Stealing property worth less than $1,000 is routinely prosecuted as a misdemeanor in most jurisdictions yet selling $25 worth of a mood-altering substance to a willing buyer can result in a felony arrest in the vast majority of jurisdictions" (p. 778). Simple assault and battery are also misdemeanors.

Felony liability marks a person as a serious criminal and effectively sets them apart from others in society in ways that are significant and lasting. For those reasons, felony liability is reserved for more serious crimes. The point is that a single incident of gram-or-less possession or sale of an illegal drug is no more deserving of felony liability—and arguably is less deserving—than one who commits a misdemeanor act of violence or theft. Given that those arrested with gram-or-less amounts of drugs are most likely addicts or very low-level employees of a drug group, felony liability for such low-level involvement cannot be justified. Felony liability "dis-integrates" the offender from family, community, and ultimately society by marking the offender as a serious criminal. (p. 779)

Making gram-or-less drug offenses misdemeanors rather than felonies would be a state-by-state project.

Economic downturns present a unique opportunity to think about the impact of current policies—from putting nonviolent offenders in prison for drug offenses to inflating prison populations by revoking parole or probation for minor drug violations. The suggestions and approaches in this section contribute to transforming the overemphasis on exacting punishment on inner city neighborhoods and the overreliance on costly and ineffective criminal justice suppression and interdiction practices.

Curbing Prosecutorial Power

Prosecutors are the most powerful—and the most unregulated—participants in the legal system (Butler, 2019). Prosecutors represent the state in criminal cases. Depending on the state, the title could be district attorney (DA), prosecuting attorney, county attorney, or state's attorney. DAs supervise assistants (ADAs). In the federal system, the equivalent to a DA is United States attorney. In 46 states, DAs are elected officials, while in 4 states DAs are appointed.

Fordham law professor John Pfaff (2017) researched prosecutors in the 1990s and 2000s and found that the number of felony filings (controlled by prosecutors) per arrest doubled. Mandatory minimums and habitual offender laws added to the power of prosecutors, who make the decision about how to charge a crime. The major concern with prosecutorial power is the high degree of discretion in the hands of a group of people, primarily white men, who share similarities across class and educational backgrounds (Karakatsanis, 2019).

The prosecutor discretion to threaten arrestees with prison time increased the use of plea bargains, which has reverberating effects on how the public experiences their civil rights. Replacing trials with deals negotiated outside the courtroom benefited judges, defense lawyers, and prosecutors by reducing their workloads. The deals also increased the power of the prosecutor, who essentially decides the sentence; judges and defense lawyers become incidental. "And so the criminal justice landscape reconstituted itself, making way for a feature that distorted the original design. It's called the trial penalty, and it's become so common in the criminal courtroom that we hardly register it anymore" (Bazelon, 2019, pp. 133–134). Defendants who accept the plea bargain, or deal, plead guilty to a lesser offense and a shorter sentence; a defendant who goes to trial and loses receives the lengthy sentence for the higher charge. "Trials remain the public face of the American justice system and a pillar of its legitimacy" (p. 134). They are, however, rare. In federal narcotics cases, the sentences after plea bargains averaged 5 years, while sentences after trials averaged 16 years. Plea bargains settle about 95% of criminal convictions, indicating that in the vast majority of criminal cases people do not access their full civil rights for comprehensive due process.

Emily Bazelon's (2019) book, *Charged: The New Movement to Transform American Prosecution and End Mass Incarceration*, places the primary blame for mass incarceration on prosecutors—and offers hope that progressive prosecutors who seek solutions other than prison can change the trajectory. Georgetown law professor Paul Butler (2019), a former federal prosecutor, cautions about being overly optimistic about a transformation of the prosecutor role and trajectory. He estimates there are about 100 progressive prosecutors among the more than 2,400 elected in the United States. Politics remains an influential factor. The dramatic reduction in crime over the last two decades created a climate in which progressive approaches could flourish. An increase in violent crime could prompt a return to repressive approaches.

Butler (2019) commented that prosecutors are political actors socialized in mass human caging. They are unlikely to dismantle the current system without a social movement articulating the necessity and demanding it. In contrast, he cited a 1973 dissent by David Bazelon (Emily Bazelon's grandfather) as a judge on the U.S. Court of Appeals for the District of Columbia. Benjamin Murdock, a Black man, killed a white marine who called him a "Black bastard." The trial judge instructed the jury to disregard Murdock's background of economic and social deprivation and repeated experiences of racism. The jury found him guilty; he was sentenced to twenty years to life. Murdock appealed the case, and the appeals court upheld the verdict. In Bazelon's dissent, he said the judge had erred in instructing the jury to ignore Murdock's deprived background and racist treatment. Bazelon said society's conduct toward defendants should be considered when determining punishment—society has no right to sit in judgment of those it has treated in a condemnable way. Today, movement away from prison sentences generally involves sympathetic nonviolent offenders. Until progressive prosecutors find effective alternatives to punishment for those who commit violent acts, they will continue to implement the cruelty of mass incarceration, and the United States will remain the world's leader in imprisonment.

Expanding Diversion Programs, Avoiding Net Widening

Thoughtfully constructed, diversion programs that replace incarceration with community-based programs provide an affirmative answer to the question in the title of this chapter. Net widening refers to policies and practices that enlarge the possibility of catching people in the net of the justice systems. Hence, if not constructed with care, even these program alternatives can expand the populations subject to punishment. Community-based programs are significantly better than incarceration when designed intentionally to address underlying systemic barriers in the lives of populations who are under the gaze of the criminal justice system.

The war on drugs is emblematic of how net widening works; the changing definitions of which substances are illegal and which punishments are applied for the use and dealing of those substances illustrates the ways that nets widen, change, and ultimately catch specific populations. (Re)writing laws widens the net, and the legal process itself multiples the likelihood of remaining trapped in the net. "For many who enter the system, their experiences of arrest and of court routines are such that these in themselves literally have become a form of punishment, and, most importantly, the U.S. is haunted by a very racialized system of mass incarceration" (Chesney-Lind, 2017, p. 106).

Labeling Theory

Frank Tannenbaum in 1938 was the first to explain how society creates the criminal by defining what behavior is acceptable based on preferred habits and values. He primarily looked at the effect of society's disapproval on juveniles, although his observations hold for other groups as well.

> American criminal activity must be related to the total social complex. The United States has as much crime as it generates. . . . The amount of crime in the United States responds to all the factors and forces in American life. . . . The relationship between the criminal and the community is a total relationship and not a partial one. He is the product of the sum of our institutions and the product of a selective series of influences within them, as are the best and the worst of the noncriminal population. The community does not set out to make a saint, and yet it does occasionally. It does not set out to make a criminal, and yet it does, more than occasionally. (Tannenbaum, 1938)

Anyone who deviates from prescribed behavior challenges established societal dictates, which then defines and sets apart the "deviant" so that the social order isn't threatened. Tannenbaum (1938) termed the process of societal reaction to disapproved behavior "the dramatization of evil" (p. 19). This is a precursor to labeling theory. Casting youthful misbehavior (e.g., shoplifting a candy bar) as deviant begins the process. "The process of making the criminal, therefore, is a process of tagging, defining, identifying, segregating, describing, emphasizing, making conscious and self-conscious; it becomes a way of stimulating, suggesting, emphasizing, and evoking the very traits that are complained of" (p. 19). Tannenbaum

(1938) believed the solution was to refuse to dramatize the evil. He saw the processes of arrest, trial, and conviction as a drama that pushed the individual further in the direction of crime and believed alternatives to punishment would be more effective.

Edwin Lemert (1951) refined labeling theory with his concepts of primary and secondary deviance. Individuals committing primary deviance do not consider their deviance fundamental to their identity—rather, the deviant acts are spontaneous responses to particular situations. With secondary deviance, the individual links deviance with his or her self-identity. For example, if an individual decides to steal a candy bar in an adventurous moment, the deviance is primary deviance. However, if the individual defines him or herself as a thief, stealing the candy becomes secondary deviance. The change from primary to secondary is usually the result of multiple negative reactions by others over time. Howard Becker (1997) refined the concept that deviance is not a quality of the act the person commits but rather the label applied by society. Social groups create deviance by making the rules. When someone breaks those rules, society labels them outsiders and applies sanctions.

The labeling perspective provides the theoretical foundation for programs that *divert* individuals from juvenile detention, jail, or prison. Legal interactions perpetuate delinquency and crime by processing cases that could be dealt with informally and more effectively in community settings. Proponents of diversion programs cite numerous studies showing that diversion programs successfully reduce subsequent deviance (Kretschmar et al., 2014). The most successful diversion projects have been those that provide comprehensive services and hire experienced workers (Schwalbe et al., 2012; Wilson & Hoge, 2012).

Ideally, a true diversion program (and the original concept behind diversion) takes individuals who would ordinarily be processed through the criminal justice system and places them into some alternative program. However, net widening occurs when new laws or policies widen the scope of who is criminalized for an offense. The alternative programs should not capture individuals whose cases would have been dismissed rather than prosecuted. We argue that diversion programs should be used for serious and chronic offending. Research shows that diversion programs can have a significant impact on that population (McClanahan et al., 2012; Petrosino et al., 2015).

A Community Based Example

Delancey Street is not specifically a diversion program. Courts do, however, refer 85% of its participants (Harris et al., 2019). It has helped many people labelled as irredeemable succeed in changing their lives. Its website includes the slogan "enter with a history, leave with a future" and talks about the foundation's belief in ordinary people's abilities to achieve extraordinary accomplishments. Delancey Street has achieved what many would think was impossible. It has over 18,000 graduates. It is a residential self-help organization for substance abusers, ex-convicts, and the homeless. The average resident has been a hard-core drug addict for sixteen years, dropped out of school in seventh grade, and has been institutionalized several times. Many were gang members; most had been trapped in poverty for generations.

Mimi Silbert (a clinical psychologist) and John Maher (former alcoholic, heroin addict, and criminal) started the Delancey Street Foundation in 1971. They decided to run Delancey Street with no staff and no government funding. Residents learn to develop their skills and to help each other. Together, 300 unemployable drug addicts, homeless people, and ex-felons learned to construct a 400,000 square foot complex on the waterfront in San Francisco near the bay. The compound includes a variety of businesses operated by ex-cons. There is an incredible restaurant (visited often by the senior author), townhouses for the workers, a Town Hall, and a park.

Today, Delancey has 6 residential education homes across the country (New York, North Carolina, South Carolina, and three California locations—Los Angeles, San Francisco, and Stockbridge) and a 17-acre ranch in New Mexico. The minimum stay at Delancey Street is two years, and the average stay is four years. Residents learn to live crime-, drug-, and alcohol-free lives through extensive rehabilitation services, substance abuse programming, and therapy. Each resident learns three marketable skills by working in the training schools; these skills include at least one manual skill, one clerical/computer skill, and one interpersonal/sales skill. Over 10,000 formerly illiterate people have received high school equivalency degrees; 50 have earned an undergraduate degree through Golden Gate University. Although it has never been subjected to a thorough evaluation according to scientific research principles, we strongly believe in the concept and wonder why it has not been replicated throughout the country.

Gender-Responsive Strategies

Chapter 6 described the characteristics of women in prison, and chapter 7 discussed historical and contemporary factors involved in the policing and incarceration of members of the LGBTQ community. The criminal justice system was designed for punishing males. Deeply embedded gender biases materialize in policies and practices that harm non-male populations. Being responsive requires acknowledging the pathways travelled to criminal offending. Several decades ago, feminist criminology promoted gender-responsive programming that recognized the unique pathways to crime for girls and women and the preponderance of backgrounds involving trauma and abuse (Kahle & Rosenbaum, 2019). To be effective, programming needed to address these differences. Sometimes overlooked is the intersection of sexual orientation with gender, which compounds the pathways to crime.

Most prison programs take a "gender-neutral" approach, which in reality means programs designed for white males. Classification, screening, and assessment techniques have not been validated for women, minorities, and nonheterosexuals. Standard practices such as searches, isolation, and restraints may re-traumatize women offenders (Bloom, 2015). Experiences in the justice system can trigger memories of earlier abuse. A survivor of sexual abuse may be traumatized by a full-body search. Research by Barbara Bloom, Barbara Owen, and Stephanie Covington (2003) found the following specific areas where men and women prisoners needed to be treated differently: (1) pat-search and strip-search procedures; (2) commissary items, especially health and toiletry items; (3) allowable personal property; (4) transportation and restraint policies for pregnant women.

A trauma-informed approach takes the trauma in women's lives into account when creating criminal justice policies, avoids triggering trauma reactions, trains counselors and other staff members to consider the individual's ability to cope, and helps women manage their trauma symptoms (Bloom, 2015). Studies show that nearly half of women in prisons have post-traumatic stress and co-occurring mental and physical health conditions (Harner et al., 2015). Likewise, the lifetime, cumulative experiences of trauma and chronic stress for LGBTQ offenders are important to understand in order to address the negative impact of the design of the criminal justice system for persons from the LGBTQ community.

As discussed in chapter 7, LGBTQ youth and adults are disproportionately represented in the juvenile and criminal justice systems, which are ill equipped to address the needs of these populations. "Being LGBT in a US jail or prison often means daily humiliation, physical and sexual abuse, and fearing it will get worse if you complain" (Marksamer & Tobin, 2014, p. 2). If victimization is reported, staff may refuse to take the reports of abuse seriously. If vulnerability is recognized, the solution is too frequently indefinite solitary confinement. Researchers highlight the importance of not using solitary confinement for the LGBTQ inmates as the sole safety mechanism against sexual assault in prisons (McCauley & Brinkley-Rubinstein, 2017). There are dire health consequences of solitary confinement (Kaba et al., 2014; Shalev, 2017). Many facilities house transgender people according to their genital anatomy, which can increase vulnerability to abuse. Policies may deny access to preferred gender-appropriate clothing or grooming items and punish people for attempting to express their gender identity.

Gender-responsive programming has been a significant contribution, and there is increasing recognition that such practices are important at every stage of the criminal justice process. However, gender is usually measured as a male-female binary, which miscategorizes individuals who do not fit one of those two gender categories (Valcore & Pfeffer, 2018). Assuming that all girls and women have identical needs renders non-heterosexual and non-gender binary identities invisible (Kahle & Rosenbaum, 2020). To provide a better environment for system-involved LGBTQ girls and women, staff training should focus on responses to sexism and homophobia and on developing cultural appropriateness and competence.

The National Council on Crime and Delinquency suggests the following expansions to gender-responsive principles for people outside the man/woman binary (Selph, 2015). (1) Acknowledge that gender makes a difference. (2) Create an environment based on safety, dignity, and respect. (3) Develop policies, practices and programs that are relational and promote health connections to children, family, significant others, and the community. (4) Address substance abuse, trauma, and mental health issues through integrated and culturally relevant services and supervision. (5) Provide opportunities to improve socioeconomic conditions. (6) Establish a system of community supervision and reentry with comprehensive, collaborative services.

In the juvenile justice system, youth of color are both hypervisible in terms of surveillance and punishment, yet relatively invisible when it comes to programming (Irvine-Baker et al., 2019). Over the past several decades, the juvenile justice system has adopted gender-responsive policies and practices. The complex interactions between race, sexual orientation, gender identity, and gender expression illuminate shortcomings of some gender-responsive programming. When gender-responsive programming is grounded in gender stereotypes that are rooted in a sex binary, it can be irrelevant for some gender-nonconforming and nonbinary youth. Other gender-nonconforming youth may be denied access to programming designed for the sex different from the one they were assigned at birth even when according to emerging studies "sexual minorities" in the juvenile justice system can be up to one-third of nonincarcerated but justice-involved populations (Hirschtritt et al., 2018). Juvenile institutions should be cautious about relying on assumptions of gender binaries; the needs of juveniles may not be associated with biological sex categories. Generally, gender-responsive programming is designed for cisgender (and heterosexual) girls. The better approach is gender-affirming programming for all youth across the gender spectrum.

Gender responsiveness, to varying degrees, has been addressed in jails and prisons nationwide (Blakinger, 2019). Sometimes the changes are small, such as allowing small dignities like makeup and jewelry or supplying underwear and tampons. There have also been programming changes, such as offering trauma-informed treatment or women-centered self-help programs. In Iowa, officers were trained to write fewer violations, to allow women more freedom, and to listen to them rather than barking orders. California created a Female Offender Programs and Services Office for state prisoners.

Las Colinas Detention and Reentry Facility, a women's jail in San Diego County, was built in 2014; it is considered a gold standard for gender-responsive corrections (Blakinger, 2019). Stephanie Covington and Barbara Bloom co-direct the Center for Gender and Justice, an organization that helps advise jails and prisons on how to address women's needs and treat them better. Two years before the new jail was built, the two women reviewed Las Colinas's policies and operations and advised officials on how to improve. They suggested policy changes, provided training for the staff, and visited regularly to make sure it was implemented properly. Covington said women in jail should experience what it is like to live in a community in a healthy way so that they can be contributing members to the community when they return.

There is no razor wire at the facility. More than 12,000 women pass through annually; the average daily population is about 860 (Blakinger, 2019). Women are not routinely strip-searched at admission. The visiting area has a playroom for children. Women have access to unlimited feminine hygiene supplies. There is a six-week trauma class; anger management programs; a few college courses; vocational programs that offer certificates in culinary arts, sewing, landscaping and gardening; and job-readiness. An on-site worker is available as a liaison with the county's child welfare services. Only one-quarter of the women at Las Colinas have access to most of the privileges. For women in the general population units, life at Las Colinas is similar to other jails.

Sally Hernandez became the sheriff of Travis County (Texas) in 2017. She found the jail could not meet the needs of women, many of whom had abusive backgrounds and were mothers (Blakinger, 2019). Jailed women had different issues than men, including being pregnant. There were no on-site women's health services or vocational programs aligned with women's interests. Hernandez formed a committee of six women to plan a new jail focused on women's specific needs. The committee report mentioned trauma-informed treatment more than three dozen times. It suggested no bolted-down furniture, clanging doors, metal bars, or congregate showers. If a particular feature is not part of the routine experience in living outside a jail, there should be serious questions about whether the feature is essential in the jail. For example, there should be no bunk beds because adults do not sleep in bunk beds. Privacy is prioritized, as is natural light. The most outspoken opponents of building the new jail have been activist community members. They believe another jail—no matter how improved the programming and services—is not reform. True reform is incarcerating fewer people. Sheriff Hernandez believes the county needs both—even with increased diversion, some women will be confined in the facility, and they need better care (Travis, 2020).

Many gender-responsive changes are about treating inmates more humanely—which could help inmates of all genders (Blakinger, 2019). Covington commented that for years advocates for women's services have said if there is improvement for women, there can then be improvement for men—but if you focus only on men, it never seems to get better for women.

Broad-Based National Strategies to Reduce Crime

There are limitations to any individual proposals that are offered as alternatives to using the criminal justice system as a response to crime if they do not address the root causes of various types of crimes. There is only so much tinkering with the justice systems that can be done. Without changing basic premises, we will continue to confront unequal justice and a "revolving door" where, under the best circumstances, we rehabilitate one offender and release him or her only to repeat the process with a new offender.

When evaluating the problem of crime, it is essential to include white-collar crime in addition to street crime. Public fear of crime relates to street crime, yet white-collar crime has extensive, devastating consequences (Horsley, 2014; Schoepfer et al., 2013). White collar-crime is not uniformly defined but can be understood as crimes including fraud, malpractice, and embezzlement. There is an ironic intersection of white-collar crime and street crime. Wealthier offenders use their power to remain outside of the grasp of courts (or less frequently to serve their time in more comfortable prisons) but are connected to the macroeconomic factors that drive inner-city poverty. The poor financial conditions of communities of color and individual families are directly traceable to the theft of indigenous land, Black farms (Newkirk, 2019), and restricted housing by companies and government agencies (Douglas, 2017). Greed frequently motivates white-collar crime—whether through outright theft of property, eliminating safety features in consumer products to cut costs, or convincing doctors to prescribe highly addictive opioids for pain relief. There should be at least equal time and talent addressing white-collar crime and its threat to public safety and public health as there is to punishing street crime.

Most street crime policies are *reactive* (Stamper, 2016). It is time to make a serious attempt to be *proactive* where appropriate—that is, to ameliorate criminogenic influences before crime happens. And it is time to make a serious attempt not to disproportionately criminalize behaviors that are rooted in economic destitution or that are better addressed through treatment than through punishment.

Elliot Currie (1989; 2013) suggested five general categories for a national strategy to address the general problem of crime. The first is early educational interventions (e.g., Head Start). The lack of preparedness for school, especially among underprivileged minorities, leads to poor school performance and dropping out, a leading cause of delinquency. Second, the United States should expand health and mental health services (including pre- and post-natal care), with a special focus on high-risk youths suffering from childhood traumas. Third, Currie suggests family support programs, especially for families dealing with child abuse and other forms of domestic violence. Abused children are far more likely than nonabused children to become abusers themselves. Fourth, Currie recommends doing something constructive with offenders after they have broken the law rather than warehousing them in criminogenic institutions. His fifth recommendation is to make drug and alcohol abuse treatment programs readily available.

Currie (2020) suggests that society needs to reduce racial inequality, poverty, and inadequate services. "If we have learned one thing from decades of experience, it is that even well-conceived initiatives, unless they are linked to more fundamental changes, ultimately will be thwarted by the overarching environment of systemic neglect and racialized inequality" (p. 180), Addressing social inequalities requires establishing access to the job market (Hannon, 2015). Currie (2013) outlines the following four goals: (1) reduction of inequality and social impoverishment, (2) an active labor market policy that aims at upgrading job skills, (3) a national family policy to strengthen that institution (for instance, a family leave law), and (4) economic and social stability of local communities.

Currie (2020) recently suggested that the racial divide in the experience of violence is one of the most profound racial inequalities in society. "When it comes to the violence that afflicts Black communities, a peculiar indifference still shapes our twenty-first-century response" (p. 178). The violence reflects the extraordinary levels of deprivation, insecurity, and thwarted opportunity experienced by individuals—problems compounded by racial segregation and a system of social control that itself adds to the dangers African Americans face rather than protecting them from it. Currie suggests similar key strategies to address the roots of violence, namely poverty reduction through meaningful employment at wages that support a decent standard of living plus good schooling and health care.

Margaret Phillips (1991) elaborated on the importance of unemployment as a key factor related to crime. Her thesis was that the stress associated with poverty and feelings of powerlessness—which are correlated—result in the tendency to be present oriented. Phillips noted the abundant evidence that poverty and economic dislocation play an important role in crime, as well as in the lack of self-control. The stress of living a marginal existence is physiologically harmful and creates feelings of powerlessness and the futility of planning for the future. These tendencies are similar to those of criminal offenders who generally do not consider the consequences of their behaviors. In contrast, full employment at livable wages and adequate health care is empowering and encourages responsibility.

Residents in marginal communities lack power and are trapped in a recurring cycle. Joblessness, poverty, undereducation, substance abuse, and social alienation create the lack of power—and the community does not have the resources to correct the problems that cause powerlessness. Social policies contribute to the disadvantages. Social control agents focus on symptoms rather than addressing root causes (Lab, 2020). For example, people who commit property crime are punished rather than identifying the reasons why people commit property crime. Focusing on disorder may clean up an area, but no steps are taken to understand and eliminate the causes of disorder. Phillips's theory combines the role of environmental (especially socioeconomic) factors with individual decision-making and powerlessness.

We Need a New Paradigm

We have established an elaborate system to respond to crime, but we have not increased public safety or improved conditions to address the *causes* of crime.

> The criminal justice system oppresses the poor and minorities. It uses punishment not primarily to effect justice or to protect public safety, but to rein in deviance and disorder, especially among the underclass. Though it pays lip service to justice and fairness, in practice it is a coercive tool of social control designed to maintain the status quo. Underneath the rhetoric of jury trials and constitutional rights lies a speedy plea-bargaining machine that uses conviction and punishment to control mostly poor, predominantly minority defendants. (Bibas, 2017, p. 64)

The criminal justice system can be succinctly summarized with a line from the television series, *Rawhide*. At the end of each episode, the trail boss mounted his horse and called out "Head 'em up, move 'em out." In the criminal justice system, one offender leaves a jail or a prison, only to be replaced by another.

The Power of Paradigms

In Thomas Kuhn's (1962) *The Structure of Scientific Revolutions*, he argued that paradigms—a collection of general agreements, models, or theories about how problems are to be understood and resolved—guide those who practice the scientific method. However, anomalies that do not fit the commonly accepted norms can create a crisis and a dramatic shift in how scientists think about a phenomenon. Classic examples include: the discoveries of Copernicus that challenged the conventional paradigm of viewing the sun as revolving around the earth and Darwin's work on evolution. When the prevailing paradigm faces overwhelming new evidence, a scientific revolution occurs. Answers to troubling anomalies require a new way of thinking—a totally different paradigm.

The paradigm of positivism is the prevailing norm of how to solve the problem of crime. More specifically, the dominant view comes from the branch of positivism that locates the causes and, hence, solutions to the problem of crime and delinquency within the individual. This approach focuses on the need to change the individual in some way—their psychological development, their general attitudes, their worldview, and/or their behaviors. It typically includes some form of punishment to force this change.

We suggest the need for a new paradigm—not just for criminal justice but for the operation of our social and economic systems. Efforts to make the existing justice system more efficient (as many recommend) miss the point. If the current system were more effective, there would be more arrests of the poor and racial minorities and more people in prison. In order to achieve "justice," we need to confront and overcome failures embedded in the current system. Because crime is still very much with us, we should be looking elsewhere for answers.

Many people are calling for reform. What does it mean to reform a system that relies on captivity and control? If changes re-form the system in its own image, the elements remain confinement, isolation, surveillance, and punishment (Schenwar & Law, 2020). Shortening sentences to reduce the number of people in prison has value but replacing time behind bars with electronic monitoring only changes the method of controlling individuals. The web of punitive sanctions targets people marginalized by race, class, gender identity, and disability—those considered surplus to society.

Will mass incarceration be dismantled—or will the architecture of the punishment bureaucracy remain with only small changes to the most flagrant abuses? As discussed in earlier chapters, there are a number of stakeholders in the status quo—police and correctional unions, prosecutors, judges, bail bond companies, private probation companies, private prisons, and the private companies that sell products and services at every stage of the process from handcuffs and Tasers for arrests to telephones and video calls in jails, to health care and food service in prisons. The bureaucracy is massive, and bureaucracies try to expand and preserve themselves.

> A person's path from crime to prison to release passes through a sprawling, poorly coordinated web of competing bureaucratic actors, each responding to different incentives put in place by different sets of constituents: city police, county prosecutors, state or county public defenders, state or county judges (who may be elected or appointed), parole boards appointed by the governor, and so on, each operating under laws passed by state legislators elected in local districts, and each usually paying only a portion of the costs they impose. (Pfaff, 2017, p. 163)

We need to shrink each stage of the system and to invest in noncarceral, empowerment solutions.

Alec Karakatsanis (2019) is a civil rights lawyer and founder of Civil Rights Corps, which challenges systemic injustices in the legal system. He uses the phrase *punishment bureaucracy* to describe the set of interlocking systems that define who is a criminal, what is criminal behavior, and the severity of the punishment for violations. Because the process itself is structured on mythical beliefs, reform of the components of the system does not bring meaningful change—only a complete transformation will bring equitable treatment.

The enforcement of laws is based on distributions of power (Karakatsanis, 2019). For example, street gambling is illegal; participants are subject to arrest and jail. Gambling on the price of the global wheat supply is perfectly legal, even if it has caused starvation for tens of millions of people. The same behavior—gambling—is viewed as morally culpable or morally praiseworthy, depending on who is engaging in what activity.

> Our criminal laws are not an objective mechanism for increasing overall well-being by efficiently reducing harmful behavior. Our criminal laws are based on some of the most arbitrary aspects of human existence, like power, racial bias, and economic self-interest—they reflect our demons, past and present. (pp. 861–862)

Criminal law is not an abstract repository of right and wrong behavior. It is implemented in institutional contexts affected by social, political, and economic realities (Dolovich & Natapoff, 2017).

> The law of policing, for example, cannot be understood apart from how, and against whom, American police officers enforce their power. In the same way, the law regulating punishment can be fully appreciated only by surveying how, as a practical matter, the state's agents mark, burden, and exclude those it labels as criminal. To understand the law governing the criminal context, we need to understand the rich and conflicted relationship between law's implementation (the law in action) and the terms set down by various legal sources (the law on the books). (p. 2)

Powerful people can create laws with harsh punishments knowing that they will not be enforced against them (Karakatsanis, 2019). True criminal justice reform requires a movement to change power dynamics.

> A good rule of thumb for identifying whether a proposal is meaningful or hollow is asking the question: would this reform result in greater or fewer resources going to the punishment bureaucracy? Virtually every major "reform" pushed by local, state, and federal punishment bureaucrats would result in either the same or more resources flowing into the punishment bureaucracy. (p. 932)

Complete transformation will be attained only when (1) reformers recognize that the criminal justice system does not operate in a silo; poverty, unemployment, lack of housing, and access to medical care are issues that must be addressed simultaneously; (2) the belief that punishment is required to fix social problems is abandoned; (3) power and control shifts away from law enforcement; (4) the focus changes to harms caused; (5) the criminal justice system shrinks; (6) resources are distributed to communities.

Too few people are aware of the punishment bureaucracy and the pain it inflicts on powerless people in the name of law enforcement (Karakatsanis, 2019).

> A major achievement of the punishment bureaucracy is that it has retained mainstream respect even though it crushes unprecedented numbers of people with no evidence of any unique social benefit while simultaneously allowing enormous amounts of lawlessness that cause massive harm. Why is it still viewed as legitimate? (p. 901)

New Paradigms in Practice: Restorative and Community Justice

One example of a paradigm shift is an approach grounded in philosophical and religious works, including eastern religions and indigenous belief systems. Restorative justice focuses on healing rather than punishment. It views crime as a violation of relationships and people, with an obligation to make things right (D. Wilson et al., 2017). Important principles of restorative justice include offender accountability and respect for all participants.

Reflecting several decades of restorative justice work in Western countries, Richard Quinney (1991) pointed us in the direction of peacemaking—seeking peace within ourselves and through various nonviolent and noncoercive alternatives to crime and crime control. The underpinning philosophy of restorative justice is restoring harmony to the community following a breech. It calls for an end to the pain and suffering of the victims of crime and all forms of human rights abuses.

The usual response to crime—especially violent crime—is a desire for retribution—to "get even" by seeking "just deserts" against offenders. But this response has always proved to be counterproductive. The underlying aim of restorative justice is to cease objectification of everyone involved in the violent act, including the victim, the offender, the families connected to those individuals, and the community at large. Restorative justice encourages all of the individuals involved to engage in a healing process through traditional mediation and conflict resolution techniques—dissolving fears, hate, and resentment in order to return to their former selves prior to victimization. Through this process, the person most directly harmed "is able to achieve a greater sense of inner-healing and closure for any traumatic loss of trust, self-worth, and freedom . . . [while] the harmed person might also achieve a modicum of reparation for his or her losses as well as be able to reduce his or her fears of being harmed" (Sullivan & Tift, 2000, p. 9). All restorative justice programs share this logic while employing various practices, such as victim-offender mediation, community circle processes, and community councils.

Retributive justice—which underpins the current criminal justice system—is contrary to virtually every religious tenet. As Gandhi and Martin

Luther King, Jr., taught and demonstrated, the only way to end violence is *not* to reciprocate in kind. In other words, we must stop the violence at the individual and institutional levels in order to end the cycle. King, in his acceptance speech for the Nobel Peace Prize in 1964, said: "The choice today is not between violence and nonviolence. It is either nonviolence or nonexistence" (Seldes, 1996, p. 253). The idea that restoration—through programs and practices that cultivate forgiveness—is the only way to rid society of injury has a long history. Alexander Pope (1688–1744), an English poet, wrote, "To err is human, to forgive divine" (Seldes, 1996, p. 376). Unfortunately, forgiveness seems out of step in our current political-economy. Forgiveness would be more in line with a political-economy system "that sees acknowledgment of a harm done, and apology for it, and forgiveness offered in return, as processes that are personally healing for all involved and simultaneously restorative of community" (Sullivan & Tifft, 2000, p. 6).

David Friedrichs (2006) argues that the positivistic focus of the criminal justice system privileges discovery, explanation, and prediction over a concern with developing the concept of justice. It views crime as a legal concept and ignores the political-economic context that defines what crime is and how it should be punished. The criminal justice system fixates on street offenders rather than victims or the communities within which crime occurs. Mainstream criminology views crime as the violation of state law. Restorative justice looks to the community that experienced the offense to identify the harm, removing the exclusive right to define crime from elite groups in society. "Crime in a humanistic approach is best defined as activity that is demonstrably harmful to human beings and their environment, regardless of the status of these activities under law" (p. 441).

Howard Zehr (2015) suggests finding lenses other than guilt and punishment in which to see both the problem of crime and the response to it. Crime victims want to know why the crime happened and what should happen next. Our understanding of what is possible is based on our constructions of reality. Those constructs can change. Restorative justice offers a way out of the harms of punitive confinement by enlisting the power of communities to help members when things go wrong.

Three principles guide restorative justice (Van Ness & Strong, 2015). (1) Work to heal victims, offenders, and communities injured by crime to achieve justice. (2) Provide opportunities for the active participation of everyone involved as early and as fully as they wish. (3) Rethink the responsibilities of government and community. "In promoting justice, government is responsible for preserving a just order and the community for establishing a just peace" (p. 47). Four important values attach to the process of restorative justice. *Inclusion* encompasses invitation, acknowledgment of interests, and acceptance of alternative approaches. *Encounter* covers meeting, understanding, and agreement. *Amends* includes restitution, changed behavior, apology, and generosity. *Reintegration* involves respect, practical and material help, and moral/spiritual guidance and care.

Todd Clear (2006) compares and contrasts restorative justice with community justice. "Restorative justice is a deeply penetrating critique of formal justice processes and a profound challenge to the adversarial due process model of criminal justice" (p. 465). Community justice advocates are equally dissatisfied with traditional criminal justice but focus on how the astounding growth of the criminal justice system has failed to make communities better, safer, or more livable. Proponents of community justice argue that the prosecution and punishment of felons should not be an end in itself; rather, it should be to make communities better places for people to live and work.

> The claim is that the growing criminal justice system has, in the end, done more damage than good, and that its strategies need to be recalibrated to take account of what communities need rather than merely what wrongdoers deserve. . . . What we need is not strategies to deal with individuals who engage in misdeeds but those that target places where these misdeeds concentrate. (p. 465)

Community justice initiatives are needed in high-impact areas (communities where both crime and criminal justice responses to crime exist in concentrated levels) because traditional methods of criminal justice have failed (Clear et al., 2011). Social injustice and crime reinforce each other in these areas.

> The aim of community justice is not merely to process criminal cases but to restore order, strengthen community cohesion, repair the damage from crime, and build partnerships that nurture a more beneficial community life. Taken together, these capacities represent social capital, which enables communities to act in defense of their interests and to pursue collective goals. (p. 4)

Community justice involves two assumptions. First, "within existing jurisdictions, such as states or large cities, there are critically important differences from one community to another, and these differences suggest that criminal justice strategies need to be tailored to fit those differences" (p. 1). The second assumption is that informal social controls (friends, families, neighbors, social organizations) rather than formal systems of social control (the criminal justice system) provide the most important foundation for public safety.

Proponents of restorative justice and community justice must overcome established attitudes about social organization as well as punishment. As Dennis Sullivan and Larry Tifft (2000) observe, the change needed "transforms all of our conceptions of political economy, that is, how we view power and money, and how we assess human worth" (p. 34). By transforming how social power is held and by whom, we recognize the "money-surplus complex" for what it really is—a manipulation of power hoarding and control over others.

A New Paradigm Requires New Discourse

Rethinking the labels we use to describe people who violate the law is a component in establishing a different discourse. As discussed in chapter 8, Jerome Miller (1996) described the evolution of labels applied to young offenders from "possessed" youths in the seventeenth century to "super-predators" in the 1990s to the "compulsive delinquent" in the twenty-first century. Labeling reassures us that the fault lies in the offender, relieving others of any responsibility.

Richard Quinney (2000) offers useful advice about the evolution of definitions and the meaning of crime and criminal law.

> A criminal definition is applied according to an *evaluation* by someone charged with the authority to enforce and administer the law. In the course of "criminalization," a criminal label may be affixed to a person because of real or fancied attributes. Indeed, a person is evaluated, either favorably or unfavorably, not because he *does* something, or even because he *is* something, but because others react to their perceptions of him as offensive or inoffensive. . . .

> Departing significantly from positivistic studies, social constructionists have exposed the problematic nature of legal order. Crime and other stigmatized behaviors are examined as categories created and imposed upon some persons by others. Crime exists because the society constructs and applies the label of crime. Criminal law, too, is not separate from society, but is itself a construction, created by those who are in power. The administration of justice is a human social activity that is constructed as various legal agents interpret and impose their order on those they select for processing. (pp. 78, 196)

We might start the process of change by looking in the mirror. We should begin by asking ourselves: Is there anything that I can do differently? Is there something wrong with *my* attitudes, *my* beliefs, *my* definitions, and *my* actions that may contribute to the problem? An early step in transitioning out of the simplistic, punitive discourse—a discourse that thrives on labeling some people as less valuable—requires that we be willing to acknowledge our own culpability in this process. For example, if serving on a jury, would you be more likely to sentence a Black man to death but not a white man for the same crime (Levinson et al., 2014; Nellis, 2016)? When a teen is charged as an adult, how willing are you to assume that the teen must be a predator (Rios, 2009)? When voting, how quick are you to choose the candidate who claims to be tough on crime (Hetey & Eberhardt, 2014)?

Commitment to a new paradigm can result in the restoration of community.

> The truth that relieves suffering lies in the concrete moment of our awareness, an awareness that frees us from conditioned judgments. . . . The source of social action is within the human heart that

has come to understand fully its own suffering and therefore the suffering of others. If human actions are not rooted in compassion, these actions will not contribute to a peaceful and compassionate world. (Quinney, 2000, p. 87)

Some Closing Thoughts

There are many great challenges ahead. We begin many of our classes by writing two words on the blackboard: "power and control"—two elements of the dominant paradigm for more than 300 years. Critical criminology argues that crime stems from oppressive conditions that are most likely to impact the poor and minorities—a result of class, gender, and racial inequalities. The elimination of crime and the achievement of justice cannot be done without the elimination of these inequalities.

Recall from the discussion of paradigms that crises can create a dramatic shift in thinking. In mid-March 2020, a global pandemic was in full swing. State orders to close businesses to flatten the curve of the virus left millions unemployed and the economy shattered. During this economic crisis, police violence targeted at Black bodies continued and was captured by smartphone technologies. On May 25, George Floyd, a forty-six-year-old Black man, was handcuffed and lying on the pavement while Derek Chauvin, a white Minneapolis police officer, pressed his knee on Floyd's neck for almost nine minutes. The chilling cellphone video of Floyd's slow death from Officer Chauvin's actions set off turbulent demonstrations against police brutality, racism, and inequality (Morrison & Sedensky, 2020). By the end of September, about 23 million people had attended protests in what experts called the largest sustained mobilization in modern history (Chan, 2020).

Throughout history, the police often have been the face of oppression (Chotiner, 2020). Before the Civil War, law enforcement tracked down fugitive slaves. After emancipation, law enforcement stood aside while Black communities were terrorized. Throughout the first half of the twentieth century, the police and the justice system allowed white mobs to lynch Black people with impunity. During civil rights demonstrations in the 1950s and 1960s, uniformed police beat and arrested protestors. The police are an extension of the larger society that has allowed violence and oppression.

The persistent refusal to view Black people as equals infuses present-day issues (Chotiner, 2020). Black and brown people must navigate the presumption of dangerousness, which increases the possibility of tragic outcomes in encounters with the police (Hetey & Eberhardt, 2018). After Floyd's death, Bryan Stevenson described the oppressive burden of such presumptions to an interviewer.

I'm sixty years old and have been practicing law for thirty-five years. I have a lot of honorary degrees and went to Harvard. And I still go places where I am presumed dangerous. I have been told to leave courtrooms because the presumption was that I was the defendant and not the lawyer. I have been pulled out of my car by police who pointed a gun on me. And I can just tell you that, when you have to navigate this presumption of guilt, day in and day out, and when the burden is on you to make the people around you see you as fully human and equal, you get exhausted. You are tired. And I would argue that the Black people in the streets are expressing their fatigue, their anger, and their frustration at having to live this menaced life in America. (paragraph 20)

The public health crisis and economic downturn of the pandemic exposed major gaps in the social safety net, which might lead to rethinking the government's role in providing basic safeguards (Bush, 2020). The pandemic highlighted the fragility of some of the most marginalized groups. For Black and Hispanic households, it added to the social and economic disparities that are deeply rooted in structural discrimination and systemic racism (Grooms et al., 2020). The pandemic altered retail commerce, moving it from brick and mortar stores to e-commerce (Seib, 2020). Some of the jobs lost may never return. Working remotely rather than in a traditional office setting may become the norm. Politics and civic life were affected. How Americans cast their votes may have changed permanently. There may be changes in the Electoral College, the Supreme Court, and police departments. Prior to 2020, the status quo of these institutions was largely accepted. The tumultuous year may push some populations, who previously went about their lives largely unaware of the widespread oppressive factors discussed throughout *Our Punitive Society,* to notice the need for change. Whether changes will extend to how people are punished and how minorities are policed remains to be seen. Will the crisis lead to a new paradigm regarding punishment and criminality after five decades of deeply seated, harsh attitudes that fostered the growth of mass incarceration?

Brian Highsmith (2020), a civil rights lawyer and researcher at Yale Law School's Arthur Liman Center for Public Interest Law, said defunding the punishment bureaucracy through significant, permanent reductions to existing policing and carceral infrastructures would address the public health, economic, and social justice crises. The fiscal crisis reinforces the need to reduce expenditures on the criminal justice system. The safety of communities will not be harmed by combining funding cuts with the decriminalization of misdemeanors, ordinance violations, and other charges that consume most of the activities of contemporary policing. Cities can divert funds away from the construction of jails and redistribute the monies to communities, which could employ medics and crisis workers to address vulnerable populations such as the mentally ill or chronically homeless. The redistributed funds would help communities find effective alternatives to policing and arrests as the primary response to social problems.

The Irish poet Seamus Heaney (1991) wrote about humans suffering and enduring wrongs. While they may be conditioned not to hope, "once in a lifetime" a tidal wave of justice can arise (p. 76). There can be hope for a sea change and healing. Perhaps the 2020 crises will precipitate the tidal wave. Change begins with individuals and communities reframing their views and working together for an equal and just society. Bryan Stevenson (2014) offers a valuable perspective.

> We are all implicated when we allow other people to be mistreated. An absence of compassion can corrupt the decency of a community, a state, a nation. Fear and anger can make us vindictive and abusive, unjust and unfair, until we all suffer from the absence of mercy and we condemn ourselves as much as we victimize others. The closer we get to mass incarceration and extreme levels of punishment, the more I believe it's necessary to recognize that we all need mercy, we all need justice, and—perhaps—we all need some measure of unmerited grace. (p. 18)

A tidal wave of just mercy could divert society from the destructive tendency to discard the most vulnerable and from the excessive punishment that has ravaged so many lives.

References

Abbott, G. (1938). *The child and the state.* Chicago: University of Chicago Press.

Abram, K. M., Choe, J. Y., Washburn, J. J., Teplin, L. A., King, D. C., & Dulcan, M. K. (2008). Suicidal ideation and behaviors among youth in juvenile detention. *Journal of the American Academy of Child & Adolescent Psychiatry, 47*(3), 291–300.

ACLU. (2019). Student drug testing: Relevant case law. New York: Author.

ACLU. (2020a). Getting rid of sodomy laws: History and strategy that led to the *Lawrence* decision. New York: Author.

ACLU. (2020b). Why sodomy laws matter. New York: Author.

Adler, J. S. (1989). A historical analysis of the law of vagrancy. *Criminology, 27,* 209–229.

Aiken, J. (2017, June 14). The downstream effect of 35 years of jail growth? A state prison boom. Northampton, MA: Prison Policy Initiative.

Al.com. (2019, March 5). Special report: Alabama leads nation in turning pregnant women into felons. Al.com.

Alexander, M. (2020). *The new Jim Crow: Colorblindness in the age of mass incarceration* (10th anniversary ed.). New York: The New Press.

Allyn, B. (2019, August 7). Cyntoia Brown released after 15 years in prison for murder. NPR.

Alper, M., Durose, M., & Markman, J. (2018, May). 2018 update on prisoner recidivism: A 9-year follow-up period (2005–2014). Washington, DC: Bureau of Justice Statistics. NCJ 250975.

Amadeo, K. (2019, June 25). Deinstitutionalization, its causes, effects, pros and cons. The Balance. https://www.thebalance.com/deinstitutionalization-3306067

Amaning, A. (2020, June 25). Advancing clean slate: The need for automatic record clearance during the coronavirus pandemic. Center for American Progress.

Amicus Curiae in Support of Respondent, Roper v. Simmons, 543 U.S. 551 (2005) (No. 03-633).

Amnesty International. (2014, July 16). USA: Prisoners held in extreme solitary confinement in breach of international law. London: Author.

Amnesty International. (2018). Executions of juveniles since 1990 as of March 2018. London: Author.

Anderson, C. (2018). *One person, no vote: How voter suppression is destroying our democracy*. New York: Bloomsbury Publishing.

Anderson, T. (2016, June 3). LAFF: Why Laverne Cox is lending her voice to the *Free Cece* documentary. *The Los Angeles Times*.

Annamma, S., Anyon, Y., Joseph, N., Farrar, J., Greer, E., Downing, B., & Simmons, J. (2019). Black girls and school discipline: The complexities of being overrepresented and understudied. *Urban Education, 54*(2): 211–242.

AP. (2017, July 31). *Miller v. Alabama* and *Jackson v. Hobbs*. https://www.ap.org/explore/locked-up-for-life/Miller-v-Alabama-and-Jackson-v-Hobbs

Arango, T. (2019, April 7). Democratic candidates rethink the death penalty, and its politics. *The New York Times*, sec. A, p. 14.

Arias, E., & Xu, J. (2019, June 24). United States life tables 2017. *National Vital Statistics Reports, 68*(7). Hyattsville, MD: National Center for Health Statistics.

Armstrong, M. (2019, September 12). Here's why abolishing private prisons isn't a silver bullet. New York: The Marshall Project.

Arnold, C. (2020, January 22). Another round of prison closures may soon be coming to New York. Democrat & Chronicle/USA Today Network.

Atkinson, T. (2016). A fine scheme: How municipal fines become crushing debt in the shadow of the new debtors' prison. *Harvard Civil Rights-Civil Liberties Law Review, 51*(1), 189–238.

Aubin, D. (2016, November 4). Bank of America accused of gouging ex-inmates with card fees. Reuters

Austin, J.,& Irwin, J. (2012). *It's about time: America's incarceration binge* (4th ed.). Belmont, CA: Wadsworth.

Ayers, E. (1984). *Vengeance and justice: Crime and punishment in the 19th century American South*. New York: Oxford University Press.

Bacigal, R. J. (2013). Watching the watchers. *Mississippi Law Journal, 82*(5), 821.

Bacon, L., Lee, G., Weber, J., & Duran, L. (2020, February). Laying the groundwork: How states can improve access to continued education for people in the criminal justice system. New York: Author.

Bailey, W. C. (1998). Deterrence, brutalization, and the death penalty: Another examination of Oklahoma's return to capital punishment. *Criminology, 36*(4), 711–734.

Baldus, D. C., Woodworth, G., & Pulaski, C. A. (1990). *Equal justice and the death penalty: A legal and empirical analysis*. Boston: Northeastern University Press.

Balko, R. (2013). *Rise of the warrior cop: The militarization of America's police forces*. New York: Public Affairs.

Barber, H. E. (1973). The Association of Southern Women for the Prevention of Lynching, 1930-1942. *Phylon, 34*, 378–389.

Barkan, S. B., & Cohen, S. F. (1994). Racial prejudice and support for the death penalty by whites. *Journal of Research in Crime and Delinquency, 31*, 202–209.

Barnert, E., Dudovitz, R., Nelson, B., Coker, T., Biely, C., Li, N., & Chung, P. (2017, January). How does incarcerating young people affect their adult health outcomes? *Pediatrics*.

Barnert, E., Perry, R., & Morris, R. (2016). Juvenile incarceration and health. *Academic Pediatrics, 16*(2), 99–109.

Barnes, H. E., & Teeters, N. (1959). *New horizons in criminology*. Englewood Cliffs, NJ: Prentice-Hall.

Barnes, R. (2019, February 20). Supreme Court limits power of state and localities to impose fines, seize property. *The Washington Post.*

Bauer, S. (2018, September 25). The true history of America's private prison industry. *Time.*

Baum, D. (2016, April). Legalize it all: How to win the war on drugs. *Harper's Magazine.*

Baumgartner, F., Grigg, A., & Mastro, A. (2015). #BlackLivesDon'tMatter: Race-of-victim effects in US executions 1976–2013. Politics, Groups and Identities, NCJ 224527.

Bazelon, E. (2019). *Charged, the new movement to transform American prosecution and end mass incarceration.* New York: Random House.

Beck, A. J., Berzofsky, M., Caspar, R., & Krebs, C. (2013, May). Sexual victimization in prisons and jails reported by inmates, 2011–2012. Bureau of Justice Statistics. NCJ 241399.

Beck, A. J., & Dilliard, D. K. (1995). Prisoners in 1994. Washington, DC: Bureau of Justice Statistics. NCJ 151654.

Beck, E. M., Massey, J. L., & Tolnay, S. E. (1989). The gallows, the mob, and the vote: Lethal sanctioning of blacks in North Carolina and Georgia, 1882–1930. *Law and Society Review, 23,* 317–329.

Becker, H. S. (1997). *Outsiders: Studies in the sociology of deviance.* New York: The Free Press.

Benjamin, R. (2012, March 30). The gated community mentality. *The New York Times,* p. 27.

Bennett, C. (2017). Invisible punishment is wrong—but why? The normative basis of criticism of collateral consequences of criminal conviction. *The Howard Journal of Crime & Justice,* 56(4), 480-499.

Benns, W., & Strode, B. (2016, February 23). Debtors' prison in 21st-century America. *The Atlantic.*

Bernard, T. J., & Kurlychek, M. C. (2010). *The cycle of juvenile justice* (2nd ed.). New York: Oxford University Press.

Bevan, G. R. (2014). Opinion of Supreme Court of the State of Idaho docket no. 38769 *Sarah M. Johnson v. the State of Idaho.*

Bibas, S. (2017). Improve, dynamite, or dissolve the criminal regulatory state. In S. Dolovich & A. Natapoff (Eds.), *The new criminal justice thinking* (pp. 61–70), New York: NYU Press.

Bierschbach, R., & Bibas, S. (2016). What's wrong with sentencing equality? *Virginia Law Review, 102,* 1447–1522.

Biggar, R. Jr., Forsyth, C., Chen, J., & Burstein, K. (2016). The poly-drug user: Examining associations between drugs used by adolescents, *Deviant Behavior, 38*(10), 1186–1196.

Birckhead, T. R. (2015). The new peonage. *Washington and Lee Law Review, 72,* 1595–1678.

Black, A. (2018, November 18). *Out in the Night*: Rethinking the New Jersey Four case. *The College Voice.*

Blackmon, D. (2008). *Slavery by another name: The re-enslavement of black Americans from the Civil War to World War II.* New York: Doubleday.

Blad, E., & Harwin, A. (2017, January 24). Black students more likely to be arrested at school. *Education Week.*

Blakely, E. J., & Snyder, M. G. (1997). *Fortress America: Gated communities in the United States*. Washington, DC: Brookings Institution Press.

Blakinger, K. (2019, October 28). Can we build a better women's prison? *The Washington Post*.

Bloom, B. (2015). Meeting the needs of women in California's county justice systems. San Francisco: Californians for Safety and Justice.

Bloom, B., Owen, B., & Covington, S. (2003). *Gender-responsive strategies: Research, practice, guiding principles for women offenders*. Rockville, MD: National Institute of Justice.

Blumstein, A., & Beck, A. (1999). Population growth in U.S. prisons, 1980–1996. *Crime and Justice, 26*, 17–61.

Bones, P., & Hope, T. (2015). Broken neighborhoods: A hierarchical spatial analysis of assault and disability concentration in Washington, DC. *Journal of Quantitative Criminology, 31*(2), 311–329.

Bowers, W. G., Pierce, G. L., & McDevitt, J. F. (1984). *Legal homicide: Death as punishment in America, 1864–1982*. Boston: Northeastern University Press.

Bowman, L. (2004, May 11). New research shows stark differences in teen brains. Scripps Howard News Service.

Boyer, T. (2020, May 19). Advocates cautious about California proposal to move state detention to counties. Kennesaw, GA: Juvenile Justice Information Exchange.

Bradford, T. (2019). Zero disenfranchisement: The movement to restore voting rights. Washington, DC: Common Cause.

Bradley, K. (1987). *Slaves and masters in the Roman empire: A study in social control*. New York: Oxford University Press.

Bradner, K., & Schiraldi, V. (2020, March). Racial inequities in New York parole supervision. New York: Columbia University Justice Lab.

Bradner, K., Schiraldi, V., Mejia, N., & Lopoo, E. (2020, August 2020). More work to do: Analysis of probation and parole in the United States, 2017–2018. New York: Columbia University Justice Lab.

Braunstein, M. (2017). The five stages of LGBTQ discrimination and its effects on mass incarceration. *University of Miami Race and Social Justice Law Review, 7*(1), 1–29.

Brenzel, B. (1983). *Daughters of the state*. Cambridge: MIT Press.

Brett, S., Khoshkhoo, N., & Nagrecha, M. (2020, June). Paying on probation: How financial sanctions intersect with probation to target, trap, and punish people who cannot pay Cambridge: Harvard Law School Criminal Justice Policy Program.

Briefing Report. (2020, February). Women in prison: Seeking justice behind bars. Washington, DC: United States Commission on Civil Rights.

Buczynski, B. (2014, February 6). Shocking facts about America's for-profit prison industry. Truthout. http://www.truth-out.org/news/item/21694-shocking-facts-about-americas-for-profit-prison-industry

Bureau of Labor Statistics. (2019, September 4). Occupational outlook handbook: Security guards and gaming surveillance officers. Washington, DC: Department of Labor.

Burley, L. (1997). History repeats itself in the resurrection of prisoner chain gangs: Alabama's experience raises Eighth Amendment concerns. *Law & Inequality, 15*, 127–155.

Bush, D. (2020, April 2). Could the coronavirus reshape America's social safety net? PBS.

Butler, P. (2019, May 5). Book Review. *The Washington Post,* sec 4, p. 4.

California Department of Corrections and Rehabilitation (CDCR). (2019). Conservation (fire) camps. Sacramento: Author.

CALPIA. (2019). CALPIA report to the legislature FY 2018–2019. Folsom, CA: Author.

Campbell, J. C. (2002). Health consequences of intimate partner violence. *The Lancet, 359,* 1331–1336.

Campaign for Youth Justice. (2018, December 10). Let's get children out of adult courts, jails, and prisons. Washington, DC: Author.

Carson, E. (2020a, February). Mortality in local jails, 2000–2016. Washington, DC: Bureau of Justice Statistics. NCJ 251921.

Carson, E. (2020b, October). Prisoners in 2019. Washington, DC: Bureau of Justice Statistics. NCJ 255115.

Carter, D. (1979). *Scottsboro: A tragedy of the American South.* Baton Rouge: Louisiana State University Press.

Carter, T. (2010). The Maricopa courthouse war. *ABA Journal, 96,* 43–49.

Catalanello, R. (2014, April 3). New Bethany Home for Girls endured 30 years of controversy, leaving former residents wondering why. *The Times-Picayune.*

Cavendish, W. (2013). Academic attainment during commitment and postrelease education–related outcomes of juvenile justice-involved youth with and without disabilities. *Journal of Emotional and Behavioral Disorders, 22*(1).

CBS News. (2018). Shocking "prison" study 40 years later: What happened at Stanford? cbsnews.com.

Center on Juvenile and Criminal Justice. (2020). Juvenile Collaborative Reentry Unit. San Francisco, Author.

Centers for Disease Control. (2019). Preventing intimate partner violence. Atlanta: Author.

Chambliss, W. S. (1975). The law of vagrancy. In W. S. Chambliss (Ed.), *Criminal law in action.* New York: John Wiley.

Chammah, M. (2015, February 25). Rape in American prison. *The Atlantic.*

Chapman, S. (2019, October 17). Barr to nonbelievers: Go to hell. *Chicago Tribune,* p. 16.

Chan, M. (2019, December 16). Fear of mass shootings fuels a thriving bulletproof business. *Time,* 24–25.

Chan, M. (2020, September 28). The price of protest. *Time,* 58–61.

Chen, S. (2009, February 23). Pennsylvania rocked by "jailing kids for cash" scandal. CNN.

Cheyney, E. P. (1913). *An introduction to the industrial and social history of England.* New York: Macmillan.

Chesney-Lind, M. (2017). Linking criminal theory and social practice: A response to Natapoff. In S. Dolovich & A. Natapoff (Eds.), *The new criminal justice thinking* (pp. 99–110). New York: NYU Press.

Chomsky, N. (1989). *Necessary illusions: Thought control in democratic societies.* Boston: South End Press.

Chomsky, N. (1993). *Year 501: The conquest continues.* Boston: South End Press.

Chomsky, N. (1996). *Class warfare: Interviews with David Barsamian.* Monroe, ME: Common Courage Press.

Chomsky, N. (2000). *Rogue states: The rule of force in world affairs.* Boston: South End Press.

Chotiner, I. (2020, June 1). Bryan Stevenson on the frustration behind the George Floyd protests. *The New Yorker.*

Christie, N. (2000). *Crime control as industry* (3rd ed.). New York: Routledge.

Chung, J. (2019, June). Felony disenfranchisement: A primer. Washington, DC: The Sentencing Project.

Cianciotto, J., & Cahill, S. (2012). *LGBT youth in America's schools.* Ann Arbor: University of Michigan Press.

Citizens Commission on Jail Violence. (2012). Report of the Citizens Commission on Jail Violence. Los Angeles: County of Los Angeles.

Civil Rights Division. (2020, February 5). Investigation of South Carolina Department of Juvenile Justice's Broad River Road Complex. Washington, DC: Department of Justice.

Clark, A. (2017). Juvenile solitary confinement as a form of child abuse. *Journal of the American Academy of Psychiatry and the Law, 45*(3), 350–357.

Clark, A. (2019, November 12). Think your house is hard to unload? Try selling a prison. *Bridge Magazine.*

Clark, C., Hendricks, P., Lane, P., Trent, L., & Cropsey, K. (2014). Methadone maintenance treatment may improve completion rates and delay opioid relapse for opioid dependent individuals under community corrections supervision, *Addictive Behaviors, 39,* 1736–1740.

Clark, N. (2018, February 14). Lawsuit, criminal investigation into Jackson County Sheriff's Office: What we know so far. Michigan Live.
https://www.mlive.com/news/jackson/index.ssf/2018/02/harassment_
lawsuit_criminal_in.html

Clear, T. (2002). The problem with "addition by subtraction." In M. Mauer & M. Chesney-Lind (Eds.), *Invisible punishment: The collateral consequences of mass imprisonment* (pp. 181–193). New York: The New Press.

Clear, T. (2006). Community justice versus restorative justice: Contrasts in family values. In D. Sullivan & L. Tift (Eds.), *The handbook of restorative justice: A global perspective* (pp. 463–472). New York: Rutledge.

Clear, T., & Frost, N. (2015). *The punishment imperative: The rise and failure of mass incarceration in America.* New York: NYU Press.

Clear, T., Hamilton, J., & Cadora, E. (2011). *Community justice* (2nd ed.). New York: Routledge.

Cloninger, D., & Marchesini, R. (2009). Reflections on a critique. *Applied Economics Letters, 16,* 1709–1711.

Coates, T. (2015, October). The black family in the age of mass incarceration. The Atlantic. https://www.theatlantic.com/magazine/archive/2015/10/the-black-family-in-the-age-of-mass-incarceration/403246/

Cockcroft, T. (2014). Police culture and transformational leadership: Outlining the contours of a troubled relationship. *Policing: A Journal of Policy and Practice, 8*(1), 5–13.

Cole, D. (1999). *No equal justice: Race and class in the American criminal justice system.* New York: The New Press.

Collins, C. F. (2010). *The imprisonment of African American women: Causes, experiences and effects* (2nd ed.). Jefferson, NC: McFarland.

Collins, S., Clifasefi, S., & Lonczak, H. (2015). Summary of LEAD program evaluation: Recidivism report. Seattle: University of Washington.

Color of Change. (2020). Normalizing injustice: The dangerous misrepresentations that define television's scripted crime genre. Oakland, CA: Author.

Comen, E. (2019, July 20). Detroit, Chicago, Memphis: The 25 most segregated cities in America. New York: 24/7 Wall Street.

Conquest, R. (1995, February 24). Playing down the gulag. *Times Literary Supplement.*

Cook, R. (2017, February 2). Private probation company settles lawsuits for over $2 million. *Atlanta Constitution.*

Costanzo, M. (1997). *Just revenge: Costs and consequences of the death penalty.* Belmont, CA: Wadsworth.

Couloute, L. (2018 August). Nowhere to go: Homelessness among formerly incarcerated people. Northampton, MA: Prison Policy Initiative.

Council of Europe. (2019, April 2). Europe's rate of imprisonment falls, according to Council of Europe survey. Switzerland: University of Lausanne.

Council of State Governments Justice Center. (2015). Locked out: Improving educational and vocational outcomes for incarcerated youth. New York: Author.

Council of State Governments Justice Center. (2019). Confined and costly: How probation and parole violations fill prisons and drive costs. New York: Author.

Cowan, B. (2019, April). *Incarcerated women: Poverty, trauma and unmet need.* Washington, DC: American Psychological Association.

Coyne, C., & Hall, A. (2017, April 12). Four decades and counting: The continued failure of the war on drugs. Washington, DC: Cato Institute.

Cramer, L., Goff, M., Peterson, B., & Sandstrom, H. (2017, April). Parent-child visiting practices in prisons and jails: A synthesis of research and practice. Washington, DC: Urban Institute.

Cullen, T. (2018, March 13). ICE released its most comprehensive immigration detention data yet. It's alarming. National Immigrant Justice Center.

Currie, E. (1989). Confronting crime: Looking toward the twenty-first century. *Justice Quarterly, 6*, 5–25.

Currie, E. (1993). *Reckoning: Drugs, the cities, and the American future.* New York: Hill and Wang.

Currie, E. (2013). *Crime and punishment in America* (rev. ed.). New York: Picador.

Currie, E. (2020). *A peculiar indifference: The neglected toll of violence on Black America.* New York: Metropolitan Books.

Curtin, M. E. (2000). *Black prisoners and their world, Alabama, 1865–1900.* Charlottesville: University Press of Virginia.

Daniel, R. (2019, December 5). Prisons neglect pregnant women in their healthcare policies. Northampton, MA: Prison Policy Initiative.

Dario, L., Fradella, H., Verhagen, M., & Parry, M. (2020). Assessing LGBT people's perceptions of police legitimacy. *Journal of Homosexuality, 67*(7), 885–915.

Davidson, J. (2016, October 27). "Invisible punishment" hits ex-felon for life: DOJ, HUD fight blanket rental bias. *The Washington Post.*

Davis, M. (2003). Fortress Los Angeles. In R. T. LeGates & F. Stout (Eds.), *The city reade,* (3rd ed., pp. 201–206). New York: Routledge.

Death Penalty Information Center. (n.d.). History of the death penalty. Washington, DC: Author.

Death Penalty Information Center. (2017, December 31). International: Abolitionist and retentionist countries. Washington, DC: Author.

Death Penalty Information Center. (2019a). Executions in the United States 1608–2002: The Espy file. Washington, DC: Author.

Death Penalty Information Center. (2019b). Former state and federal judges, prosecutors and law enforcement officials, and families of murder victims urge federal government to call off executions. Washington, DC: Author.

Death Penalty Information Center. (2020a, October 2). Facts about the death penalty. Washington, DC: Author.

Death Penalty Information Center. (2020b). Executions by county. Washington, DC: Author.

Death Penalty Information Center. (2020c). Executions overview. Washington, DC: Author.

Death Penalty Information Center. (2020d). Race, rape, and the death penalty. Washington, DC: Author.

Death Penalty Information Center. (2020e). Size of death row by year. Washington, DC: Author.

Death Penalty Information Center. (2020f, June 18). States with no recent executions. Washington, DC: Author.

Department of Justice. (2019, March 7). Hate crime laws. Washington, DC: Author. https://www.justice.gov/crt/hate-crime-laws

Development Services Group, Inc. (2014, August). LGBTQ Youths in the juvenile justice system. Literature review. Washington, DC: Office of Juvenile Justice and Delinquency Prevention.

Dezhbakhsh, H., & Rubin, P. (2011). From the "econometrics of capital punishment" to the "capital punishment" of econometrics: On the use and abuse of sensitivity analysis. *Applied Economics, 43,* 3655–3670.

Dickson, J., & LeBlanc, B. (2019, February 17). Whitmer: "Michigan values" led to blocked sale of shuttered prison. *The Detroit News.*

Dierkhising, C., Lane, A., & Natsuaki, M. (2014). Victims behind bars: A preliminary study of abuse during juvenile incarceration and post-release social and emotional functioning. *Psychology, Public Policy, and Law, 20*(2), 181–190.

DiFonzo, J. H. (1995). Deprived of "fatal liberty": The rhetoric of child saving and the reality of juvenile incarceration, *University of Toledo Law Review, 26*: 855–900.

Dilawar, A. (2019, June 30). Inmates are using Instagram to raise awareness of inhumane jails. *Pacific Standard.*

Dilulio, J. L. (1996). Broken bottles: Alcohol, disorder, and crime. *The Brookings Review, 14,* 14–17.

Dobash, R. E., Dobash, R., & Gutteridge, S. (1986). *The imprisonment of women.* New York: Basil and Blackwell.

Docherty, J. P. (2017, October 20). Creating new hope for mental illness and the criminal justice system. Arlington, VA: National Alliance on Mental Illness.

Dollar, C. B. (2018). Criminalization and drug "wars" or medicalization and health "epidemics": How race, class, and neoliberal politics influence drug laws. *Critical Criminology, 27,* 305–327.

Dolovich. S., & Natapoff, A. (2017). Introduction: Mapping the new criminal justice thinking. In S. Dolovich & A. Natapoff (Eds.), *The new criminal justice thinking* (pp. 1–30). New York: NYU Press.

Donziger, S. R. (1996). *The real war on crime: The report of the national criminal justice commission.* New York: Harper Perennial.

Douglas, L. (2017, June 26). African Americans have lost untold acres of land over the last century: An obscure legal loophole is often to blame. *The Nation.*

Dow, M. (2004). American gulag: Inside U.S. immigration prisons. Berkeley: University of California Press.

Drug Policy Alliance. (2019). Drug war statistics. New York: Author.

Du Rose, N. (2015). *The governance of female drug users: Women's experiences of drug policy.* Chicago: Policy Press.

Eason, J. (2017a). *Big house on the prairie: Rise of the rural ghetto and prison proliferation.* Chicago: University of Chicago Press.

Eason, J. (2017b). Prisons as panacea or pariah? The countervailing consequences of the prison boom on the political economy of rural towns. *Social Science,* 6(1), 1–23.

Economist. (2017, August 10). America's cheeriest prison town does not want to lock more people up. *The Economist.*

Editorial. (2007, October 28). The right model for juvenile justice. *The New York Times,* p. 411.

Editorial. (2018a, February 12). New York's parole problem. *The New York Times,* p. 22.

Editorial. (2018b, December 28). A woman's rights. *The New York Times.*

Editorial. (2020, March 1). In Idaho, orange is the new black. *Lewiston Tribune.*

Editors. (2020, July 15). James Byrd, Jr. Biography.com; A&E Television Networks.

Eisen, L. (2017a, December 13). What is the best way to hold private prisons to account? New York: Brennan Center for Justice.

Eisen, L. (2017b, November 6). When a small town's private prison goes bust. New York: The Marshall Project.

Eisen, L. (2018, November 14). Down under, more humane private prisons. *The New York Times.*

Eisenstein, Z. R. (1988). *The female body and the law.* Berkeley: University of California Press.

Ellerbe, H. (1995). *The dark side of Christian history.* San Rafael, CA: Morningstar Books.

Ellison, R. (1986). *Going to the territory.* New York: Random House.

Elias, R. (1993). *Victims still: The political manipulation of crime victims.* Thousand Oaks, CA: Sage.

Elejalde-Ruiz, A. (2019, October 22). Chase open to hiring former criminals. *Chicago Tribune,* sec. 2, pp. 1, 3.

Elkins, S. M. (1976). *Slavery: A problem in American institutional and intellectual life.* Chicago: University of Chicago Press.

Emmer, P., Lowe, A., & Marshall, R. (2011). This is a prison, glitter is not allowed: Experiences of trans and gender variant people in Pennsylvania's prison systems. Philadelphia: The Hearts on A Wire Collective.

Epstein, R., Black, J., & González, T. (2017, June). Girlhood interrupted: The erasure of black girls' childhood. Washington, DC: Georgetown Law Center on Poverty and Inequality.

Equal Justice Initiative. (2017). *Lynching in America: Confronting the legacy of racial terror* (3rd ed.). Montgomery, AL: Author.

Equal Justice Initiative. (2018, November 5). Former guards at North Carolina jail allege abuse and mismanagement. Montgomery, AL: Author.

Equal Justice Initiative. (2020). Death penalty. Montgomery, AL: Author. https://eji.org/issues/death-penalty/

Erdely, S. (2014, July 30). The transgender crucible. *Rolling Stone.*

Escobedo, D. (2004, December 2). Secrets in the schoolhouse. *Independent News.* http://www.inweekly.net/article.asp?artID=713

Eskridge, W. N. (1999). *Gaylaw: Challenging the apartheid of the closet.* Cambridge: Harvard University Press.

Ewing, M. (2017, March 20). What's propelling second-chance legislation across America? Pacific Standard.

Fagan, J. (2006). Death and deterrence redux: Science, law and causal reasoning on capital punishment. *Ohio State Journal of Criminal Law, 4,*255–320.

Fahmy, D. (2018, July 31). Americans are far more religious than adults in other wealthy nations. Washington, DC: Pew Research Center.

FBI. (2020a). Crime in the United States 2019. Clarksburg, WV: Uniform Crime Reports.

FBI. (2020b). Hate crime statistics 2019. Clarksburg, WV: Uniform Crime Reports.

Feeley, M. (1979). *The process is the punishment.* New York: Russell Sage Foundation.

Feld, B. (1999). *Bad kids: Race and the transformation of the juvenile court.* New York: Oxford University Press.

Fellner, J. (1996). Stark racial disparities found in Georgia drug law enforcement. *Overcrowded Times, 7*(5).

Fellner, J., & Mauer, M. (1998). Nearly 4 million Americans denied vote because of felony convictions. *Overcrowded Times, 9*(5).

Finkel, E. (2018, December 1). 2018 guarding report: Changing times for the guarding industry. *Security Magazine.*

Fitz-Gibbon, K., & Walklate, S. (2018). *Gender, crime and criminal justice* (3rd ed.). New York: Routledge.

Fitzpatrick, K., & Myrstol, B. (2011). The jailing of America's homeless: Evaluating the rabble management thesis. *Crime & Delinquency, 57,* 271–297.

Fitzsimons, T. (2019, November 12). Nearly 1 in 5 hate crimes motivated by anti-LGBTQ bias, FBI finds. NBC News.

Fogel, R. W. (1995). *Time on the cross: The economics of American Negro slavery.* New York: W.W. Norton.

Ford, A. (2013, May 2). Florida sheriff reintroduces chain gang. *USA Today.*

Ford, M. (2019, April 5). The everyday brutality of America's prisons. *New Republic.*

Forman, J., Jr. (2012). Racial critiques of mass incarceration: Beyond the new Jim Crow. *New York University Law Review,* 87, 101–146.

Forman, J., Jr. (2018, October 9). How 20 years of stop and search has widened America's racial divide. *The Guardian.*

Foucault, M. (1979). *Discipline and punish: The birth of the prison.* New York: Vintage.

Fowler, S. (2007). *The workhouse: An everyday tale of ultimate degradation.* Surrey, UK: National Archives Press.

Frankel, A. (2020, July). Revoked: How probation and parole feed mass incarceration in the United States. New York: Human Rights Watch and ACLU.

Freedonia Group. (2019). Private security services. Cleveland, OH: Author. https://www.freedoniagroup.com/Private-Security-Services-In-The-Us.html

Freedman, E. (1981). *Their sisters' keepers: Women's prison reform in America, 1830–1930.*Ann Arbor: University of Michigan Press.

Freedman, E. (2013). *Redefining rape: Sexual violence in the era of suffrage and segregation.* Cambridge: Harvard University Press.

Fremont County. (2020). Colorado's correctional capitol. Author. https://www.fremontco.com/colorados-correctional-capitol-fremont-county

French-Marcelin, M., & Hingeer, S. (2017, April). Bullies in blue: The origins and consequences of school policing. New York: American Civil Liberties Union.

Frey, W. (2018, December 17). *Black-white segregation edges downward since 2000, census shows.* Washington, DC: Brookings.

Friedman, L. J. (1970). *The white savage: Racial fantasies in the postbellum South.* Englewood Cliffs, NJ: Prentice-Hall.

Friedrichs, D. O. (2006). Restorative justice and the criminological enterprise. In D. Sullivan & L. Tift (Eds.), *The handbook of restorative justice: A global perspective* (pp. 439–451). New York: Routledge.

Garcia, R. J. (2018, September 3). U.S. prisoners' strike is a reminder how common inmate labor is. CBS News.

Garfinkel, H. (1956). Conditions of successful degradation ceremonies. *American Sociological Review, 61,* 420–424.

Garland, D. (2001). *The culture of control: Crime and social order in contemporary society.* Chicago: University of Chicago Press.

Garrett, B. (2017). *End of its rope: How killing the death penalty can revive criminal justice.* Cambridge: Harvard University Press.

Geiger, A. (2019, June 26). 5 facts about marijuana. Washington, DC: Pew Research Center.

Georges-Abeyie, D. (1990). The myth of a racist criminal justice system? In B. Maclean & D. Milovanovic (Eds.), *Racism, empiricism, and criminal justice.* Vancouver, Canada: Collective Press.

Gertner, N. (2020). Women and sentencing. *American Criminal Law Review, 57:* 1401–1410.

Gibson, R. A. (1979). *The Negro holocaust: Lynching and race riots in the United States, 1880–1950.* New Haven: Yale-New Haven Teachers Institute.

Giddens, A. (1971). *Capitalism and modern social theory.* New York: Cambridge University Press.

Gilmore, R. W. (2007). *Golden gulag: Prisons, surplus, crisis, and opposition in globalizing California.* Berkeley: University of California Press.

Gilna, D. (2018, March). Settlements in Arizona DOC, BOP lawsuits over release debit card fees. *Prison Legal News,* p. 18.

Ginger, J. (Ed.). (1998). *Handel's trumpeter: The diary of John Grano.* (Originally written in 1728.) London: Pendragon Press.

Glassner, B. (2018). *The culture of fear* (updated edition). New York: Basic Books.

Glazer, Y. (1996). The chains may be heavy, but they are not cruel and unusual: Examining the constitutionality of the reintroduced chain gang. *Hofstra Law Review, 24*(4), 1195–1224.

Glionna, J. (2015, August 13). In Colorado's Prison Valley, corrections are a way of life. *Los Angeles Times.*

Goffman, I. (1961). *Asylums.* New York: Doubleday.

Goldfarb, R. (1965). *Ransom: A critique of the American bail system.* New York: Harper & Row.

Goldfarb, R. (1975). *Jails: The ultimate ghetto of the criminal justice system.* New York: Doubleday.

Goldstein, D. (2020, June 12). Some districts remove police from the schools, seeing them as a threat. *The New York Times,* p. A20.

Gomez, L. (2017, October 20). For $1 an hour, inmates fight California fires. *The San Diego Tribune.*

Goode, E. (2013, July 25). U.S. prison populations decline, reflecting new approach to crime. *The New York Times,* p. 11.

Goodland, M. (2020, February 7). Fight over private prisons heats up in Colorado House. *Journal-Advocate.*

Gorman, S. (2019, October 9). California set to end private prison and immigration detention camps. Reuters.

Gotsch, K. (2018, April 24). Families and mass incarceration. Washington, DC: The Sentencing Project.

Gottschalk, M. (2015). *Caught: The prison state and the lockdown of American politics*. Princeton: Princeton University Press.

Gould, E., & Wilson, V. (2020, June 1). Black workers face two of the most lethal preexisting conditions for coronavirus—racism and economic inequality. Washington, DC: Economic Policy Institute.

Gramlich, J. (2019, January 3). 5 facts about crime in the United States. Washington, DC: Pew Research Center.

Gramlich, J. (2020, May 3). Black imprisonment rate in the U.S. has fallen by a third since 2006. Washington, DC: Pew Research Center.

Grant, J., Mottet, L., Tanis, J., Harrison, J., Herman, J., & Keisling, M. (2011). Injustice at every turn: A report of the national transgender discrimination survey. Washington, DC: National Center for Transgender Equality and the National Gay and Lesbian Task Force.

Grattet, R., & Lin, J. (2014). Supervision intensity and parole outcomes: A competing risks approach to criminal and technical parole violations. *Justice Quarterly, 33,* 565–583.

Greenblatt, A. (2019, April 16). Why the death penalty has lost support from both parties. Governing.com

Greenfeld, L. A. (1998, April). Alcohol and crime: An analysis of national data on the prevalence of alcohol involvement in crime. Washington, DC: Bureau of Justice Statistics.

Grooms, J., Ortega, A., & Rubalcaba, J. (2020, August 13). *Economic crises leave vulnerable populations exposed*. Washington, DC: Brookings Institution.

Gross, K. N. (2015). African American women, mass incarceration, and the politics of protection. *The Journal of American History,* doi: 10.1093/jahist/jav226, 25–33.

Grovier, K. (2008). *The Gaol: The story of Newgate—London's most notorious prison.* London: John Murray.

GTL. (2018). GTL's VisitMe Video Visitation Solution. *Global Tel Link.*

Guerino, P., Harrison, P., & Sabol, W. (2011). Prisoners in 2010. Washington, DC: Bureau of Justice Statistics. NCJ 236096.

Guttmacher Institute. (2019, October 1). Substance use during pregnancy. New York: Author.

Haberman, C. (2018, October 2). For private prisons, Detaining immigrants is a big business. *The New York Times*, sec. A, p. 17.

Hager, E. (2017, December 15). A mass incarceration mystery: Why are black imprisonment rates going down? Four theories. New York: The Marshall Project.

Halladay, S. (2007). *Newgate: London's prototype of hell.* London: The History Press.

Hallett, M. (2006). *Private prisons in America: A critical race perspective.* Champaign: University of Illinois Press.

Hamilton, Z., & Campbell, C. (2013). A dark figure of corrections: Failure by way of participation. *Criminal Justice and Behavior, 40,* 180–202.

Hanna, W. (2015). *Varying levels of morality awareness in corrections officers* [Doctoral dissertation, Walden University].

Hannon, L. (2015). White colorism. *Social Currents, 2*, 13–21.

Harding, D., Morenoff, J., Nguyen, A., & Bushway, S. (2017, October). Short- and long-term effects of imprisonment on future felony convictions and prison admissions. Proceedings of the National Academy of Sciences. DOI: 10.1073/pnas.1701544114.

Harki, G. A. (2018). Horrific deaths, brutal treatment: Mental illness in America's jails. *The Virginian-Pilot.* https://www.pilotonline.com/projects/jail-crisis/article_5ba8a112-974e-11e8-ba17-b734814f14db.html-2

Harner, H., Budescu, M., Gillihan, S., Riley, S., & Foa, E. (2015). Posttraumatic stress disorder in incarcerated women: A call for evidence-based treatment. *Psychological Trauma: Theory, Research, Practice, and Policy, 7*(1), 58–66.

Harries, K., & Cheatwood, D. (1997). *The geography of execution: The capital punishment quagmire in America.* Lanham, MD: Rowan and Littlefield.

Harrington, M. (1962). *The other America: Poverty in the United States* (50th anniversary ed.). New York: Touchstone.

Harris, A. (2016). *A pound of flesh: Monetary sanctions as punishment.* New York: Russell Sage Foundation.

Harris, K., Moreno, V., & Rudolph, A. (2019). Re-entry housing issues in Illinois. Chicago: Illinois Justice Project and Metropolitan Planning Council.

Harshbarger, D., & Perry, A. (2019, February 26). *The rise of black-majority cities.* Washington, DC: Brookings.

Hart, A. (2018, September 28). Texas lawmakers are rethinking criminal justice in light of swollen prison population. Kut.org Austin's NPR Station.

Harvard Law Review Association. (1989). The disenfranchisement of ex-felons: Citizenship, criminality, and the purity of the ballot box. *The Harvard Law Review, 102*, 1300–1317.

Haskins, G. L. (1969). A rule to walk by. In R. Quinney (Ed.), *Crime and justice in society* (pp. 33–54). Boston: Little Brown.

Hatchel, T., Espelage, D., & Huang, Y. (2017). Sexual harassment victimization, school belonging, and depressive symptoms among LGBTQ adolescents: Temporal insights. *American Journal of Orthopsychiatry, 88*(4), 422–430.

Haviland, D. (2017, November 15). Grays Harbor County settles ACLU lawsuit over teen solitary confinement. KBKW.

Hay, D., Linebaugh, P., Rule, J., Thompson, E., & Wilslow, C. (Eds.). (1975). *Albion's fatal tree: Crime and society in 18th century England.* New York: Pantheon.

Heaney, S. (1991). *The cure at Troy: Sophocles's* Philoctetes. New York: Farrar, Straus, and Giroux.

Heaton, L., Cantor, D., Bruce, C., Ren, W., Hartge, J., & Beck, A. (2016). Facility-level and individual-level correlates of sexual victimization in juvenile facilities, 2012. Washington, DC: Bureau of Justice Statistics. NCJ 249877

Hedges, C. (2015, April 5). Boycott, divest and sanction corporations that feed on prisons. Truthdig.http://www.truthdig.com/report/item/boycott_divest_and_sanction_corporations_that_feed_on_prisons_20150405

Heilbroner, R. L. (1985). *The nature and logic of capitalism.* New York: W.W. Norton.

Helmer, J. (1975). *Drugs and minority oppression.* New York: Seabury Press.

Herbert, C., Morenoff, J., & Harding, D. (2016). Homelessness and housing insecurity among former prisoners. Bethesda, MD: National Center for Biotechnology Information.

Herman, C. (2018, September 19). County jails struggle to treat mentally ill inmates. NPR, September 19.

Herman, E. (1997). Privatization: Downsizing government for principle and profit. Third World Traveler.

Herrick, J. (2020a, March 7). Centennial South, a Colorado prison shuttered in 2012, reopens. *Colorado Independent.*

Herrick, J. (2020b, February 6). Polis signals he wants private prisons like Kit Carson kept shut. *Colorado Independent.*

Hetey, R., & Eberhardt, J. (2014). Racial disparities in incarceration Increase acceptance of punitive policies. *Psychological Science, 25*(10), 1949–1954.

Hetey, R., & Eberhardt, J. (2018). The numbers don't speak for themselves: Racial disparities and the persistence of inequality in the criminal justice system. *Current Directions in Psychological Science: A Journal of the American Psychological Society, 27*(3), 183–187.

Highsmith, B. (2020, June 2). Defund our punishment bureaucracy. *The American Prospect.*

Hirschtritt, M. E., Dauria, E. F., Marshall, B. D. L, & Tolou-Shams, M. (2018). Sexual minority, justice-involved youth: A hidden population in need of integrated mental health, substance use, and sexual health services. *Journal of Adolescent Health, 63*(4), 421–428.

Hitchcock, D., & Miringoff, M. (2008). Social indicators: The *real* health of the states. *ISSP Insight.*

Ho, V. (2019, June 6). "Outdated and expensive": San Francisco to close juvenile hall in pioneering move. *The Guardian.*

Hoag, A. (2020) Valuing black lives: A case for ending the death penalty. *Columbia Human Rights Law Review, 51*(3), 985–205.

Hockenberry, S. (2020, June). Juveniles in residential placement, 2017. Washington, DC: OJJDP.

Hockenberry, S., & Puzzanchera, C. (2020). Juvenile court statistics 2018. Pittsburgh, PA: National Center for Juvenile Justice.

Hooks, G., Mosher, C., Genter, S., Rotolo, T., & Lobao, L. (2010). Revisiting the impact of prison building on job growth: Education, incarceration, and county-level employment, 1976–2004. *Social Science Quarterly, 91*(1), 228–244.

Hope Rises. (2020). Ten facts about women in prison. Little Rock, AR: Author.

Horn, S. (2019). CoreCivic bilked rural Oklahoma town, forced to pay back money in lawsuit. *Prison Legal News*, p. 60.

Horsley, M. (2014). White-collar crime. In R. Atkinson (Ed.), *Shades of deviance: A primer on crime, deviance and social harm* (pp. 139–142). New York: Routledge.

Huling, T. (2002). Building a prison economy in rural America. In M. Mauer & M. Chesney-Lind (Eds.), *Invisible punishment: The collateral consequences of mass imprisonment* (pp. 197–213). New York: The New Press.

Human Rights Watch. (2014, February 5). Profiting from probation: America's "offender-funded" probation industry. New York: Author.

Hussey, H. (2015). Beyond 4 walls and a roof: Addressing homelessness among transgender youth. Washington, DC: Center for American Progress.

Hutchison, E. D. (2017). *Essentials of human behavior: Integrating person environment, and the life course* (2nd ed.). Thousand Oaks, CA: Sage.

Hyland, S. (2019, November 7). Justice expenditure and employment extracts, 2016–Preliminary. Washington, DC: Bureau of Justice Statistics.

Ignatieff, M. (1978). *A just measure of pain*. New York: Pantheon.

Illinois Justice Project and the Metropolitan Planning Council. (2019, July). Re-entry housing issues in Illinois: The current situation, challenges, and possible solutions. Chicago: Authors.

Independent Lens. (2017, May 5). The prison economy: How do prisons affect the places we live? PBS.

International Commission of Jurists. (1997). Administration of the death penalty in the United States. *Human Rights Quarterly 19*(1), 165–213.

Irvine-Baker, A., Jones, N., & Canfield, A. (2019). Taking the "girl" out of gender-responsive programming in the juvenile justice system. *Annual Review of Criminology, 2*(1), 321–336.

Irwin, J. (1985). *The jail: Managing the underclass in American society*. Berkeley: University of California Press.

Ishay, M. R. (Ed.). (1997). *The human rights reader*. New York: Routledge.

Jackson, T. A. (2017). Dilution of the black vote: Revisiting the oppressive methods of voting rights restoration for ex-felons. *University of Miami Race & Social Justice Law Review, 7*, 81–106.

James, M. (2020, January 23). What a landmark LGBTQ case reveals about two clashing visions of America. *Time.*

James, S., Herman, J., Rankin, S., Keisling, M., Mottet, L., & Anafi, M. (2016). The report of the 2015 U.S. transgender survey. Washington, DC: National Center for Transgender Equality.

Janos, A. (2019, April 29). The offenders behind 3 court cases that changed lifetime imprisonment laws for juveniles. A&E Television Networks.

Jardine, C. (2018). Eroding legitimacy? The impact of imprisonment on the relationships between families, communities, and the criminal justice system. In R. Condry & P. Scharff Smith (Eds.), *Prisons, punishment, and the family* (pp. 167–181). Oxford: Oxford University Press.

Jessie, B. O. (2020). *On the patio: Serving time in a women's correctional facility*. Long Grove, IL: Waveland Press.

Johnson, A. (2019, August 25). Ex-sheriff Joe Arpaio, pardoned by Trump, wants his old job back. NBCnews.com

Johnson, C. (2001). *Blowback: The costs and consequences of American empire*. New York: Metropolitan/Owl Books.

Johnson, C. (2014, September 26). California bans coerced sterilization of female inmates. Emeryville, CA: The Center for Investigative Reporting.

Johnson, R. (1998). *Death work: A study of the modern execution process* (2nd ed.). Belmont, CA: Wadsworth.

Johnson, R., Rocheleau, A., & Martin, A. (2017). *Hard time: A fresh look at understanding and reforming the prison* (4th ed.). Malden, MA: Wiley.

Johnson, S., & Beletsky, L. (2020, May). Helping people transition from incarceration to society during a pandemic. Northeastern University School of Law Research Paper No. 375-2020.

Johnson, S., Blum, R., & Giedd, J. (2009). Adolescent maturity and the brain: The promise and pitfalls of neuroscience research in adolescent health policy. *Journal of Adolescent Health, 45*(3), 216–221.

Johnston, N. (2009). Prison reform in Pennsylvania. The Pennsylvania Prison Society.

Jones, A. (2018, December). Correctional control 2018. Northampton, MA: Prison Policy Initiative.

Jones, J. (2019, November 25). Americans now support life in prison over death penalty. Gallup.com

Joyce, K. (2011, August). Horror stories from tough-love teen homes. *Mother Jones.*

Joyce, K., & Mechanic, M. (2011, August). Survivor snapshots from teen-home hell. *Mother Jones.*

Juvenile Law Center. (2010, January 15). Lessons from Luzerne County: Promoting fairness, transparency and accountability. Philadelphia: Author.

Kaba, F., Lewis, A., Glowa-Kollisch, S., Hadler, J., Lee, D., Alper, H., Selling, D., MacDonald, R., Solimo, A., Parsons, A., & Venters, H. (2014). Solitary confinement and risk of self-harm among jail inmates. *American Journal of Public Health, 104*(3), 442–447.

Kaeble, D., & Alper, M. (2020, August). Probation and parole in the United States, 2017–2018. Washington, DC: Bureau of Justice Statistics. NCJ 252072.

Kaeble, D., & Cowhig, M. (2018, April). Correctional populations in the United States, 2016. Washington, DC: Bureau of Justice Statistics. NCJ 251211.

Kahle, L., & Rosenbaum, J. (2019). Making gender-responsive programming more queer responsive. *Women, Crime, and Justice,* DOI: 10.1093/acrefore/9780190264079.013.532.

Kahle, L., & Rosenbaum, J. (2020). What staff need to know: Using elements of gender-responsive programming to create safer environments for system-involved LGBTQ girls and women. *Criminal Justice Studies,* DOI: 10.1080/1478601X.2020.1786281.

Kajstura, A. (2019, October 29). Women's mass incarceration: The whole pie 2019. Northampton, MA: Prison Policy Initiative.

Kappeler, V., & Potter, G. (2018). *The mythology of crime and criminal justice* (5th ed.). Long Grove, IL: Waveland Press.

Karakatsanis, A. (2019). The punishment bureaucracy: How to think about "criminal justice reform." The *Yale Law Journal* Forum, pp. 848–935.

Keefe Group. (2020). https://www.keefegroup.com/home-100

Kennedy, D., & Wong, S. (2012). The High Point drug market intervention strategy. Washington, DC: Office of Community Oriented Policing Services.

Kennedy, J., Unah, I., & Wahlers, K. (2018). Sharks and minnows in the war on drugs: A study of quantity, race, and drug type in drug arrests. *UC Davis Law Review,* 52, 729–801.

Kennedy, R. (1997). *Race, crime and the law.* New York: Vintage.

Kilborn, P. T. (2001, August 1). Rural towns turn to prisons to reignite their economies. *The New York Times.*

Kim, C. (2019a, June 27). Bank of America cuts ties with the private prison industry. Vox.

Kim, C. (2019b, December 1). Private prisons face an uncertain future as states turn their backs on the industry. Vox. https://www.vox.com/policy-and-politics/2019/12/1/20989336/private-prisons-states-bans-califonia-nevada-colorado

King, B. A., & Erickson, L. (2016). Disenfranchising the enfranchised: Exploring the relationship between felony disenfranchisement and African American voter turnout. *Journal of Black Studies, 47*(8), 799–821.

King, R., Mauer, M., & Huling, T. (2003, February). Big prisons, small towns: Prison economics in rural America. Washington, DC: The Sentencing Project.

Kinsey, A., Pomeroy, W., & Martin, C. (1948). *Sexual behavior in the human male.* Philadelphia: Saunders.

Knappman, E. W. (1994). *Great American trials: From Salem witchcraft to Rodney King*. Detroit: Visible Ink Press.

Kochanek, K., Murphy, S., Xu, J., & Arias, E. (2019, June 24). Deaths: Final data for 2017. *National Vital Statistics Reports, 68*(9). Hyattsville, MD: National Center for Health Statistics.

Kohler-Hausmann, J. (2019). *Getting tough: Welfare and imprisonment in 1970s America.* Princeton: Princeton University Press.

Kolchin, P., & Foner, E. (1995). *American slavery, 1619–1877*. London: Penguin Books.

Kreager, D., & Kruttschnitt, C. (2018). Inmate society in the era of mass incarceration. *Annual Review of Criminology, 1*(1), 16.1–16.23.

Kretschmar, J., Butcher, F., Flannery, D., & Singer, M. (2014). Diverting juvenile justice-involved youth with behavioral health issues from detention: Preliminary findings from Ohio's Behavioral Health Juvenile Justice (BHJJ) Initiative. *Criminal Justice Policy Review, 27*, 302–325.

Krimsky, M., & Foster, L. (2019, January 4). Eliminate court fines and fees that penalize poverty. *USA Today*.

Krisberg, B. (2005). *Juvenile justice: Redeeming our children.* Thousand Oaks, CA: Sage.

Krugman, P. (2007). *The conscience of a liberal*. New York: W.W. Norton.

Krysan, M., & Crowder, K. (2017). *Cycle of segregation*. New York: The Russell Sage Foundation.

Kuhn, T. (2012). *The structure of scientific revolutions* (50th Anniversary Edition, originally published in 1962). Chicago: University of Chicago Press.

Kushner, R. (2019, April 17). Is prison necessary? Ruth Wilson Gilmore might change your mind. *The New York Times Magazine,* p. 37.

Kuttner, R. (2015). *Debtors' prison: The politics of austerity versus possibility.* New York: Vintage Books.

Lab, S. (2020). *Crime prevention: Approaches, practices, and evaluations* (10th ed.). New York: Routledge.

LaChance, D. (2016). *Executing freedom: The cultural life of capital punishment in the United States*. Chicago: University of Chicago Press.

Lakoff, G. (2016). *Moral politics: How liberals and conservatives think*. Chicago: University of Chicago Press.

Lambda Legal. (2015). Protected and served? New York: Author.

Land, K., Teske, R., Jr., & Zheng, H. (2012). The differential short-term impacts of executions on felony and non-felony homicides. *Criminology and Public Policy, 11*(3), 541–563.

Landis, T. (2002, June 1). Hard time: Illinois is among those states looking for ways to downsize the prison industry. NPR Illinois. https://www.nprillinois.org/post/hard-time-illinois-among-those-states-looking-ways-downsize-prison-industry#stream/0

Law, V. (2019, May 21). When abuse victims commit crimes. *The Atlantic*.

Lawrence, S., & Travis, J. (2004). The new landscape of imprisonment: Mapping America's prison expansion. Washington, DC: Urban Institute.

LeFlouira, T. (2016). *Chained in silence: Black women and convict labor in the New South*. Chapel Hill: The University of North Carolina Press.

Legal Dictionary. (2015, December 6). Inalienable rights.

Lemert, E. (1951). *Social pathology*. New York: McGraw-Hill.

Lepore, J. (2009, April 13). I.O.U. How we used to treat debtors. *The New Yorker*. http://www.newyorker.com/reporting/2009/04/13/090413fa_fact_lepore#ixzz0Xp2NZDFq

Levin, D. (2019, December 28). As more mothers fill prisons, children suffer "a primal wound." *The New York Times*, sec. A, p. 14.

Levin, S. (2020, May 20). "People are sick all around me": Inside the coronavirus catastrophe in California prisons. *The Guardian*.

Levinson, J., Smith, R., & Young, D. (2014). Devaluing death: An empirical study of implicit racial bias on jury-eligible citizens in six death penalty states. *New York University Law Review, 89*(2), 513–581.

Lewis, W. D. (2009). *From Newgate to Dannemora: The rise of the penitentiary in New York, 1796–1848*. Ithaca, NY: Cornell University Press (originally published in 1965).

Lieber, D. (2016, April). Watchdog: Pay-or-go-to-jail policy makes probation officers bill collectors. *The Dallas Morning News*. https://www.dallasnews.com/news/watchdog/2016/04/01/watchdog-pay-or-go-to-jail-policy-makes-probation-officers-bill-collectors

Liebman, J., Fagan, J., & West, V. (2000). A broken system: Error rates in capital cases, 1973–1995. Columbia Law School, Public Law Research Paper No. 15.

Liebowitz, S., Eliasberg, P., Winter, M., & Lim, E. (2011, September). Cruel and usual punishment: How a savage gang of deputies controls LA county jails. Los Angeles: ACLU of Southern California and Washington, DC: ACLU National Prison Project.

Liptak, A. (2019, April 2). Death penalty ruling bares friction on Supreme Court. *The New York Times*, sec. A, p. 20.

Lithwick, D. (2002, July 3). Urinalysis: The Supreme Court's torturous justification of high-school urine tests. Slate.com. http://www.slate.com/id/2067710/

Lithwick, D. (2012, March 5). Extreme makeover: The story behind the story of *Lawrence v. Texas*. *The New Yorker*.

Lockhart, P. R. (2019, July 2). Florida faces an intense legal battle over restoring former felons' voting rights. Vox.

Longley, R. (2019, July 28). What you should know about the prison industrial complex. New York: ThoughtCo. https://www.thoughtco.com/what-you-should-know-about-the-prison-industrial-complex-4155637

Lopez, G. (2020a, September 18). The state of ex-felon's voting rights, explained. Vox.com.

Lopez, G. (2020b, April 22). Why US jails and prisons became coronavirus epicenters. Vox.com.

Love, M., & Schlussel, D. (2020). The many roads to reintegration: A 50-state report on laws restoring rights and opportunities after arrest or conviction. Collateral Consequences Resource Center.

Low, S. (2003). *Behind the gates: Life, security, and the pursuit of happiness in fortress America*. New York: Routledge.

Low, S. (2017). *Spatializing culture: The ethnography of space and place*. New York: Routledge.

Lozano, J. (2020, April 21). Doctors: Execution drugs could help COVID-19 patients. USnews.com

Lyon, E. (2019, February 4). Imprisoning America's mentally ill. *Prison Legal News*.

Lyons, K. (2019, November 4). U.S. Department of Justice investigating conditions at Manson Youth Institute. *The CT Mirror*.

Macallair, D. E. (2015). *After the doors were locked: A history of youth corrections in California and the origins of twenty-first century reform*. Lanham, Maryland: Rowman & Littlefield.

Macallair, D. E., & Males, M. (2004). A failure of good intentions: An analysis of juvenile justice reform in San Francisco during the 1990s. *Review of Policy Research, 21,* 63–78.

MacBride, E. (2018, December 29). AI security camera software aims for $5 billion threat detection market. *Forbes.*

Magliocca, G., Bingham, G., & Bingham, J. (2013). *American founding son: John Bingham and the invention of the Fourteenth Amendment.* New York: New York University Press.

Mai, C., Belaineh, M., Subramanian, R., & Kang-Brown, J. (2019, November). Broken ground: Why America keeps building more jails and what it can do instead. New York: Vera Institute of Justice.

Majd, K., Marksamer, J., & Reyes, C. (2009). *Hidden injustice: Lesbian, gay, bisexual, and transgender youth in juvenile courts.* Washington, DC: National Juvenile Defender Center, The Equity Project.

Mallett, C. (2003). Socio-historical analysis of juvenile offenders on death row. *Criminal Law Bulletin, 39*(4), 455–468.

Mallett, C. (2016). *The school-to-prison pipeline: A comprehensive assessment.* New York: Springer Publishing.

Mallory, C., Hasenbush, A., & Sears, B. (2015). *Discrimination and harassment by law enforcement officers in the LGBT community.* Los Angeles: The Williams Institute.

Mancini, M. J. (1978). Race, economics, and the abandonment of convict leasing. *Journal of Negro History, 63*(4), 339–352.

Mancini, M. J. (1996). *One man dies, get another: Convict leasing in the American South, 1866–1928.* Chapel Hill: University of North Carolina Press.

Manza, J., & Uggen, C. (2006). *Locked out: Felon disenfranchisement and American democracy.* New York: Oxford University Press.

Marksamer, J., & Tobin, H. (2014). Standing with LGBT Prisoners: An advocate's guide to ending abuse and combating imprisonment. Washington, DC: National Center for Transgender Equality.

Marquart, J., & Sorensen, J. (1988). Institutional and post-release behavior of *Furman*-commuted inmates in Texas. *Criminology, 26,* 677–693.

Marrett, S. (2015). Beyond punishment: Constitutional violations associated with the isolation and discrimination of transgender youth in the juvenile justice system. *Boston College Law Review, 58,* 351–378.

Marshall, J. (2018, August 22). The world's most committed Christians live in Africa, Latin America—and the U.S. Washington, DC: Pew Research Center.

Martin, K., Smith, S., & Still, W. (2017). Shackled to debt: Criminal justice financial obligations and the barriers to re-entry they create. Laurel, MD: National Institute of Justice.

Martinson, R. L. (1974). What works?—Questions and answers about prison reform. *The Public Interest, 35,* 22–54.

Maruschak, L., & Minton, T. (2020, August). Correctional populations in the United States, 2017–2018. Washington, DC: Bureau of Justice Statistics. NCJ 252127.

Marx, K. (1977). *Capital.* New York: Vintage Books.

Maselli, C. (2019). *The new debtor's prison: Why all Americans are in danger of losing their freedom.* New York: Skyhorse Publishing.

Massey, D., & Denton, N. (1998). *American apartheid: Segregation and the making of the Underclass.* Cambridge: Harvard University Press.

Masur, L. P. (1989). *Rites of execution: Capital punishment and the transformation of American culture, 1776–1865.* New York: Oxford University Press.

Matthews, C. (2020, May 1). America's Covid-19 hot spots shed a light on our moral failures. Vox.

Mauer, M. (2001). The causes and consequences of prison growth in the United States. *Punishment and Society, 3*, 9–20.

Maxwell, S. (2018, June 6). Florida spends too much money jailing people awaiting trial on petty crimes. *TC Palm*.

May, R. (Director). (2014). *Kids for Cash* (documentary). FilmBuff.

Mays, D. A. (2004). *Women in early America: Struggle, survival, and freedom in a new world*. Santa Barbara, CA: ABC-CLIO.

Mazareanu, E. (2019, August 28). Security services industry in the U.S.—Statistics & Facts. Statista.

McCarthy, N. (2017, August 31). Private security outnumbers the police in most countries worldwide. *Forbes*.

McCarthy, P., Schiraldi, V., & Shark, M. (2016). The future of youth justice: A community-based alternative to the youth prison model. National Institute of Justice, NCJ 250142.

McCauley E., & Brinkley-Rubinstein, L. (2017). Institutionalization and incarceration of LGBT individuals. In K. Eckstrand & J. Potter (Eds.), *Trauma, resilience, and health promotion in LGBT patients* (pp. 149–161). New York: Springer.

McCauley, E., Eckstrand, K., Desta, B., Bouvier, B., Brockmann, B., & Brinkley-Rubinstein, L. (2018). Exploring healthcare experiences for incarcerated individuals who identify as transgender in a southern jail. *Transgender Health, 3*(1), 34–41.

McClain, D. (2015, July 2). Black women vilified as a "lesbian wolf pack" speak for themselves in a new film. *The Nation*.

McClanahan, W., Kauh, T., Manning, A., Campos, P., & Farley, C. (2012). Illuminating solutions: The youth violence reduction partnership. New York: Public/Private Ventures Issue Lab.

McConville, S. (1995). Local justice: The jail. In N. Morris & D. Rothman (Eds.), *The Oxford history of the prison: The practice of punishment in Western society* (pp. 297–327). New York: Oxford University Press.

McCormack, S. (2012, December 10). Prison labor booms as unemployment remains high: Companies reap profits. Huffpost News.

McCormick, S., Peterson-Badali, M., & Skilling, T. (2017). The role of mental health and specific responsivity in juvenile justice rehabilitation. *Law and Human Behavior, 41*(1), 55–67.

McCue, J. (2019, January 31). Home security cameras market to surpass $9.7 billion by 2023. *Forbes*.

McGraw, J. (2017, February 28). Former Elk Grove cop sues over treatment as a gay officer. CBS Sacramento.

McKelvey, B. (1968). *American prisons*. Montclair, NJ: Patterson Smith (originally published 1936).

McKernan, P. (2018). Homelessness and prisoner re-entry. Alexandria, VA: Volunteers of America.

McLeod, A. (2015). Prison abolition and grounded justice. *UCLA Law Review, 62*(5), 1156–1239.

Meadows, M. (2019, October 19). Wheelwright prison to re-open. *The Paintsville Herald*.

Meagher, T., & Thompson, C. (2016, June 14). *So you think a new prison will save your town?* New York: The Marshall Project.

Mears, B. (2009, January 16). Court to hear case of teen strip-searched for ibuprofen. CNN.

Meares, T. (1996, February). For many, commercializing the chain gang is akin to commercializing slavery. *The University of Chicago Magazine.* https://magazine.uchicago.edu/9602/9602Voices.html

Medwed, D. (2020, January 28). Black deaths matter: The race-of-victim effect and capital punishment. Northeastern University School of Law Research Paper No. 367-2020.

Mendel, R. A. (2010) The Missouri model: Reinventing the practice of rehabilitating youthful offenders. Baltimore, MD: The Annie E. Casey Foundation.

Mennel, R. M. (1973). *Thorns and thistles: Juvenile delinquents in the U.S., 1820–1940.* Hanover, NH: University Press of New England.

Mettler, K. (2017, April 5). New sheriff in town to close Joe Arpaio's outdoor tent city jail, of pink underwear fame. *The Washington Post.*

Metz, N. (2020, February 13). No badge of honor for many cop shows. *Chicago Tribune,* sec. 4, pp. 1–3.

Midgette, G., Davenport, S., Caulkins, J., & Kilmer, B. (2019) What America's users spend on illegal drugs, 2006–2016. Santa Monica, CA: RAND Corporation.

Miethe, T., & Lu, H. (2005). *Punishment: A comparative historical perspective.* New York: Cambridge University Press.

Miller, J. (1996). *Search and destroy: African American males in the criminal justice system.* New York: Cambridge University Press.

Miller, J. (1998). *Last one over the wall* (2nd ed.). Columbus: Ohio State University Press.

Mitchum, P., & Moodie-Mills, A. (2014, February). Beyond bullying: How hostile school climate perpetuates the school-to-prison pipeline for LGBT youth. Washington, DC: Center for American Progress.

Miranda, L., Dixon, V., & Reyes, C. (2015, September 30). How states handle drug use during pregnancy. Propublica.

Mogul, J., Ritchie, A., & Whitlock, K. (2011). *Queer (in)justice: The criminalization of LGBT people in the United States.* Boston: Beacon Press.

Monocchio, R., & Burns, C. (2019, September 30). From jail to an apartment: Secure housing is key for those pulling their lives back together. *Chicago Tribune,* p. 14.

Moore, L. (2016). Women, property, and the law in the Anglo-American world, 1630–1700. *Early American Studies: An Interdisciplinary Journal, 14*(3), 537–567.

Morgan, E. S. (1975). *American slavery, American freedom.* New York: W.W. Norton.

Morlock, T. (2017). *LGBTQ human rights movement.* New York, PowerKids Press.

Morris, E., & Perry, B. (2017). Girls behaving badly? Race, gender, and subjective evaluation in the discipline of African American girls. *Sociology of Education, 90*(2), 127–148.

Morrison, A., & Ben-Menachem, J. (2019, June 11). A troubled Virginia jail looks to add guards, but advocates push for decarceration. The Appeal.

Morrison, A., & Sedensky, M. (2020, June 5). The fallout from the death of George Floyd. *Chicago Tribune,* pp. 1, 7.

Mountz, S. (2016). That's the sound of the police: State-sanctioned violence and resistance among LGBT young people previously incarcerated in girls' juvenile justice facilities. *Affilia, 31*(3), 287–302.

Moynhan, J., & Stewart, E. (1990). *The American jail: Its development and growth.* Chicago: Nelson-Hall.

Murch, D. (2015). Historicizing Ferguson: Police violence, domestic warfare, and the genesis of a national movement against state-sanctioned violence. *New Politics, 15*(3), 5–16.

Murphey, D., & Cooper, P. (2015, October). Parents behind bars: What happens to their children? Washington, DC: ChildTrends, publication #2015-42.

Myers, M. (1998). *Race, labor and punishment in the New South*. Columbus: Ohio State University Press.

Naeger, J. (2004). And then there were none: The repeal of sodomy laws after *Lawrence v. Texas* and its effect on the custody and visitation rights of gay and lesbian parents. *St. John's Law Review, 78*(2): 397–425.

Natapoff, A. (2017). The penal pyramid. In S. Dolovich & A. Natapoff (Eds.), *The new criminal justice thinking* (pp. 71–98). New York: NYU Press.

Natapoff, A. (2018). *Punishment without crime: How our massive misdemeanor system traps the innocent and makes America more unequal*. New York: Basic Books.

National Center for Transgender Equality. (2012, July). LGBT people and the Prison Rape Elimination Act. Washington, DC: Author.

National Registry of Exonerations. (2020). http://www.law.umich.edu/special/exoneration/Pages/Exoneration-by-Year-Crime-Type.aspx

National Resource Center on Justice-Involved Women. (2016). Fact sheet on justice involved women in 2016. Washington, DC: Author.

Neff, J., & Santo, A. (2019, June 26). Corporate confession: Gangs ran this private prison. New York: The Marshall Project.

Nellis, A. (2016). The color of justice: Racial and ethnic disparity in state prisons. Washington, DC: The Sentencing Project.

Newkirk, V. R., II. (2019, September). This land was our land. *The Atlantic Monthly, 324*, 74–85.

Newman, G. (2008). *The punishment response* (2nd ed.). New York: Routledge.

Norton, J. (2018, April 19). Life and jail in southern Colorado. New York: Vera Institute of Justice.

Nussbaum, M. (2010). Mill's feminism: Liberal, radical and queer. In G. Varouxakis & P. Kelly (Eds.), *John Stuart Mill—Thought and influence: The saint of rationalism* (pp. 130–145). New York: Routledge.

Oakford, P., Brumfield, C., Goldvale, C., Tatum, L., diZerega, M., & Patrick, F. (2019). Investing in futures: Economic and fiscal benefits of postsecondary education in prison. New York: Vera Institute of Justice.

OJJDP Statistical Briefing Book. (2020, May 15). One day count of juveniles in residential placement facilities, 1997–2018. https://www.ojjdp.gov/ojstatbb/corrections/qa08201.asp?qaDate=2018

Office of Minority Health. (2017, November 9). Infant mortality and African Americans. Rockville, MD: Author.

Oliver, L. (2015). W. E. B. Du Bois, Charlotte Perkins Gilman, and a suggestion on the Negro problem. *American Literary Realism, 48*(1), 25–39.

Ortiz, A. (2020, January 16). Former L.A. county sheriff is ordered to prison for obstruction of justice. *The New York Times*.

Osgood, R. K. (1984). John Clark, Esq., Justice of the Peace, 1667–1728. In D. R. Coquillette (Ed.), *Law in colonial Massachusetts* (pp. 106–151). Charlottesville: University Press of Virginia.

Oshinsky, D. M. (1996). *Worse than slavery: Parchman Farm and the ordeal of Jim Crow*. Detroit: Free Press.

Palacios, L. (2017, February 17). The Prison Rape Elimination Act and the limits of liberal reform. The Gender Policy Report.

Palast, G. (2000). *The best democracy money can buy.* New York: Penguin Books.

Paltrow, L., & Flavin, J. (2013). Arrests of and forced interventions on pregnant women in the United States, 1973–2005: Implications for women's legal status and public health. *Journal of Health Politics, Policy and Law, 38,* 299–343.

Pasulka, N. (2015, June 30). How 4 gay black women fought back against sexual harassment—And landed in jail. NPR.

Pasulka, N. (2016, March 17). The criminal black lesbian: Where does this damaging stereotype come from? WBUR News, NPR.

Paton, E., & Zarate, A. (2019, February 24). Made on the inside, worn on the outside. *The New York Times*, sec. BU, p. 1.

Patterson, H., & Conrad, E. (1950). *Scottsboro boy.* New York: Doubleday.

Patterson, O. (2020, June 6–7). The long reach of racism in the United States. *The Wall Street Journal*, pp. C1, C2.

PCSO Media Center. (2010). PCSO chain gang program has multiple benefits for community. Pueblo, CO: Pueblo County Sheriff's Office.

Pauly, M. (2019, February 6). Mississippi's prison bribery scandal is in the past, but the state still hasn't learned its lesson. *Mother Jones.*

Pearl, B. (2018, June 27). Ending the war on drugs: By the numbers. Washington, DC: Center for American Progress.

Pearl, B., & Perez, M. (2018, June 27). Ending the war on drugs. Washington, DC: Center for American Progress.

Peternelj-Taylor, C. (2008). Criminalization of the mentally ill. *Journal of Forensic Nursing, 4,* 185–187.

Petersilia, J. (2009). *When prisoners come home: Parole and prisoner reentry.* New York: Oxford University Press.

Petersilia, J., & Threatt, J. (2017). Release from prison. In K. R. Kerley (Ed.), *The encyclopedia of corrections.* Hoboken, NJ: John Wiley & Sons.

Petrosino, A., Campie, P., Pace, J., Fronius, T., Guckenburg, S., Wiatrowski, M., & Rivera, L. (2015). Cross-sector, multi-agency interventions to address urban youth firearms violence: A rapid evidence assessment. *Aggression and Violent Behavior, 22,* 87–96.

Petrosky, E., Blair, J., Betz, C., Fowler, K., Jack, S., & Lyons, B. (2017). Racial and ethnic differences in homicides of adult women and the role of intimate partner violence—United States, 2003–2014. *MMWR. Morbidity and Mortality Weekly Report, 66*(28), 741.

Petrow, S. (2014, May 23). Civilities: What does the acronym "LGBTQ" stand for? *The Washington Post.*

Pettit, B., & Sykes, B. (2017). Incarceration. Palo Alto: Stanford Center on Poverty and Inequality.

PEW Charitable Trusts. (2018, September 25). Probation and parole systems marked by high stakes, missed opportunities. Philadelphia: Author.

PEW Charitable Trusts. (2020, April). Policy Reforms Can Strengthen Community Supervision A framework to improve probation and parole. Philadelphia: Author.

Pfaff, J. (2017). *Locked in: The true causes of mass incarceration.* New York: Basic Books.

Phelps, M. (2020). Mass probation from micro to macro: Tracing the expansion and consequences of community supervision. *Annual Review of Criminology, 3,* 261–279.

Phillips, E. (2014, June 6). DOJ says Los Angeles County jails violating constitutional requirements. *Wall Street Journal.*

Phillips, M. B. (1991). A hedgehog proposal. *Crime and Delinquency, 37,* 555–574.

Piaggio, A., & Vidwans, P. (2019, August 7). The costs and consequences of the war on drugs. New York: Human Rights Foundation.

Picard-Fritsche, S., Rempel, M., Tallon, J., Adler, J., & Reyes, N. (2017). Demystifying risk assessment: Key principles and controversies. New York: Center for Court Innovation.

Pickett, R. (1969). *House of refuge.* Syracuse: Syracuse University Press.

Pierce, G., Radelet, M., & Sharp, S. (2017). Race and death sentencing for Oklahoma homicides committed between 1990 and 2012. *Journal of Criminal Law & Criminology, 107*(4), 733–756

Pilkington, E. (2015, October 21). Pay up or go to jail: How a Mississippi town resurrected the debtors' prison. *The Guardian.*

Pisciotta, A. (1982). Saving the children: The promise and practice of *Parens Patriae,* 1838–98. *Crime and Delinquency, 28,* 410–425.

Piven, F., & Cloward, R. (1972). *Regulating the poor: The functions of social welfare.* New York: Vintage Books.

Platoff, E., & Greene, S. (2018, June 26). Fifteen years after landmark gay rights case, same-sex couples in Texas still face challenges in court. *The Texas Tribune.*

Polantz, K. (2020, March 31). Inmates sue for soap and paper towels as coronavirus spreads in jails. CNN.

Polkey, C. (2019, July 30). Most states have ended SNAP ban for convicted drug felons. Washington, DC: National Conference of State Legislatures.

Pollock, J. M. (1996). Gender, justice, and social control: A historical perspective. In A. V. Merlo & J. M. Pollock (Eds.), *Women, law, and social control.* New York: Allyn & Bacon.

Porter, N. (2020, May 7). Voting in jails. Washington, DC: The Sentencing Project.

Poteat, V., Scheer, J., & Chong, E. (2016). Sexual orientation-based disparities in school and juvenile justice discipline: A multiple group comparison of contributing factors. *Journal of Educational Psychology, 108*(2), 229–241.

Potter, R., Lin, H., Maze, A., & Bjoring, D. (2011). The health of jail inmates: The role of jail population "flow" in community health. *Criminal Justice Review, 36*(4), 470–486.

Powell, J. C. (1891). *The American Siberia.* Chicago: H.J. Smith.

President's Commission on Law and Administration of Justice. (1967a). *The challenge of crime in a free society.* Washington, DC: U.S. Government Printing Office.

President's Commission on Law and Administration of Justice. (1967b). Task force report: Corrections. Washington, DC: U.S. Government Printing Office.

Primeau, A., Bowers, T., Harrison, M., & Xu, X. (2013). Deinstitutionalization of the mentally ill: Evidence for transinstitutionalization from psychiatric hospitals to penal institutions. *Comprehensive Psychology, 2,* 1–10.

Prison Policy Initiative. (2018, February 7). Census bureau will count incarcerated people in the wrong place once again in 2020 Census, continues to distort democracy. Northampton, MA: Author.

Prison Policy Initiative. (2019a, May 14). Policing women: Race and gender disparities in police stops, searches, and use of force. Northampton, MA: Author.

Prison Policy Initiative. (2019b, April 25). Prison populations and the Census. Northampton, MA: Author.

Prison Policy Initiative. (2020a). Prison and jail visitation: Major victories. Northampton, MA: Author.

Prison Policy Initiative. (2020b, June 16). Responses to the COVID-19 pandemic. Northampton, MA: Author.

Provost, C. (2017, May 12). The industry of inequality: Why the world is obsessed with private security. *The Guardian.*

Pyke, A. (2019, August 26). The DEA just made a huge change to how the government treats medical marijuana. ThinkProgress.

Quinney, R. (1970). *The social reality of crime.* Boston: Little, Brown.

Quinney, R. (1991). The way of peace. In H. E. Pepinsky & R. Quinney (Eds.), *Criminology as peacemaking.* Bloomington: Indiana University Press.

Quinney, R. (2000). *Bearing witness to crime and social justice.* Albany: State University of New York Press.

Quinney, R. (2006). The life inside: Abolishing the prison. *Contemporary Justice Review, 9*(3), 269–275.

Rable, G. C. (1985). The South and the politics of anti-lynching legislation, 1920–1940. *Journal of Southern History, 51,* 201–220.

Radelet, M. L. (1989). Executions of whites for crimes against blacks: Exceptions to the rule? *The Sociological Quarterly, 30,* 529–544.

Radelet, M., & Cohn, B. (2019). The decline of the judicial override. *Annual Review of Law and Social Science, 15,* 539–557.

Radelet, M., Bedau, H., & Putnam, C. (1992). *In spite of innocence: Erroneous convictions in capital cases.* Boston: Northeastern University Press.

Rafter, N. H. (1990). *Partial justice: Women, prisons, and social control* (2nd ed.). New Brunswick, NJ: Transaction Books.

Raper, A. A. (1933). *The tragedy of lynching.* Chapel Hill: University of North Carolina Press.

Reed, J. S. (1968). An evaluation of an anti-lynching organization. *Social Problems, 16,* 172–182.

Reiman, J., & Leighton, P. (2020). *The rich get richer and the poor get prison: Thinking critically about class and criminal justice* (12th ed.). New York: Routledge.

Reinarman, C., & Levine, H. (Eds.). (1997). *Crack in America: Demon drugs and social justice.* Berkeley: University of California Press.

Renaud, J. (2019, February 26). Grading the parole release systems of all 50 states. Northampton, MA: Prison Policy Initiative.

Rendleman, D. (1979). *Parens patriae*: From chancery to juvenile court. In F. Faust & P. Brantingham (Eds.), *Juvenile justice philosophy* (2nd ed.). St. Paul, MN: West.

Reynolds, G. H. (2018, August 7). The next step in criminal justice reform is fewer laws. *USA Today.*

Rhine, E., Mitchell, K., & Reitz, K. (2019). *Levers of change in parole release and revocation.* Minneapolis: Robina Institute of Criminal Law and Criminal Justice.

Right on Crime. (2019). Prisons. http://rightoncrime.com/category/priority-issues/prisons/

Rios, V. M. (2009). The consequences of the criminal justice pipeline on black and Latino masculinity. *The ANNALS of the American Academy of Political and Social Science, 623*(1), 150–162.

Rippey, S. (2020). Incarcerated parents and child welfare in Washington. *Washington Law Review, 95:* 531–554.

Ritchie, A. (2017). *Invisible no more: Police violence against Black women and women of color.* Boston: Beacon Press.

Roberts, D. (2019, November 8). Abolition constitutionalism. *Harvard Law Review, 133*(1), 1–122.

Roberts, A., & Willits, D. (2015). Income inequality and homicide in the United States: Consistency across different income inequality measures and disaggregated homicide types. *Homicide Studies, 19*(1), 28–57.

Robinson, R. (2011). Masculinity as prison: Sexual identity, race, and incarceration. *California Law Review, 99*(5), 1309–1408.

Rodriguez, C. M. (2013). Saving the nation's expendable children: Amending state education laws to encourage keeping students in school. *Family Court Review, 51*(3), 469–484.

Rodriguez, I. (2019, December 10). Changing the culture of community supervision. *The Crime Report.*

Roodman, D. (2017, September 25). Reasonable doubt: A new look at whether prison growth cuts crime. San Francisco: Open Philanthropy Project.

Roth, A. (2018). *Insane: America's criminal treatment of mental illness.* New York: Basic Books.

Rothman, D. (1971). *The discovery of the asylum.* Boston: Little, Brown.

Rovner, J. (2020, February 25). Juvenile life without parole: An overview. Washington, DC: The Sentencing Project.

Rugaber, C. (2020, September 21). Soaring wealth during pandemic highlights rising inequality. APnews.com

Ruhland, E. (2016). The impact of fees and fines for individuals on probation and parole. Minneapolis: Robina Institute of Criminal Justice.

Russell, E. (2017). Queer penalties: The criminal justice paradigm in lesbian and gay anti-violence politics. *Critical Criminology, 25*(1), 21–35.

Salisbury, D. (2019, January 30). New suit alleges Jackson's sheriff office was incubator for racism, bigotry. *Jackson News.* https://www.mlive.com/news/jackson/2018/07/new_suit_alleges_jackson_sheri.html

Sarat, A. (2020, June 9). The illusory quest to execute only "the worst of the worst." *Verdict.*

Sawyer, W. (2016, December 8). Punishing poverty: The high cost of probation fees in Massachusetts. Northampton, MA: Prison Policy Initiative.

Sawyer, W. (2018). The gender divide: Tracking women's state prison growth. Northampton, MA: Prison Policy Initiative.

Sawyer, W. (2019). Youth confinement: The whole pie, 2019. Northampton, MA: Prison Policy Initiative.

Sawyer, W., & Wagner, P. (2020, March 24). Mass incarceration: The whole pie 2020. Northampton, MA: Prison Policy Initiative.

Schaeffer, K. (2020, February 7). 6 facts about economic inequality in the U.S. Washington, DC: Pew Research Center.

Schaffer, K., Tylek, B., & Callahan, R. (2019). Paying for jail: How county jails extract wealth from New York communities. New York: Worth Rises, Brooklyn Community Bail Fund.

Schenwar, M., & Law, V. (2020). *Prison by any other name: The harmful consequences of popular reforms.* New York: The New Press.

Schnabel, L. (2018). Education and attitudes toward interpersonal and state-sanctioned violence. *PS: Political Science & Politics, 51*(3), 505–511.

Schoepfer, A., Leeper Piquero, N., & Langton, L. (2013). Low self-control versus the desire-for-control: An empirical test of white-collar crime and conventional crime. *Deviant Behavior, 35,* 197–214.

Schuetz, J. (2017, December 8). *Metro areas are still racially segregated.* Washington, DC: Brookings Institution.

Schuppe, J. (2016, June 19). 30 years after basketball star Len Bias' death, its drug war impact endures. NBC News.

Schwalbe, C., Gearing, R., MacKenzie, M., Brewer, K., & Ibrahim, R. (2012). A meta-analysis of experimental studies of diversion programs for juvenile offenders. *Clinical Psychology Review, 32*(1), 26–33.

Schwartz, H. (2014, September 26). Following reports of forced sterilization of female prison inmates, California passes ban. *The Washington Post.*

Schwartz, M. (2020, June 15). Federal executions set to resume after nearly 2-decade hiatus. NPR.

Schwartzapfel, B. (2009, February 12). Your valentine, made in prison. *The Nation.*

Schwartzapfel, B. (2017, April 4). Probation for profit just got less profitable. New York: The Marshall Project.

Seib, G. (2020, October 6). Turning point year heads to parts unknown. *The Wall Street Journal*, p. A4.

Seldes, G. (Ed.). (1996). *The great thoughts.* New York: Ballantine Books.

Sellin, J. T. (1944). *Pioneering in penology: The Amsterdam houses of correction in the sixteenth and seventeenth centuries.* Philadelphia: University of Pennsylvania Press.

Sellin, J. T. (2016). *Slavery and the penal system* (40th anniversary edition). New Orleans: Quid Pro Books.

Selph, M. (2015, March 13). Expanding gender-responsive principles to incorporate trans females. Madison, WI: National Council on Crime and Delinquency.

Semuels, A. (2016, October 12). No, most black people don't live in poverty—or inner cities. *The Atlantic.*

Sentencing Project. (2008, October 20). Federal crack cocaine sentencing. Washington, DC: Author.

Sentencing Project. (2018). Capitalizing on mass incarceration: U.S. growth in private prisons. Washington, DC: Author.

Sentencing Project. (2019a, June 6). Incarcerated women and girls. Washington, DC: Author.

Sentencing Project. (2019b, June). Women and girls serving life sentences. Washington, DC: Author.

Sentencing Project. (2020a, August 17). Disenfranchisement news: Iowa governor ends lifetime ban on voting for people with felony convictions. Washington, DC: Author.

Sentencing Project. (2020b, August). Trends in U.S. corrections. Washington, DC: Author.

Shafer, S., & Lagos, M. (2019, March 12). Gov. Gavin Newsom suspends death penalty in California. NPR.com

Shalev, S. (2017). Solitary confinement as a prison health issue. In S. Enggist, L. Moller, G. Galea, & C. Udesen (Eds.), *WHO guide to prisons and health* (pp. 27–35). Copenhagen: World Health Organization.

Shapiro, J., Pupovac, J., & Lydersen, K. (2018, October 15). In prison, discipline comes down hardest on women. NPR, *All Things Considered.*

Shay, G., & Strader, J. (2012). Queer (in)justice: Mapping new gay (scholarly) agendas. *Journal of Criminal Law & Criminology, 102*(1), 171–193.

Shelden, R. G. (1979). From slave to caste society: Penal changes in Tennessee, 1840–1915.*Tennessee Historical Quarterly, 38,* 462–478.

Shelden, R. G., Brown, W. B., Miller, K. S., & Fritzler, R. B. (2016). *Crime and criminal justice in American society* (2nd ed). Long Grove, IL: Waveland Press.

Shelden, R. G., Tracy, S. K., & Brown, W. B. (2013). *Youth gangs in American society* (4th ed.). Belmont, CA: Cengage.

Shelden, R. G., & Troshynski, E. (2020). *Delinquency and juvenile justice in American society* (3rd ed.). Long Grove, IL: Waveland Press.

Shelden, R. G., & Vasiliev, P. V. (2018). *Controlling the dangerous classes: A history of criminal justice in America* (3rd ed.). Long Grove, IL: Waveland Press.

Siegel, L. (1997). The pregnancy police fight the war on drugs. In C. Reinarman & H. Levine (Eds.), *Crack in America: Demon drugs and social justice* (pp. 249–259). Berkeley: University of California Press.

Slack, P. (1995). *The English Poor Law, 1531–1782.* London: Cambridge University Press.

Smialek, J. (2020, September 29). Savings rise but fed sees persistent inequality. *The New York Times*, sec. B, p. 1.

Smith, A. E. (2012). *Colonists in bondage: White servitude and convict labor in America, 1607–1776.* Chapel Hill: University of North Carolina Press.

Smith, D. (2017, February 26). Man sues Elk Grove Police Department, claims anti-gay treatment, discrimination. *Sacramento Bee.*

Smith, D., Campbell, C., & Kavanagh, B. (2017). Trends in state courts 2017. Williamsburg, VA: National Center for State Courts.

Smith, E., & Stroop, J. (2019, December). Sexual victimization reported by youth in juvenile facilities, 2018. Washington, DC: Bureau of Justice Statistics, NCJ 253042.

Smith, S., Zhang, X., Basile, K., Merrick, M., Wang, J., Kresnow, M., & Chen, J. (2018). National intimate partner and sexual violence survey: 2015 data brief—Updated release. Atlanta: Centers for Disease Control and Prevention.

Snapp, S., Hoenig, J., Fields, A., & Russell, S. (2014). Messy, butch, and queer: LGBTQ youth and the school-to-prison pipeline. *Journal of Adolescent Research*, *30*(1), 57–82.

Solzhenitsyn, A. (1970). *The gulag archipelago*. New York: Bantam Books.

Southern Poverty Law Center. (2017, March 14). AL town agrees in settlement to stop operating debtors' prison. Montgomery, AL: Author.

Spitzer, A., & Scull, A. (1977). Privatization and capitalist development: The case of the private police. *Social Problems, 25*(1), 18–29.

Spruk, R., & Kešeljević, A. (2018). Institutional origins of subjective well-being: Estimating the effects of economic freedom on national happiness. *Journal of Happiness Studies, 17*(1), 659–712.

Stamper, N. (2016). *To protect and serve: How to fix America's police.* New York: Nation Books.

Staples, B. (1995, September 17). The chain gang show. *The New York Times Magazine,* sec. 6, p. 62.

Statista. (2020). Security: United States https://www.statista.com/outlook/281/109/security/united-states

Stebbins, S. (2019, July 16). America's most violent state? *USA Today.*

Stebbins, S., & Comen, E. (2020, January 11). The worst cities for black Americans. New York: 24/7 Wall Street.

Stellin, S. (2019, November 5). Is the "war on drugs" over? Arrest statistics say no. *The New York Times.*

Stemen, D. (2017, July). The prison paradox: More incarceration will not make us safer. New York: Vera Institute of Justice.

Stephan, J. (2008). Census of State and Federal Correctional Facilities, 2005. Washington, DC: Bureau of Justice Statistics. NCJ 222182.

Stevens, H. (2020, February 27). Mothers in prison should still get to be parents. *Chicago Tribune*, p. 3.

Stevenson, B. (2014). *Just mercy.* New York: Spiegel & Grau.

Stevenson, B. (2017). A presumption of guilt: The legacy of America's history of racial injustice. In A. Davis (Ed.), *Policing the black man: Arrest, prosecution, and imprisonment* (pp. 3–30). New York: Vintage Books.

Stevenson, B. (2019, August 14). Slavery gave America a fear of black people and a taste for violent punishment. Both still define our criminal-justice system. *The New York Times,* The 1619 Project.

Stillwell, S. (2014). *Slavery and slaving in African history.* Cambridge: Cambridge University Press.

Stotzer, R. L. (2014). Law enforcement and criminal justice personnel interactions with transgender people in the United States: A literature review. *Aggression and Violent Behavior, 19,* 263–277.

Streib, V. L. (2004). The juvenile death penalty today: Death sentences and executions for juvenile crimes, January 1, 1973–February 29, 2004. Ada: Ohio Northern University College of Law.

Stretton, T., Kesselring, T., & Kesselring, K. (2014). Married women and the law: Coverture in England and the common law world. Quebec: McGill-Queen's University Press.

Stunson, M. (2020, April 13). States asked to hand over lethal injection drugs to fight coronavirus. *The Sacramento Bee.*

Subramanian, R., Delaney, R., Roberts, S., & Fishman, N. (2015). *Incarceration's front door: The misuse of jails in America.* New York: Vera Institute.

Substance Abuse and Mental Health Services Administration (SAMHSA). (2019). Key substance use and mental health indicators in the United States: Results from the 2018 National Survey on Drug Use and Health. Rockville, MD: Center for Behavioral Health Statistics and Quality.

Sullivan, J. (2009, March 8). A corrupt judge, a damaged life. *Philadelphia Inquirer.*

Sullivan, S. P. (2017a, January 28). N.J. likely under-reports sexual abuse behind bars, experts say. *New Jersey Real-Time News.*

Sullivan, S. P. (2017b, January 23). 4 N.J. corrections officers indicted over sex abuse claims. *New Jersey Real-Time News.*

Sullivan, D., & Tifft, L. (2000). *Restorative justice as a transformative process.* Voorheesville, NY: Mutual Aid Press.

Sutton, J. R. (1988). *Stubborn children: Controlling delinquency in the United States.* Berkeley: University of California Press.

Swavola, E., Riley, K., & Subramanian, R. (2016). *Overlooked: Women and jails in an era of reform.* New York: Vera Institute of Justice.

Talbott, J. A. (2004). Deinstitutionalization: avoiding the disasters of the past. *Psychiatric Services, 55,* 1112–1115.

Tannenbaum, F. (1938). *Crime and the community.* Boston: Ginn.

Taylor, J. (2018, August 2). Jim Crow's lasting legacy at the ballot box. New York: The Marshall Project.

Taylor, S., Buchanan, J., & Ayres. T. (2016). Prohibition, privilege and the drug apartheid: The failure of drug policy reform to address the underlying fallacies of drug prohibition. *Criminology & Criminal Justice, 16*, 452–469.

Teitelbaum, L., & Harris, L. (1977). Some historical perspectives on governmental regulation of children and parents. In L. Teitelbaum & A. Gough (Eds.), *Beyond control: Status offenders in the juvenile court.* Cambridge, MA: Ballinger.

Telford, T. (2019, September 26). Income inequality in America is the highest it's been since Census Bureau started tracking it, data shows. *The Washington Post.*

Teplin, L., McClelland, G., Abram, K., & Mileusnic, D. (2005). Early violent death among delinquent youth: A prospective longitudinal study. *Pediatrics, 115*, 1586–1593.

Teplin, L., McClelland, G., Abram, K., Mileusnic-Polchan, D., Olson, N.,& Harrison, A. (2015, September). Violent death in delinquent youth after detention. Washington, DC: Office of Juvenile Justice and Delinquency Prevention. NCJ 248408.

Thompson, C. (2014, December 18). Everything you ever wanted to know about private prisons . . . is none of you damn business. New York: The Marshall Project.

Thorbecke, C., & Mitropoulos, A. (2020, June 28). Extreme inequality was the preexisting condition: How COVID-19 widened America's wealth gap. ABCNews.com

Tolnay, S., & Beck, E. (1995). *Festival of violence.* Chicago: University of Illinois Press.

Tonry, M. (1995). *Malign neglect: Race, crime, and punishment in America.* New York: Oxford University Press.

Tonry, M. (2006). *Thinking about crime: Sense and sensibility in American penal culture.* New York: Oxford University Press.

Travis, A. (2020, February 11). Travis County sheriff wants to reduce jail capacity, meanwhile plans for new women's jail move forward. Kxan.com

Travis, J. (2002). Invisible punishment: An instrument of social exclusion. In M. Mauer & M. Chesney-Lind (Eds.), *Invisible punishment* (pp. 15–36). New York: The New Press.

Travis, J., & Western, B. (2017). Poverty, violence and black incarceration. In A. Davis (Ed.), *Policing the black man: Arrest, prosecution, and imprisonment* (pp. 294–321). New York: Vintage Books.

Tsolkas, P. (2019, September 8). Plans for a new federal prison on coal mine site in Kentucky withdrawn. *Prison Legal News,* p. 31.

Turner, J. (2003). Almshouse, workhouse, outdoor relief: Responses to the poor in southeastern Massachusetts, 1740–1800. *Historical Journal of Massachusetts, 32.*

Tuskegee Institute. (2010). Lynching, whites & negroes, 1882–1968. Archives. Tuskegee, AL: Author.

Uggen, C., Larson, R., & Shannon, S. (2016). 6 million lost voters: State-level estimates of felony disenfranchisement. Washington, DC: The Sentencing Project.

Uggen, C., & Manza, J. (2002). Democratic contraction? Political consequences of felon disenfranchisement in the United States. *American Sociological Review, 67*(6), 777–803.

United States National Commission on Law Observance and Enforcement (Wickersham Commission). (1931). *Reports.* Washington, DC: U.S. Government Printing Office.

Ura, A. (2017, June 30). Texas Supreme Court throws out ruling that favored same-sex marriage benefits. *The Texas Tribune*.

Valcore, J., & Pfeffer, R. (2018). Systemic error: Measuring gender in criminological research. *Criminal Justice Studies, 31*(4), 333–351.

Van Ness, D., & Strong, K. (2015). *Restoring justice: An introduction to restorative justice* (5th ed.). New York: Routledge.

Varenne, H., & McDermott, R. (1999). *Successful failure: The school America builds*. Boulder, CO: Westview Press.

Vélez Young, M. (2017). Students as threats: Schooling inside a youth prison. *Anthropology & Education Quarterly, 43*(8), 301–317.

Vélez Young, M., Phillips, R., & Nasir, N. (2010). Schooling in a youth prison. *Journal of Correctional Education, 61*(3), 203–222.

Vélez Young, M., Phillips, R., & Nasir, N. (n.d.). Unmaking and remaking school connectedness: Students navigating barriers to connectedness inside a youth prison school (unpublished manuscript).

Violence Policy Center. (2019). When men murder women: An analysis of 2017 homicide data. Washington, DC: Author.

Vito, G., Koester, P., & Wilson, D. (1991). Return of the dead: An update on the status of *Furman*-commuted death row inmates. In R. M. Bohm (Ed.), *The death penalty in America: Current research* (pp. 89–99). Cincinnati, OH: Anderson.

Von Drehle, D. (2019, March 15). The death penalty makes a mockery of our justice system. Abolish it. *The Washington Post*.

Vuori, J., Blonk, R., & Price, R. (2015). *Sustainable working lives: Managing work transitions and health throughout the life course*. New York: Springer.

Wacquant, L. (2001). Deadly symbiosis: When ghetto and prison meet and mesh. *Punishment and Society, 3*, 95–133.

Wacquant, L. (2010). Prisoner reentry as myth and ceremony. *Dialectical Anthropology, 34*, 605–620.

Wagner, D. (2005). *The poorhouse: American's forgotten institution*. Lanham, MD: Rowman and Littlefield.

Wagner, P., & Jones, A. (2019, February). State of phone justice: Local jails, state prisons and private phone providers. Northampton, MA: Prison Policy Initiative.

Wagner, P., & Rabuy, B. (2017, January 25). Following the money of mass incarceration. Northampton, MA: Prison Policy Initiative.

Wakefield, L. (2020, January 24). There are 16 states in the US that still have sodomy laws against "perverted sexual practice." PinkNews.

Waldrep, C. (2006). *Lynching in America: A history in documents*. New York: New York University Press.

Walker, S., Spohn, C., & DeLone, M. (2018). *The color of justice: Race, ethnicity and crime in America* (6th ed.). Boston: Cengage Learning.

Wallace, J., Goodkind, S., Wallace, C., & Bachman, J. (2008). Racial, ethnic, and gender differences in school discipline among U.S. high school students: 1991–2005. *Negro Educational Review, 59*(1-2), 47–62.

Walmsley, R. (2018). *World prison population list* (12th ed.). London: Institute for Criminal Police Research.

Wang, H., & Devarajan, K. (2019, December 31). Your body being used: Where prisoners who can't vote fill voting districts. National Public Radio.

Waters, E. (2016). Lesbian, gay, bisexual, transgender, queer, and HIV-affected intimate partner violence in 2015. New York: National Coalition of Anti-Violence Programs.

Watkins, M. (2019, February). Misdemeanors matter #2: Alexandra Natapoff on a legacy of injustice. New York: Center for Court Innovation.

Watson, S. (2019, June 18). When jails replace in-person visits with video, what happens when the technology fails? Northampton, MA: Prison Policy Initiative.

Watterson, K. (1996). *Women in prison: Inside the concrete womb* (rev. ed.). Boston: Northeastern University Press.

Weber, M. (1958). *The Protestant ethic and the spirit of capitalism.* New York: Scribner.

Weiss, R. P. (1987). Humanitarianism, labour exploitation, or social control? A critical survey of theory and research on the origin and development of prisons. *Social History, 12,* 331–350.

Welch, M. (1999). *Punishment in America.* Thousand Oaks, CA: Sage.

West, P. A. (2017, May 4). Hold Sheriff David Clarke accountable. *Wisconsin Gazette.*

Western, B., & Pettit, B. (2010, Summer). Incarceration & social inequality. *Daedalus*, 8–19.

Wheelock, D. (2005). Collateral consequences and racial inequality: Felon status restrictions as a system of disadvantage. *Journal of Contemporary Criminal Justice, 21,* 82–90.

White, C. (2016). Incarcerating youth with mental health problems. *Youth Violence and Juvenile Justice, 14*(4), 426–447.

White Paper. (2019, July). U.S. contract security industry. Greensboro, NC: Robert H. Perry & Associates, Incorporated.

Whitford, E. (2016, January). When walking while trans is a crime. The Cut.

Whitman, J. (2003) *Harsh justice: Criminal punishment and the widening divide between America and Europe.* New York: Oxford University Press.

Widra, E. (2017, December 7). Tracking the impact of the prison system on the economy. Northampton, MA: Prison Policy Initiative.

Wildeman, C., Fitzpatrick, M., & Goldman, A. (2018). Conditions of confinement in American prisons and jails. *Annual Review of Law and Social Science, 14,* 29–47.

Wildeman, S. (2015). Agonizing identity in mental health law and policy. *Dalhousie Law Journal, 38*(2), 619–643.

Williams, T. (2018, April 4). Trial uncovers casual horrors at private jail. *The New York Times,* sec. A, p. 1.

Williams, T., & Oppel, T., Jr. (2018, April 11). Escapes, riots and beatings. Behind bars in private prisons. *The New York Times,* sec. A, p. 11.

Wilson, B., Jordan, S., Meyer, I., Flores, A., Stemple, L., & Herman, J. (2017). Disproportionality and disparities among sexual minority youth in custody. *Journal of Youth and Adolescence, 46*(7), 1547–1561.

Wilson, C. (2017, April 25). Every execution in US history in a single chart. *Time.*

Wilson, D., Olaghere, A., & Kimbrell, C. (2017, May 12). Effectiveness of restorative justice principles in juvenile justice: A meta-analysis. Washington, DC: National Criminal Justice Reference Service, 250872.

Wilson, H., & Hoge, R. (2012). The effect of youth diversion programs on recidivism: A meta-analytic review. *Criminal Justice and Behavior, 40,* 497–518.

Wilson, J. Q. (1975). *Thinking about crime.* New York: Vintage Books.

Wiltz, T. (2019, April 23). Where "returning citizens" find housing after prison. Washington, DC: PEW Charitable Trusts.

Wisconsin Gazette. (2018, July 12). Vote Earnell Lucas for Milwaukee County sheriff.

Wolfe, A., & Liu, M. (2020, January 9). *Think debtors' prisons are a thing of the past? Not in Mississippi.* New York: The Marshall Project.

Wolfgang, M., & Riedel, M. (1973). Race, judicial discretion, and the death penalty. *The Annals of the American Academy of Political and Social Science, 407*(1), 119–133.

Wolfgang, R., Figlio, R., & Tracy, P. (1981). The seriousness of crime: The results of a national survey. Washington, DC: Bureau of Justice Statistics. NCJ 96017.

Wood, G. (2017, June 14). From our prison to your dinner table. Santa Barbara, CA: Pacific Standard.

Woolard, J. (2019, June). Waiver of counsel in juvenile court. National Criminal Justice Reference Service, document number 253015.

Workhouses.org. (2018). http://www.workhouses.org.uk/intro/

World Health Organization. (2013). Global and regional estimates of violence against women: Prevalence and health effects of intimate partner violence and non-partner sexual violence. Geneva, Switzerland: Author.

Worth Rises. (2019, April). The prison industrial complex: Mapping private sector players. New York: Author.

Wright, G. C. (1997). By the book: The legal execution of Kentucky blacks. In W. F. Brundage (Ed.), *Under sentence of death: Lynchings in the South.* Chapel Hill: University of North Carolina Press.

Xidias, J. (2017). *The souls of black folk.* London: Taylor & Francis Group.

Yacka, S. (2014, September 29). LGBTQ allied organizations alarmed by trend of prosecution of survivors for self-defense. New York: Family Equality Council.

Yohanna, D. (2013). Deinstitutionalization of people with mental illness: Causes and consequences. *AMA Journal of Ethics, 15,* 886–891.

Zangrando, R. L. (1991). About lynching. In E. Foner & J. Garraty (Eds.), *The reader's companion to American history* (pp. 684–686). Boston: Houghton Mifflin.

Zaveri, M., & Garcia, S. (2019, June 9). Ohio governor increases oversight of Cleveland jail where several inmates died. *The New York Times,* sec. A, p. 27.

Zehr, H. (2015). *Changing lenses: Restorative justice for our times* (25th anniversary edition). Harrisonburg, VA: Herald Press.

Zeng, Z. (2020). Jail inmates in 2018. Washington, DC: Bureau of Justice Statistics. NCJ 253044.

Court Cases

Atkins v. Virginia, 536 U.S. 304 (2002).

Batson v. Kentucky, 476 U.S. 79 (1986).

Baze v. Rees, 53 U.S. 35 (2008).

Bearden v. Georgia, 461 U.S. 660 (1983).

Board of Education of Independent School District No. 92 v. Earls, 536 U.S. 822 (2002).

Bowers v. Hardwick, 478 U.S. 186 (1986).

Breed v, Jones 421 U.S. 519 (1975).

Bucklew v. Precythe. 587 U.S.__ (2019).

Callins v. Collins, 510 U.S. 1141 (1994).

Coker v. Georgia, 433 U.S. 584 (1977).

Commonwealth v. Fisher, 213 Pa. 48 (1905).

Doe v. Grays Harbor County et al., 3:17-cv-05186 (W.D. Wa. 2017).

Dunn v. Ray, 586 U.S. __ (2019).

Eddings v. Oklahoma, 455 U.S. 104 (1982).

Ex Parte Crouse, 4 Wharton (Pa.) 9 (1838).
Flowers v. Mississippi 588 U.S. __(2019).
Foster v. Chatman, 578 U.S. __ (2016).
Furman v. Georgia, 408 U.S. 238 (1972).
Gagnon v. Scarpelli, 411 U.S. 778, 782 (1973).
Glossip v. Gross, 576 U.S. __ (2015).
Graham v. Florida, 560 U.S. 48 (2010).
Gregg v. Georgia, 428 U.S. 153 (1976).
Hall v. Florida, 572 U.S. 701 (2014).
Herrera v. Collins, 506 U.S. 390 (1993).
Hurst v. Florida, 577 U.S. __ (2016).
In re Gault, 387 U.S. 1 (1967).
In re Winship, 7 U.S. 358 (1970).
Jackson v. Hobbs, 567 U.S. 460 (2012).
Kennedy v. Louisiana, 554 U.S. 407 (2008).
Kent v. United States, 383 U.S. 541 (1966).
Lawrence V. Texas, 539 U.S. 558 (2003).
Lockett v. Ohio, 438 U.S. 586 (1978).
Madison v. Alabama, 586 U.S. __ (2019).
McCleskey v. Kemp, 481 U.S. 279 (1987).
McKeiver v. Pennsylvania, 403 U.S. 528 (1971).
McKinney v. Arizona, 589 U.S. __ (2020).
Miller v. Alabama, 567 U.S. 460 (2012).
Montgomery v. Louisiana, 577 U.S. __ (2016).
Moore v. Texas, 581 U.S. __ (2017).
Moore v. Texas, 586 U.S. __ (2019).
Morrissey v. Brewer, 408 U.S. 471 (1972).
Murphy v. Collier, 587 U.S. __ (2019).
New Jersey v. T.L.O., 469 U.S. 325 (1985).
People ex rel. O'Connell v. Turner, 55 Il1. 280 (1870).
People v. Watkins, 282 P.3d 500 (Colo. App. 2012).
Obergefell v. Hodges, 576 U.S. __ (2015).
Reed v. Louisiana, 580 U.S. __ (2017).
Richardson v. Ramirez, 418 U.S. 24 (1974).
Ring v. Arizona, 536 U.S. 584 (2002).
Romer v. Evans, 517 U.S. 620 (1996).
Roper v. Simmons, 543 U.S. 551 (2005).
Safford United School District v. April Redding, 557 U.S. (2009).
Schall v. Martin, 467 U.S. 253 (1984).
Stanford v. Kentucky, 492 U.S. 361 (1989).
Strickland v. Washington, 466 U.S. 668 (1984).
Thompson v Oklahoma, 487 U.S. 815 (1988).
Timbs v. Indiana, 586 U.S. ___ (2019).
United States v. Booker, 543 U.S. 220 (2005).
United States v. Windsor, 570 U.S. 744 (2013).
Vernonia School District v. Acton, 515 U.S. 646 (1995).

Index

construction boom in, xii, 22–23
custodial vs. reformatory, 148
differential treatment of Black
    women in, 218
geography of, 24
history of, 144–148
parents in, 20–21, 158–159, 162
privatization of, 55–62
reform, 70, 115, 146, 147, 187, 225
reinvention of, 4
religion's historic role in, 7–10
rural, economic boost from, 44–55
women's, history of, 144–150
Probation. *See also* Supervision
conditions of, 235–237
cost, 17
disproportionate sanctions,
    238–239
fees, 36–38, 77, 233–235
feeding mass incarceration, 225,
    230–231
history of, 226–227
length of supervision, 234–235
levels of, 228
monitoring focus, 5
population, 17–18, 151, 225, 228
revocation, 229, 230–231, 233,
    235, 237–238, 239
violations of, 77, 152, 210, 213,
    228, 230, 235
widening the net, 227, 250
Prosecutorial power, 98, 261–262
Public housing, denial to parolees, 104
Punishment
bureaucracy, 272–273
business of, 31–64
change in tone of discourse about, 3
conservative philosophy of, 6–7
European vs. American, 12–13
excessive, 95, 280
inability to address causes of crime,
    3, 271
inflexibility of, 13
as market for capitalism, 39–42
racial bias in, 32, 99, 105, 123, 124,
    273
religion's role in, 7–10
social and political factors involv-
    ing, 10–12

Whitman's measure of harshness, in
    US, 13
of women offenders, 143–174

Quetelet, A., 254
Quinney, R., xv, 274, 277, 278

Race/racism
Baldus et al. study on death penalty,
    120, 123, 124
bias in punishment and, 87–108
death penalty bias and, 123
executions by race, 1608–1972,
    111
lynching as expression of, 111–115
racial profiling, 100
society's need to reduce racial
    inequality, 270
Racial Justice Act of 1994, 124
Recidivism rates
for juveniles, 222
parole revocation and, 126
Redfield, I., 199–200
Redlining, 101
Reed v. Louisiana, 118
Reformatory movement, 148
Rehabilitative ideal, decline in, 2
Reiman, J., 231, 256
Religion
peacemaking paradigm, 274
role in punishment, 7–10
Restorative justice, 20, 274–276
Retribution and vengeance, as pur-
    poses of crime control, 8
Richardson v. Ramirez, 107
Ring, K., 81
Ring v. Arizona, 117
Ritchie, B., 98
Rogers, H., 48–49
Rockefeller drug laws, 164–165
Romer v. Evans, 184, 189
Roodman, D., 19–20
Roper v. Simmons, 127–128, 130
Rural communities, prison construc-
    tion in, 22

Safety in community, growth in infra-
    structure of, 4
Sayre, Oklahoma, 44–45